FAMILY CAPITALISM

FAMILY CAPITALISM

Wendels, Haniels, Falcks,

and the

Continental European Model

HAROLD JAMES

THE BELKNAP PRESS OF HARVARD UNIVERSITY PRESS
Cambridge, Massachusetts · London, England
2006

Printed in the United States of America

Library of Congress Cataloging-in-Publication Data
James, Harold, 1956–
Family capitalism : Wendels, Haniels, Falcks, and the continental European model / Harold James.
p. cm.
Includes bibliographical references and index.
ISBN 0-674-02181-9 (alk. paper)
1. Family-owned business enterprises—Europe—History. 2. Family-owned business enterprises—Case studies. I. Title.
HD62.25.J355 2006
338.7—dc22 2005045637

Contents

Figures · vii
Maps · ix
Abbreviations · xii

Introduction: The Familiarity of Capitalism · 1

Part I. The Age of the Individual
1. The Wendels and the French State · 41
2. The Pioneer in German History · 73
3. The Industrial Origins of the Falcks · 99

Part II. The Age of the Corporation
4. The Gutehoffnungshütte as a Joint-Stock Company · 119
5. French Companies in Two Countries · 136
6. An Italian Joint-Stock Company · 161

Part III. The Age of Organizationalism
7. The Politician as Businessman · 179
8. A Family Concern · 204
9. Models of Italian Industrial Development · 245

Part IV. The Age of the Postwar Miracle
10. A Costly Miracle in Italy · 263
11. A New Kind of Family Togetherness · 273
12. Postwar Reconstruction in France · 298

Part V. The Age of Globalization
13. Wendel Becomes a Conglomerate, French Style · 325
14. The Crisis of Italian Steel · 341
15. German Diversification and Internationalization · 353
16. Family Capitalism and the Exit from Steel · 369

Conclusion: Family Entrepreneurship · 377

Appendix: Family Trees · 387
Notes · 393
Acknowledgments · 423
Index · 427

Figures

1. Dollar stock index for France, Germany, Italy, and the United States, 1906–1998 33
2. Charles de Wendel, 1809–1870 64
3. Madame François de Wendel (Madame Joséphine), 1784–1872 67
4. Franz Haniel, 1779–1868 86
5. Franz Haniel and grandchildren, ca. 1865 97
6. Giorgio Enrico Falck, 1802–1886 100
7. Family of Giuseppe Rubini 104
8. Irene Rubini Falck, 1840–1919 107
9. GHH iron and steel production, 1870–1940 120
10. Hugo Haniel and family, ca. 1885 122
11. GHH Martin Works 125
12. GHH-constructed dock at Qingdao 134
13. Madame Henri de Wendel with her children 154
14. The Wendel chateau in Joeuf 155
15. Ballot of Reichstag for Henri de Wendel 157
16. François de Wendel, 1874–1949 181
17. Return of the Wendels to Hayange, November 1918 183
18. Propaganda against the "200 Families" 193
19. Paul Reusch, 1868–1956 207

20. Prisoners of war in GHH, First World War 209
21. The GHH *Konzern* in the 1920s 217
22. GHH Aktienverein profits and dividends, 1924–1944 236
23. Giorgio Enrico Falck, 1866–1947 251
24. San Giorgio delle Ferriere 253
25. Enrico Falck, 1899–1953 265
26. Cardinal Montini visits the Falck Montessori school, 1952 267
27. The GHH before and after reorganization, 1953 276
28. Alfred Haniel, 1883–1964 285
29. Share prices of major French steel companies, 1961–1971 311
30. Reorganization of Wendel holdings, 1975 318
31. Wendel stock prices, 1989–2003 337
32. Market capitalization, CGIP/Wendel Investissement, 1998–2002 338
33. Price charts, CGE&Y and Valeo, 1998–2003 339
34. Long- and short-term debt of Falck, 1961–1980 342
35. Falck stock prices, 1935–2003 350
36. Falck profits and share prices, 1935–2000 351
37. Haniel as a new company in the 1980s and 1990s 363

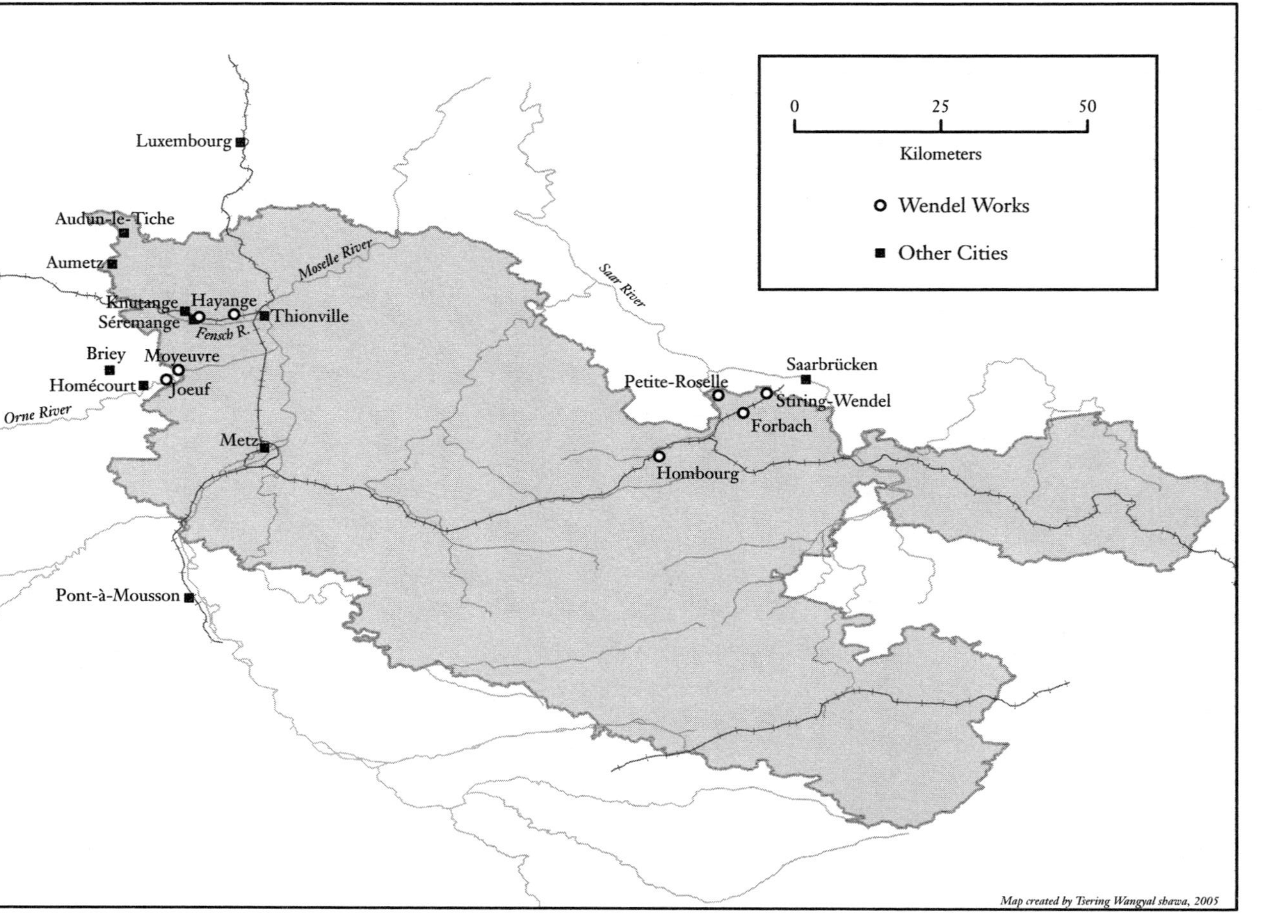

Lorraine, showing the area occupied by Germany, 1871–1918

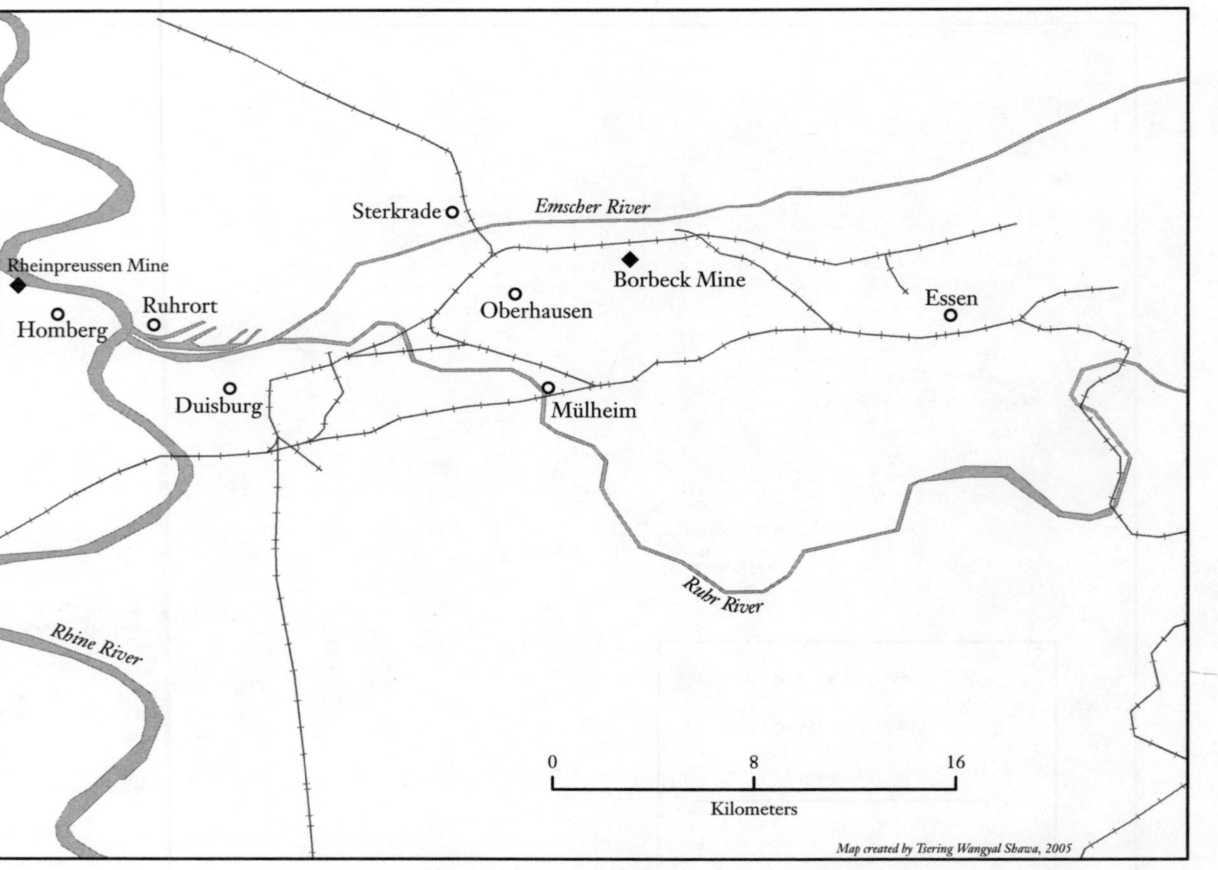

The Ruhr valley

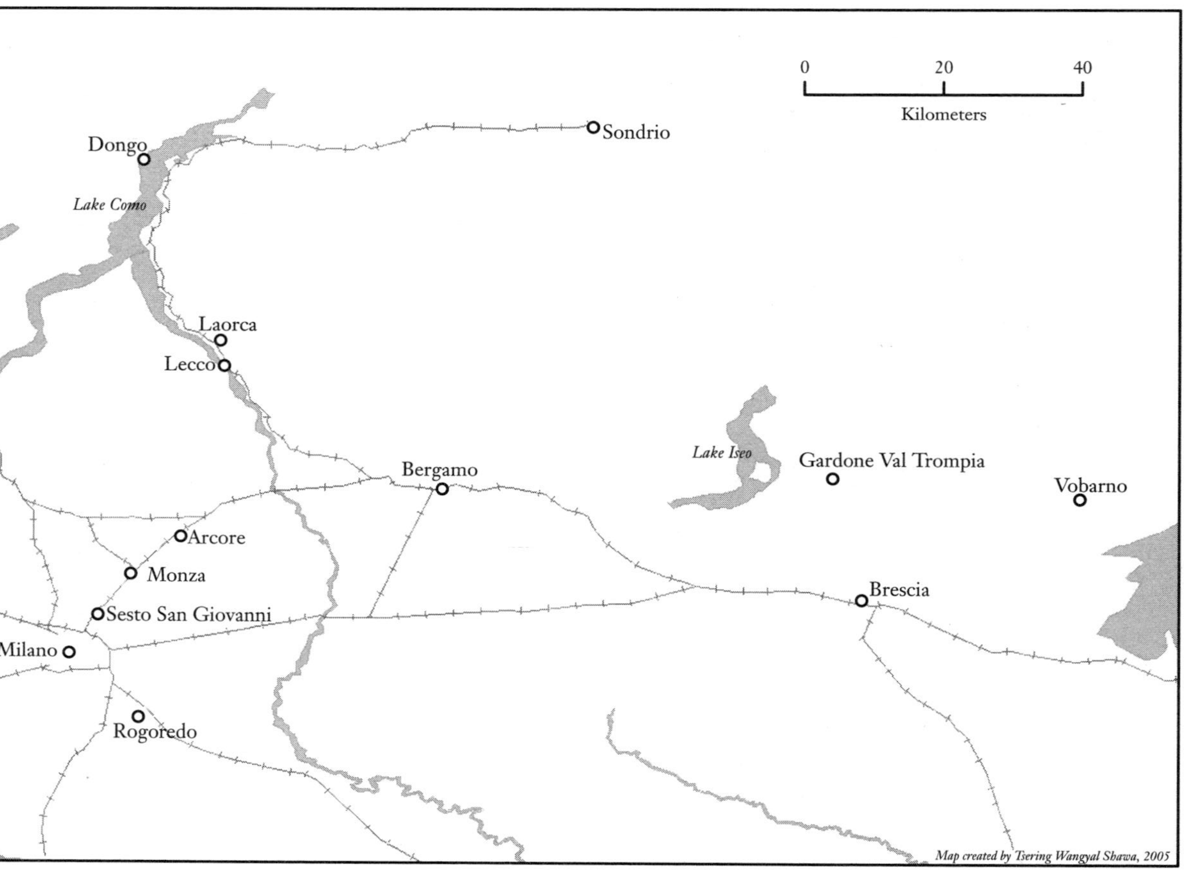

Lombard iron- and steel-producing area

Abbreviations

AFL	Società Anonima Acciaierie e Ferriere Lombarde
AG	Aktiengesellschaft (joint-stock company)
AN	Archives Nationales, Paris
BAGR	Beteiligungs-Aktiengesellschaft Ruhrort
BCI	Banca Commerciale Italiana
CGIP	Compagnie Générale d'Industrie et des Participations
ECSC	European Coal and Steel Community
FHC	Franz Haniel & Cie. GmbH
GHH	Gutehoffnungshütte
GmbH	Gesellschaft mit beschränkter Haftung (private limited liability company)
IRI	Istituto per la Ricostruzione Industriale
MAN	Maschinenfabrik Augsburg-Nürnberg AG
NA	National Archives, Washington, D.C.
OMGUS	Office of the Military Government of the United States
OPDR	Oldenburg-Portugiesische Dampfschiffs-Rhederei
PFFW	Société Les Petits-Fils de François de Wendel et Cie
RWWA	Rheinischwestphälisches Wirtschaftsarchiv, Cologne
SA	Société Anonyme (joint-stock company)
Sacilor	Société Aciéries et Laminoires de Lorraine
Sollac	Société Lorraine de Laminage Continu

Introduction

The Familiarity of Capitalism

There is no capitalism that is not familiar. The anomaly of capitalism is the [stock] market.

Ernest-Antoine Seillière,
Le Monde, 30 July 2002

THIS BOOK is about the interplay of three powerful social constellations, families, states, and markets, in the European context. Recently a great deal of literature has been devoted to demonstrating that there is no simple opposition between state and market; in particular, that a well-functioning market needs a secure institutional framework that can be provided only by well-functioning states. Without a state, there is no way of enforcing contracts, which are at the heart of the market process. Where states become abusive, arbitrary, or corrupt, the scope for rent-seeking increases, and economic agents in the market, instead of looking for technical improvements or innovations as a way of expanding their activities, try to capture the state.

The proposition that the state requires the market is perhaps more controversial; but it really should not be so. The extreme example of the malfunctioning of Communist systems demonstrated that when states arbitrarily seek to replace markets, they lose legitimacy by extending themselves into too many areas in which individuals have strong feelings.

A great deal of the discussion about the efficient and just operation of markets and states ignores the contribution of the family to their functioning. This is surprising, because the family can be understood as providing a link across generations, and with this a perspective on time. The process of building institutions and markets fails if there is no long-term outlook. Children are an investment in the future, and societies that do not adequately reproduce themselves have great problems in all areas that demand equity and justice.

The family has played and continues to play a decisive role in the form of economic organization characterized by the legal transfer of ownership rights, a type of organization best described by the term "capitalism." The family molds capitalism. Human beings have a biological urge to pass their assets on to other humans linked to them by spirals of DNA. The DNA chains are the real chains that bind the capitalist economy, not the allegorical chains whose loosing Marx and Engels demanded at the end of the *Communist Manifesto*. But there is a continual tension at the heart of the relationship between capitalism and the family. The Schumpeterian creative destruction of capitalism always throws up new challenges and changes, making for an instability that tears away at the fabric of the family.

The simple fact of the literal familiarity of capitalism perplexes many commentators, and many indeed simply wish to deny it. Conceiving of capitalism as a vast, inhuman process, based alternately on swindle and exploitation, that dwarfs and destroys individuals, they cannot see that it has anything to do with the affection and emotional warmth of family life or any sense of personal responsibility.

The linkage between capitalism and the family is clearest in the type of business organization that developed most fully outside the United States and the United Kingdom. Although the following pages present a history set in three rather different national cultures in continental Europe, it would be just as possible to set the story in Japan, China, or India.

The major business role played by family firms in a large number of countries has largely escaped serious comparative historical analysis.[1] This omission is surprising given the recent upsurge of interest in two issues related to the operation of markets that are central to the question of family businesses.

The first issue is the linkage between macroeconomic performance and the microeconomic problems of firms' balance sheets and profitability. What sorts of firms contribute most to long-term economic growth? How do world economic conditions and the varying phases of globalization and deglobalization correspond to developments in enterprise structure and behavior?[2] In particular, is there a "relationship capitalism" in continental Europe and Japan that has in the past been sustained by the localization of national capital markets and limits on the international mobility of capital, and is now facing inevitable decline as a consequence of the impact of financial globalization?[3] Is "relationship capitalism" more suited to some sorts of technology, which require long-term skill development (such as mechanical engineering in Germany or production of luxury goods in Italy), but less suited to branches with very rapid and sudden patterns of innovation (such as biotechnology or information technology)? In practice, "relationship capitalism" in continental Europe has almost always meant family relations.

The second issue relates to the way in which different legal traditions molded the development of quite different types of companies. A new orthodoxy asserts that common-law societies have produced more successful firms than the largely continental European Roman law traditions because owner or shareholder rewards and remuneration are more closely aligned with those of the company. Shareholders are more powerful and influential because they can litigate more easily. The long-term consequence is that there is more information about company behavior and results available in the public domain. It is therefore possible for owners to make more informed and thus more rational or better decisions on the allocation of capital. Most of this discussion has focused on the consequences of different degrees of shareholder protection for investment strategy. But the issue of common-law versus continental codified firm is also central to the particular issue of governance in family-owned and -controlled companies.[4]

There are two obvious ways in which this kind of legislative intervention limits the scope of family firms, if the major vehicle of family enterprise is a joint-stock corporation (as is frequently but not necessarily the case). First, it is obviously harder for families to use biased or weighted voting in order to maintain control as they dilute capital. Second, investor protection makes the stock market more efficient and thus attractive to many members of big families who do not necessarily want to keep their money in a traditional firm rather than allocating risk more widely. Most European legal systems were happy with unequal voting until the 1990s, when large (and in many cases foreign) institutional investors exerted strong pressure for change. In a recent survey of European companies, only seventeen of forty-three adhered to a simple one-share one-vote principle. Over a third allowed multiple voting rights.[5] The big families that dominate Swedish capitalism rely on this way of maintaining control.

But this type of explanation holds only for quite recent events and not for a broad or long historical development. Legislation restricting multiple voting is relatively recent, dating to the 1930s in the United States, and to the 1980s in the United Kingdom. Family firms in those countries had largely lost control before then. Continental Europe may be moving to a similar type of regulation, at the initiative of big (and in many cases foreign) institutional investors, especially mutual funds. Germany introduced a reform that eliminated some kinds of multiple votes in 2001. France had imposed this control in the 1930s, but it was subsequently dismantled, and the country is resistant to restoring it today. Indeed the recent Hellebuyck commission on corporate governance in France endorsed double voting rights as a way to reward the loyalty of "certain shareholders."

An obvious objection to the literature on common-law superiority is that if family firms with nontransparent ownership and control mechanisms are such an inefficient way of managing the allocation of capital, they should not exist in such numbers. But in fact more than three-quarters of registered companies in the industrialized world are family businesses, and—especially in continental Europe—they include some very large companies. Historians of the subject are often surprised by the extent to which this business phenomenon has survived.[6] According to one recent calculation, 17 of the largest 100 companies in Germany are in family hands, 26 in France, and 43 in Italy.[7] France and Italy still consider themselves to be the "champions of family capitalism."[8] In France at the beginning of the twenty-first century 33.8 percent of the total market value of listed corporate assets was controlled by just fifteen families (and 22.0 percent by five families). For Italy the equivalent figures are 21.9 percent and 16.8 percent, and for Germany 25.0 percent and 15.7 percent. By contrast, in the United Kingdom the equivalent figures are 6.6 and 4.1 percent.[9] This is not to say that there are no long-lived family firms in the United States and Canada—the often eccentric du Ponts and the highly secretive Cargills are obvious examples. But many of the most outstanding North American family dynasties are relatively recent. Family capitalism in the United States is exceptionally vibrant, but it usually involves first- or second-generation startups.

Such crossnational comparisons raise obvious questions of definition: Could it be argued, for instance, that the Ford Motor Company is still a family firm because its chief executive is the great-grandson of Henry Ford? By the 1960s less than 10 percent of the capital was in family hands, although the family-owned stock had greater voting power. Even the same levels of ownership mean different outcomes in different settings: Andrea Colli, for instance, points out that while it is impossible to dominate a company with 5 percent stock ownership in the United States, the same level of ownership may be enough to ensure effective control in Italy.[10]

The controversy about whether family firms promote or retard general economic performance centers upon a qualitative evaluation of the implications of statistics on how common family firms are. In Asian capitalism, the special trust that exists among members of often very extended families is often interpreted as a source of greater resilience.[11] In a similar vein, the mid-nineteenth-century conservative French social theorist Frédéric Le Play argued that industrial success was a reflection of the spirit of the family. The beginning of the twenty-first century saw renewed emphasis on the positive sides of family business, especially in debates outside the United States and the United Kingdom.

Family ownership has the advantage of being visible and identifiable, in contrast to the anonymous capitalism of large numbers of individual investors or the facelessness of institutional investors. If ownership is an important or even the defining feature of the capitalist process, transparency may be desirable. The greater difficulties that arise when disposing of ownership offer a guarantee of continuity and make property part of a stakeholding and relatively permanent pattern of institutional arrangements, in which there are higher levels of commitment. In such a setting it may be easier to motivate managers and workers than in one ruled by uncertainty about whether tomorrow the (faceless) owners will walk away. Families in business recently responded to this sort of analysis by developing a concept of "professional ownership," an obligation of owners to inform themselves in depth about the financial and business position of the companies they own, so that they can exercise more effective control. The family and its long-term vision thus offer a striking and reassuring alternative to the emphasis on "shareholder value" that was so fashionable in the 1990s and was linked with the "Americanization" of business conduct.

With the collapse of ideas about a "New Economy," the end of the dot.com bubble, and revelations of corporate corruption and scandal, businesses looked for a new model of responsible conduct. Family interests reasserted themselves in continental Europe, especially against managers and executives who seemed to have become too Americanized. The Mohn family ousted the leading manager of Bertelsmann, Thomas Middelhoff, who had wanted to turn a family company into an internationalized or even a denationalized enterprise. In France Jean-Marie Messier was similarly deposed from Vivendi Universal, and the Lagardère dynasty tried to regain control of Vivendi. Unlike Messier, the Lagardères were seen as deeply French; the wife of the president of the republic, the prime minister, and five cabinet ministers attended the funeral of Jean-Luc Lagardère in 2003. The left-wing newspaper *Le Monde* published a striking defense of a national form of capitalism: "at a time when the stock exchange keeps on falling, family capitalism, privileging long-term patrimonial interest over short-term operations, seems to have all the virtues."[12] One recent study of U.S. businesses also concluded, on the basis of a broad definition that counted one-third of the companies in the S&P 500 as family firms, that they performed significantly better than nonfamily firms.[13]

But more often family capitalism is still presented as a negative phenomenon that obstructs development and instills corrupt practices. The concept is often used, particularly in the United States, to explain deviation from some notion of an ideal-typical American path, of the kind best described by Alfred Chandler.[14] Firms in this tradition should move smoothly from an entrepreneurial to a managerial type of organization, with the movement to the multidivisional firm being taken as the key indicator that such a transition to business modernity has been achieved. The dominance of family business has historically been used, notably by David Landes, to explain poor French economic performance until the second half of the twentieth century, when the deficiencies of such organizations were overcome by a transition to planning in which technically trained business elites replaced dynastic control.[15] The economist Charles Kindleberger echoed this view in asserting that the French family firm "sinned against economic efficiency."[16] The financial limitations that keep family firms small are also generally held to explain why Italian modernization remained incomplete and polarized between a large and until recently state-dominated industry and myriad small producers.[17] The idea of the family firm is thus at the heart of a debate over the costs of the divergence of a continental European model of capitalism from the "Anglo-Saxon" one. According to this view, path dependence locked continental economies on a suboptimal institutional track.[18]

This model is also used to explain failure in other countries. A perhaps idiosyncratic interpretation of the business experience reflects the common criticism, particularly intense in the interwar period, of the limited investment horizons of British firms. Alfred Chandler in *Scale and Scope* portrays late twentieth-century Britain as being still in thrall to "personal capitalism," in which family relations still play a big part. The term refers to a style of management, and not exclusively to the actual structure of ownership. William Lazonick uses a similar diagnosis for the ills of British capitalism.[19]

One variant of the gloomy depiction of family business holds that such firms may play a useful role in resolving the problems of trust that arise in small-scale local economies, but that large family firms still impose a heavy price in terms of efficiency.[20] The penalty of family ownership is thus far heavier for larger enterprises. Such an interpretation lies outside Chandler's portrayal of family firms as a childlike stage on the path to the mature managerial enterprise. It allows interpretations in which economies thrive on the interplay of a dualism between a small family-based sector and large modern enterprise.

On the other hand, it is hard to claim that German or Japanese business life was sluggish in the century after 1870, although family firms there dominated large as well as smaller-scale business. Nor were family firms particularly undynamic. Jeffrey Fear has recently used the impressive development of August Thyssen's firm in the late nineteenth century to challenge the Chandlerian tradition, and to show how innovative and responsive personal capitalism could be.[21] In the late nineteenth- and early twentieth-century U.S. "Gilded Age," owner-dominated firms like Singer and Carnegie Steel were often more bent on growth than managerial enterprises, including the large company formed by a merger in 1901 that absorbed Carnegie Steel, namely U.S. Steel.[22]

Perhaps surprisingly, it is not economists or economic historians but rather anthropologists, notably Jack Goody, who have mounted a sustained challenge to the simple idea that family capitalism is inevitably replaced by a modern rational individualistic managerial capitalism. Goody concludes:

> The aspect of the managerial approach that sees the evolutionary replacement of the family firm by impersonal forms of economic organisation has little empirical justification and neglects the continuing role of the family not only in smaller enterprises but also in many larger ones. Firstly it gives insufficient weight to the growth of new businesses that are bound to be centred on the family . . . Secondly, even where control may be transmitted in a bureaucratic way, the property people possess at death normally passes to family members, whether this consists of jewellery, a house or shares.

In short, across the world, from Ahmadabad to Toulouse to Bradford, "the structure of the enterprise tended to duplicate the structure of the family."[23]

In general, the changing role of the family in the classic story of industrialization is impossible to separate from the organizational development of enterprises. The evolution of a strong sense of family was a crucial part of the creation of the nineteenth-century bourgeoisie.[24] The information gains achieved over time by expanding networks of relationships provided a social capital that complemented financial capital, contributing to efficiency by reducing transaction costs.[25]

The idea and structures of family capitalism revive in a particularly startling way at moments when the idea and the capacity of the state to act as a provider of economic growth and opportunity falter. Continental European history is especially rich in such moments of crises of "state capitalism," and this, I suggest, is the most fundamental reason for the striking success and dynamism in Europe of the family model. The transition to a third "industrial revolution" at the end of the twentieth century has produced another big and perhaps final challenge to state-based concepts of development. The last quarter of the twentieth century brought a widespread questioning of the state-centered model of economic development, and thus might well be expected to produce new opportunities for entrepreneurship, including entrepreneurship in the family setting.

Any discussion of the family firm has to consider a number of important distinctions among enterprises that are often simply labeled as "family." There are quite different instruments and degrees of influence available to family-owners.

1. Is the family firm a publicly quoted joint-stock company, with a family exercising control, in some cases with special voting shares, in some cases through pyramided holding structures? Or is it a nonquoted company? Many firms combine both, with an unlisted family holding company controlling substantial shares in public companies.

2. Is the management dominated by executives from the controlling family or not? Almost every study of family businesses makes the point that a preponderance of family directors over outside directors leads to suboptimal behavior by the family.[26] Some commentators follow Alfred Chandler in holding that when family members are not directly engaged in full-time management, the firm should no longer be described as a family company but rather as a managerial firm. Others see this as some sort of intermediate form. Such distinctions are made difficult by differences in national company laws: for instance, German law provides for a supervisory board *(Aufsichtsrat)* that is not directly involved in management, and on which family members may well be represented (as well as the German but not the foreign employees of the company). Some supervisory boards are quite interventionist, and they are required to be so at moments of managerial failure.

3. Is the company recent or long-established? A long-term vision can be articulated most clearly in companies that span many generations of ownership, while short-term interests, divergent family interests, and struggles among individual members often lead to the breakup of firms in the second or third generation.

Old companies do not have to be spectacularly successful companies. Indeed a recent study found that the overwhelming majority of the 18 U.S. companies from the first *Forbes* listing of the largest 100 American corporations in 1917 that survived to 1987 underperformed the market as a whole, and that the group's average returns were 20 percent below the compound growth rate of the market as a whole.[27] Long life thus does not necessarily mean continuous outperformance.

The question whether family firms *in general* perform better in the long run cannot be definitively answered by a comparative study of a few. The very fact of a long history, and therefore of success by some measure, renders them unrepresentative. Evaluating performance through large samples raises similar problems: a choice of modern firms will leave out historical failures. Even samples that involve frequent cross-sections of data often leave out private companies in early eras because of data unavailability and thus exclude a big section of the family-enterprise sector. Above all, large samples even with a perfect sampling technique do not examine what is peculiar in the family setting about decisionmaking and entrepreneurial choice: a detailed investigation of this must depend on case studies.

A working hypothesis is that some sectors, activities, or technologies hold out more opportunities to the family firm than others. Families offer a particular way of casting the contracts that constitute a firm.[28] Family-controlled enterprises are more likely to be found in industries and technologies that demand a long-term perspective, and less likely to be found in very fast-growing industries with very high capital requirements. Case studies help to identify the particular strategic choices made by families and their firms, as well as the consequences of failure to make the right choices.

This book considers three families from different countries, the Wendels in France, the Haniels in Germany, and the Falcks in Italy. They have been selected because of their longevity and because for most of their business history they were active in a sector that was strategic in European industrialization efforts, in military preparation, and in the management of social conflict. They are all literally representative of "Rhineland capitalism" in that all three families began their business activities in the industrial areas of the Rhine and Moselle valleys. But the families are not "typical"; indeed it would be hard to think what the criteria would be for a typical family. Neither are they iconic figures of national family capitalism; such a choice would have involved other, more notorious, dynasties: the Schneiders in France, the Krupps in Germany, the Agnellis in Italy. In the twentieth century, all three firms were shaped by the political cataclysms of defeat, occupation, and large-scale industrial reorganization. In the 1960s the Haniels substantially sold their steel and iron interests; in 1978 the Wendel steel business was nationalized (by a conservative French government). Both family enterprises then developed into conglomerates with a wide range of holdings. Those of Haniel are centered in retail and wholesale trading (in particular through the control of Metro, the world's second-largest retailer, and a pharmaceutical distributor, Celesio). They are also substantially more globalized than the Wendel holdings, which are still based mostly in France, with a concentration on abrasives (Wheelabrator), energy, and real estate (Orange Nassau), but also a very internationalized risk-management company (Bureau Veritas). Falck moved away from steel production in the mid-1990s, after nearly two decades of almost uninterrupted losses. One of the Falcks' new areas of activity, energy, continues the family interest in hydroelectric power in the early twentieth century that contributed crucially to the success of the dynasty. Thus the family enterprises have reverted from industrial production to the mercantile (for Haniel) or political (for Wendel) backgrounds of the families in the eighteenth century. It is easy to see this trend as a microcosm of European economic development: first, the strong commercial tradition, then the embrace of heavy industry, followed by deindustrialization and the shift to a financial and service economy. Europe's big dramas focused on iron and steel in the nineteenth century, and on the legacy of steel in the late twentieth century.

The three families differ in regard to the presence of family management, governance, and corporate structure. The Wendels and Falcks retained much greater family influence in management than the Haniels. The firms also vary in the extent to which they used the joint-stock company as a way of perpetuating family capitalism. In the midst of great crises of national capitalism, both the Falcks and the Haniels pursued a course that made them less like joint-stock corporations and more like family firms, in an apparent reversion to an older historical model.

My survey of the stages of European business organization treats the national and company stories in parallel. It moves from the individualistic capitalism of the late eighteenth century (Part I), through the rise of the modern corporation in the second half of the nineteenth century (Part II), the new and massive involvement of the state in economic organization as a consequence of the twentieth-century world wars (Part III), and postwar reconstruction in Europe (Part IV), to the modern challenge of globalization (Part V).

The Family as Intermediary between State and Markets

It is worth examining why families can play a very dynamic role in several specific social and economic settings. Society is polarized between formal hierarchical organization in political institutions (what might be termed the state in a very broad sense) and the anarchic interplay of individual decisions and wishes in a market. Neither one by itself provides a viable way of managing social and economic interaction. States can command only at the price of inflexibility, while markets require codes of conduct and rules, which are most easily determined by some form of political negotiation. The family, as an intermediary organization, is particularly effective when both states and markets are chaotic and disrupted. This has obviously been the case in many parts of continental Europe over the past two centuries, when political stability was exceptional.

Family capitalism has thus been particularly important in countries and societies experiencing profound shocks and discontinuities. It is a way of managing risk in a high-risk environment. This historical role is confirmed by recent work which suggests that in developing countries undergoing economic transition family firms play a major role. They can generate better access to market capital because they create a degree of trust that offers a response to market failure. They provide a higher degree of human or social capital. Thus with the liberalization of the Indian economy since 1991, family groups (which many predicted would disappear) have become more important.[29] The European experience, which was politically turbulent until the mid-twentieth century, offers some important lessons. It is directly relevant to the problems of developing resilient companies and robust corporate governance throughout most of the world. Two of the family groups studied in the following pages, the Wendels and Haniels, remade themselves under the threat and challenge of the French Revolution, when property relations were challenged and transformed. The Haniels and Falcks survived as industrial families and, contrary to initial expectations, were substantially strengthened by the transition from totalitarian to representative democratic rule in Germany and Italy. There are obvious analogies in Japan, where after 1945 the U.S. occupation dissolved the industrial conglomerates, or *zaibatsu*, and purged fifty-six members of *zaibatsu* families, but within a decade the family groupings had effectively reconstituted themselves.[30]

There is no simple one-way track from family firm to dispersed ownership that corresponds to a rational development or modernization of the economic process. For example, one of the family firms considered here, Falck, started in 1906 as a joint-stock company (Acciaierie e Ferriere Lombarde) substantially controlled by banks, and Giorgio Enrico Falck was really a manager, with little of his own rather meager capital in the company. During the 1930s the enterprise became a family firm. Following different paths, the major instruments of the Wendel and Falck families were joint-stock companies for most of the twentieth century, but the availability of vigorous capital markets in the late twentieth and early twenty-first centuries made a private holding more attractive again.

One way of understanding how family firms not only survived but took advantage of profound social and political transitions is to examine how the families conceived of themselves and their role. Large-enterprise families (as opposed to small-scale artisanal family firms) frequently and explicitly compared themselves to monarchs of the ancien régime: they preserved the dynastic principle and what it represented into modern times.[31] After the Italian electorate rejected the monarchy, Gianni Agnelli became "the uncrowned king of the nation," with intense press interest in the firm's succession struggles and difficulties. The family and its organization in a company could offer a self-consciously aristocratic or even royal vision. At the beginning of the twentieth century, an influential German handbook referred to the corporation as having an "aristocratic mold." The Krupps saw themselves as monarchs.[32]

At one level, then, the family seems to offer an alternative locus of loyalty to political allegiances—in other words, to the state. At another level, it can substitute for the anonymous abstractions of the market. Companies in general—following the classical analysis of Ronald Coase—are ways of substituting control for market operations in a climate of information uncertainty. Family firms offer a particularly clear logic of control. Economic development is thus best understood as the story of the interplay of families, states, and markets and of the differing ways in which they understood themselves and one another.

Property is a central concept in explaining this interplay. Critics from Karl Marx and Friedrich Engels onward have attacked the family as an economic rather than an emotional construct: the bourgeois family was kept in place by a sense of property rather than by romantic love or tender paternal and maternal feelings. The intangible assets and networks of the family thus became quite material and tangible. In this tradition Pierre Bourdieu (in an article illustrated by a photograph of Wendel family members lined up at the funeral of the dynastic patriarch) concluded that "the family spirit and even the affection that create family cohesion are transfigured and sublimated forms of the interest specifically attached to the membership in a family group, or to participation in capital whose integrity is guaranteed by family integration. By this . . . collective alchemy, the membership in an integrated family assures every individual the symbolic profits corresponding to the cumulative connections of all members of the group."[33]

The supposed incompatibility between love and rationality then produced continual psychic crises and made the institution of the family emotionally and in the end psychologically dysfunctional. The family did change, however, in response to changed ideas about affection. In the Wendel and Haniel dynasties, for example, marriage between cousins was extremely common in the nineteenth century but quite rare after the First World War. There is an economic reason for this shift, as well as the more obvious reason of changing cultural norms. Without a joint-stock company as a way of organizing and limiting family owners' control of the company, family members needed to be tightly controlled in some other way. Parental choice of marriage partners avoided the dissipation of wealth through the marriage of heiresses to aristocrats, wastrels, or charming adventurers. Thus it was not a coincidence that when joint-stock companies with limited liability became generally available on the European continent in the 1860s and 1870s, some of the necessity for parental discipline disappeared. Bad behavior by heirs no longer had the capacity to wreck the whole family unit. In consequence young men became free to spend their inherited fortunes on racehorses, and young women could have exciting and insolvent husbands.

Changes in family firms thus reflected changing notions of property.

The Precarious Stability of the Family

The family firm played a central role in the early stages of European industrialization, before the institutional innovations associated with the joint-stock limited liability corporation (generally a feature only of the mid-nineteenth century and later). At first there was little alternative to the family as a way of establishing a link based on trust between individuals. There was no way legally of enforcing trust, so it had to depend on family piety and duty. Religiously pious families often did much better in commerce because they established trust more easily.

But families remained important even after the emergence of the joint-stock company as a way of establishing a solid long-term business relationship among people with potentially divergent interests. The cynic might have asked: If you have a company, why do you need a family that behaves like a company? But the old models of behavior were deeply entrenched in the European psyche. At the beginning of the novel *The Man of Property*, John Galsworthy describes the Forsytes, a British dynasty:

> Those privileged to be present at a family festival of the Forsytes have seen that charming and instructive sight—an upper middle-class family in full plumage. But whosoever of these favored persons has possessed the gift of psychological analysis (a talent without monetary value and properly ignored by the Forsytes), has witnessed a spectacle, not only delightful in itself, but illustrative of an obscure human problem. In plainer words, he has gleaned from the gathering of this family—no branch of which had a liking for any other, between no three members of whom existed anything worthy of the name of sympathy—evidence of that mysterious concrete tenacity which renders a family so formidable a unit of society, so clear a reproduction of society in

> miniature. He has been admitted to a vision of the dim roads of social progress, has understood something of the patriarchal life, of the swarmings of savage hordes, of the rise and fall of nations.

In the family enterprise, the close relationship of family members solved a number of problems that would otherwise have impeded economic growth. In an age of great demographic uncertainty, with high mortality rates, it offered a way of securing the future of an enterprise. Relatives who were brought into the firm could give security, lend money, and provide reliable business contacts in distant cities. Daughters could be used in the same way they were treated by the royal families (also a sort of business) that governed Europe: to make strategic alliances between firms on a secure and long-term basis. Marriage remained, long into the age of romantic love (and longer than for other social classes), a business transaction. In the twentieth century, André Michelin was still urging his family to preserve wealth by marrying cousins (a strategy common in such long-lived dynasties as the Rothschilds, Haniels, and Wendels).

In fact in the premodern world women also played a central role in business management, a much more substantial role than that played by women in business in most twentieth-century European societies. A study of the French iron industry during the French Revolution found a large number of iron businesses headed by women as political turmoil and persecution drove male business leaders into flight; the iron mistresses included the widows of Charles de Wendel and of Jean-Albert Frédéric de Dietrich, and Madame du Bourg de Bozas.[34] The French and German business dynasties examined in this book were controlled by powerful widows during the upheavals of the 1790s; and the French and Italian ones in the 1870s, again at moments of great national trauma. From the mid-nineteenth century, however, joint-stock companies held out an attraction to an increasingly patriarchal world in that they were ways of bringing in professional (male) managers and excluding female relations. In this respect there is an element of truth in the widely supported notion that "the rise of capitalism is the root cause of the modern social and economic discrimination against women, which came to a peak in the last [nineteenth] century."[35]

Families are of course not always harmonious. As Tolstoy reminds us at the opening of *Anna Karenina*, they can be unhappy in quite different and ingenious ways. In a business context, family quarrels required some sort of legal management and institutional solution in order to stop feckless or irresponsible or simply irrepressibly entrepreneurial individuals from endangering the whole enterprise. The Wendel family disputes produced two highly complicated and long-drawn-out legal cases in the early nineteenth century. In the same period the brothers Haniel were infuriated by the scroungingly parasitical behavior of their brother-in-law, to whom they were bound in a joint business venture. At the end of the twentieth century, after a series of business setbacks, the Falcks split their family enterprise between two branches.

Keeping the family together was not an easy exercise before the creation of the legal concept of a limited liability corporation. Then, when limited liability offered a new way of protecting wealth, it also endangered the ideal of family control, in that family members might sell their shares in a publicly quoted corporation.

Demographics could also hurt a long-lived family venture. Since about a fifth of nineteenth-century marriages produced no children, there was a strong likelihood of families' dying out. Alternatively, there could be too many children, too many heirs, and too much subdivision of family wealth.

Influences on Organization

In examining what Galsworthy called "a reproduction of society in miniature," this book addresses four questions related to how the family firm crucially shaped national styles of capitalism:

- Are there cultural as well as national differences in entrepreneurial behavior?
- What is the relationship between owners and managers?
- How does business interact with politics?
- What impact does crossnational business activity have on the formulation of business strategy?

First, what sense does it make to use "nation" as a concept in analyzing cultural differences in entrepreneurial behavior? It may be that well-developed extended families were and to some extent still are more a part of social life in large parts of Catholic Europe than in the more individualistic and atomistic Anglo-Saxon world. Anyone who has had lunch on a Sunday in a restaurant in provincial

France will have been struck by the large multigenerational family groups; and there are similar sights in Italy and Germany. Of course, there are great dynastic families in other cultures, but they are less frequently bound together in business transactions. Galsworthy's Forsytes, intensely money-centered as they are, do not share in any commercial enterprise. They go their own ways, some to demand returns of 5 percent, some to be content with government bonds yielding 3 percent. By contrast, the continental family firm is a community of interest, with (today) 750 family owners in the case of the Wendels and 550 in the case of the Haniels. (There are more descendants than there are owners: in 1990 there were 1,259 living descendants of the nineteenth-century François de Wendel). Even in the mid-nineteenth century, the number of partners struck a visiting English observer as the most extraordinary feature of the Haniel firm.

> This house has realized what John Cockerill was unable to do at Liège, and perhaps the success of Messrs. Haniel is traceable to their depending on their own skill and industry, instead of ambitioning the alliance and the capital of kings or governments . . . this family is strong in the number of its members, who, especially the younger portion, are indefatigable in their superintendence of works, while they live in an enviable harmony that is in itself a source of wealth.[36]

But the social-religious explanation of Catholic family life is not entirely compelling: a great many of the great French family businesses in industry were Protestant (though the Wendels and Seillières were Catholic); and the Haniels, like the Krupps, were Protestant; while the Catholic Thyssens had spectacularly and notoriously bad family relations (as did the Wendels in the first half of the nineteenth century). Each confession was aware that the other embodied different traditions: the great German industrialist Hugo Stinnes, for instance, described the Haniels and Krupps as "Anglo-Saxons" who were more reliable than Thyssens.[37] But each had strong notions of the links between family and faith.

What appear to be cultural differences are frequently in reality the results of different national legal and fiscal traditions. In particular, the continental European tradition initially owed a great deal to the principles of equal inheritance introduced by the French Revolution and the Code Napoléon, which was also applied in many western areas of Germany. European law made it problematic and legally contestable to leave property principally to an eldest son; the *droit d'aînesse*, or right of the oldest, was rejected as a part of the feudal order. The division of property made for longer-lived family firms, and more difficulty in "exiting," since the capital of many members of the family was locked together in the company, and an attempt to separate the components might well render it worthless. By contrast, the common-law traditions of Britain and the United States had no such restrictions on the testamentary disposition of property. There was no problem in an elder son's deciding that it conformed to his interest to go to the stock market and raise outside capital. In Japan, complex and formalized family codes regulated inheritance and characteristically limited the ability of family members to incur debts or guarantee the debt of others.[38] Charles de Wendel in the mid-nineteenth century helped to launch an initiative aimed at abolishing partible inheritance, but the proposal was widely (and successfully) attacked as a restoration of the ancien régime and an overthrow of revolutionary principles.

The partible inheritance provisions could be circumvented only by new legal devices—in particular, from the middle of the nineteenth century, the joint-stock company, in which the company's statutes established a model of governance and made the multiplicity of owners irrelevant to the day-to-day life of the corporation. But sometimes this type of protection was not chosen. There was an older alternative, which had a feudal flavor: the entail, or *Fideikommiss*. In Germany, the steel dynasty with the most obviously feudal pretensions, the Krupps, adopted the *Fideikommiss* as a means to pass on the inheritance intact. But it had its odd consequence: the family home, for instance, was then treated as a part of the factory.[39]

Europe (including Britain) had very strict bankruptcy laws, which increased the incentives to make family groupings that would save members who had made business miscalculations. Since entrepreneurship is inherently concerned with taking risks, and some risks inevitably end badly, many analysts now see bankruptcy figures as an indication of a society's entrepreneurial capacity. Julian Hoppit produced a pathbreaking study of bankruptcy as an indication of industrial success in eighteenth-century Britain.[40] One of the features that contributed greatly to nineteenth-century U.S. economic success was the relaxed attitude to bankruptcy: American society did not need family support as a mechanism to help with the bad consequences of failed entrepreneurial strategies (as well as simple fecklessness), since failure was not judged as harshly.

In the twentieth century, fiscal issues, in particular capital gains and inheritance taxes, have been major determinants of business structure: holdings are kept for a long time in order to avoid capital gains liabilities.

The second comparative issue is one that is raised by any firm, and increases with the size of the firm. It is now generally discussed as the principal-agent issue, but businessmen were clearly aware of the issue of whether they could trust their managers well before the term was introduced. Are there mechanisms to ensure that the management does not promote its interests at the expense of the owners? A high dependence on managers may promote growth at the expense of profitability, as the managers benefit from increased activity that makes their functions more important. Having managers who come from the owning firm removes this problem to some extent, but at the price of depriving the firm of access to the best skills and qualifications for management. In the late nineteenth and early twentieth centuries, visitors to the Wendel works were struck by the almost complete absence of a managerial layer: the owners supervised almost every detail and discussed matters directly with the foremen on the shop floor. By contrast, the Haniel-owned companies were managed from the mid-nineteenth century by "directors," and in the early twentieth century one of these, Paul Reusch, made an energetic push to expand.

Managers often develop some philosophy to explain their preferences for expansion, and one of the most common ways of doing this over the past two centuries was through appeals to national issues: prestige, security provisions, and then increasingly the expansion and maintenance of high levels of employment. They presented themselves as allies of the state in a quest for bigness. They were national managers. An alternative vision for the managerial mission was *techne:* the pursuit of better scientific solutions to practical problems. Especially in Germany, in the nineteenth century there developed a vision of the rationality of enterprise that was based on its capacity to produce technical innovation.

Much of the search for a national business *raison d'être* looked futile by the end of the twentieth century. Over the past twenty years, the divided interests of owners and managers have again become a topic of intense discussion. But the rather faddish concept of the 1990s, "shareholder value," did not provide an effective solution. Instead shareholder value was instrumentalized chiefly by managers as a way of linking their rewards to short-term indicators of performance. By the twenty-first century, disillusionment set in, and there is a new search for a way of making motivation effective throughout a large enterprise.

The third major question is implicit in the first two considerations of national peculiarities: What is the relationship between business and the state, and how does it vary among countries? In what circumstances can states be captured by particular interests, and how does political history affect ownership structure? Mark Roe has produced an interesting explanation of the divergence of ownership patterns in the United States from those of continental Europe which rejects the idea that a particular legal tradition creates a simple path-dependency (as in the common-law link to shareholder protection). Instead, social democracies in the twentieth century put a high value on employment in the firm, and thus wished to restrict measures that might lead to a more effective representation of shareholder interests. By contrast, a widely diffused ownership is a response to the ability of shareholders to influence corporations. Thus the major feature of the U.S. trajectory is the absence of a strong social democracy. Roe concludes: "Where social democracy was strong, the public firm was unstable, weak, and unable to dominate without difficulty; where social democracy was weak, ownership diffusion of the large firm could, if other economic and institutional conditions prevailed, begin."[41] The argument could be put more generally: the strong continental European state and family business traditions are intertwined. A less interventionist state would not produce such strong clusters of family bonds as a counterpole to its power.

If this pattern does in fact exist, it should show some dramatic effects in the history of iron and steel. The iron and steel business is politically an especially sensitive one, in the first place because it was required for armaments production, and was the base of military and thus ultimately of political power. During the twentieth century it was at the center of political disputes about employment, the responsibility of business to maintain jobs (exactly the kind of issue Roe believes to be central), and co-determination in corporate governance.

The intertwining of families and politics is readily visible as social history in that modern politics required a social role for business. Social contacts presented a way of obtaining political and economic leverage. Economists describe this sort of process as obtaining rents. The Wendels were rapidly ennobled primarily as a reward for their military services (and it was a military officer who started the family's excursion into iron). During the 1790s the Haniels developed a thriving business out of supplying iron for munitions for the armies of the counterrevolution. Franz Haniel was on good terms with the Prussian royal family: as a young man he danced with the princess who became the tragic Queen Louisa of Prussia; as an older businessman he welcomed the crown prince of Prussia (later Frederick William IV) to his coal mines.

The Wendels developed substantial political interests, and sat in French parliaments from immediately after the Restoration of 1815 (and also in the German Reichstag after 1871, where two Wendels were members for Lorraine). François (II) de Wendel became the most powerful French businessman of the interwar period and the subject of many attacks on the power of the 200 families said to control the policies of the Banque de France. From 1997 to 2005 his great-nephew, Ernest-Antoine Seillière, was chairman of the major employers' organization, now known as Medef, and was at the forefront of the fight against the Jospin government's imposition of the thirty-five-hour week. The London *Financial Times* snidely observed in 2000 that "taking on the French government may not be bad for your business career."[42] The Haniel-controlled Gutehoffnungshütte (GHH) was at the center of discussions about political intervention in wage determination in the Weimar Republic, and of the co-determination debates of the 1950s. For the Falcks, the greatest problem of the 1960s and 1970s was dealing with politically diverse labor unions in the steelworks. Politics mattered everywhere in industry in the twentieth century.

The intertwining of strong state and family business does not necessarily produce a climate of mutual sympathy. In order to understand the dynamic, it is necessary to contemplate how countries interpreted their industrial histories. In Germany, France, and Italy the search for influence by business took place in the context of political debates around the issue of backwardness and catching up. The wish for some alteration of the existing order involved profound social criticism. For much of the nineteenth century the external reference point was the British experience, and for much of the twentieth the American. (In the twenty-first century the Asian model may compel attention and force structural change.) Given the importance of business families during the debate about backwardness, it is unsurprising that many policymakers concluded that family business and backwardness were coterminous, and thus that the dominance of family firms was a barrier to adopting best practice from abroad.

The state also became the focus of attempts to catch up or to modernize and was viewed as an instrument of a development strategy. In mobilizing forces for change, the state identified enemies/scapegoats that could be used to explain the resistance, failure, and disappointment inevitably encountered during the modernization project. Thus policymakers came to believe that the state could supplant or succeed the family as a form of social and economic organization.

The statist focus has the deepest historical resonance in France. Indeed the phenomenon of state-run economics is often described as "Colbertism," after Louis XIV's minister, economic planner, and modernizer. Colbert also identified enemies—in his case, the traditional aristocracy. In the nineteenth century, Napoleon attempted to make good the damages done by revolutionary upheaval and to systematize the legal and institutional bases of the French economy, and his nephew Napoleon III launched a new push to drive the French economy forward. The Third Republic by contrast seemed politically and institutionally crippled by what was from the 1930s widely described as "Malthusianism," the limitation not just of population growth, but of every other sort of growth in a kind of collective self-restriction.[43] From the collaborationist Vichy period in the 1940s until the 1980s, the state again came to be regarded, in very different ideological settings, as the generator of growth that would overcome the Malthusian propensity.

Much of the debate on ways of overcoming backwardness was focused on heavy industry, and especially on iron and steel, because of their importance for national defense, and thus for the projection of the national image. Steel was the backbone of a new economy and a new state. The most striking physical embodiment of the legacy of the French Revolution, erected on the centenary in 1889, was the iron Eiffel Tower.

The quest for control over iron and steel played a major part in France's political development over two centuries: ample though they were, the coalfields of northern France proved to be less productive than those of the great Ruhr valley basin. The consequence was that the large iron-ore reserves of the Lorraine area were frequently separated politically from the greatest coal resources in Europe, and the most basic components of industrialization needed to be shipped across national frontiers. Lorraine thus became a geopolitical hinge for European power politics. Steel became a political obsession because of its importance in the manufacture of military equipment, and for a long time national success was gauged in terms of statistics on population and crude steel output.

The state interacted with owners of the steel business. Often their interests did not coincide, with the result that they tried to influence each other. Because iron and steel were the business of the state as well as the business of business, the business dynasties sought political leverage in order to affect entrepreneurial outcomes. They cultivated first the courts of the ancien régime, and then the postrevolutionary parliaments and ministries. A substantial number of deputies and senators came from the steel-producing Chagot, Coulaux, Dietrich, Petot, and Wendel families. Even in the 1970s, it mattered politically that Valéry Giscard d'Estaing was related to the Schneider dynasty. And as late as 1968, the economic historian Bertrand Gille noted the "permanence of the large owners in the political life of the nation."[44]

The political centrality of steel tied the Wendel industrial dynasty inextricably to the history of the French state. During the French Revolution, Wendels were accused of providing the aristocrats, royalists, and foreign powers with munitions to be used against the French people. Their assets were confiscated. In the late nineteenth century, Wendels were often suspected of being unpatriotic because they had steelworks on both sides of the German-French border in Lorraine. During and after the First World War, socialists and reformist Catholics accused the Wendels of having prolonged the war by obstructing the destruction of their Lorraine steel mills by artillery or aerial bombardment, with the result that Germans were able to use the steel for munitions. The accusers ignored the fact that their chief target, François de Wendel, was probably the most committedly nationalist and most Germanophobe member of the whole dynasty. Similar charges circulated during the Second World War, culminating in the post-Liberation barring of François de Wendel from political office because as a senator he allegedly had voted full powers to Marshall Pétain (in fact he was one of the very few senators deliberately to absent himself from the meeting, so that he did not have to vote on this issue).

In the postwar era, the attacks continued. François de Wendel was the model for a hugely popular novel by Maurice Druon portraying the decline and disintegration of an ironmaster's family and business, and in general the decay and decadence of French capitalism. Not until the late 1970s, when a conservative government nationalized the French steel industry, did the Wendels move into relative political obscurity. Finally in the 1990s, with extensive privatization and the opening of the French economy to outside investment, in a surprising turn family capitalism was strengthened, as it had been in previous times of upheaval. The head of the Wendel enterprises, a family member, once again became a major and controversial political figure as a result of his leadership of the employers' organization Medef.

In France the debate about stagnation retained a high profile from the mid-nineteenth to the mid-twentieth century; today it has resurfaced with a series of popular books devoted to unmasking those responsible for poor French economic performance.

In Germany, by contrast, the most acute period of national reflection about backwardness was the first half of the nineteenth century. Especially in the impoverished 1840s, many reformers looked to the English experience as a model, arguing that the alternative to English-style industrialization was Irish-style rural impoverishment and famine. Entrepreneurs could see themselves as heroes of the national drama, whereas before German unification the plethora of conservative and bureaucratic states was a limiting force. But there were a multitude of paths to English business practice and success: while some advocated a classical liberalism that had plenty of room for the heroic entrepreneur, others (notably Friedrich List, who was largely ignored during his short and mostly unhappy life) thought that the state should intervene in the promotion of growth. By the end of the nineteenth century the statist view had triumphed over the liberal option.

After the 1850s Germany experienced a period of substantial growth, characterized by great and, in the last phases of the boom, euphoric optimism. This growth, described by W. W. Rostow as the German "take-off," coincided with the process of political integration and to some extent drove it. The influential journalist and commentator Ludwig August Rochau characterized German unity in the 1860s as "a simple business calculation, nothing more or less."[45] Germany subsequently became a model for other states, notably Japan and Italy, seeking shortcuts to modernization.

After the enactment of the Prussian law on joint-stock companies in 1870 and the establishment of the German empire in 1871, there came a wave of speculative company creations. It was followed by a crash, and a long period of sobering up. The survivors of the *Gründerkrach* of the 1870s became the great dynastic firms of German heavy industry: in metallurgy, the Thyssens, Krupps, Stumms, Röchlings—and Haniels.

Textbooks frequently attribute a substantial and even definitive role in German industrialization to the new universal banks, which were themselves largely creatures of the 1870s. According to Alexander Gerschenkron's classic interpretation, banks made up for some of German backwardness by mobilizing otherwise unavailable capital. The Gerschenkron hypothesis has not survived modern scholarship, for although banks undoubtedly played a major part in one of the defining industries of German modernity, the capital-intensive electrotechnical industry, they played almost no role in the equally dynamic chemical industry. The steel and engineering dynasties borrowed relatively little, and relied for their investments mostly on internally generated funds.[46] It is more useful to think about the peculiarities of German development as a process of organizing in order to manage competition.

At the turn of the twentieth century, a new economic crisis prompted a search for new ways of expanding and consolidating industrial empires. It was then that banks briefly came into their own as the managers of takeovers, mergers, and cooperative associations. These reorganizations were not driven by operations on the capital market, and until the 1990s there were no major hostile takeovers in German business life (the Thyssen-Krupp merger is the first example, and even in this case an initially hostile bid became by 1998 a friendly liaison). Instead the move to industrial gigantism was pushed by definitions of areas of common interest, and banks played a large role in brokering consensus. The real period of bank dominance of German industry was relatively brief, from around 1900 to the Great Depression, and—in terms of its macroeconomic results—not particularly successful. The banks were responding at first to a clear market failure, in particular of the capital markets, which were stunted by a highly restrictive stock-exchange law of 1896. Bank influence was weakened by the great inflation after the First World War, and the banks only briefly managed to rebuild their positions precariously with borrowed foreign money, before they were destroyed by waves of financial panic during the Great Depression.

After the First World War and the associated and subsequent inflation and hyperinflation, many of the largest German heavy industrial enterprises attempted to build trusts as a way of managing their cost structures and planning sales more precisely. The idea of a planned economy, with or without the participation of the state in the planning process, took hold. The Nazi dictatorship was able to build on previous attempts to manage a collectivized economy, and suppressed price signals in a way that had already been begun in the First World War.

During and after the Second World War there was a substantial debate about the responsibility of the business community for Germany's political disaster. There were two contrasting approaches, both substantially colored by ideology. According to one interpretation, influentially advocated by the U.S. occupation authorities in the immediate aftermath of the war, it was capitalism that had produced the dictatorship. The dynasts of German industry looked particularly sinister, and were later memorably evoked in Luchino Visconti's 1969 film *The Damned* (*La Caduta degli dei*). The appropriate policy response was the breakup (or decartelization and detrustification) of German industrial holding structures. An alternative vision, held by German liberals, made state dirigisme responsible for the catastrophe and saw the market as a solution.

Neither of these ideological programs was ever fully realized; detrustified industries reshaped and recombined, and the idea of more competition was undermined by the maintenance of much of the regulatory system of the 1920s and 1930s. In practice Germany's road to economic recovery lay in a double strategy, which first emphasized cooperation between "social partners," labor and capital, as a way of overcoming the destructive distributional politics of the past. This was the pattern later celebrated as the *Modell Deutschland.* The idea of long-term responsibilities of owners fitted well with some of the paternalist traditions of German industry, which could be neatly tweaked in order to adjust to a new climate. Second, there was a greater push to internationalize business activities earlier than in the other major continental European economies.

The economic success of the Federal Republic was built on twin pillars. One consisted of small-scale family enterprise in the so-called *Mittelstand* sector, which began to run into major problems in the late twentieth century. New family firms found the succession problem difficult to manage, and the whole sector was in general badly undercapitalized and hence not resilient to shocks. The other pillar consisted of big firms, many of which were also family enterprises, and most of which were skeptical about the possibilities of the capital market until the late twentieth century. They faced severe problems in adjusting to the changing structure of the world economy, and many of the famous names of German industrial history—the Flicks, Thyssens, and Krupps—disappeared from the industrial landscape and retreated to high society and gossip-page glitz. With a slowdown in German growth and a controversial push to adopt "Anglo-Saxon" reforms of the capital as well as the labor markets, it became tempting once again to think of a German lag and to offer organizational explanations for economic problems.

The history of Italian economic development through much of the nineteenth century is one of economic backwardness and of poor resource endowment for the crucial technologies of the European industrial revolution—in particular, the absence of large iron-ore reserves and coalfields. What Italian advantages there were lay in a network of relationships, with a strong family content, that was combined with an interest in technical progress. The great Milanese economist Carlo Cattaneo developed a theory according to which intelligence formed the major principle of public economy:

"Control of new arts gave plentiful and reliable food to a number of families. They took their secrets from land to land; their wealth was the idea they had developed. They often remained divided from the crowd owing to their foreign origin and their different religion. Their knowledge became an inheritance, a perpetual privilege; they became a caste."[47] Especially in Lombardy, the commitment to technical education became institutionalized at an early stage through the Milan Society for the Encouragement of Arts and Sciences, established in 1838.[48]

From the last years of the nineteenth century, Italian politicians searched for institutional mechanisms for overcoming backwardness. The principal feature of Italian backwardness appeared to be the underdevelopment of the capital market. At first many business leaders believed that the best device for transcending Italy's institutional limits lay in financial institutions that could mobilize domestic investment resources and also attract foreign investments. But such institutions were themselves quite vulnerable. In 1893 there was a general banking crisis following a severe economic downturn, in which two of the largest Italian commercial banks, Credito Mobiliare and the Banca Generale, failed. After this episode there was more or less continual political intervention in business structures, with the result that business, financial, and political interests became closely interconnected. A new set of banks, closely linked to a German model of industrialization, became very powerful, but also immediately became the focus of political attention. Periodic crises destroyed financial values and demanded restructuring. After the First World War, such restructuring usually occurred at the public initiative and with public funds. The financial story of twentieth-century Italy can be summarized as the repeated destruction of capital, both of investors in the stock market and of government contributions.

The steel sector took a major part in this story. It was in general particularly adept at capturing the state, with the result that some critics, like the Socialist Ernesto Rossi, referred to steel as "la grande parassitaria."[49] But to speak of "steel" as a single interest is misleading. It was a particular type of steel industry, the large integrated works, usually sited on the coast in order to have access to imported ore, that was generally most effective at "capture," at first of the banks and then of the state. The family firm of Falck staked its strategy on resistance to those sectors that were particularly effective in the capture maneuver.

The first hope of liberal Italy at the beginning of the twentieth century was that the country could be made financially and economically more robust through the operations of two large and newly established German-style universal investment banks in northern Italy, the Banca Commerciale Italiana (BCI, also often called the Comit) and the Credito Italiano (Credit). These Milanese banks rapidly became intertwined with factions in the political elite of liberal Italy.[50] In addition to a German business model, these institutions initially operated with German capital. They derived most of their earnings from underwriting, and promoted quite speculative enterprises. After a sharp setback in the stock market following the U.S. crisis of 1907, the stock-buying public turned away from this kind of asset, and the banks had to retrench.[51]

The banks' hold was further shaken by the inflation during and immediately after the First World War, and then by the postwar deflation. The major crisis of the steelmaker Ansaldo severely affected the banks, and in a dramatic and conspiratorial conflict, the BCI undermined the ministry of the liberal politician Francesco Nitti. The major steel producer Ilva was restructured in 1920, with new share capital (as well as loans) from the two big commercial banks. The banks emerged as the effective controllers of much of Italian heavy industry, and in particular of steel. But that dominance made them highly vulnerable in the deflationary business climate of the 1920s, following the stabilization of the Italian lira in 1927 at the overvalued *quota novanta*, or ninety liras to the British pound. Their industrial assets lost value during the depression, producing a de facto insolvency of the major Italian credit institutions. The industrial hegemony of the universal banks was thus finally destroyed by new deflation during the world depression at the end of the 1920s and in the early 1930s.

The Italian government tackled the problems of the financial sector by demanding that the banks sell their industrial securities to holding companies that were eventually concentrated in the giant state holding company Istituto per la Ricostruzione Industriale (IRI), established in January 1933. IRI made virtually all of Italy's large-scale industry dependent on the state, and ensured that this sector was the least dynamic and least flexible in the postwar recovery. The Italian economic miracle depended instead on large numbers of small-scale family firms.

After the Second World War a new industrial bank emerged, backed by the Christian Democratic government, with the aim of providing a new way of organizing an inherently Italian structure of enterprise that was not dominated by the big state-run institutions. Enrico Cuccia's Mediobanca (established in April 1946) was initially in ownership terms a creature of IRI, which at first held 68 percent of the stock; but its policy was controlled by a voting trust of leading private-sector industrialists, who with only 3.75 percent of the shares were given an equal voice in the new bank. The idea of Mediobanca was bitterly opposed (predictably) by the representatives of the state industrial sector, notably by Donato Menichella, the powerful head of IRI.[52] The imbalance between state provision of financing and private control of policy was widely seen as the key to an Italian phenomenon of "capitalism without capital." An influential governor of the Bank of Italy, Guido Carli, described Cuccia's role as that of the sentinel "protecting the empty barrel of Italian capitalism."[53]

Mediobanca had shareholdings in big Italian family companies, such as Fiat and Pirelli, and also organized interlocking shareholdings among family groups. Its role has sometimes been regarded as quite mysterious, with opaque links to politics and to religion, including the Holy See.

The Italian financial system had been hostile to the development of a stock market, but over the past thirty years it began to change, largely as a result of pressures to reform and modernize, arising from Italy's membership in the European Community. The Consob, an agency to supervise the stock market, modeled on the U.S. Securities and Exchange Commission, was established in 1974. In 1983 European Community provisions gave a larger role to mutual funds, which over the next two decades became major presences on the Italian financial scene. In 1991 EC law required the publication of consolidated balances for firms and groups. In 1998 the *lex Draghi* increased the legal protection of shareholders. With this opening, the role of large family businesses at first increased, but then began to fall away. Financial liberalization and the growth of the capital market thus destroyed important aspects of the institutional framework that had favored family business for the previous century. By one estimate, family-controlled pyramid companies accounted for 30 percent of the market capitalization of the Milan stock exchange in 1950, 40 percent by the mid-1980s, and 20 percent by the end of the 1990s. Deaths of major figures in Italian business life were now interpreted as the end of the era of family capitalism. The demise of Enrico Cuccia in June 2000 and of Giovanni ("Gianni") Agnelli in January 2003 were heralded as the unsticking of a glue that held family capitalism together.[54]

There is a consensus that the Italian economic miracle owes a great deal to the flexibility of small and medium enterprises, particularly in sectors such as textiles and clothing, where constant innovation, and rapid response to changing fashion demands, can create value in an industry that would otherwise seem logically destined to move to low-wage production countries.

The legacy of Italy's family capitalism for larger enterprises is more controversial. Fiat spent a great deal of the late twentieth century stumbling from one entrepreneurial disaster to the next. Many critics—as in France—accused family enterprises of being badly managed. In some industries, such as steel, it was possible to destroy wealth on a big scale. Indeed, the head of my case study in the 1990s, Alberto Falck, told me that it was the wealth of his family that allowed him to continue to bear continuing heavy losses in the 1970s and 1980s.

Bad times and business losses obviously meant the erosion of much capital. The large family companies were then controlled by families that continued to possess in fact only a minority of the shares, and that managed to assert ownership by complicated shell companies. This was the real meaning of Italian "capitalism without capital."

What other sort of wealth-holding might have stood a better chance of preserving value? In fact, Italian stock markets and publicly quoted companies have—with very short-lived exceptions—fared very badly (see Figure 1).[55] One Italian twentieth-century peculiarity in comparison with other industrial countries was the weakness of the stock market. Between 1960 and 1975 there was a dramatic loss of real value of Italian stocks. But even during the subsequent period of institutional reform and modernization, the performance of the Italian market has been exceptionally weak in

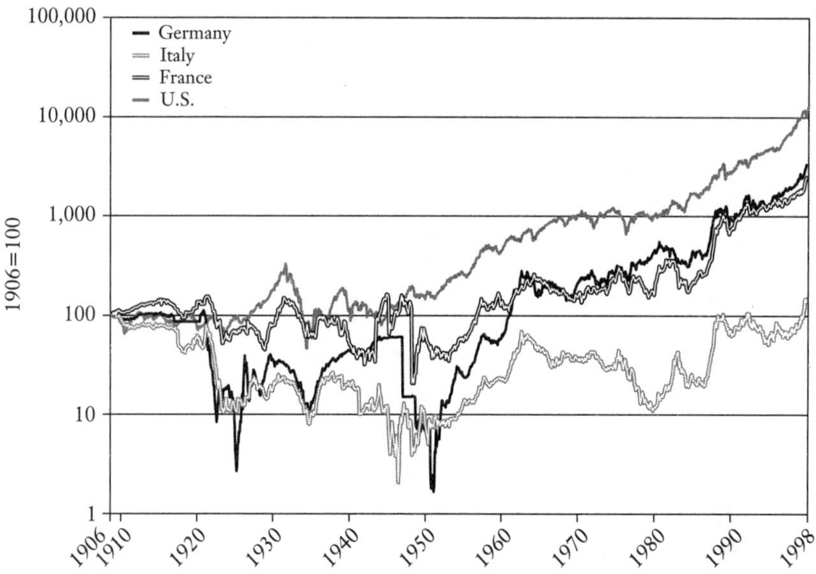

1. *Dollar stock index for France, Germany, Italy, and the United States, 1906–1998*

comparison not only with the United States but also with France and Germany. The weakness should be interpreted as a reflection of the inadequate protection of minority shareholders and correspondingly of the power and influence of insiders. The lack of returns on the stock market in turn encouraged family members to keep their wealth concentrated in the family groups. In turn, outsiders launched big battles for corporate control, seeking to become insiders in their turn. "Capitalism without capital" was thus very directly a consequence of the poor transparency of corporations and hence of the feebleness of the Italian stock market. The Italian case is an extreme example of development distorted by an inadequate capital market, but it also raises the question whether this is a common European problem that arose in weaker forms in other national settings. Backwardness (and specifically the poor state of the capital market) and dependence on state guidance look like two sides of a coin that became the standard currency of political debate in continental Europe.

Fourth, and finally, then, national businesses may want to look outside the national political setting for other outlets for activity in an effort to internationalize or globalize their activities. All three family businesses examined in the following pages had from their beginnings substantial international contacts: the entrepreneurs looked abroad, to England in the late eighteenth and early nineteenth centuries, to the United States in the late nineteenth century and beyond, and (in the cases of Wendel and Falck) to Germany. Thus the story of the steel dynasties is a European one, and not one confined to particular national cultures.

The first initial surge in growth of the Haniels occurred during the French revolutionary wars. In 1870–71 the Franco-Prussian war brought much of ore-rich Lorraine into the German empire, and thus into the same political unit as the Ruhr coal reserves. The settlement was a major blow to French political, economic, and military power. Yet the Germans quickly viewed the outcome as unsatisfactory, since the Treaty of Frankfurt left the substantial ore reserves of the Longwy-Briey basin (whose potential had largely not been recognized in 1870) in French hands. German plans for expansion thus involved more annexation—of Longwy-Briey, as well as of industrial resources in Luxembourg and Belgium.

In the twentieth century, the creation of a new holding of a diversified group of assets required geographic extension. After the First World War the Haniel interests were extended to southern Germany, and their activity in the Netherlands and Switzerland increased. Since the 1960s, and in particular with the move to discounted shopping through Metro, the internationalization has become much more dramatic; in the 1990s especially, the search for new markets in central and eastern Europe and in China has produced new strategies. The Wendels also first expanded out of Lorraine to sites for steel production in the north and on the Mediterranean coast, where access to cheaper imported iron ore was easier. In the 1990s they looked for a much broader kind of diversification, with more high-technology and electronic interests and assets.

Businesses will continually adapt to new market conditions, at least if they are to continue to be successful. The success of family firms in continental Europe was due to a broad carapace of protective institutions—some in the law of inheritance and in tax law, some in political contacts, some in market organization (through the nineteenth-century German cartel system). None of this protection could guarantee success, but it created the conditions for an effective evolution. It also made the firms controversial. There are thus two major intertwined themes in the following pages, one of the family as a focus for business activity, and the other of the idea of backwardness in continental European capitalism that produced a constant demand that the state intervene and compensate for industrial and economic retardation.

PART ONE

The Age of the Individual

The European ancien régime was a family affair, at every level of society. The most obvious embodiment of the dynastic principle was the hereditary divine-right monarchy; but poor peasant farmers also treated their activity as a household enterprise. At every level, families looked to dynastic marriage strategies to find greater wealth and power. The marriage of a Bourbon prince to a Habsburg princess was only the highest-level exemplification of the logic of family existence; farmers could try to marry additional land. (Analogies between the world of business and the world of royalty continue today: the Queen of England apparently habitually refers to the monarchy as "the firm.")

Family values meshed especially well with craft traditions in manufacturing. Ironworking and textiles abounded in all sorts of arcane techniques and secret tricks that needed to be carefully guarded from competitors. Businesses were continually prying and trying to lure skilled workers away from their rivals, and industrial espionage evolved into a major ancien-régime activity. The best defense against defecting craftsmen was to restrict the most important secrets to sons or even daughters: the sons would be locked into the business, and the daughters would be useful bargaining chips in the strategic game of dynastic marriage.

For some people in the eighteenth century, the collectivism and anti-individualism of their family-dominated world looked strange and irrational. It was also at odds with the relatively new idea that states had identities that went beyond the person of the ruler, and that an Enlightened ruler should be, as Frederick the Great memorably put it, the first servant of the state. Among royal marriage alliances, for example, Louis XVI's union with the Habsburg Marie-Antoinette was seen as an affront to French national interest.

During and after the French Revolution, a cult of romantic individualism released men and women from family ties, which were reinterpreted as being conventional and restrictive. In economic life, territorial changes, the upheavals of markets, and the search for new technologies that would yield military advantage all helped to shape an image of a creative individual entrepreneur driven by a demon. The new man both created and destroyed: he was a sort of

Napoleon of the business world. But there was an irony in all this Napoleonic emulation: Napoleon depended on his family for influence and power and became an archetypal dynast.[1]

Some comparisons:

Wendel, 1850: 22,000 tons of cast iron and 2,000 workers (11 tons per worker)

Jacobi, Haniel & Huyssen, 1867: 18,730 tons of cast iron and 1,220 ironworkers (15 tons per worker)

Rubini & Falck, 1858: 1,000 tons of cast iron and 400 workers (2.5 tons per worker)

Chapter 1

The Wendels and the French State

It seems to me that I am well placed to deserve the goodwill of a just government.

François de Wendel, 1824

THE WENDEL FAMILY began its industrial existence in part in France, and in part in the Duchy of Lorraine. Ancien-régime France was far from being a static society, in which a rigid feudal order blocked attempts at social mobility. Between the nobility and the peasantry there were many intermediate groups: minor gentry who cultivated their fields, small-scale officers, producers and merchants who sought prosperity and status. But the nobility for a long time imposed its values on the rest of society—which consequently tried as hard as it could to join the nobility.[1] Since this was a quite commercialized society, money could buy titles, privileges, patents of nobility, and shares in royal influence, royal power, and royal revenue. Thus a quarter of the aristocracy of France consisted of parvenus ennobled, like the Wendels, in the eighteenth century.

A century before the French Revolution destroyed this society and created new paths to social mobility, the Wendels were just such a family: originating in Bruges, in Flanders (the Van Daëls), a branch of the family had moved to the Rhineland and as officers fought in the service of Catholic small princes. Jean-Georges Wendel had been a colonel in a Croat regiment fighting in central

Europe during the Thirty Years' War; his son Christian Wendel was a cavalry captain in the army of Duke Charles IV of Lorraine.

One of Christian's sons, Jean-Martin Wendel, made an advantageous marriage to Anne-Marguerite Meyer, the daughter of a substantial *fermier* (more likely to have been a cog in the enormous privatized tax-collecting bureaucracy of the *fermiers-généraux* than a simple agricultural farmer, or *fermier*). In 1704 Jean-Martin used his wife's money to buy, for 9,000 livres (around $2,000)[2] and an annual rent of 100 livres, the iron forge of Hayange from the king of France. This was a substantial but not overwhelming amount of money at a time when a skilled craftsman could expect to earn around 200 livres a year. Iron had been extracted at Hayange since 1260, and in 1446 the first forge had operated there. This small town was situated in a deep valley of the river Fensch, where the water cut through layers of ore-bearing rock. In 1704 there was a little industrial settlement, including a forge (named Rodolphe after its creator, Rodolphe de la Roche), a furnace (called the Magdelaine), a hammer mill, and a cutting mill. The latter two were incomplete, and the rest of the equipment was crumbling. The whole works had been sold two years previously to the commissioner of artillery in Thionville, Louis de Ridouet-Sancé, for 1,500 livres; he had probably also needed to put in around 9,000 livres, and had still failed to make a successful business.

The monarch sold the right to use forges essentially as a revenue-raising device, and the mastership of a forge was especially attractive to purchasers in that it carried with it a noble title. In 1723 a royal decree stated that letters patent from the king were required before a new iron factory could be established.[3] Wendel was by then a *maître de forges* and a seigneur—the seigneur d'Hayange. The title went with the forging, one of the few commercial activities that was permitted to noblemen (it did not "derogate" from their nobility); shipbuilding and glass manufacture were the other permitted trades. These activities thus had an unusual status in a world in which most industrial or commercial activity was literally debasing. The attraction of iron and ships lay in the fact that they represented weapons for conflict, which was unambiguously *the* noble profession. On the other hand, if the master were to abandon the forge, the title would also be forfeit. Hayange had in fact been traded in this way quite actively: the first forge there had been built by Rodolphe de la Roche, who had obtained a royal patent, and four subsequent would-be ironmasters had taken over the forge before Wendel. Wendel seems to have prepared himself, and had already directed a forge at Ottange, slightly to the north of Hayange.

But he needed a substantially larger sum than the purchase price to make anything of Hayange. In total, he needed some 30,000 livres ($6,200), which he borrowed from bankers in Metz and Thionville.[4] This kind of investment made sense only if the basis of the operation was to be expanded. In 1709 Martin Wendel demanded the cession of another ruined Hayange forge, named de la Morelle, whose owner, Benoît de Malzy, had failed to pay the feudal dues to the seigneur d'Hayange, namely Wendel. By 1711 he had successfully confirmed the acquisition of this forge. Wendel also bought territory, and above all woodland, which he needed to supply the charcoal for the forges. By 1720 he was operating five furnaces. He also rebuilt the chateau in Hayange about 1720, and in 1727 obtained letters patent from the duke of Lorraine, confirming his noble quality independent of his iron activity. The patent added that the nobility could not be formally proved since the titles had been "lost in the misfortune of war."[5] Already in 1711 he had obtained from the French monarchy "an office as king's secretary" in the chancellery of the Metz *parlement*, a minor royal office that finalized his ascent into the lesser nobility.[6]

In the 1930s the Wendels reacted with considerable indignation to the suggestion of the American magazine *Fortune* that they were arms producers and dealers, merchants of death.[7] But armaments is exactly how the family started its long engagement in the French iron and steel industry. Wendels had in fact not made armaments as such since the early nineteenth century, but from the point of view of the French state—as under the ancien régime—iron and steel were fundamentally important because of their potential military use.

The only customer of the Wendel forge for most of the eighteenth century was the royal artillery works in Thionville. Wendel established his business at a propitious time, in that there was a great demand as a consequence of the War of Spanish Succession. The only risk was military: as Louis XIV was increasingly isolated politically, a forge situated in the far east of France was vulnerable to the attacks of the Habsburg and British coalition. The chaotic circumstances of war finance, and the inflationary schemes designed to stabilize the government (this was the time of John Law's famous monetary experiment), in fact made it easy for individuals as well as the state to borrow, and easy to repay debt. It thus produced a wave of quite speculative business foundations. (The late eighteenth century proved to be a much harder financial environment.)

When Martin de Wendel died in 1737, his estate was valued at 700,000 livres. His eldest son, Charles, inherited the works; two years later he made another important strategic marriage, to the daughter of the king's receiver of finances in Lorraine, Marguerite d'Hausen, who brought a dowry of some 60,000 livres. Again, as with his father, there was a dynastic link to the fiscal bureaucracy of ancien-régime France; though at the same time as Charles worked with the French state, like his nineteenth-century successors he also dealt with another political unity, in this case the Duchy of Lorraine. Like his father, he benefited from the expansion of wartime demand for armor and bullets, in his case during the Seven Years' War.

Charles was determined to expand the ironworks further, and in particular bought substantial tracts of land in order to prospect for ore, and also to secure the necessary supply of charcoal. He bought woodland to the west of Hayange, in Longwy. The search for wood touched one of the most sensitive social issues of ancien-régime France, since woodlands were used extensively for animal forage, and deforestation thus put the livelihood of French villagers at stake. The peasants of Ranguevaux, on the hill just above Hayange, took their complaint about deforestation to the Financial Court in Bar, which limited Charles's felling of wood to 600 arpents annually, while Hayange consumed 18,000–20,000 *cordes*.[8] The locals also complained about the pollution of the river Fensch, which led to the periodic death of fish (and a consequent diminution of their income). Constrained in Hayange, Charles de Wendel bought another forge in eastern Lorraine, at Sainte-Fontaine, on the river Merle, from the duke of Lorraine, again with a hereditary title; here he had the right to fell up to 11,000 arpents from the forest of Bouzonville. In 1749 he obtained from the duke an authorization to operate a blast furnace at Hombourg. In view of the wood problem, Wendel also began to experiment with the use of coal in 1768.

By this time his forges were producing 1,370 tons of iron annually.[9] After 1769, however, iron prices fell as competition among the Lorraine and Saar manufacturers became more intense.

Searching for markets for his products, Charles de Wendel saw little alternative to state orders. In 1779 he obtained an exclusive contract to supply the French navy with bullets and cannonballs. When he died, in 1784, there seemed little reason to worry about the dynastic future; indeed his eldest son had already established a brilliant reputation as a metallurgist, and also very substantial political patronage.

Ignace de Wendel saw clearly where the logic of the family business lay. It required good political contacts, which Ignace cultivated, in order to secure sales. He was trained in the royal artillery school and fought in the French army. On 23 June 1758 he was slightly wounded at the battle of Krefeld. In 1772, still relatively young, he made a spectacular marriage, with Françoise-Cécile de Tronville, the daughter of the president of the *parlement* at Metz. The substantial dowry (60,000 livres) allowed him to buy a stake in the arsenal (weapons factory) of Charleville on the Meuse. Here was an early example of the logic of vertical integration, in which an iron business looked for industries that consumed iron. Eventually Ignace became a knight of the order of Saint Louis.

But Ignace was also an intellectual, who read widely. He was aware both that France's industry was backward in relation to those of other European powers, and that relative retardation was becoming an obsession with a monarchy recently isolated and humiliated in the Seven Years' War and later financially exhausted by the war of American independence. In 1757, just after the outbreak of the Seven Years' War, the finance inspector and director of hedges and roads Daniel-Charles Trudaine had sent the scientist and mining engineer Gabriel-Jean Jars to research the iron-ore mines and the forges of Bohemia, Hungary, Tyrol, and Saxony. Jars was then supposed to reorganize iron production in the east and center of France on the basis of his observation of the best foreign practice.[10] Wendel obtained instructions in 1768 from the royal minister of war, the duc de Choiseul, to explore alternative methods of fabrication, and also undertook his own very extensive journeys of industrial exploitation: in France, in the Franche-Comté, in the

Rhineland, Bavaria, Styria, and above all in what was then the most innovative metallurgical region, namely England. He wrote numerous treatises on mining and on the advantages of free trade.

As early as January 1769 Ignace de Wendel opened the first French coke-burning forge at Hayange in collaboration with Jars. After visiting central Europe, Jars had traveled to England, where he had studied, and then urged French imitation of, coke-smelting. But in 1773, when Wendel tried to repeat the experiment in Hayange, he obtained only very crumbly iron.

In 1779 the French government sent Wendel to inspect a foundry established in 1775 at Indret, at the mouth of the Loire, intended to supply material for royal armaments manufacture. The minister of the navy, Antoine-Raymond-Jean-Gualbert-Gabriel de Sartine, had wanted these works to become an English-style factory, and indeed they were initially managed by William Wilkinson, the brother of the English coke-smelting pioneer, John Wilkinson, but were not producing substantial quantities of iron. Wendel, who managed the negotiations with Wilkinson, concluded that new coke-fired blast furnaces needed to be built; but the government was unwilling to pay, and Wendel concluded a fifteen-year lease on his own behalf.

In 1780 Wilkinson had given a favorable report of the iron ore near Montcenis, at Le Creusot in central France. The next year Louis XVI authorized the establishment of blast furnaces there "founding by the English method." The state's hope was to create a model that the rest of French business would imitate. To raise the necessary capital, Wendel approached a cousin, Gabriel Palteau de Veymerange (a grandson of Martin Wendel), who held a prominent position as inspector of armies and mails; an uncle, Jean-François de Longlaville (a son of Martin); and the general treasurer of war, Megret de Sérilly. The family and its connections were a substantial source of industrial finance, but more money was required, and this could come only from the monarchy, which was already strained financially. The initial financing was complete in 1782, with the state providing 600,000 livres in 1783 and another 600,000 two years later. In 1785, when the large factory at Le Creusot began to operate, Wendel used the secret English method of ironmaking for the first time. The process depended on a steam-powered bellows that could deliver 3,000 cubic feet of air per minute. Le Creusot was soon producing 5,000 tons of iron annually, dwarfing the 900 tons manufactured by the old methods at Hayange. It was quite literally at the technological cutting edge of Europe.

With his new works in Indret and Le Creusot, Ignace de Wendel left Hayange and moved to Paris. Hayange was now marginal to his interests, and he left it in the control of his mother, Marguerite d'Hausen, who became generally known as Madame de Hayange. The summit of Ignace de Wendel's ambitions was reached when Louis XVI created a big industrial conglomerate, the Manufacture des Fonderies Royales d'Indret et de Montcenis et des Cristalleries de la Reine. Simon Schama describes the result as "the most formidable concentration of both workers and capital in western Europe."[11] It dwarfed anything occurring at that time in England's "industrial revolution." The new enterprise combined the forges at Indret and Le Creusot, managed by Ignace de Wendel, as well as iron-ore mines at Chalency, Antully, and de la Pâture; Ignace was one of three administrators (with Sérilly and Palteau de Veymerange). The capital was fixed at 10 million livres, divided into 4,000 shares, of which only half seem to have been issued initially. Of these the king held 333, and Ignace de Wendel, Sérilly, and Palteau de Vermerange a total of 1,756. But the production was quite expensive, and when there was a demand for cannons it was cheaper to import pig iron from England than to do the smelting in Le Creusot.[12]

Wendel was a victim of the increasingly desperate state of royal finances. The 600,000 livres promised by the king to the Manufacture des Fonderies Royales never materialized. In the major financial crash of the summer of 1787, Sérilly went bankrupt, and the production of the enterprise slowed. In 1789 Marguerite d'Hausen reminded Finance Minister Necker of the 100,000 livres owed by the king. Necker refused to pay for reasons that he justified in terms of the new liberal ideas about economics as worked out by the physiocrats, who advocated a more limited role for the state: "public authority should not involve itself in individual industry except in order to share the results when they are developed."[13] Without state support, however, French industry was in a precarious position, including the Wendel businesses. The mundane reality behind Necker's statement was the bankruptcy of the ancien régime.

The Revolution

During the 1780s, feudalism became a highly political issue as some titleholders tried to revalue or restore claims that had dwindled away over time. The Wendels were drawn into the case of an almost 1,000-year-old claim of an abbey to possess the seigneurie of Hayange. Marguerite d'Hausen quickly spent 117,000 livres (in addition to legal costs) to buy off the abbess. The feudal backlash led to a politicization of every sort of demand.

By 1789, a family as politically well connected as the Wendels was highly vulnerable. Old scores could be settled in a new environment. With their new opportunity to express grievances, the peasants of the Fensch valley again protested against the water pollution emanating from the forges of Hayange. The formal letter of grievances, solicited by the newly constituted Estates General, stated that the river Fensch was "one of the most beautiful in the kingdom," but

> since a certain time the Sieur Wendel d'Hayange who owns the forges has used the river to wash his ore. In response to the complaints made several times by different villages, he replied that since he worked in making bullets and artillery for the king, he was entitled to use the stream as he wished. The communities have never risked any action against a man so rich and so powerful; and the result has been a decline in the number of farmers working in the riverside villages and to losses of cattle, to sterility and abortions in cows and mares, because of the pollution of the stream by the forge.[14]

On 18 March 1790 a decree required the suspension of all woodcutting. At the same time, demand collapsed. French ironmasters rapidly complained that there "has never been such a stagnation of trade in iron. The demand of commerce is not one-tenth part of the manufacture."[15]

As war with the monarchical powers of Austria and Prussia became more likely, Ignace de Wendel may have thought that the political upheavals would improve his financial situation, and he worked loyally with the constitutional monarchy to supply weapons: he received an order from the minister of war, Louis de

Narbonne-Lara, to find 150,000 rifles (which he bought with credit from his cousin, Gabriel Palteau de Veymerange); and Le Creusot supplied eighty-four large cannons for the royal navy. In August 1792 Hayange was invaded by Austrian and Prussian forces, which besieged Thionville before retreating. Early the previous year Ignace de Wendel had set out his political philosophy in letters to his son in which he produced a conventional justification of the demolition of the absolute monarchy and of feudalism, as the revolution of the productive fighting against the idle. Versailles had been a den of splendor and voluptuousness. By contrast, "in agriculture and commerce, everything worked only because of the Third Estate. Is one surprised that the people who did everything do not want to be inferior to those who do nothing?" He placed this critique of the old in the context of a plea for constitutional monarchy, and above all for the rule of law. The kings of France, he thought retrospectively, had lapsed into a despotism "like the Turkish sultans."[16]

After the proclamation of the Republic, however, Ignace de Wendel was dismissed from his positions in Le Creusot and in the Manufacture des Fonderies Royales. He now returned to the ancestral enterprise in Hayange, where the mayor, Jacques Tourneur—a former coachman of the Wendel family—tried to provoke him into fleeing so that as an émigré his property would be confiscated. The Wendel family was vulnerable on a number of counts. Benoît de Wendel, a younger brother of Ignace, had taken part in an assembly of the nobility at Thionville and had since disappeared, presumably into exile. A grandson of Marguerite d'Hausen, an army officer, Louis-Ignace de Balthasar, had fled from Hayange after being arrested in Metz as a royalist. But he did not run very far, was soon rearrested, and was executed in Metz in October 1793. Before the guillotine fell, the executioner solemnly burned the picture of Louis XVI that Balthasar had carried with him at the time of his arrest. Louis's father had already been arrested in April 1793, but was freed at the request of Marguerite d'Hausen, and in November 1793 fled to Germany.

Quite quickly (though the writings cannot be precisely dated) Ignace de Wendel made clear his abhorrence for the Jacobins and the new republican regime: "the revolutionary government is supported by a million factious people and led by five or six scoundrels." But his objections were based on more than the bad character of the new leaders: a republic, he believed, could not last in France because of its inherently democratic and anti-wealth-producing propensities. "Big enterprise cannot be made except by big capital accumulated in a few hands. Thus there need to be a certain number of rich men in France, the big profits need to go to these men, and the inequality of fortunes needs to increase with the property of the state. If this empire is made into a democratic republic, every day property will be exposed to the invasion of the multitude, power will be placed in the hands of envy, and the state's law will be the strongest law; that is the most terrible despotism." Thus the industrialist concluded that some brake on democracy, and some support of the aristocracy, in the form of legal certainty, were required for the good of France.[17]

Ignace fled France, probably at the end of October 1792, first to a small forge he owned at Berchiwé, in Luxembourg. In April 1794 the Berchiwé forge was destroyed by local protesters and soldiers, presumably French revolutionary troops.[18] He then went on to Germany, from where in 1795, after Thermidor and the fall of Robespierre, he addressed a number of pleas to be allowed to return to France and to have his property restored, on the grounds that in emigrating he had simply been trying to save his life from injustice and oppression.

Alone of her family, Madame de Hayange remained in France and continued to supervise the operation of the forges, which she seems to have done with considerable skill. In late 1793 the commissar ("representative of the people") attached to the army of the Moselle protected her and intervened to protect the factory employees from the recruiting squads mobilizing men for the defense of the nation. Presumably his motive was to ensure continued production of much-needed munitions. Madame continued her management when, eventually, after the radicalization of the Revolution, the defeat of the Girondins, the execution of Louis de Balthasar, and the flight of her son, the Wendel manufacture was sequestered (December 1793). She herself was arrested on 5 April 1794, the day Danton was executed, and was not released until October 1795.

The state management of ironworks proved to be ineffective. By 1796 the cost of making iron in France had tripled from the early 1790s, in part because it was harder to obtain high-quality English pig iron while France was at war and in part because there was a shortage of skilled workers. Garnier, the representative of Paris ("of the people") in the department of the Allier, wrote in a report that "national factories are a perpetual source of wastage and extravagance."[19] From Year IV (1795–96) the Council of Mines advised the sale of national property.

Marguerite d'Hausen, who knew many of the secrets of the iron trade, remained as the manager in Hayange under the direction of a trustee imposed by the Revolution. Other, politically less threatening women remained as the managers of works: the widow Hardy managed a similar business in Longuyon; across the Rhine, in the Ruhr basin, the widow Krupp played an analogous role; and Aletta Noot Haniel managed the family's trading house for eighteen years while her children were minors. Women had played a substantial role in eighteenth-century business households, and their lack of empowerment in the Revolution gave their functions an unpolitical cast that could be useful in the midst of political turmoils.

The Wendels, however, were very exposed politically. In 1797 the leases of the forges at Hayange and Sainte-Fontaine were auctioned for the benefit of the state, and sold to a speculator in confiscated property, Louis Granthil. Marguerite d'Hausen, who had protested bitterly against the sale on the grounds of the family firm's sixty years of demonstrated patriotism in arming the French nation, was rewarded for having supplied munitions for the Republic with the right to live in two rooms in the chateau at Hayange. She died in Metz in 1802. In 1800 Granthil succeeded in buying the ownership of the Hayange forges in a new auction, in which the bidding, driven by the land speculators who had flourished in the wake of the Revolution, had been heavy. Such overbidding at auctions for nationalized property was a common feature of the late 1790s, driven by the combined effects of an active property market resulting from the confiscations and expropriation of church and nobles' land, extreme monetary instability, the renewed threat of hyperinflation, and a belief in future national prosperity.[20] The initial guide price for Hayange was 1.25 million francs; Granthil paid 16 million, or 500 times the revenue of the forges (around 3 million). The extent of his miscalculation became obvious when the market for his products disappeared with the Treaty of Lunéville. In 1803 Granthil was forced to declare bankruptcy.

Meanwhile Ignace went first to Hesse, where he was offered a position as director of the ruler's ironworks, which he declined because they were in such a poor condition; and then to the enlightened court of Karl August of Saxony-Weimar-Eisenach. Here he tried in vain to introduce English smelting methods. Karl August's minister and friend, Goethe, described the sad fate of the French engineer as a conflict of Enlightenment ideas and technological modernization against ancien-régime conventionality:

> Several émigrés were well received at court and by society, but not all contented themselves simply with these social advantages. Some had the intention, here as elsewhere, to support themselves by laudable activity. A brave man named von Wendel, already advanced in years, found out that in Ilmenau some shares of a hammerwork company belonged to the ducal household. This works was used in an odd way, in that the hammermasters operated according to a rotation, in which everyone worked on his own account but then quickly left the works to the next in line. Such a method was thinkable only in a very old-fashioned setting. A man used to freedom could not really find himself in this activity, although the ducal rights were immediately ceded to Wendel for a small fee that perhaps was never even collected. His order-loving and active spirit led him to attempt to quench his unrest by further plans, either to buy up more shares, or the whole of the hammer mill. But both solutions were impossible, because the ordinary existence of a few quiet families depended on this business.
>
> The spirit directed itself to something else. He built a reverberator furnace, to melt and cast old iron. He hoped that the concentrated heat would have a great effect, but it was great above all expectation, for the furnace roofing collapsed with the heat as the iron melted. He tried other experiments without great success. The good man, believing in the end that he was quite out of his element, sank into despair and took an excessive dose of opium, which killed him perhaps not immediately but in its effects. His sorrow was so great that neither the support of the prince nor the charitable activity of the princely advisers who had been instructed to help could restore him. Far removed from his fatherland, in a quiet corner of the Thuringian forest, he, too, fell as a victim to a revolution without frontiers.[21]

In April 1795, before taking the fatal dose of opium, Wendel drew up a brief will, in which he wrote: "Reputation is what is dearest to us. Goodbye, my children, may you not be so unhappy as was your father during his life."[22] From being the incarnation of Enlightenment rationalism and scientific thought, he had become a worthy inhabitant of the pages and the mental world of Johann Wolfgang von Goethe.

A Restoration Career

Two diametrically opposed clichés are applied to early nineteenth-century French business existence. According to one cliché, family firms, and especially French family firms, never borrow, because their owners are anxious about letting outsiders into family secrets and watering down the essence of family control. According to the other cliché, life in Restoration France was all about borrowing, speculating, and the making and losing of gigantic fortunes. This was, for instance, the France of Balzac's Rastignac. The French Revolution and the profound legal uncertainty it generated had made French capitalism a madly dizzying casino rather than a rationally ordered market.

The consequence of on the one hand a very active property market, dramatic swings in valuations, and new market and technological opportunities and, on the other, a systematic codification of law as a result of the Revolution and above all of the Napoleonic reforms, meant that society became obsessed by the interplay of law and property. Equality and the partition of inheritance, as laid down by the Code Napoléon, seemed to be at odds with the possibilities opened by the new business world. The consequence was to set family members against one another, with dramatic quarrels and complex and long-lived legal cases ensuing. The new language of the law required the specification of grievances, and increased rather than calmed conflict between siblings and between generations.

The younger son of Ignace de Wendel, François, was more like Rastagnac than a conventional French family businessman, except that he was not a self-made man. He was proud of his family tradition, and in particular of its military tradition and its service to the French state and the French monarchy. A characteristic document of this mentality is his will, which explained that originally he did not want to be a businessman. It opens with the statement: "I the undersigned, François de Wendel, former cadet in the royal navy, officer in the hussars' regiment and in the light cavalry, and now, against my will, ironmaster and owner of several establishments that have prospered despite and against everything . . ."[23] He had had to leave the naval academy at the age of fifteen because of the Revolution and had spent some time in his father's forges in Luxembourg before joining the counterrevolutionary armies. He fought in Italy against the French revolutionary army of General Bonaparte, had his horse shot from under him at the battle of Friedberg (24 April 1796), and was wounded in the thigh during the fighting on the river Mincio (May 1796). But in 1802 Napoleon appealed to the émigrés to return to France, and François de Wendel made his way back to Metz via Hayange. At this time he was almost penniless, his total assets amounting to 30 louis.

When he learned that the estate and the forges of Hayange were for sale, he organized a general Wendel family bid through an intermediary, Aubertin, a Metz merchant, who bought the forges for 222,000 francs ($44,000)—a remarkable contrast with the inflated sum paid by Granthil. Alexandre-Georges de Balthasar (an uncle of François by marriage, and the younger brother of the Balthasar executed in 1793), François's older brother Charles, who had served in the Republican armies at Santo Domingo, and François de Wendel acted as a consortium to reestablish the Wendel industrial fortunes. At this stage Charles found himself financially strained by the businesses he was running in the department of the Saar.

On 9 January 1805 (29 Nivôse, Year XIII) Charles and François reached an agreement to share their father's inheritance, with Charles abdicating his rights to the forge at Hayange but keeping control of works at Charleville and Tulle. A third brother, Louis, was not in France at this time and was left out of the partition of property, though a later share was reserved for him should he return. He seems to have accepted this result, at least for the moment. In 1813 François reached an agreement with Louis, under which the successful younger brother paid his elder brother a *rente*, or annuity, of 3,000 francs (which would be raised to 4,000 if François won his case against Sérilly, the former royal treasurer, bankrupt, and associate of Ignace de Wendel, who was trying to press a financial claim against the estate of Ignace). Louis in turn renounced his rights of inheritance.

Paying such *rentes* to impoverished older brothers required cash, but the most important demand for funds stemmed from the reconstruction and modernization of works that had long been neglected and run down by careless management. The skilled technicians of the ancien régime had been dispersed by the Revolution, and there was a general knowledge deficit. To get money, François de Wendel in 1802–1804 sold the remaining assets of Madame de Wendel for 77,352 francs and went to the bankers of Mulhouse and Metz.

François de Wendel borrowed a substantial amount of money for the purchase and then the modernization of the works. Initially he borrowed 150,000 francs from Jacob Cahen of Mulhouse, which he proposed to repay from the proceeds of the forges: but he eventually borrowed much more in order to expand the factory and to buy the mines and woodlands he needed to supply his forges.[24] Wendel's accounts from 1808 show that by then he had borrowed 539,924 francs from Cahen and had paid 26,987 in interest. By the time of the Restoration, in 1815, Cahen was bankrupt and wrote a pathetic letter to Wendel begging for support; it is not clear whether he had any response. In 1807 Wendel received permission to build a sheet mill on the River Fensch below Hayange at Montminou. He also bought a large foundry in Moyeuvre in 1811 from Jean François Marin; this venture involved borrowing from the financier who had originally supported Marin's acquisition of Moyeuvre.[25] François de Wendel thus signed two bonds of 120,000 and 180,000 francs for a loan from the Lorraine banker Florentin Seillière (who later established himself in Paris). By 1819 Wendel had borrowed a total of 250,000 from the Seillières and another 200,000 from the allied banking house of Louis Poupillier.[26]

Since his father had taken his many technical secrets with him to his Weimar grave, François de Wendel had no knowledge or experience of English methods of coke-smelting. The obvious nearby source of coal, the Saar coalfields, which in 1814 were in France under the terms of the first Treaty of Vienna, in 1815 lay outside France as punishment for Napoleon's 100 days.

François was also beset by family difficulties. He fell out with his brother Charles, who had returned to France too soon from Santo Domingo, been arrested, and when released had tried to work as an iron merchant in the Saar, where he had—like Granthil—paid much too much for a forge. Believing that François, who had ceded the Wendel property in Charleville, Tulle, and Berchiwé to him, had cheated him over the repurchase of Hayange, he launched a lengthy and highly acrimonious lawsuit. By 1811 Charles de Wendel's works had run into great difficulties.

In 1814 Charles brought a court case against François, whom he accused of having "outspent his inheritance and of having used deception to obtain his [Charles's] agreement to the division of the belongings of our father and grandmother." He prepared a pamphlet detailing how he had been "deprived of my rights by my brother François de Wendel." He renewed the case in 1817, and in 1818 a court in Thionville ruled in favor of François, with its judgment upheld by the royal court in Metz. The judges' decision ruled that the contract between the two brothers had been valid. It stated: "Considering that the correspondence of Charles de Wendel, his actions, the disposition of property made by him as well as that which he announced as his intention under the terms of the partition of 1805 after that act, his actions and his promises in the six years after that partition all prove that this was a final and serious contract between the two brothers."[27]

In 1820 the other Wendel brother, Louis, brought his own case against François. Louis argued to the court in support of his claim to payment that he had been abominably treated: "stripped by François de Wendel, the youngest of my brothers, of the rights that nature and law guaranteed to me in the estate of my father and my grandmother, reduced to misery, when he built a colossal fortune upon my ruin, I should have my just complaints heard . . . It is therefore necessary finally to break the silence, to announce the scandal of his wealth and the scandal of my misery." François submitted to the court his brother's old and generally supportive letters, as well as his brother's declarations that he did not intend to marry and thus might live modestly: evidence that Louis was simply being litigious because of all the post-Restoration possibilities for redress. In 1806, for instance, Louis had written to his brother to ask for some small payment: "I feel like you, and more than you, the difficulty that you must have in helping me with my needs, and perhaps also in regard to Charles; and it is for this reason that I ardently hope to find employment that will at least allow me to be less of a burden to you." And in 1811 he had declared: "I would be able to live on a modest allowance because I do not have any passions any more. If my brother does not decide that we can make something of our little foundry and if he does not give me any way of being useful for his business, I will solicit a job, and when peace comes I will with his help make another long trip or two." Then in 1812 he had stated: "As for me, I tell you that I am in no way jealous of your fortune and your bustling business; that if I wanted to get involved, it would be to help you, to keep myself busy and to give evidence of my gratitude, which I will do whenever you deem me ready. From now on I hope for an honest, steady comfort, and a job to keep me busy."[28]

The court again ruled in favor of François de Wendel, who added a preface to the collection of the court documents that he kept in his papers and thus became part of the Wendel archive:

> Louis de Wendel brought an unjust lawsuit against me. I have been denounced as the despoiler of my brothers' fortune, although it was decided that they received even more than what my parents' inheritance could offer them; although it is proven above all, that he who, at the last minute objected to a division with me, had more interest in carrying out a transaction that put him happily under the shelter of good fortunes that are associated with the title of heir. My brother saw in this trial the opportunity to vent his spite and hatred; he seized upon it with eagerness, with ardor.[29]

Just a few months after the court had settled the issue against him, Louis wrote to Charles and now took a conspicuously reasonable tone:

> François acquired, like you, at his risk and dangers, the Hayange ironworks from which both of you derived a return. He succeeded through good management and conduct that you perhaps did not copy. You were unlucky, I know, but you had the same means, perhaps more knowledge of ironworks, since you did not leave my father. Fortune turned her back on you as on me; follow my moderation, ask reasonably, without bitterness, for the resources to make up for your losses; but leave this unsettled life;

> restrain the spiteful passions that make you hated by men and by yourself.[30]

While he was building up Hayange and Moyeuvre, François de Wendel also engaged in a cooperative venture in Quint (just north of Trier on the Moselle), where he held eight of thirty shares, with twelve owned by M. de Balthasar, the brother-in-law of François's father, who emerged as a key adviser to François de Wendel in a wide range of business decisions. A great deal of technical expertise had been lost as the Revolution dispersed skilled workmen. Quite how technically and financially fragile these metallurgical ventures were at the beginning of the new political era can be judged from a letter from Balthasar to François de Wendel in 1810:

> You promised me a month ago that you were going to send me a horse, a cart, and some weights; meanwhile nothing has arrived, and every time M. Seillière [the banker from the Nancy and Paris house] or M. Mesnil [another financier] sees me he asks when it will arrive . . . The warehouse has been in order for three or four days and is already stocked with a considerable amount of iron, which could be started if there were weights. The merchants believe there is trouble, but you know that that is their usual way of talking, and I am not frightened, because there is always need for iron. I think it is necessary to stock the warehouse with high-quality iron, which is the side where the reputation of these ironworks is the least well established.

The same letter shows that speculators who believed that they could manipulate the future of the iron industry were rushing to get credit in order to expand their holdings:

> I spoke with M. Mesnil about M. Moreau's trip and he told me that he knew from a good source that the latter through his employment at the Bank of France had procured a loan of two million [francs] at 4 percent; that his speculation concerned primarily steel and iron of the best quality, which is completely lacking here. He may also want to buy more of them. However that may be, in this state of uncertainty could not you get the prefect to intervene? The main wealth of his department lies in ironworks, which would be harmed by the import of Swedish iron; it seems

> to me that it is justified to attract the government's attention to this subject before the harm is done. The customs duties that existed in 1804 did not increase with the price of iron in the Empire.[31]

After the Restoration of 1814–15, the French iron industry was in a parlous state. It had been cut off for many years from best practice by the Continental System of Napoleon; French works had lost relative to the new businesses of the Rhine valley; and after the conclusion of the peace there was the threat of a vigorous English competition. A letter from Balthasar to his partner Serre in 1817 after the ceramics workshop burnt down as a result of an accident is illustrative of the Restoration malaise: the event was not a catastrophe, Balthasar argued, because the workshop was hopelessly outdated anyway, and had not been renovated only because of a shortage of funds:

> You know that the potter's workshop was falling into ruins, that there was discussion of rebuilding it in 1815, and that the desire to economize, in that period of tight circumstances, hindered us; in 1816 I was stopped by the same consideration; it seemed to me that it would be better to employ some ovens for the preparation of the mill . . . but it would hardly have been possible to proceed like that for more than one season, because one of the sections of the wall was leaning considerably and all the woodwork was decayed. The damage actually was restricted to the loss of wooden implements, such as lanterns and small planks, and a part of this we would have been able to repair by using planks that were still good and by giving free drinks to people who would help . . . I estimate the entirety of the damage at about 500 francs. This is nothing compared to the danger we have run, which has inspired a healthy fear in us. It is also fortunate that the pottery orders are completed for this season and do not pick up again until summer. Wendel should have explained to you where we would rebuild the mill, where the first copse was; there will be a sawmill next to it, and I think that it will be very profitable.[32]

François de Wendel, notwithstanding the acrimonious lawsuits against his brothers, seems to have had a strong sense of family tradition. In 1804 he married a distant relative, the great-granddaughter of Martin Wendel, Joséphine de Fischer de Dicourt. Later he rebuilt the Hayange chateau, which had been severely damaged during the Revolution, in a modest style appropriate to a post-revolutionary age. He developed a considerable range of business interests and activities, extending his industrial capacity even in the rather poor years that followed the peace. This seemed at the time like another gamble. In 1816 he built rolling mills at Sérémange and Jamailles, and in 1820 rolling mills and a cutting mill at Moulin-Neuf (all in the vicinity of Hayange). He also requested permission to build a blast furnace at Knutange, near the Moselle, which he hoped to fuel with Saar coal, despite the relatively high tariffs. Later he prospected for coal on the French side of the frontier in the Saar basin, near Forbach. He also directed four forges in Luxembourg, all in the vicinity of Bitburg: the Eichelhütte, Wenzelhausen, Laschmidt, and Malberg. These new enterprises demanded considerable skill, which was scarce in the desolate France of the Restoration, and in 1816 François de Wendel went to England and Wales, labored as an ironworker for a time (in order to learn the new methods), and then employed some English workers who were familiar with best practice. When he returned he concluded that Hayange needed a coke-fired blast furnace. He also brought back the English technique of puddling (stirring iron in order to burn off carbon).

English workers became the most obvious solution to a French shortage of skills. In Charenton, coke was made almost entirely by English workers, who were paid much more than their French equivalents. The English iron specialist Dobson in 1802 was arrested by the British government after returning to his native country: he was accused of stealing plans and inciting English workers to emigrate. (The British government at this time prohibited the emigration of skilled workers on mercantilist grounds.)[33] Even when Wendel could recruit skilled Englishmen, there was no guarantee that they would stay, or that they would keep his secrets. Some ironmasters in the Ardennes, for instance, in turn lured workers away from François de Wendel and copied his machines.

One prefectural report on Wendel explained that he had rebuilt his family's ruined factories and rapidly established a "very honorable fortune": his credit, the report stated, was almost without limit.[34] Indeed, he seems to have been able to borrow a great deal. A list of François de Wendel's debts in 1828 shows a total of 2,764,814 francs (around $532,000), borrowed at rates of 5 and 6 percent. (At the time the yield on government debt was below 4 percent, so Wendel only paid a relatively small risk premium.) In the early 1820s, however, Wendel was close to despair. He noted "a general distrust, demands for repayment from all sides; abandonment by the Ministry of War; English production disparaged, so that we don't want it; a reduction of 20 percent in all iron prices; many difficulties with the new production."[35] At this point he was close to absolute despair: "I should liquidate everything, by any possible means; anything, even death, rather than staying like this." He contemplated returning from Paris and national politics to Hayange and industry, leading a very modest life with only one servant, one cook, and one maid, and thus saving more than 30,000 francs.[36]

One way out of the quagmire was through politics. François de Wendel already had some political leverage. In 1807 he had become mayor of Hayange, and in 1808 he became a member of the general council of the Moselle department. At the Restoration, he became much more prominent. In September 1814 he received the duc de Berry at Hayange, and in January 1815 he became a knight of the order of Saint Louis. In August 1815 he was elected to the Chamber of Deputies for the Moselle department, although he could no longer stand in 1816 because at thirty-eight he was below the minimum age of forty designed to assure the deep conservatism of the new parliament. He was elected, however, to the same seat in 1818 and 1822. In 1817 he became a knight in the Légion d'Honneur. In addition, from 1819 he was a member of the General Council of Manufactures. He used these positions to press for protectionist legislation so as to exclude Swedish and English iron, and in 1821 and 1822 French tariffs on iron products were indeed raised. By the beginning of 1823 he had shaken off all the old pessimism: "The greatest ill is often quite close to the good; the human heart should never give up. The distrust has disappeared; the English production is going very well; iron prices have recovered; I am free."[37] By 1824 he was calculating that there would be a tremendous demand for iron in Paris—and for nonmilitary purposes. There would be canals built, iron railroads (for horse-drawn traffic), water conduits, gas lighting. In fact François de Wendel was quickly sketching out the entire story of the economic development of the nineteenth century.

He also translated what this new demand for iron would mean

for him, both in business and in personal terms. In business, he would need to "perfect manufacture so that we can produce at low prices; and accustom the workers here to produce all detailed products." Politically and personally, he saw two major objectives: first, "to establish my fortune on a solid base, and leave a good reputation to my children, as the best of all inheritances"; and second, "to derive from my political position the goal that I must reasonably expect, the peerage." He concluded this optimistic assessment: "Why, with things arranged like this, with good ancestors, real services given to the state, descendants who are nobly established, some means which I can spend, why can I not get to a peerage, which so many others have achieved only by low intrigues and cowardly compliance? It seems to me that I am well placed to deserve the goodwill of a just government."[38] There were just two problems. One was that the government was shifting to the right, away from the pragmatic liberal constitutionalism with which François de Wendel had affiliated himself since the days of the Empire, and toward the power of the *ultras*. In 1820 he had been quite close to the peerage that he yearned for, but then the duc de Berry was assassinated, and the reactionary Count Joseph de Villèle, who thought of Wendel as a major enemy, formed a government. The second was that on 11 March 1825 François de Wendel died suddenly in Metz.

Families were enormously vulnerable to politics, but also to chance events. Unanticipated death and the devolution of wealth to underage children brought the likelihood of a round of legal disputes between heirs. In this situation, widows played a central role. Women in fact had a much greater part in the formulation of business strategies than later in the nineteenth century, when the corporation and its statutes and the bureaucratization of corporate existence left less to chance and to the skillful operation of dynastic politics.

Wrestling with Primogeniture

In the year of François de Wendel's death, the mining engineer Théodore de Gargan, who had conducted the most elaborate survey of the ore resources of the Moselle department, wrote in a memorandum: "the ore of Hayange is in horizontal layers in the chalk of the surrounding hills. It is part of an oolitic formation. It seems to be an extension of the field that is being mined two hours by foot away, in Moyeuvre. The seam is between 1.6 and 2 meters thick, and comes to the surface in all the neighboring valley folds. Its quantity is extraordinary."[39] Under the mining law of 1810 the excavation of underground ore required state permission, but François de Wendel's application had lain unanswered, gathering dust in the prefectural offices. The great coup of François's widow, Madame Joséphine de Fischer de Dicourt, was to marry her daughter, Marguérite-Josephine (in 1826), to the one man who not only knew exactly where the iron-ore fields lay but also could work the complexities of bureaucracy—and who happened to be a widower.

The new son-in-law, Théodore de Gargan, at once left the Corps Royal des Mines and applied himself decisively to furthering the Wendel interests. In December 1827 he submitted an application to the prefect of the Moselle for a concession of 7,840 hectares, stretching from north of the river Fensch to south of the Orne. The application was publicly posted, and sometime after the deadline for objections another foundry operator, Felix de Hunolstein of Ottange, registered a protest on the ground that his family had worked iron in the area longer than the Wendels. The case took a long time to be settled, but in 1834 the royal concession was granted to the Wendels: a grant of mining in an area of 2,763 hectares in Hayange and 1,496 hectares in Moyeuvre. The area of the concession was altered in 1863, without the total amount of territory being affected; but in 1869 the family enlarged its award. This concession was by far the largest of any of those awarded in the Lorraine iron field, and by the end of the Second Empire amounted to over half of the total Lorraine concessions. The grant by itself practically guaranteed the prosperity of the family.[40]

Madame Joséphine also had two sons. The younger, Charles de Wendel, was sixteen when his father died. He set out to acquire technical rather than commercial skills. In 1828 he entered the Ecole Polytechnique; on graduating, he went to England to study mining and metallurgy and did not return to France until 1834. His older brother, Victor-François, was more interested in landowning, and moved away from Hayange to estates on the river Seille. Charles developed into a major business figure. The Wendel historian Jacques Marseille points out that while in 1834 the Wendels produced only one percent of French iron, by 1870 they were the premier iron dynasty, accounting for 11.2 percent of national pro-

2. *Charles de Wendel, 1809–1870*
COURTESY OF THE WENDEL ARCHIVE, PARIS

duction.[41] Nevertheless, Charles de Wendel always felt that his considerable industrial triumphs were incomplete. He never had full control over his enterprises, because of the knowledge and activity of the powerful team of Gargan and his mother. In later life he also saw himself overtaken by the meteoric rise of the Schneider dynasty, and came greatly to resent his eclipse.

Charles de Wendel focused much of his resulting sense of grievance on French law. The Code Napoléon and its insistence on the equal rights of heirs had a considerable and redistributive effect on the way in which business successions were handled. It was no longer possible simply to leave property to one favored or elder son; such arrangements would have smacked of the ills of feudalism. The National Assembly had abolished primogeniture in March 1790, and in 1791 it had passed a resolution requiring equal division among heirs. The Code Napoléon stepped back from an endorsement of complete equality, allowing a parent to dispose freely of one-quarter of the property if there were three or more children. Gifts between the living were permitted, but any transfer above the disposable share permitted had to be repaid on the death of the parent.[42] A family compact of the type that the Rothschilds concluded in 1810 and 1812, and that threatened females with disinheritance, would thus have been illegal in France.

Divisible inheritance had been one of the major demands of opponents of the ancien régime and of proponents of economic rationality. The economic irrationality of single-heir "feudal" inheritance had been pilloried in Adam Smith's *Wealth of Nations*, and large estates were blamed for the backwardness of agricultural production.[43] After the radical reform program was implemented in revolutionary France, however, the tone of economic argument shifted, and some business figures and many aristocrats now maintained that it was partition and division which threatened national prosperity by producing nonviable small land holdings and business units. The answer to the business issue lay in the legal framework that would allow corporations and shareholding systems, but it was not implemented until the middle of the nineteenth century. In the meantime, the personal tensions arising out of partible inheritance created major difficulties for those heads of family firms who saw themselves as seigneurs. Subdivision of agricultural holdings also remained a major topic of political debate until the mid-twentieth century.

In the 1830s the matriarch of the Wendel dynasty, Madame Joséphine, had drawn up contracts specifying how the share of each child and grandchild of François de Wendel could be paid off through a notional cash alternative that would bear a fixed and purposefully low rate of interest. In the versions of 1831 and 1833 each child agreed to cede the right of inheritance for a sum of 400,000 francs, which would be left in the firm as operating capital but would yield a meager 2.5 percent, with the intention that the rest of the income could be reinvested in the company. In the 1835 contract the interest rate was lowered further, to 2 percent, for ten years after each child reached the age of majority. This contract is worth quoting as an example of a family compact of the time:

> Between the undersigned Marie Françoise Joséphine Fischer widow of M. Fr. de Wendel landowner domiciled at Hayange . . . for one part, and for the other part Marguerite Joséphine de Wendel wife of M. Gargan landowner residing, at Hayange; Victor François de Wendel landowner residing near Thionville;

> Alexie Charles de Wendel landowner residing at Hayange and Mademoiselle Caroline de Wendel. It has been agreed that modifying the contracts of 12 March 1831 and 5 May 1833, by which all children gave up their rights in the succession of M. de Wendel their father, for the sum of 400,000 francs, paying interest of 2 percent for ten years from the moment when each one should participate in the return, and after that 5 percent with the right to dispose of the capital.[44]

After the death of Gargan in 1851 the company was managed solely by Charles de Wendel, but without full ownership (because of the inheritance clauses protecting Charles's siblings and their offspring). The contract of 1835 was superseded by the establishment of a company *en commandite*, or partnership (at this time, joint-stock companies required a complex process of governmental approval, and the *commandite* form was highly popular). In such a corporation, almost all the authority (as well as unlimited liability) rested with one or more *gérants* (managing partners), while the other shareholders had limited liability but no control over the *gérant.* The only time they could exercise any influence was when the *gérant* died or was incapacitated and a new manager needed to be selected. On 24 April 1857 a deed between Madame veuve de Wendel, her son Charles de Wendel, and Baron Théodore de Gargan (junior) established Le Fils de François de Wendel et Cie. Almost all its capital was brought in by Madame de Wendel, a very substantial 30,406,329.88 francs ($5.8 million), and the widow Wendel pledged further support of 8,177,872.97 francs ($1.6 million). Charles de Wendel and Baron de Gargan invested no capital but pledged their "special knowledge and hard work." Of the profits of the company, 80 percent were to be paid to Madame de Wendel and 20 percent to the *gérants*, Charles de Wendel (12 percent) and Gargan (8 percent). The preamble stressed the "spirit of preservation and of family . . Madame de Wendel wanted to keep in her children's inheritance the fine factories created by her husband and his son-in-law."

In a letter of March 1862 Madame Joséphine had again declared her intention of creating equal shares for each of her children and their descendants, and in May 1862 she had given 100,000 francs to each child. But then she seems to have been pressed by Charles to

3. *Madame François de Wendel (Madame Joséphine), 1784–1872*
COURTESY OF THE WENDEL ARCHIVE, PARIS

take a different course. On 4 December 1862 she wrote a letter to Charles and a parallel letter to the company Fils de François de Wendel et Cie., giving Charles 1,481,251.93 francs that had already been advanced by the company, and an equal sum for the future. Gargan contested this highly problematic promise, which was contrary to the provisions of the Code Napoléon on equality of inheritance. Gargan's lawyer offered as a legal opinion: "The law required two things: first, it required that the mother and father's fortune be preserved for the children insofar as it was possible; this result having been attained, it also required insofar as possible that equality between the children be maintained. Let the most dear and the best-loved not complain about the law!"[45]

In 1867 the new law on the establishment of joint-stock companies, under which government permission was no longer required for the establishment of a company, set off a wave of speculative foundations. It offered a way of protecting industrial property against the regular divisions resulting from the inheritance law of the Code Civil. The Wendels reworked their company at this time, without, however, creating a share company. The major effect was to establish a notional debt owed by the company to Charles de Wendel of 1,639,597 francs and to the estate of Gargan 285,976.[46]

During the period of Charles's management, the company expanded dramatically, thanks to the new supplies of minette ore as a result of the grant negotiated by Gargan. In 1834 there were three blast furnaces in Hayange, six in 1850, and eight in 1857; the whole works was the most modern in France. The output of cast iron amounted to 6,000 tons in 1828, and 23,000 in 1847, 22,000 in 1850, and then rose sharply as the economy recovered from the revolutionary disturbances: to 88,000 in 1862, and 134,500 in 1869. In 1828 there were 325 workers, in 1850 2,000, and in 1869 7,000. These works attracted widespread admiration. It was a visit to "the fine establishments of M. de Wendel" in 1834 that persuaded the engineer François Alexandre to convince the Schneider brothers that the old works at Le Creusot, originally established by Ignace de Wendel, could be restarted with great profit. Achille Schneider noted that "the ironworks are destined to take on a very large growth in France, and in Le Creusot we will always produce it. In this way there will always be money to be made."[47] This was the beginning of the great dynastic rivalry of the Wendels and the

Schneiders, who started their works at Le Creusot in 1836. The mutual hostility lasted until the steel restructuring of the 1970s. The Schneiders began with modest means and a very small equity stake, but were bankrolled by the former ally of the Wendels, the Seillière bank.

The production of iron generated a greater need for energy, and Charles de Wendel looked east to the big Saar field, where his father had already developed some sites in the vicinity of Forbach. Charles's initial involvement came by chance: a coal mine at Schoeneck, near Saarbrücken, was leased in 1840 to the owner of a Hombourg forge, who in 1846 asked Gargan and Charles de Wendel to participate in the Compagnie des Houillières de Stiring. In 1847 the company reached a seam in the Petite-Rosselle field, in the forest of Forbach on the large Saar coal basin; then came additional pits (Saint-Charles, Saint-Joseph, Vuillemin, Wendel). In 1847 production amounted to 32,000 tons; by 1870 it was 223,000 tons. But the coal was not suitable for producing coke for use in iron-smelting, and could be used only for heating furnaces. Thus the Wendels needed to buy German or Belgian coke if they wanted to move beyond the limits imposed by charcoal smelting; in 1865 Charles de Wendel bought a site in Seraing, near Liège (where the great Cockerill ironworks were situated), which he converted into a cokery.

Having acquired coal, Wendel could produce more iron. At the same time as he began his coal investment in the Saar basin, in 1846, Charles de Wendel also explored the possibility of building an ironworks at Stiring, near the Rosselle mines in the Saar basin. The new plant began production in 1853. Since the new works were built in an isolated part of the Forbach forest, Wendel had to build a new town, which he intended as a model not only of industrial, but also of religious and social life. Five parallel streets, given the names of saints, created a grid pattern around a central square dominated not by a secular *mairie*, but by an impressive ecclesiastical edifice. The town was to be held together by devotion. In 1857 the new iron city, now called Stiring-Wendel, was inaugurated by a visit of Emperor Napoleon III.

Wendel set a model for business in other ways also. As early as 1836, he introduced a pay scale with a supplement for seniority (an additional month's pay after five years' work, and two months' pay after ten years) that was based on that used in the army. There were also pensions based on the principle of rewarding long-term employees. In Hayange and Moyeuvre in 1857, Wendel constructed workers' hostelries, and in 1863 company shops. The management of the works involved a strong measure of paternalism, driven by a Catholic piety. In 1836 funds were created for the assistance of the sick and injured, and in 1866 the scheme was extended with funds introduced to pay the families of those injured in work accidents. From 1859, boys' education in Hayange, Moyeuvre, and Stiring occurred not in state institutions but in company schools run by Marianist friars. The company also built a girls' school in Hayange run by the nuns of Providence de Peltre. In 1869 the Stiring works started a medical fund.

The major demand for iron came from the new railroads. Charles de Wendel owned shares in the company operating the railroad line between Metz and Clouange. He also built private lines linking Hayange and Moyeuvre to the Moselle ports, where the coking coal arrived; in addition, he tried to promote the canalization of the river Moselle. In 1851 Stiring was connected to the main Metz-Saarbrücken line, which was completed in 1852. The completion of the line was taken as an opportunity for the celebration of a new internationalism. It was opened by French and Prussian ministers, and a triumphal arch announced: "In 1552, war separated Metz from Germany. In 1852, industry reunites them."[48] In 1854 Thionville was linked to Metz by rail, and in 1859 the line reached Luxembourg. From 1860 the Belgian coalfields were linked by rail with the ore fields of Lorraine.

The development of the iron industry was shaken by major crises: in 1826–27; from 1847 to 1852, when the economic crisis contributed to a new wave of revolution and regime transformation; and again in the 1860s. Wendel survived in 1848 with the help of credit from the Banque de France; but he had to reach an agreement with the rival works at Le Creusot and Fourchambault on a joint liability for the 300,000 francs advanced by the Banque de France "as a consequence of the financial crises brought about by the sudden change in government": in other words, the revolution of 1848.[49] The Empire of Napoleon III created political stability, but the highly authoritarian and centralized government was less responsive to business pressures.

The great free trade treaty of 1860, the Cobden-Chevalier agreement, dramatically lowered iron prices in France as British products entered the French market. A ton of cast iron cost 176 francs in 1855, 129 in 1860, and only 91 by 1869. When the emperor asked Wendel (retrospectively) about the treaty, he replied: "I regret only one point, that Monsieur Schneider was consulted before, while I was faced with a *fait accompli.*"[50] In 1863 the works were temporarily closed down as part of a major renovation program, with three new blast furnaces and more puddling. By 1865 there was a large increase in production.

Charles de Wendel entered politics only after the collapse of the July Monarchy. He was elected in May 1849 as deputy for the Moselle department, running on the slogan "Order, Property, Religion." He remained a parliamentarian for eighteen years. He never felt entirely happy with Bonapartism and the Empire, and did not hide his royalist sympathy. His major political concern directly reflected his experience of difficulties in business life as a manager who did not own his enterprise. The rights of his sister and mother and their descendants, seemed to him personally irritating and economically irrational. Wendel presented his concern as a worry about the effects of splitting inheritance. In April 1865 he was one of forty-two deputies who voted to change the law of succession to give family heads more freedom to dispose of their property, and to end the revolutionary principle of partible inheritance in equal shares that had then been enshrined in the Code Napoléon. There was obviously a considerable irony in his position, in that as the younger son of François de Wendel he would presumably have been excluded from his inheritance by the bill he proposed, and would have had to seek a career in the church or the army.

The parliamentary debate turned into a polemic on the legacy of the French Revolution. The motion's defenders emphasized that they did not want to restore the ancien régime or the *droit d'aînesse.* They made a liberal argument about freedom to make wills and about the needs of industry, commerce, and agriculture. But above all they argued that the "rights of the father of the family" needed to be increased. Their opponents argued that they did not want France to be like England. "In England testatory freedom has a corrective in jobs in India, ecclesiastical titles, purchased military ranks: you don't want any of that. Here this holds as well. We have civil liberty, economic freedom, and, if I should be so bold to say, political freedom."[51] This issue was taken up by the social reformer

Frédéric Le Play, the government's general commissioner at the universal expositions designed as a showcase for French industrial expertise, who incidentally was also an iron engineer. Le Play linked the debate about partible inheritance to the popularity and danger of the joint-stock corporation: "In France, joint-stock companies are multiplying beyond the actual needs of our day; but rather than being seen as a regular movement, they should be seen as a tacit reaction of all the interests against the consequences of forced partition."[52] In the late twentieth century, Pierre Bourdieu argued that the *grande famille* had rescued itself only by using the device of the company as a legal means of protecting itself against the code's requirement of partition. But there were in fact many industrial families in the northern textile industry who destroyed themselves by the need to create too many positions in the management of family enterprises for too many sons and grandsons.[53]

The aftermath of the free trade debate over the Chevalier treaty also provoked a greater degree of institutional organization in the French iron industry as it tried to demand some measure of protection. Charles de Wendel at this time proclaimed: "I think the unlimited liberty of commerce is fatal."[54] In 1864 the Comité des Forges was established, at first under Eugène Schneider, who also became president of its Corps Législatif. Wendel sat as a member, but resented Schneider's dominance. The Comité des Forges was intended to respond to the Cobden-Chevalier treaty by collecting information about foreign prices, to look for potential export markets, and to cultivate better relations with the government. The organization of pressure groups began to play a substantial role in the late, liberalizing phases of the Empire, but above all after another political upheaval in 1870–71, in the new Republic.

At the same time, as a consequence of the new company law of 1867, corporations began to be organized. Did the legal precision of the new business form make dynastic politics less important? The return of Madame de Wendel to center stage demonstrated the continued role of demographic accident, for Charles de Wendel died in April 1870, on the eve of a new European war that led to the demise of the Empire and seemed—for the moment—to show the weakness of France and the supremacy of everything German: the needle rifle, the Prussian schoolmaster, and of course also the new power of German industrialism.

Chapter 2

The Pioneer in German History

Perhaps the success of Messrs. Haniel is traceable to their depending on their own skill and industry, instead of ambitioning the alliance and the capital of kings or governments.

T. C. Banfield, *Industry of the Rhine*, 1848

IN THE BEGINNING of industrial history is the pioneer. Particularly in the third quarter of the nineteenth century, Germany celebrated the figure of the *Gründer* (founder), who provided a link between a simultaneous reshaping of commercial life and of politics. In the beginning? Actually, not quite: contrary to mythology, the pioneer does not simply emerge fully formed like Venus from a seashell. The pioneer needs a quite specific milieu; and in the case of Franz Haniel, who has often been presented as the archetype of the Schumpeterian entrepreneur in Germany,[1] that milieu was a family. It was defined quite precisely and intimately by the traditions of German Protestant pietism. In that tradition, the function of the family was to restrain excesses and to promote respect for longer-term continuities.

Some of the most impressive testimonies to the power of the pietist tradition appear in the Barmen family of Engels, which was distantly related to the Haniels, and indeed lost a good deal of money in loans to the Noots, a family more directly related to the Haniels. The package containing the Engels family correspondence carries the inscription for posterity: "Do not burn, but learn, how your great-grandparents were pious, godfearing souls." Friedrich

Engels senior wrote to a friend about the radicalism of his subsequently famous son: "I don't want to quarrel with him. This would just lead to stubbornness and embitterment. His conversion must come from above. At his confirmation he had, as I know certainly, pious inclinations, and I am confident that a man who has once experienced the power of God in his heart will not in the long run be satisfied with shallow new systems. But he will have to take a tough path, before he comes down from his proud heights and puts his heart in humility under the strong hand of God."[2]

Both restraint and a long-term vision actually do not fit easily with entrepreneurial vigor in its most red-blooded form. Pioneers, at least according to a widely held stereotype, are likely to invest too many resources in pioneering technical ventures that do not pay off, at least in the time frame envisaged or determined by their creditors. Consequently, some of the most famous and ultimately successful pioneers are repeat bankrupts; and many failed entrepreneurs have done a great deal to advance the cause of technical change. One function of a family—particularly at a time of wild speculation and business uncertainty, such as the early nineteenth century—was to restrain the expansionist instincts of the pioneer.

In German economic history, the really frenzied entrepreneur, the entrepreneur in his purest form, is quite rare. The cotton- and ironmasters of western Germany are generally described as a group phenomenon, whose collective socialization in industry demands explanation, rather than as iconoclastic individualists. They are, in theoretical terms, better described by Max Weber and Werner Sombart than by Joseph Schumpeter. At a later stage, German business adopted rationalized and routinized forms of management that went beyond the confines of individual companies. The outcome has frequently been described as "organized capitalism" or "corporatism," and it began to be demolished (very tentatively) only in the closing years of the twentieth century.

Franz Haniel was unusual in the range of his interests and activities, and he also saw himself as a figure in an explicitly English tradition of entrepreneurship. He greatly admired James Watt and Matthew Boulton and thought that Germany needed more figures like them (and him). He was well aware during his lifetime how much of a pioneer, and also how unusual, he had been. Throughout his life he regularly recorded important moments on small pieces of paper, which he carefully preserved. As a very old man, in 1858 during a stay in the spa of Wiesbaden, he decided to write an autobiography: a rare interest of businessmen, at least at that time, and a labor of love that he intended as a guide to his children and their heirs. The consequence is that his writing largely shapes the interpretation of posterity: he founded not only a dynasty but provided a narrative that would motivate and inspire it. As with the first François de Wendel, who provided an inspirational will intended not just to distribute property but to drive a family forward to economic and social conquest, the patriarch created an image during his lifetime, a sort of corporate brand.

The family narrative was at the center of Haniel's idea of how to describe his life; and it was a family transaction, in the middle of the turmoil of the Napoleonic Wars, which brought the beginning of a great industrial enterprise. What is striking about Franz Haniel's account, however, is that the problems and tensions of linking commercial life with often strained family relationships are addressed with clarity and candor, and actually form the human heart of Haniel's story of a German technological revolution.

The relationship of the Haniels with the state was quite different from that of the French family, which from the beginning invested heavily in the cultivation of political interests, whether under the ancien régime, Napoleon, or the Restoration monarchy. France's discontinuous politics made the politics of business speculative and dangerous. By contrast, and despite the catastrophic defeat of 1806, there was a fair measure of continuity in Prussian politics. The Haniel businesses developed and expanded during the political and territorial confusions of the revolutionary and Napoleonic Wars, and benefited considerably from artificial price differentials produced by French policies, tariffs, and controls. Political uncertainty (and, it will be seen, corruption) offered a great number of profitable opportunities.

European political and business conditions changed radically, but Prussian politics remained quite constant, especially in the Rhineland. Haniel went out of his way to emphasize the intimate connection of his dynasty with that of the austerely incorruptible Hohenzollerns. Frederick William III was the godfather of his seventh son, appropriately named Friedrich Wilhelm (it was an ancien régime custom for the monarch to be a godfather to seventh sons);

and Frederick William IV was godfather to his eighth son, Friedrich Wilhelm Theobald. At the age of twelve or thirteen Franz Haniel had attended a public ball at Schloss Broich in honor of the new prince of Hessen-Darmstadt (Ludwig X). The prince asked him to dance with two young princesses of Mecklenburg-Strelitz, Auguste Wilhelmine Amalie Louise, who must have been fifteen at the time, and Friederike. Louise later became famous as the inspirationally beautiful queen of Prussia, wife of Frederick William III (and mother of Frederick William IV, and of William I), who mobilized resistance to Napoleon and died young, to be commemorated in Schadow's coldly erotic neoclassical tomb effigy. And as an old man, Haniel's inspiration to write his memoirs came from a royal suggestion during the inaugural voyage of a steamship on the Rhine, named after Princess Augusta of Prussia (the wife of the crown prince who would become king and then German emperor as William I).[3] Haniel's business career also owed a great deal to his long-term friendship with the chief Prussian administrator in the west, the president of Westfalen province, Ludwig von Vincke. The more Haniel looked back, the more he came to the conclusion that his life was part of the great exercise of Prussian state-building. But that was the perspective of the 1850s and 1860s. It was not always that way. Indeed, in a critical period, the greatest business opportunities derived from the incompetence and venality of the French occupation regime.

The Family

The Haniels as a family were first mentioned as millers, bakers, and brewers in Tournai, in Flanders, in the thirteenth century.[4] In the sixteenth century part of the family fled the persecution of Protestants in the Netherlands and settled in Pomerania, under the protection of the Hohenzollern dynasty. They frequently adopted Hohenzollern first names as a token of dynastic loyalty: there is, for instance, a record of a Joachim Haniel who studied at the university of Wittenberg.

Jacob Wilhelm Haniel moved to Duisburg, where he established a wine trading firm with his brother in 1760. In 1761 he married Aletta Noot, the daughter of a customs official, Jan Willem Noot, in nearby Ruhrort, at the confluence of the rivers Rhine and Ruhr.

She seems to have had courage and initiative: in 1758 she reportedly freed her father from French captivity by giving the French commanding officer a kiss. In 1756 Noot received a patent signed by Frederick the Great, permitting the building on land formerly part of the fortified castle; there Noot constructed a trading house, the Packhaus, which was for a long time the center of the Haniel business and which indeed still stands as a historical museum next to the headquarters of the modern company Franz Haniel & Cie. GmbH. When Jan Willem Noot lay dying in 1770, he expressed a wish that a member of the Haniel family continue trading from the Ruhrort Packhaus; he presumably meant his son-in-law, Jacob Haniel, and both his widow and his daughter encouraged Haniel to make this move and to expand the trading business on the Ruhr. Jacob Haniel had eleven children, seven of whom died in infancy. At the time of his early death in 1782, Wilhelm was eighteen years old, Sophia eight, Gerhard seven, and Franz (the youngest) two. Aletta Noot continued the business, which was now known as Jb. Wm. Haniel seel. Wittib (Widow of the late Cb. Wm. Haniel). She extended its sphere of activities from shipping to the coal trade. But by the mid-1790s Gerhard and Franz were effectively running much of the firm.

Eighteenth-century women who became prominent in business were almost always widows. They, too, faced considerable problems and obstacles in inheriting as well as in practicing a trade. Aletta Noot, for instance, was not allowed to inherit the Packhaus, which remained subject to joint control by her father's heirs until the property was bought out in 1800. Where guilds were strong, they frequently stopped women from continuing their husbands' businesses.[5] Such guild restrictions did not apply in agriculture and in commerce, and guilds in Prussia were less powerful than in most of the German lands. But Aletta Noot still encountered a substantial hostility from other Ruhrort merchants.

When the Packhaus had been built by Jan Willem Noot, it was connected to the river by a canal so that goods could easily be taken to the warehouse. In 1796, however, with a need for better fortification as the revolutionary wars swept over the Rhineland, the town built a high dike that cut off the Noot house altogether from the river. The other and better-established Ruhrort merchants were not severely affected by the new defenses, as they had sheds directly on the river Ruhr on land held by hereditary tenure. Aletta Noot Haniel made repeated requests for equivalent rights, or at least permission to build a coal warehouse on common land: she wrote to the royal administration in Cleves in 1796, 1797, 1799, and then directly to the king of Prussia in 1800. In this last appeal she made her suspicions of the Ruhrort establishment very explicit. She described the canal constructed by her father as principally responsible for the commercial prosperity of Ruhrort, and she explained how she had continued and extended her father's and her husband's business "to general applause and general utility." She then told the king: "In every other country, such useful enterprise would have received the greatest support from the authorities, and here too I might have had such support as a widow with four children, had not commercial envy and disfavor undermined all my activities." She was in danger of "gradually losing my whole business" if her goods could no longer be properly stored while her competitors were given the right to create sheds on the lands of the Cleves royal domain.[6] This final appeal was eventually successful, but only because her son Franz took up the case and appeared in the War and Domain Council in Wesel, securing an agreement that allowed the widow Haniel to use one-third of the common lands for the storage of traded goods.

Haniel and the Coal Trade

When Franz Haniel was born, the Ruhr was not really navigable, but by the 1780s it was open to some shipping, which stimulated the development of the coal trade. In consequence, Franz remembered the first time he burnt coal in the grate at home, as a boy, as a decisive event in the story of his life and his region. Coal and its possibilities remained the guiding principle of his life, and he is today best remembered as a coal pioneer.

The main feature of the 1790s, for any Rhinelander, was political turmoil. The young Haniel saw a great number of French émigrés fleeing the violence of the Revolution, including the marquis de Lafayette, who, as he explained to his Rhineland hosts, "did not want to let himself be guillotined."[7] But Franz Haniel also saw a commercial opportunity in supplying heavy bombs and bullets from the iron forges St. Antoni and Neu Essen to the Austrian army engaged in the siege of Valencienne.[8] The Haniels also later managed the sales of munitions produced by the Gute Hoffnungs Hütte (which at the time they did not own). Haniel thus supplied ammunition fired at French positions protected by the products of Wendel.

After 1795, when France concluded a truce with Prussia, the Ruhr towns of Duisburg and Ruhrort played a major part in the shipping of coffee, tobacco, sugar, and pelts from the Netherlands to major cities farther up the Rhine and Main: Mainz, Cologne, and Frankfurt; while the French armies across the Rhine also wanted to make large-scale purchases of imported goods. Haniel in old age recalled the considerable economic stimulus provided by the political chaos of the mid-1790s to those with entrepreneurial initiative: "Our house had made fortunate speculations in the purchase of coffee, sugar and wine, and other goods; only the purchase of Dutch gin, which I myself suggested, proved a failure, as did our taking of several thousand French assignats that were offered to us at a low rate, and which I still possess and are worth nothing; but in general our house prospered between 1794 and the end of 1798."[9]

Franz Haniel's mother had originally suggested that he serve an apprenticeship in the famous Cologne bank of Schaaffhausen, but he did not want to work in a bank (where he said he would be trained "one-sidedly"); he would rather see the world.[10] This disdain for financial activity remained with him throughout his life, and indeed became part of a family tradition. The dynasty that he founded took a generally conservative approach to financial leverage. Repelled by the insufficient worldliness of banking, Franz Haniel worked in a Mainz trading house, J. Hr. Weingärtner Sohn, which was substantially more exciting. It was managed by a flirtatious widow, who eagerly explained to the newly arrived nineteen-year-old that she was only twenty-eight. In Mainz, Haniel quickly established his mastery at shipping goods across newly established customs barriers (and also in smuggling operations at the cost of the French army). In his memoirs he explained how he drank several bottles of wine with the French official, as well as some coffee, and then managed to get his goods passed through the customs at the lowest possible rate. The revolutionary occupation regime proved to be obligingly corrupt.

In 1799 Franz Haniel began to worry about his family. In 1795 his oldest brother, Wilhelm, had married Diederike Noot, a relative of his mother, and established an independent trading house in Duisburg, which in Franz's words "made many unfortunate speculations and businesses." Wilhelm was respected locally and became a municipal councilor, but he was unfortunate. His wife died in 1798 after the birth of a daughter; by 1810 he was bankrupt. The collapse of Wilhelm's business demonstrated in a very painful fashion the importance of limiting liability for family business ventures and of defining separate areas of financial responsibility. Thus, when in 1800 Franz and Gerhard's sister Johanna Sophia married Gottlob Jacobi, the managing director of the ironworks of St. Antoni and Neu Essen, and started to engage her capital in his business, Franz Haniel demanded a separation of property of his siblings. The parental assets were inventoried, and any surplus not required for the household of the mother was to be shared between Franz and his brother Gerhard. In return the two brothers guaranteed the sum of the parental assets.[11] Wilhelm's daughter, though impoverished, was not excluded altogether from the family. She eventually married a talented house tutor in the household of Franz Haniel's brother-in-law who had become the business manager of part of the family enterprise.

From 1799 to 1805 Franz and Gerhard expanded their business, with a substantial trade in wood, coal, and wine, and also a large smuggling operation in which wheat, whose export the French authorities prohibited, was moved at night to the right bank of the Rhine. Considerable quantities were sold in the 1800s via the Netherlands to England, so that French wheat ended up feeding British bellies, and in this way undermining Napoleon's idea of a blockade on England.[12] The business depended once more on the bribing of French officials, on the supply of French certificates (including one signed by Napoleon himself), and on the collaboration of the French general Jean-Baptiste Bernadotte (who took an eighth part in the profits of the business). This kind of political corruption operated on an infinitely greater scale than the small-scale business of French customs officials in revolutionary Mainz in the 1790s. It took Franz Haniel into a quite different sort of business activity.

Haniel and Iron

Franz Haniel's decision to move into ironworking came in response to the territorial changes accompanying Napoleon's destruction of the Holy Roman Empire. In the Rhineland the geopolitical reordering had the effect above all of enlarging the Prussian state. As compensation for the cession of territory on the left bank of the Rhine to France, Napoleon transferred the lands of the abbess of Essen to the Hohenzollern dynasty. In the early 1790s the Haniels had already shipped munitions from the St. Antoni and Neu Essen forges, which were in the personal possession of the abbess, and from the Gute Hoffnungs Hütte to the counterrevolutionary armies in northern France. These three forges were geographically quite close (and are all in the modern city area of Oberhausen), but in ancien-régime Germany they lay in separate territories. The Gute Hoffnungs Hütte was in the Duchy of Cleves (held by the Hohenzollerns); St. Antoni was in the territory of Recklinghausen, belonging to the archbishop of Cologne; and Neu Essen was part of the property of the Abbey of Essen and "Reich immediate" (that is, directly held from the Holy Roman Empire, and thus legally equal in status to the larger territorial states).

St. Antoni, the oldest blast furnace in the Ruhr area, had begun—unsurprisingly given its location—as a clerical venture: a member of the cathedral chapter, Franz Ferdinand Freiherr von Wenge zu Dieck, had obtained permission from the archbishop of Cologne in 1741 to prospect for iron. In 1752, when he wanted to build a blast furnace, the nuns of nearby Sterkrade protested on the grounds that the washing of the ore would poison fish and make it impossible to use the water for brewing or washing. The furnace in consequence started operating only in 1758.[13] There was also a shortage of suitable charcoal, and in 1771 Wenge tried to use coal for smelting (inevitably unsuccessfully, because of the damage done by the sulfuric content of the coal).

Another blast furnace (Neu Essen) was established in 1790 by the abbess of Essen, who employed a young man, the son of a Sayn mine and forge inspector, Gottlob Jacobi; and in 1796, with Cologne occupied by French soldiers, the abbess managed to acquire the St. Antoni forge too. Both forges were now managed by Jacobi, who introduced a domed furnace, in the English style, and who, in return for his endeavors, received a quarter share of the two forges.

A third Ruhr valley forge had been established in 1780 in the Prussian territory of Cleves, in Sterkrade. Gute Hoffnung's owner, Eberhard Pfandhöfer, originally an imaginative and innovative businessman, had engaged in a diverse series of speculative investments, descended into alcoholism, and borrowed extensively, in particular from Helene Amalie Krupp in Essen (another of the remarkable women such as Madame de Hayange who managed many of the leading continental ironworks in the late eighteenth century; she had been left a widow at the age of twenty-five in 1757). In 1799 the widow Krupp bought the foundry at an auction, and by 1807 it was in the possession of her grandson.

The new military and political changes that put an end to the Holy Roman Empire, abolished almost all the tiny "immediate" principalities, and reordered the territorial map of Germany also produced a great wave of property transactions, analogous to that following the nationalizations and secularizations in the French Revolution. In 1805 the Haniel brothers bought three-quarters ownership of St. Antoni (for 23,800 Reichsthalers, the equivalent at the time of U.S. $16,500) and Neu Essen (for 8,000 Reichsthalers, or $5,500) from the abbess of Essen, with payment due by 1809. Had they, like Granthil in Hayange and so many others in France, been so swept up in the speculative current that they lost all sense of the relationship between investment and return when they bid for a strictly limited number of properties, in the hope that they might come to assume a monopoly position? In practice the brothers found it difficult to make the payments, and they quickly came to the conclusion that the manufacture of iron would be profitable only if the Gute Hoffnung were included in a large iron business.[14] A common reaction to disappointment in a business venture is to think that lack of success is due to an only incomplete engagement, and that it can be overcome by an even larger venture. But such a response required more capital, which came to the Haniel brothers by marriage.

Franz Haniel met Friederike Huyssen at a ball in Essen in November 1805 and married her in July 1806. In 1808 Gerhard married Friederike's sister. The Huyssen girls were attractive, and Franz had a close, companionate, and long-lasting marriage with "Fritze," as he called her from the beginning. But they also almost certainly brought financial resources with them, as their father, Arnold Huyssen, was a wealthy and highly respected senator of the city of Essen. The two Haniels, married to two sisters, now conducted separate businesses, in accordance with the idea of separating risk within the greater family unit. But such separation, which was based on the logic of preserving wealth in the family against the consequences of business mistakes, ran counter to the other logic calling for larger-scale investment in order to achieve a measure of strategic control. In the particular case of the three western Ruhr ironworks, there was a particularly powerful argument for the economies of scale that would be brought by amalgamation.

The Haniels could not deal easily with the widow Krupp about a potential purchase, because they were locked in dispute over the water consumed by the St. Antoni forge, which was being taken from the same water basin used by the Gute Hoffnung. Franz Haniel thought that the difficulties in obtaining water were one reason why Krupp might be inclined to sell the Gute Hoffnung; but obviously he might not be the most appropriate person to suggest the transaction himself. So in 1808 he employed as an intermediary his and Gerhard's brother-in-law, Heinrich Huyssen, whom he later described as an idle unemployed layabout, maintained by his father, and altogether lacking in business capability.[15]

The only detailed account of the transaction is that left by Franz Haniel, who was considerably irritated by his brother-in-law's behavior. But the story as told by Haniel seems plausible. Gottlob Jacobi, who was married to Sophie Haniel (a sister of Franz and Gerhard), and Gerhard Haniel originally asked Franz to buy the Gute Hoffnung for a maximum of 30,000 Cleves Reichsthaler, or 15,000 French crown thalers. When Franz failed to reach an agreement with the widow, he sent Huyssen with a commission to make the transaction on behalf of Jacobi and the two Haniel brothers. Huyssen, however, also failed to persuade Krupp to sell. Then he talked to an Essen lawyer, Tuttmann, who suggested a different form of transaction, in which Huyssen would buy the Gute Hoffnung for around 19,000 crown thalers ($26,400), with a guarantee by the Haniels and Jacobi. Huyssen promised to conclude a second transaction, transferring the property to the three intended new owners; but whereas the first contract was concluded in the presence of Krupp, Tuttmann, other lawyers, and the three associates, the second was not, and offered ample room for fudging and indeed for deception. Tuttmann and Huyssen were jubilant, and declared that now "they had the sword in their hands, and we would have to agree to everything." When he wrote this account, in 1859, Franz Haniel still emphasized his "bitterness."[16] Huyssen had no money, his father could not lend him any, and so the three original partners had to put in the money; Huyssen still insisted on being paid a dividend, and the three partners "in order to avoid scandal and even worse enmities" took the loss. The result was that the Haniels did not want to deal with Huyssen any more, and Huyssen remained in Sterkrade. Jacobi, who blamed Franz Haniel for having brought the incompetent and duplicitous Huyssen into the transaction, fell out with him, with the consequence that Haniel rarely went to Sterkrade, and until the death of Jacobi took no dividend or interest from the forge.[17] In April 1810 a contract was drawn up in which each of the four partners had an equal share in the three ironworks.

Matters seem to have calmed somewhat after the death of Gottlob Jacobi in 1823. The chief reason was the arrival on the scene of a new personality unburdened by the old family disputes. In 1812 Jacobi had employed a farmer's son, Wilhelm Lueg, as a teacher for his children. Lueg was exceptionally competent, and from 1817 worked as an inspector in the forge. In 1819 Lueg made it into the charmed family circle: he married Sophia, daughter of the bankrupt Wilhelm Haniel. After Jacobi's death, Lueg managed his family's interest. The four principal owners now arranged a rotating management process: Franz Haniel supervised the works for one-quarter of the year (the months of April, August, and December); Gerhard Haniel for March, July, and November; Lueg in February, June, and October; and Heinrich Huyssen in May, September, and January. They thus successfully avoided any personal contact with each other, an arrangement that they seem to have disliked. It can hardly have been a very efficient way of directing an enterprise, and it is not surprising that Franz Haniel subsequently wanted to conduct new ventures on his own, and not in any business association with his relatives.

One collective action problem that is often believed to plague family firms is that multiple owners try to take too much income out of the business, and that consequently there is insufficient capital reinvested. The unpleasant negotiations and bitter quarrels over the origins of the company in this case produced the opposite effect. The two Haniel brothers, who originally had to subsidize Huyssen, did not take dividends from the company. Later Franz thought that this was the foundation of the extraordinarily successful expansion of the firm. "Through our personal presence, our conviction, and our performance, the business interests of the firm expanded quite extraordinarily. We, my brother Gerhard and myself, could live because our private business and wealth produced more returns than we required for household and other expenses, and we thus left our money in the firm. The success was the result of my insistence, in almost constant struggle with the other three partners."[18] The quarrel, and Franz Haniel's constant suspicions about the demands and extravagances of his partners, meant that two parallel business structures developed: the metallurgical firm of Jacobi, Haniel & Huyssen, which paid few dividends; and Franz Haniel's trading companies, which produced the basis of his livelihood.

This proved to be a very effective way of spreading risk. Franz Haniel's entrepreneurial drive led him to move into many new types of business, including ones that required great amounts of capital (prospecting and sinking new mines for coal). Had they not worked out, and had he been tied into Jacobi, Haniel & Huyssen, he could easily have wrecked the family partnership. As it was, he could be part of the family (contentiously), and he could also stake out new business ventures.

In the meantime Jacobi, Haniel & Huyssen prospered; in 1830 it added a plate rolling mill, and in 1835 began puddling steel. At this point there were some forty-four hearths in the plant. By 1858 the works had 3,558 employees.[19]

An Individualistic Entrepreneur

As a response to the family struggles and quarrels, and driven by his considerable personal dynamism, Franz Haniel concentrated at first on his Ruhrort businesses. They continued to depend during the French occupation on the possibility of a considerable amount of smuggling. On one occasion his house in Ruhrort, the Packhaus, was searched by French officials, who did not find the 1,500 pounds of coffee hidden under sheets of cloth.[20] Haniel also delivered iron products, bombs, bullets, and shell cases to the French army and navy; he stopped delivering only when the Russian campaign of 1812 threatened to make it hard for the French ministry to pay for deliveries.

4. *Franz Haniel, 1779–1868*
COURTESY OF FRANZ HANIEL & CIE. GMBH, DUISBURG-RUHRORT

In 1815 Aletta Noot died (aged seventy-three), and her property was divided among Gerhard, Franz, and Sophia (Wilhelm was excluded). The Packhaus and the surrounding courtyard, garden, and barn were auctioned, and bought by Franz. The year 1815 was also a political caesura of stability in the Rhineland.

At this point Haniel faced a hard choice: the military orders that had maintained business during the Napoleonic Wars were now too uncertain; the coal business with the Netherlands was drying up; and his Amsterdam bankers, Braunberg & Co., advised him to buy Prussian and Russian state bonds, which were selling at only 30 percent of their nominal value. This was an attractive speculation on the victory of the anti-Napoleonic coalition, but Haniel refused, on the grounds that "he had never speculated, or won, on such paper."[21] He again made a conscious and deliberate decision not to be a financier. Now he saw the major task of the future as developing new technologies, which he thought would transform the economic and social landscape.

In the economically and politically depressed years after the Restoration, Franz Haniel tried a large number of diverse economic activities. In response to two disastrous harvests in 1816 and 1817, he tried to expand into grain trading, buying grain from the eastern provinces of Prussia and from Russia. But the reloading of the grain in Amsterdam presented problems, and in 1818 improved harvests suddenly pushed prices down, and the business environment became harshly deflationary.

At the same time he wanted to experiment with manufacturing; he contemplated sugar refining, the making of Delft porcelain, and a glassworks, and in fact built an oilseed mill. He also bought extensive territories in Homberg, across the Rhine from Ruhrort, in the Duisburg forest, and in Driesenbusch. His most notable entrepreneurial action was to establish a shipbuilding business in Ruhrort, which expanded rapidly. In 1824 Haniel built a steam engine for the oil mills and set about winning a contract to build steamships for the Cölner Dampf Schifffahrtsgesellschaft.

In 1820 he obtained permission from the president of Westphalia, Freiherr Ludwig von Vincke, who was also the director of Ruhr shipping and who became a good friend of Haniel's, to build an extensive harbor in Ruhrort. At the time, Haniel implored Vincke not to reduce the size of the harbor, since it should be built to last for 100 years.[22] But in fact the harbor, completed in 1824, quickly required further enlargement, which Franz Haniel also financed and directed. The capital for this business was apparently taken from the account of Jacobi, Haniel & Huyssen, but in practice it came mostly from the two Haniel brothers.

Haniel was a sensitive entrepreneur, who recognized where the major sources of innovation in metallurgy lay. Like François de Wendel almost a decade earlier, he wanted to learn from English manufactures. In 1825 he set off for England along with his brother Gerhard, Wilhelm Lueg, and a Wesel manufacturer related to the Haniels and Noots, Georg Luyken. After a short stay in London, the Haniels headed to the Midlands, and in particular to James Watt's Soho workshop. Haniel had already encountered Watt in 1817, when Watt had tried out a steamship on the Rhine, which had broken down and required repairs in Sterkrade in the Gute Hoffnung workshop. At that time Watt had stayed for several days in Ruhrort. Seven years later he invited Haniel to lunch along with a number of Birmingham manufacturers; but to Haniel's great disgust, Watt refused to let him see the famous Soho works, with the consequence that Haniel turned down the lunch invitation and quickly left. Watt was clearly concerned about the possibility of industrial espionage. Watt's resistance to visits that might compromise his trade secrets gradually became well known throughout Europe. A French mint master, who was profoundly interested in the applications to coinage of a steam press, related a story of how Watt had turned even Admiral Nelson away from his Soho works, saying, "Milord, I can't respond favorably to your request, but I am glad you asked."[23] In 1825 Watt's German guests did manage to see a 100-Lachter (210-meter) deep coal mine, where a steam engine was used to raise coal and lower food for the mine horses.[24]

Understanding that the future of ironworking lay in coke-smelting, Haniel set about developing coal mines in the Ruhr basin. In 1808 he started a notebook with observations on coal and mining. "I had," he later recalled, "for many years wished for coal or coke to be used in our blast furnaces, and thus I needed to convince our firm to build a mine in Oberhausen. Since I was on my private account heavily engaged in coal mining, I knew how important coal was for our mills and puddling works, and if the firm [Jacobi, Haniel & Huyssen] had refused, I would have been obliged to end my participation."[25] He plowed back most of his revenue from the oil mill and from coal and wood trading into the purchase of coal mines and the extension of the Ruhrort shipyard.

The most important transplantation of English ironworking to continental Europe was the giant Seraing works, owned by John Cockerill in Belgium. His father, William Cockerill, had set up a spinning plant in Verviers in 1799 and moved to expand after the Restoration. In 1815 John developed links with a dynamic Prussian official, Peter Christian Beuth, and began to operate a warehouse in Berlin. In the same year he built a steam engine and in 1823 began the construction of a blast furnace at Seraing. In the 1830s John Cockerill started an even quicker expansion, enticed by the continental possibilities of the railroad. But this was a high-risk strategy, and in February 1839 his Belgian firm was forced into liquidation. Cockerill saw the way out as developing industry farther east, in Prussia and Russia, and he died in Warsaw in 1840 as a result of an infection contracted on his business mission to Russia.[26] At the moment of crisis for the Cockerill dynasty, Franz Haniel saw an attractive opportunity to acquire a matrimonial link that would probably have been out of his reach in more prosperous times. He was not so much interested in dowries for his sons as in acquiring industrial skills. Consequently, in 1839 his son Max married Cockerill's niece, Friederike Cockerill. Fourteen years later, Thusnelde Haniel married Heinrich Cockerill. (Franz Haniel also cemented his own dynastic business link through the marriage in 1837 of his son Hugo to Bertha Haniel, the only daughter of his brother Gerhard.) There were also intermarriages with other business families, including those of Böcking, de Greiff, Böninger, and Liebrecht. The marital diplomacy of business dynasties continued on these lines until the First World War. There were Haniel alliances with other important entrepreneurial families. Thus, for instance, Max's youngest son from his first marriage, John (and thus a grandson of Franz), married in 1879 Fanny Stinnes of Mülheim, the daughter of Gustav Stinnes. John's mother, Friederike, was a Cockerill, and thus John united the dynastic lines of some of the most important technological innovators.

An alternative to strategic alliances was to keep the family together by marriages to cousins or other relatives. Hugo, who had already married Bertha Haniel, had a daughter, Adeline, who in

1857 was actually engaged to marry a younger brother of her father's, though he died before an actual nuptial could be celebrated. She instead married into a Duisburg family, the Böningers, but always kept a picture of her fiancé Richard Haniel in her room, and eventually ensured that her daughter married a young Hugo Haniel. Clara Haniel (born in 1848) married her second cousin Max Berthold Haniel. August Haniel in 1880 married Eugenie Wiesner, the only child of his mother's sister. Such cousin marriages remained common practice until 1914. August Haniel's daughter Gerda in 1904 married the second cousin of her father, Franz Liebrecht. In 1912 Erich Haniel married the second cousin of his brother-in-law.

During Franz Haniel's life, the focus of his business shifted to the production of energy. Coal became the core business of the "second industrial revolution": it decisively raised productivity by allowing the application of infinitely greater energy than the limited resources of human or animal power. Franz Haniel devoted more and more of his attention to solving the issue of how to extract coal from the Ruhr basin. The problems were both technical and administrative. Mining was a closely regulated business in ancien-régime Prussia, with very complex regulations that by the 1820s were widely perceived by liberal bureaucrats and by independent businessmen as restricting innovation. Between 1826 and 1848 there were seven separate reform initiatives to recast Prussian mining law, but a new code was implemented only in 1851, after the revolution of 1848.

The technical problem that the Ruhr coal business faced was how to produce coke of adequate quality, in order to feed the new demands of the iron industry. This was the issue that Pfandhöfer had struggled with unsuccessfully in the 1780s. The Essen mine Saelzer & Neuack later supplied coke for the Krupp works and also for the Gute Hoffnung, but the Gute Hoffnung at first complained bitterly about the poor and unreliable quality of the coke.

In 1821 Franz Haniel built a first coking oven, and throughout the rest of his life tried to improve Ruhr coke. By 1842 he was easily the largest coke producer of the Ruhr area, employing forty-six burners and a total of 184 workers.[27] In 1841 he built a double coking oven next to the Saelzer & Neuack mine, and an even larger one in another Essen mine, Schölerpad (he ordered the oven from the machine shop of Jacobi, Haniel & Huyssen). In 1843 there were in the Ruhr area thirty-six simple coking ovens and thirty-three double ovens. Haniel owned two-thirds of the simple ones and almost all the double ones.[28] He had made himself indisputably the region's dominant coal consumer, and he now wanted to dominate the production side of the business as well. But this project to dominate the new business of Rhine-Ruhr required great confidence and also deep pockets, as the development of the coalfield proved difficult and expensive.

By 1833 he had bought 21 of the 128 mining shares of the Gewerkschaft Schölerpad; his brother Gerhard owned another 6. The Gewerkschaft Schölerpad had been the site of mining since the seventeenth century, and it was now locked in a legal battle with the two adjacent mines, Saelzer & Neuack and Hagenbeck, over the direction that lateral mining galleries could take. When Schölerpad won the court battle to expand, Haniel proposed an ambitious plan for a deep shaft, which started producing profits in 1838. But at the same time Haniel also bought up shares in Hagenbeck, the oldest of all the Ruhr mines, next door; by 1835 he owned 33 1/3 of the 128 shares, and by 1842 he controlled the majority of shares.

One of the greatest problems of the Ruhr valley was how to extract coal seams lying beneath a marl coverage, which frequently produced large quantities of salty water that obstructed mining operations. Haniel started to explore how to deal with marl in territory adjacent to the Jacobi, Haniel & Huyssen works. In 1832 he asked for preliminary permission to excavate near Borbeck, a move that the Prussian mining authorities initially resisted. Once Haniel started, he found coal, but at a great depth (56 meters). The technical solution depended on high-volume steam pumps, made by the Gute Hoffnung Hütte, and in 1835 he obtained the final ownership of a newly authorized mine (Zeche Franz). The total cost of the preliminary mining operation mounted to 10,000 thalers by 1835, and Haniel was getting impatient: "I wish that this costly works would at last produce some results."[29] But this mine never produced any coal. In 1833 he started work at another site near Borbeck, adjacent to the Zeche Franz. In October 1833 the boring reached a thick seam, and soon afterward Haniel acquired the rights. In 1835 water broke through into the shaft, and a more powerful steam engine was required. In 1837 the miners discovered a promising 15-inch-thick seam, and in 1839 a 30-inch seam, but at a depth of 190 meters, and liable to continual flooding. In 1838 the Zeche Kronprinz was approved. By the end of 1842, a total of 131,010 thalers had been invested in the mine, which unlike Zeche Franz did produce some coal. But four-fifths of the coal was used to fuel the pumping engines working against the underground water.[30]

In the later 1840s Franz Haniel had more luck, at the northern edge of the coalfield near Essen. In 1847 he had proposed to drill fourteen boreholes, of which the Prussian authorities permitted only one, where coal was found at a depth of 114 meters. But between 1849 and 1851 he managed to open up what became the most productive of all Ruhr mines, the Zollverein. By 1853 it produced 100,000 tons, and by 1867 the annual rate was 200,000 tons. Franz Haniel's descendants owned this mine until 1920.

These were independent mines; for Haniel, however, the central commercial feature of the English method was the linking of mines and iron production. In 1845 Haniel described his plans: "In order to expand our ironworks, we need to possess our own mines, as is the case in almost all the larger English and Belgian ironworks, and for this purpose I have made geological explorations."[31] In 1853 he returned to this theme: "It is unmistakable that it is very dangerous for the larger ironworks to be without their own coal, because the increase in coal production can scarcely keep pace with the increase in sales, and thus there can easily be an increase in the coal price." In 1847 he carried out an initial boring at Oberhausen, which started to produce coal in 1857, in the middle of the first big economic crisis since the revolution of 1848. This mine (initially named Königsberg) was the first major mine of the Ruhr valley. Its ownership overlapped with the ownership of Jacobi, Haniel & Huyssen: Franz Haniel owned 39 shares, his son Hugo and his brother Gerhard's eldest son Carl 26 2/3 shares each, and Heinrich Huyssen 40 shares. In 1858 the Prussian mining office agreed to a transfer of the ownership to Jacobi, Haniel & Huyssen, thus creating the first combined coal- and ironworks of the Ruhr.[32]

Franz Haniel's most ambitious, and most costly, coal venture was the exploration that began in 1851 on the left bank of the Rhine for what eventually became the Rheinpreussen mine, and remained until the 1960s a formidable industrial base for the family.[33] It faced major technical obstacles: the equipment repeatedly sank in the soft ground and was also regularly destroyed in mine explosions. The mine never produced any coal during Franz Haniel's life, but it eventually provided the major coal supply for the Gutehoffnungshütte (as the major Haniel company began to be called in the 1870s) in imperial Germany.

These extremely costly mining investments created a substantial entrepreneurial risk. The extent of that risk became clear in the case of another iron man, the Mülheim merchant Mathias Stinnes, whose death in 1845, on the eve of the business downturn of 1846, led to the collapse of the firm.

By the 1840s it was clear that the greatest demand for iron products would come from the railroads. The siting of the railroads was also critical for the way in which coal mining and ironworking could be combined. These were political decisions, and again, as in the case of the coal-mining authorizations, Haniel was dependent on the fiat of the Prussian state authorities.[34] His first request, for a line from Ruhrort to Oberhausen and then to the old trade route, the Hellweg at Stalleicken, was turned down by the Prussian administration in Düsseldorf because this was "merely a commercial speculation."[35] He later supported a large-scale plan for a line from Ruhrort to the Emscher valley, with the main goal of transporting large quantities of coal, but it was made superfluous by the government-backed Cologne-Minden railroad, which opened in 1848 and could be linked to Ruhrort with a side line.

Politics became important for the development of the iron business in another way in the 1840s. The German iron trade (like its French equivalent) was worried about British competition, and in particular about the British trading offensive that followed from Prime Minister Peel's tariff reform policy. In 1842 English iron prices had fallen, and the Rhenish producers became very agitated. The Rhineland iron manufacturers sent four deputies to Berlin, including Wilhelm Lueg, in order to move the Prussian administration. In 1844 the Prussian government imposed a 20 Silbergroschen-per-100-kilogram (or 20 Marks per ton) tariff.[36] In 1845 Franz Haniel was elected as a deputy to the Prussian Landtag. His major and indeed almost exclusive concern was trade protection. Already in 1839 he had submitted a memorandum asking for a small increase in tariffs on iron rods and plate, and concluding: "We trust in the wisdom and paternal care of our government that it will be resolute in rejecting all petitions for the reduction of protective tariffs on iron, which can be based only on specious arguments."[37] In 1843 and 1845 he had produced lengthy papers on the need to protect steamship building on the Rhine. But the government refused to consider seriously the demands of Rhine-Ruhr, thus fueling the political resentment of the Rhineland business community, which would eventually express itself in the political upheaval of 1848. Answering the business petition, the responsible government official commented: "I cannot avoid pointing out to the petitioners that in my opinion the interests represented by them would be better devoted to uninterrupted devotion to their own business than by the discussion of collective petitions, which only contain a repetition of attitudes often expressed in newspapers and pamphlets." The Prussian trade official Rudolf von Delbrück, a man generally unsympathetic to protectionist appeals, was appalled by this treatment of men who "had devoted their energies to completion of their own trades and had reached from lowly beginnings positions of eminence." He later commented on the way in which his colleagues handled complaining businessmen as representing very particular interests: "Herr Diergardt might understand velvets, Herr Haniel coal, or Herr Böninger tobacco, but the understanding of general interests was a preserve of the officials."[38]

Haniel clearly did not see his political activity as simply a particularistic rent-seeking. On the contrary, he had a vision of major political transformation. In the 1840s Haniel named two iron barges the *Zollverein* (Customs Union) and *Industrie*, the new concepts that seemed to be creating a new Germany. The more he thought about his business, the more it seemed to fit into the story of the political maturation of the country.

The 1840s were also of course a decade of much wider political mobilization, in part the result of the change in monarch in Berlin and of Frederick William IV's wish to make himself a popular figure, but in large part a response to the beginnings of industrialization and the harvest and food crisis of 1846–47.

Franz Haniel experienced 1848 in part as a protest against aristocratic rule in Prussia. In a tavern in Düsseldorf he was told that educated young bourgeois were bullied by stupid Junkers in the army.[39] In Cologne and Mainz he was forced to pay out wages to unemployed workers, but eventually stopped the payments and threatened to stop all shipping on the Rhine. The year 1848 was at the same time an opportunity and a threat.

Paternalism

One response of Jacobi, Haniel & Huyssen to the revolutionary upheaval of 1848 was to strengthen and coordinate welfare measures for the workforce, extending an already existing tradition of paternalism. In 1832 the Sterkrade engineering works had a fund to pay sickness benefits. From 1840 there was a parallel fund in Oberhausen. In both cases, workers had to contribute regular sums in return for the promise of benefits. In 1847, however, with the onset of the business crisis, the company decided to pay the contributions itself, and in 1848 the Oberhausen and Sterkrade institutions were merged. The workers were to contribute four silbergroschen per month, but the enterprise would also put in a monthly figure of 200 thalers. After 1848 such institutions were widely imitated, for instance by Krupp in 1853.[40] But some sort of social insurance was clearly insufficient on its own to cushion employees in a downturn as dramatic as that of the 1840s. As early as 1844, Franz Haniel wrote to the Prussian finance minister (in the context of a plea for enhanced tariff protection) that he had, through Jacobi, Haniel & Huyssen, ordered a steamship, a steam-powered tug, and two iron Rhine barges in order to employ 220 workers who had lost their jobs.[41]

The company also sponsored saving, with a savings bank at St. Antoni and Neu Essen established in 1842. In 1844 it began the construction of housing in Osterfeld, with seven one- and two-family houses for masters, and thirteen four-family houses for workers. The idea of workers' settlements came to be a standard in Rhine-Ruhr: in 1858 there was a second settlement, and between 1898 and 1912 fourteen new settlements were built for Gute Hoffnung workers.

Ownership

Franz Haniel's own businesses were extensive, and though by the 1840s they were concentrated mostly in coal, he still ventured into other areas. In 1847, in the midst of a general food crisis, he again ventured into the Baltic grain trade, this time making substantial profits. At some times the businesses were referred to as Franz Haniel & Cie., although it is not clear that there was any formal incorporation. Franz worked in this business closely with his sons, above all with Hugo, who began working in the family business when he was sixteen, in 1826, and by 1835 had power of attorney to purchase mining and other real estate.

Meanwhile, Jacobi, Haniel & Huyssen was getting bigger, and consequently harder to manage. When Wilhelm Lueg took over as director in 1823, there had been 200 employees; by the time of his death in 1864, there were 5,000. As manager and owners grew older, there was also the question of the succession. For most of the reign of Lueg, Franz Haniel remained in the shadows as far as the Jacobi, Haniel & Huyssen was concerned, and concentrated on his ventures as an individual entrepreneur.

With the expansion of the various Haniel families, the ownership of Jacobi, Haniel & Huyssen became an increasingly problematical issue. Gottlob Jacobi had left four sons and a daughter, Clementine, who was married to a skilled English engineer, Nicholas Harvey. Harvey had played an important part in attracting a number of skilled English workers to work for the company. The Harveys had no children and wished to sell their fifth part of the original Jacobi quarter share in the firm. Since the other four children of Jacobi did not wish to buy these shares, and Huyssen refused the price calculated by Franz Haniel's son, Franz Haniel bought the shares on his private account. After the transaction was complete, Carl Haniel, the heir of Gerhard, complained and argued that this sale should have been made to the firm as a whole. In his memoirs Franz Haniel explained that he gave in "in order to avoid quarrels."[42]

In 1847 Franz Haniel brought another mine into the company (Königsberg, renamed Zeche Oberhausen). Huyssen, Carl Haniel, and Wilhelm Lueg now proposed that the family enterprise be turned into a joint-stock company, in line with the legal changes that made such companies the rage in Germany in the 1850s. In 1843 Prussian law had been changed to allow the creation of joint-stock companies, but only where they served the "higher interest of the common good," and where the goal of the company could not be realized in any other way: the legislation was above all in-

5. *Franz Haniel and grandchildren, ca. 1865: from left, Max Haniel, Caroline Liebrecht (née Haniel), Franz Haniel, and Adeline Böninger behind their grandfather.*

COURTESY OF FRANZ HANIEL & CIE. GMBH, DUISBURG-RUHRORT

tended to promote railroad building. Only a more liberal law of 1870 prompted a flood of new corporations.

Franz Haniel was outraged by his partners' suggestion, which smacked of the financial dealing that he had always disdained and detested, and he threatened simply to break the company up into three parts. He concluded: "as a consequence, the swindle with shares was prevented, and the works and the company still remain. How much unpleasantness I have experienced in the course of my almost sixty-year-long most selfless and strenuous activity for the company, but ingratitude is the reward of the world."[43]

In practice, Haniel's threat left his heirs little choice but to transform the company into the joint-stock venture of the kind that Franz Haniel had always despised. Otherwise the enterprise would collapse in fragments. The legal form of the company was by now the only way of controlling the fissiparous impulses of a large family that now lacked the guiding hand of the patriarch. At Franz's death, five of his sons (Hugo, Max, Julius, Louis, and Theobald), as well as Thusnelde Cockerill, were still living, and all inherited shares in the family business. If each went his or her own way, Franz's legacy would be destroyed. Incorporation offered a way of extending that hand beyond the grave.

Thus in 1870, only a few years after his death (on 24 April 1868), the trading company Franz Haniel et Comp., embracing Franz Haniel's diverse interests, was registered in the Ruhrort official court with sixty shares, divided equally among five of the six branches of Franz Haniel's descendants (the exception being Max and his descendants).[44] In the same year Jacobi, Haniel & Huyssen was transformed into the joint-stock corporation Gute Hoffnungs Hütte. With this move there was less room for the intervention of individual owners, and more power for the organization and the management. The initial golden age of entrepreneurship in Germany had come to an end.

Chapter 3

The Industrial Origins of the Falcks

Italy has a very beautiful display, but it is more artistic than industrial.

G. E. Falck, 1885

SMALL-SCALE ENTREPRENEURSHIP as the crucial determinant of the industrial landscape lasted much longer in Italy than in Germany. The Alpine north Italian iron industry had a very old history: like the industry of Lorraine and the Rhineland, it at first depended on local ore and charcoal smelting, with long-lived dynasties of craftsmen working the foundries: Badonis (indisputably the premier dynasty of the Como area), Bolis, Redaellis, and Rubinis. The major locational advantage lay in the abundant availability of water power to drive mills and hammers. There were analogous industries in the neighboring mountain areas, Grisons (Switzerland) and the Austrian territories of Styria and Carinthia.[1] At the beginning of this story, the Alpine iron-producing areas of northern Italy were under Habsburg rule. Each locality had its own specialty: thus the Val Trompia produced cutting instruments and firearms, the Val Camonica agricultural tools, and Lecco wire that could be used to make nails and pins. The manufacturers around Lake Como, however, supplied not just local agricultural demand, but also the demand of Milanese craftsmen for iron for the manufacture of armor. Even at the beginning of the nineteenth century, they derived some of their iron not from local ore but from what they called "broken iron" or scrap.

6. *Giorgio Enrico Falck, 1802–1886*

COURTESY OF THE FALCK ARCHIVE, MILAN

The Falcks came not from Italy, but from an area long contested between France and Germany. Georges Henri (later Giorgio Enrico, although he always preferred to write in French rather than Italian) Falck was born in 1802 in Wissembourg, in Alsace, close to the border with the Palatinate, which at the time was under French rule. His father, Jean Didier, was the French commander of the gendarmerie in Landau in the Palatinate. In the early 1820s he worked in the local metallurgical industry, and then in 1826 moved south, to Switzerland, where he honed his engineering skills. A Protestant, he married a Catholic girl from the Upper Rhine valley, Barbara Noblat, and in 1827 in Cernay, near Mulhouse, their first son, Henri (Enrico), was born. Once in Switzerland, he traveled on farther south.

In 1833 Falck was invited to Lombardy (then under Austrian rule) as a technical adviser to the iron manufacturer Gaetano

Rubini e Figlio at an old-established metallurgical site at Dongo, on the western shore of Lake Como. Pietro Rubini had taken over the works in 1791 from Count Giulini,[2] and in 1801 his son Gaetano had bought out the count completely and established a new company. In 1794 it produced around 320 tons of iron.[3] During the Restoration Rubini developed as an important maker of iron bridges, and in the 1830s it moved into railroad building. The enterprise was trying to break out of the small-scale production of the late eighteenth century, and for this it needed foreign technicians and skills. In a similar way, the Wendels and Haniels had tried to hire English technicians.

The problems of the traditional and small-scale Lombard iron industry was highlighted in 1839, when the brothers Balleydier petitioned to be allowed to import pig iron at a reduced rate for a new engineering plant at Lambro, near Milan, on the grounds that the quality of existing native production was too low to make reliable equipment or to build up any industrial base. At this time Giorgio Enrico Falck settled permanently in Dongo, and the company was renamed Rubini, Falck, Scalini e Comp. Falck put up some of his own money, 30,000 Austrian liras (or $5,600), a relatively small sum; and Giuseppe Rubini contributed one-third (250,000 Austrian liras, or $47,000) of the total capital. The new firm tried to mobilize opinion against the Balleydiers' proposal, arguing that it would damage rather than advance the cause of "national industry" and would reduce employment and increase poverty (the dispute ended with a characteristically Austrian compromise, in which the Balleydiers were allowed for five years to import half the amount of iron they had originally demanded).[4]

Falck was the technical director at Rubini, and he immediately started to innovate; the investment of his own money simply offered his employer a guarantee that he would not move on and abandon the works with a half-finished modernization program. When he arrived, he had been an itinerant craftsman of a quite characteristic kind for ancien-régime Europe, who would sell knowledge and then pass on. Ownership was a means to commitment. Like François de Wendel and Franz Haniel, Falck applied English ironworking and mechanical technology. He introduced what he called the "sistema inglese" (English system), using hot air, and using the heated gases to fire a puddling oven. Falck built a much higher furnace than was customary and in the 1840s started to manufacture plate iron. He also looked for alternatives to the use of charcoal, and in 1842 became interested in using peat for smelting, proposing to use the large peat reserves near Turin.

Falck had a regular correspondence with leading French and Swiss engineers, such as Sulzberger from Frauenfeld. His major attraction for his employer and partner, Rubini, was his range of contacts with foreign best practice (or at least better practice). In 1842 he wrote: "I am proud to be better in puddling than the Wasseralfingen works [a famous Württemberg mine, foundry, rolling mill, and mechanical workshop]."[5] He remained an enthusiastic advocate of more investment in new technologies, with an engineering rather than a commercial standpoint. In 1843, for instance, Falck wrote to a friend: "It is very true that this cost us more expense and energy than I had originally believed. As to the money spent, we will make it up I am sure, but the work and the tiredness have ruined my health."[6]

The products of the firm included some of the first examples of industrial design in northern Italy. In 1841 the Austrian government gave an official recognition to Rubini and Falck as representing the "essential conditions of civilization."[7] In 1842 Rubini and Falck built a pioneering iron bridge in Milan. In the same year, the almanac of the Como province praised the Dongo works as highly modern and noted that it had received the gold medal for arts and industry from the Austrian government. Its output increased from an average of 420 tons a year in the early 1840s to 1,000 tons in 1858, by which time the works employed 400 workers.[8]

As Rubini had recognized, Falck would not be likely to confine his activities to one particular manufacturing site, and he continued to look around for new places where he might apply the new industrial knowledge. As long as these sites were sufficiently distant from Dongo, there was no competitive threat. Giorgio Enrico Falck thus also worked as a consultant in the development of iron in other regions. He advised Gervasone di Aymaville in the Valle d'Aosta on the use of anthracite and gas in puddling; and also worked in Liguria at Fiorino and Voltri, and at Prà.

The initial end to Falck's commitment to Dongo ironmaking came not as a result of wanderlust, but because of political upheaval. First, the economic crisis of 1846–47 hit the firm very hard: it asked in 1847 for a subsidy from the Austrian government's Central Welfare Commission, but was turned down on the grounds that it had had a subsidy once before (in fact, thirty years earlier). The rebuff from the Austrian government may have helped to transform the firm's owners into Italian patriots.[9] In 1848 the Dongo works provided 70-millimeter cannons for the revolutionary provisional government in Milan, as well as ammunition. On 9 June 1849 Rubini and Falck ended its business activity for a short while, and a period of stagnation followed when it revived itself as Rubini e Scalini.[10]

Falck then worked with one of the industrial leaders sympathetic to the movement of 1848, Giuseppe Badoni, who had gone into exile after the failure of the anti-Austrian revolution. With some political normalization, Badoni returned to Lombardy in 1852, and opened relatively large-scale works in Castello, Bellano, and Mandello, on the eastern shore of Lake Como. Castello (next to Lecco) produced 1,300 tons annually, and Bellano 900 tons of wire and 270 tons of plate.[11] As a way of securing the industrial loyalty of the father, Badoni also tried to bring the young Enrico Falck, who in 1853 had engaged in a metallurgical apprenticeship in Franche-Comté (at Audincourt). In 1856 Enrico came back to Italy, to the Bellano works.

Meanwhile G. E. Falck had begun his own metallurgical works, with his own machinery, at Arlenico, near Lecco, in a building, the Seminario, that he rented from the Badonis. Using Belgian coal for fuel, he started work on the construction of a steam engine. In 1855 a pamphlet published in Lecco described how "the inhabitants of the territory, during the last period of peace, threw themselves into speculation and industry."[12] But the peace was not long-lived.

On 5 June 1859 Garibaldi came to Lecco with a group of Alpine troops. Falck enthused patriotically: "Quickly to arms! Whoever has a weapon should use it, a gun or a sword? What about the Germans? With a name like ours? Because we produce steel for the weapons!"[13] This time, political events turned out well for the Falcks, and Austrian rule in Lombardy ended.

By the early 1860s Arlenico had a fermenting oven and a steam engine with 14 horsepower. Meanwhile the Rubini works had also expanded. At Lecco itself there was a puddling furnace, and at Bellano two gas reverberators. In 1862 Rubini e Scalini produced 1,600 tons of iron, and the Badoni works 1,100. In the second half

7. *The family of Giuseppe Rubini*

COURTESY OF THE FALCK ARCHIVE, MILAN

of 1860 or in 1861 the ever-peripatetic G. E. Falck left his own small-scale ironworks in the charge of his son and embarked once more on extended travels, to Liguria, the Valle d'Aosta, Savoy, and France. His son, who in 1861 engaged to marry the daughter of Giuseppe Rubini, became increasingly independent, and in 1865 G. E. Falck returned to his native soil in Alsace and resided at Dannemarie, halfway between Mulhouse and Belfort. He died on 7 April 1885.

Enrico Falck married Irene Rubini, one of twelve children of the patriarchal ironmaster, in 1863 in the cathedral of Como.[14] In a long letter to his prospective father-in-law he had explained the "beautiful future" of his ironworks and his intention to process the scrap that was now being produced in larger quantities as a waste product of other works. He also thought that his business would be helped by the completion of a railroad extending to Lecco, and that it would also thrive once Venezia was liberated from the Austrians.[15]

In fact the new political developments produced setbacks rather than success. The Austrian mining law of 1854, which was applied in Lombardy in 1857, was essentially continued by the Kingdom of Sardinia after the military victories of Magenta and Solferino in

1859, and seemed ill fitted to the scattered and diverse character of the still nascent Italian metallurgical industry. The metal produced in the small works around Lake Como was more expensive than that of other Italian producers. And in general, iron was produced more cheaply abroad, and in the 1870s imports soared. For the Italian producers, there was an even greater threat: agreements had been concluded in 1869 and 1871 for the construction of a railroad tunnel through the Gotthard, which would bring German products easily and cheaply across the Alps to the Italian market (the tunnel opened in 1882). Italians responded to the new environment by calling for tariff protection; but Falck also thought of some bold strategic gambles. In the early 1870s he explored the idea of developing production in the Valle d'Aosta. But then he resolved to develop the site at Malavedo by Lecco. He wrote to Giuseppe Rubini: "The position is rather far from the lakeshore, but there is sufficient water power in this location, and sufficient space to establish a puddling furnace . . . The iron industry in the valley of Lecco if it is well worked will have a long life."[16] The strategy proposed was "aggressive."[17] Rubini was at first not very encouraging, and was probably concerned about the depressive and melancholic character of his son-in-law.

Nevertheless in October 1871 Falck successfully established the Società del Laminatoio (Rolling Mill Company) at Malavedo, which was alternately known as Falck, Bolis, and Redaelli, with a mechanical hydraulically driven wheel and hammer. It was formally constituted as a partnership *(en commandite)* in July 1873, with 25 percent of the stock held by the sons of Giuseppe Redaelli, 25 percent by the sons of Pietro Redaelli, 30 percent by Giovanni, Carlo, and Giuseppe Bolis, and 20 percent by Falck; but Enrico Falck was the general manager. The Redaelli family had already built one of the first shops producing metal wire in Italy. Falck then brought his family from Dongo, on the other side of the lake, to live in a new villa in Malavedo. He formulated ambitious goals, with apparently great, even manic, optimism: "The iron industry has been the base and the origin of the area around Lecco, flourishing and enriching itself . . . With the help of additional capital, and using the favorable natural resources, the iron industry in the area of Lecco will develop in such vast proportions that we will not envy all the other manufacturing countries . . . With the financial help established, the project cannot fail, and will be secured by the constitution of a company with sufficient capital."[18] The business of the new works would be aided by the development of railroads, with one line from Bergamo to Lecco, linking Lecco with Venezia, Milan, and Genoa, and another line under construction between Monza and Calolzio.

The Badonis immediately responded to the new local challenge by expanding production. Apparently there was also a great deal of local opposition. On the night of 2–3 August 1874, Enrico Falck was sitting with Costante Redaelli and some other ironmasters in a tavern at Malavedo when he was hit on the head by a large stone thrown through the window. Investigators found that the assailant was a small-scale local manufacturer who had quarreled with Falck over the water supply.[19]

The considerable business difficulties of the 1870s probably contributed to a new onset of Falck's psychological depression. He died in September 1878, leaving two daughters, Luigia (aged thirteen) and Camilla (aged nine), and a son, Giorgio Enrico, who was born in 1866. At first the business was run by Irene Rubini Falck, and as in the French and German families, a widow played a crucial role in rescuing the family business after a demographic and business disaster. Her father was no longer restricted in his willingness to pour in funds by his low opinion of the character of his son-in-law. In 1882 Irene put in new money, expanded the Malavedo works, and set out to preserve a business for her son as a prospering venture. She also made some dynastic alliances: her daughter Luigia in 1884 married Costante Redaelli.

Irene Falck sent her son, G. E. Falck, at age sixteen to study in Zurich, where he spent two and a half years and eventually won admission to the new and highly prestigious Federal Technical High School. But instead of staying on in Zurich, he took an apprenticeship in the industrial heartland of Germany, working for the Dortmund "Union" from December 1884 to June 1885. He then worked for a wireworking company, Allhoff & Müller, at Plettenberg (in the old metalworking area of the Sauerland), and subsequently for the Cologne engineering company Kalker Werkzeugmaschinenfabrik. He also made trips to look at the industries of Luxembourg and the Saar, in particular the Dillinger Hüttenwerke, Röchling, and the Burbacher Hütte; as well as examining ways of

8. *Irene Rubini Falck, 1840–1919*

COURTESY OF THE FALCK ARCHIVE, MILAN

processing iron rods in Osnabrück. Unlike his father, but like his grandfather, he was aware of the realities of Italian industrial backwardness. When he visited an international exposition in Antwerp in October 1885, he noted: "Italy has a very beautiful display, but it is more artistic than industrial."[20] Like his grandfather, he resolved to apply a foreign model to revolutionize Italian business conduct.

In 1886 he returned to Italy and served a commercial apprenticeship with a metal utensils and trading company, Figli di Ippolito Sigurtà. At this time the Redaelli brothers were building a large new works at Gardone Valtrompia, a traditional ironworking location, for the manufacture of bridges and metal equipment. This was exactly what Falck had studied in Germany, and he considered himself a preeminent expert.

Falck made more trips to Germany, including Hagen, in Westphalia. He was also appointed director of the Malavedo plateworks in 1889, and general manager in 1893, with sole responsibility for the technical side of the business. The output of Malavedo increased from a daily 50 tons in 1894 to 70 tons in 1896. Falck's share of the Malavedo ironworks was raised from 20 percent to 30 percent. Under Falck's direction, the Malavedo works started to expand.

In 1895 Malavedo took over an ironworks at Rogoredo—a highly risky operation in the wake of the major business downturn and the widespread bankruptcies of 1892–93. Rogoredo lay far away from the Alpine valleys, just to the south of Milan. The purchase marked the beginning of Falck's shift away from the old locations and into the heart of the Lombard plain, where there were many big customers. Falck's rescue plan characteristically involved a big expansion and modernization with a large Siemens-Martin hearth (the first to be built in Italy) with a capacity of 16 tons, working with scrap metal and with cast iron with a manganese content. The new plant was completed in 1901, in the midst of a new (but relatively mild) recession. It began with the production of steel plate, which was also a new departure for Falck. By 1904 it was producing 30,000 tons.

To work on the new processes, Falck again made numerous trips abroad, but in the late 1890s mostly to Britain: to London, but also to the Welsh and Scottish industries (Cardiff and Glasgow). He concluded from these trips that in order to succeed, the north Italian industry would require substantial investments of capital. And in fact in the first decade of the twentieth century there were major mergers in all the major steel-producing countries; this was the age of the steel trust.

While the major expansion was occurring, in 1898, Giorgio Enrico Falck married Irene Bertarelli. She came from an old-established Lecco family that had first specialized in silk production and then moved into gas lighting in the 1870s. It is likely that the Bertarelli marriage, like Luigia's Redaelli marriage, helped to bring in additional capital. Falck also started to involve himself in industrial politics on a national level, and quickly demonstrated a charismatic quality. In October 1899 a meeting of leading iron and steel industrialists in Rome led to the creation of an Association of the Metal Industry, which was constituted in 1901. Falck, still only thirty-five years old, was elected president by acclamation.

The requirements for capital for the new steel industry exceeded anything that could be raised from an immediate network of relatives and friends. So businesses started to look to the new Italian banks, established on a German model with German capital, and committed to a program of industrial engagement and expansion. The largest of the new industrial ventures involved the establishment of coastal plants for the working of ore. In 1905, under the tutelage of the Credito Italiano, represented by Giacomo Durazzo Palavicini, the giant Ilva steel company was established. It worked with ores from Elba in a number of coastal sites: Savona, Piombino, and Naples. Italy was beginning the age of the modern corporation, and G. E. Falck saw the financial opportunities as making possible new technical advances.

PART TWO

The Age of the Corporation

The widespread institution of joint-stock corporations radically changed the way Europeans did business. The modern corporation posed a new threat to family business because of the greater efficiencies and economies of scale it potentially provided, but it also created new opportunities for families to use those efficiencies. On the one hand, it held out the possibility of dispersing ownership more widely and allowed entrepreneurs to exit from their achievements by selling their stock on the secondary securities markets and thus gain immediate rewards for having taken risks. This novel advantage gave rise to the impression that there was a one-way street from the individualistic entrepreneur to the atomized ownership of a bureaucratized corporation. On the other hand, the corporation gave families a means of institutionalizing themselves that appeared especially attractive as the passage of generations led to larger and less cohesive families, less immediately connected by personal memory to the founder generation. For the family, it offered a way of replacing trust (which could be problematic, especially as families got larger) by contract. It thus allowed family firms to survive on a big scale, and not just as the microenterprises of the early industrial revolution.

The corporation as legally defined was not a completely stable entity, and definitions of responsibility and structure were subject to dramatic changes and revisions. Corporations had existed before the middle of the nineteenth century, but they almost always required state licensing, and above all the stockholders were not protected by limited liability. They provided some advantages over a traditional partnership, in that the precise value of the partnership did not need to be ascertained for each transfer of ownership, but could instead be fixed via the stock market. But there was also a clear and potentially large risk to each owner of stock. Companies thus demanded a high level of trust in the company and its management, and were consequently quite rare.

The history of the rise of the joint-stock company is a fine example of the way in which institutions have effects that transcend national boundaries and consequently often require legal changes. In the middle of the nineteenth century, the idea of the corporation appeared to be the best way of organizing the basis for general prosperity, and hence of a solution to the pressing social issue, and it spread like wildfire. Britain in 1844 eased restrictions on joint-stock corporations imposed by the Bubble Act after the early eighteenth-century South Sea Bubble, but not until 1855 did British law provide for limited liability.

Since the late seventeenth century, France had had a tradition of share companies *en commandite*, in which share owners had limited liability but almost no control over the company. In the 1830s a surge in corporate foundations ended in many failures, and investors began to believe that incorporation in neighboring countries provided superior levels of investment protection. France first moved to regularize the position of Belgian and then other foreign corporations in France in 1857, and ten years later the Senate and the Chamber of Deputies passed a law allowing the unlicensed creation of joint-stock companies in France. Their constitution required simply a general meeting of stockholders and the appointment of a board of directors.

Prussia permitted railroad corporations from 1838, and other corporations after 1843, but they required official permission. The general German commercial code of 1861 recognized only certified companies. Not until passage of the law of 11 June 1870 could corporations be formed without government permission and operated without state supervision or regulation. The new law represented a dramatic shift from a state-ordered economy to the market. The result was a free-for-all in a speculative rush to create joint-stock corporations. Later critics complained of the radical nature of the liberalization and the absence of requirements about prospectuses for new issues. After bitter debate, a law of 1884 clarified the tasks and responsibilities of a corporation and of its boards, required prospectuses and definitions of corporate activity, and took a small step in the direction of more regulation. It set a high minimum value (1,000 Marks, or $240) for each share in larger companies, in order to discourage speculation by small investors.

Italian joint-stock companies became possible as a result of the new commercial code introduced in 1882, which substantially took over the provisions of the French law of 1867. But it was not until the beginning of the twentieth century that a big wave of company foundations began.

The corporation brought transformative changes for company

organization, corporate governance, and the financing of enterprise; but the extent of these changes was not immediately apparent, and their implications were realized only incrementally. The new rules apparently gave great powers to owners, represented in general meetings. But the practice was different; as the owners often knew little about the company and about one another, they found it hard to organize effectively at the general meetings. Information deficiencies rather than law tipped the power advantage to the managers. Hence the attempts that began after the scandals and crashes of the 1870s and 1880s in France and Germany to introduce more regulation. The pendulum that had swung from heavy regulation to dramatic liberalization began to swing back toward cautious regulation.

In France, the top level of management in a joint-stock company, the *conseil d'administration*, was conceived of as a committee of shareholders (article 22 of the 1867 law), with shareholders having the right to choose a nonshareholder as their representative(s): "un mandataire étranger à la société." A director general could thus be chosen by the general meeting or by the administrative council. A relatively high value (500 francs, or around $100) was set as the minimum share for large companies as a way of discouraging small share owners, who might be hurt by speculative collapses. The French terms had their exact counterpart in the Italian code of 1882, with a *consiglio di administrazione*, which might have a president, but also a *consigliere delegato*, who as chief executive represented the corporation.

The German law of 1870 distinguished quite sharply between a managing board *(Vorstand)* and a supervisory board *(Aufsichtsrat)* selected by a general meeting of shareholders. The *Vorstand* was charged with the day-to-day management of the company, and the supervisory board had a responsibility that was legally defined as controlling. Most commentaries on the supervisory board, however, emphasized that its role was in practice much more extensive than that provided for in the law. It exercised a "control," gave advice, and above all selected the management and the management board.[1] Its practical power is often supposed to have depended on the presence of bank representatives: this was how bankers saw what was going on in the corporation, and they could consequently make credit decisions. It was the ability to turn the financial spigot off or on that gave bankers a decisive voice, and bank lending is often held to be the major source of external finance for German corporations.[2] Family owners actually also appeared as major creditors, especially in the early years of the corporation, as well as owners of stock; this was the case with the Haniels and the Gutehoffnungshütte (GHH) in the 1870s.

In many large family-owned firms, such as Siemens, family members remained on the managing board right through the twentieth century; but the institution generally lent itself to a separation of management from ownership. Members of the *Vorstand* had no obligation to own shares in the corporation, and very often they did not. But the provision of shares offered a way of binding managers and giving incentives, and the leading managers of the GHH, the Reuschs (father and son), in fact held stock, as did Johann Welker in the trading company Franz Haniel & Cie. GmbH. The legal separation of the *Vorstand* and the supervisory board made a separation of ownership from management in the German case much clearer than in France or Italy, or indeed in Great Britain, where family owners remained on boards of directors or "administrative councils." Managers were keen to cultivate a culture of the enterprise that was quite distinct from the "property" of owners: the enterprise should also be the "property" of the nation or of the workers, and managers should be the ones who interpreted these collective (stakeholding) interests.

While it was the responsibility of the *Vorstand* to draw up the profit-and-loss account, decisions on dividend payments were formally made by the general meeting. In practice, it was very rare to override the management suggestions, and the shareholders had to take the package as prepared by the management. Already in the 1890s, Max Weber pointed out that the fundamental decisions in capitalist enterprises were made by the *Vorstand*.[3] The development of a management with its own interest in U.S. corporations led Adolf Berle and Gardner Means to claim in a celebrated book of 1932, *The Modern Corporation and Private Property*, that the "atom of property" had been split: that shareowners and managers were developing different interests.[4] Management had its own type of "property," and a separate interest. Managers were salaried, although members of the *Vorstand* as well as the supervisory board were entitled to the payment of a special dividend, or *Tantième*, that reflected the company's performance.

The major advantage of the joint-stock corporation is not so much that it raises money on the stock exchange, as that it allows founders or entrepreneurs who have invested capital and energy in a venture that is nonliquid to retrieve or recoup their original investment and thus derive a return on their entrepreneurial initiative. Owners could sell on a secondary market. The possibility of sale obviously provided a major threat to control in a family firm, and the management of the family firm was consequently continually engaged in elaboration covenants that would restrict the ability to sell to other members of the restricted family circle. Particularly in periods of great turmoil, as in the aftermath of the First World War, such covenants played an important role.

The threat to owner control created a demand for alternative forms of incorporation, for those who feared that the joint-stock corporation gave too much power to anonymous capital. The German law of 1892 allowed the establishment of a private limited liability company, the *Gesellschaft mit beschränkter Haftung* (GmbH), which required no supervisory board and no general meeting, and had consequently much reduced reporting requirements (until European Community legislation of 1987). By the end of the century there were almost 2,000 such corporations, and they mushroomed during the war and the postwar inflation: by 1924 there were 79,257. An analogy to the GmbH was not required in France, as the company *en commandite* offered the same sort of possibilities.

The characteristics of the stock market help to explain how German and U.S. corporate experience began to diverge at the beginning of the twentieth century. For most nineteenth-century economies, securities markets really involved the trading of government bonds, railroad stock and bonds, and some corporate bonds. In the United States the market for industrial securities did not really develop until the big merger movement after 1898. The Dow Jones index for industrial securities began to be calculated in the mid-1890s, and from 1900 John Moody published a manual of industrial securities.[5]

Germany, by contrast, had a highly developed market for industrial securities by the last third of the nineteenth century. Weber believed that by the 1890s 1.5 to 2 million Germans owned securities and that one billion Marks had been invested in securities.[6] The law of 1884 had tried to restrict share ownership by making the minimum shareholding 1,000 Marks, hence excluding the really small investor: but Weber nevertheless observed that "one should resist the conclusion that the owners of shares are necessarily to be found principally in the circles of 'Great Capitalists.'"[7]

The 1896 stock-exchange law in Germany was severely restrictive and was driven by anticapitalist ressentiments of the agrarian right. It limited forward dealings in securities as well as in commodities. Just at the moment when a securities culture was developing in the United States, it paralyzed development in Germany. The consequence was that Germany became more of a bank-run economy and less a market-driven one. France had analogous legislative debates to those that led to the new German law, but attempts to introduce a restrictive law were never realized, in part perhaps because the possibility of incorporating in Belgium gave companies a way of circumventing possible French controls. Twelve years after the promulgation of the German stock law, it was revised. Chancellor Bernhard von Bülow had explained that it disadvantaged Germany in competition with foreign markets; but by this time the damage had been done. Institutional arrangements, syndicate agreements, and cartels had been deployed to reorganize German business and had set it on a path where the capital market mattered less. Correspondingly, banks and the search for cooperative arrangements mattered more. The German proclivity for cartelization triumphed as the institutional solution to a struggle between the strategies of owners and managers within the new joint-stock corporations.

Some comparisons:

Wendel, 1913: 848,000 tons of iron in Germany and 394,000 tons in France; 770,000 tons of steel in Germany and 330,000 tons in France

GHH, 1913: 787,000 tons of iron and 801,000 tons of steel

AFL (Falck), 1913: 72,000 tons of steel

Chapter 4

The Gutehoffnungshütte as a Joint-Stock Company

The unbearable pressure of the wretched bank credits.
Hugo Haniel, 1878

THE BUSINESS CLIMATE of a maturing industrial economy is quite different from that of the energetic experimentalism of the early years. And Germany in the decades after the death of Franz Haniel was a very different society from that of the small provincial business networks that had functioned in the world of the French Revolution and the Napoleonic Wars. After 1871 there was a stable and secure political and legal environment. The law allowed forms of business organization that transcended the confines of old-fashioned small family firms. The existence of the joint-stock company solved the problem of trust that had been a central dilemma for early nineteenth-century businessmen and that had caused great strains in many families, including the Haniels: after all, relatives cannot always be trusted not to go bankrupt. But the search for organization did not stop at the legal institution of the firm. Especially in heavy industry, in the face of volatile markets and a globalizing world economy, with substantial international competition, there was a demand that the state supply protection. That protection, when it came in the form of the iron and steel tariff of 1879, then created incentives to organize domestically in order to derive full advantage from the possibilities offered by government

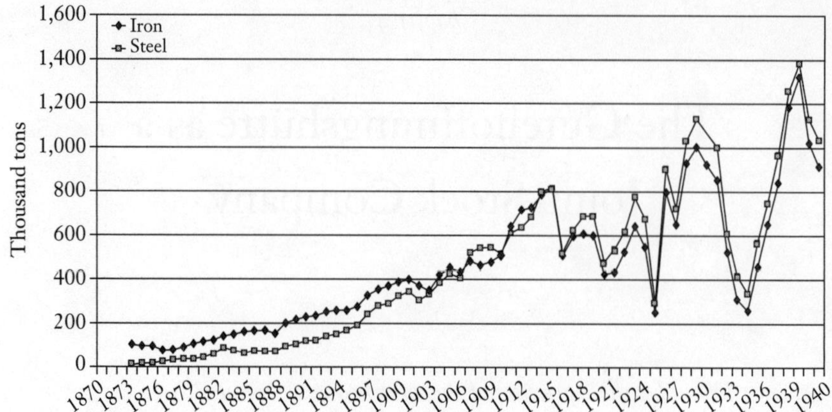

Source: Fritz Buchner, 125 Jahre Geschichte der Gutehoffnungshutte, Oberhausen, 1935; RWWA, GHH 40011112/33

9. *GHH iron and steel production, 1870–1940*

policy. The outcome was a proliferation of price- and market-stabilizing instruments, and in particular of cartels, which came to be widely regarded as a central feature of German industrial life.

The phase of the Haniel history that followed the death of the founder generation was thus very different from the first. Instead of looking for new activities and entrepreneurial diversification, the most urgent tasks entailed first updating technology and then investing in order to increase output. The story of the Haniel fortunes in the period 1870–1914 is one of a remarkably steady focus of activity on steel, and of a continual increase in production.

The main challenge faced by the joint-stock companies was one of financing: How could the sums required for the new investments be raised? The owners were required to forgo dividends in order to channel resources back into the company. But since there were many owners, and they no longer saw their whole existence as being associated with the company, such renunciation of current income was no longer intrinsically appealing. Current sacrifice could be justified only through appeal to the prospect of future income; but at the beginning of a new business development, such a prospect was obviously uncertain, and indeed one of the characteristics of the early 1870s was that a great many business investors lost a great deal of money. The early years of the new Haniel company, the GHH (formally the Aktienverein Gute Hoffnungs Hütte, but usually called the Gutehoffnungshütte), were very perilous, and this was by no means an exceptional story. Business failure became a widespread topic of debate and reflection. There were even novels about the collapse of business empires, such as Friedrich Spielhagen's *Sturmflut* (Storm Flood), which was loosely based on the collapse of the railroad empire of Baron Bethel Strousberg. Later in the nineteenth century, a pattern of bourgeois expectations would be solidified, in which wise investment and the deferral of consumption and pleasure produced great long-term gains. But just as these assumptions had become really ingrained in the world of the German commercial and industrial classes, they were dramatically shattered by the monetary disasters of the First World War and the great inflation. In the 1870s, all that was in the future; for the moment, the political setting was secure, but the economic environment was exceedingly precarious as the *Gründerkrach* succeeded the optimism of the foundation years of the empire.

The Possibilities and Dangers of Joint-Stock Companies

Beginning in 1870, Germany allowed the establishment of joint-stock companies without a special license, with a new law analogous to the French reform of 1867. The new legal form offered a substantial attraction to a family that was getting bigger. The forty-seven owners of stock in the new company, Aktienverein für Bergbau und Hüttenbetrieb Gute Hoffnungs Hütte, created in 1870, were almost all descendants of the two Haniel brothers. The only significant exception was Friedrich Jacobi, who owned 1/16 of the 10,000 shares of 1,000 thalers in the new corporation. The two largest shareholders, with 1,041 shares each (5/48), were the widow of Gerhard's son Carl Haniel, and the other son, Alphons Haniel. The big shareholders thus owed their property to the chance of the succession of Gerhard Haniel, who had fewer offspring than the large Franz family. Of Franz Haniel's heirs, the eldest son, Hugo, and his only son, Franz (who was married to a Jacobi), each received 5/64 of the stock, or 781 shares. The surviving four younger sons of the patriarch, Max, Julius, Louis, and Friedrich Wilhelm, as well as the daughter, Thusnelde Cockerill, each received 5/96 of the stock, or 520 shares. In line with the division of the estate of Franz Haniel, the eldest son and his heirs thus had three times (1,562 shares) the

10. *Hugo Haniel and family, ca. 1885: from left, Hugo Haniel (1810–1893), with crossed legs and top hat; Bertha Haniel (née Haniel) (1813–1899), with white lace cap; Johanna Haniel (née Jacobi) (1860–1953), standing, with light hat; Franz Haniel junior (1842–1916), standing, with bowler hat; Thusnelde Cockerill (née Haniel)(1830–1903), sitting with her husband, Heinrich Cockerill (1821–1903)*

COURTESY OF FRANZ HANIEL & CIE. GMBH, DUISBURG-RUHRORT

part of other family branches. There were no longer any Huyssen owners of GHH stock, although the old company (Jacobi, Haniel & Huyssen, of Sterkrade) continued to exist, with thirty-seven Huyssen heirs owning 360 of the 1,152 shares, and Friedrich Jacobi 72 shares.[1] The new company, the GHH, had a total capitalization of 10 million thalers, or 30 million Marks ($7.3 million).

The first chairman of the executive board of the GHH was Carl Lueg. The management was thus separated from the Haniel dynasty (as it had already been in the antecedent company), but the new director as the son of Wilhelm Lueg represented what began to look like a dynasty of managers to parallel the owning dynasty. Moreover, Lueg had a family link: he was the grandson of Wilhelm Haniel, the luckless elder brother of Franz and Gerhard. Wilhelm Lueg had married Wilhelm Haniel's daughter, and had then built up the Oberhausen ironworks, which were the heart of the new company. There had been a puddlingwork since 1835, and in 1849 and 1853 rod trains were added. On the death of Wilhelm Lueg in 1864, the company had employed some 5,000 workers. Carl Lueg added a second rolling mill, Neu Oberhausen, between 1865 and 1872.

Some members of the Haniel dynasty, who may have resented the way in which the new Haniel company escaped their own influence, or who may also simply have felt the entrepreneurial impetus to do something new, established separate companies. In 1864 Louis Haniel, the sixth son of Franz Haniel, had become the managing director of Jacobi, Haniel & Huyssen. When the GHH was created, he left the management and joined the new supervisory board. But this was clearly not an adequate occupation for an energetic man, and with a nephew, Franz (the son of Hugo), he joined with a Düsseldorf engineer, Heinrich Lueg, in creating an engineering firm, Haniel & Lueg. (During the First World War this firm was brought back into the main Haniel stable of companies controlled through the GHH.) In a letter to his father, Hugo, the young Franz Haniel explained his reluctance to participate in the new GHH: "With regard to the expected profit, I also believe that it will be higher and more secure, together with that of other solid companies, than with the extended GHH. The GHH will not in the long run be able to provide such a secure return as smaller works, which do not need to fear business cycles, strikes, etc. to the same extent."[2]

Max Haniel's second daughter, Nancy, had married a Belgian iron man of considerable entrepreneurial vigor. Barthold Suermondt had started as a major manager of the Cockerill ironworks at Seraing. But he also developed interests in Germany, and in 1838, at the moment of the crisis of the Cockerill works, had founded the Metallurgische Gesellschaft, which eventually became Stolberger Zink Aktiengesellschaft (AG). At the start of the speculative wave of Prussian company foundations, precipitated by the new law of 1870, he worked with Belgian and French investors to create the Société Anonyme (SA) des Aciéries Rhénanes à Meiderich (very close to Ruhrort); the name was quickly Germanicized after the Franco-Prussian War as Rheinische Stahlwerke AG. But the company quickly fell on hard times with the collapse of the *Gründer* boom. One indication is that Suermondt, who had also become an important art collector, had to sell his Rubenses, Murillos, and

Velásquezes to what later became the Kaiser Friedrich Museum in Berlin. Max Haniel's oldest son, Max Berthold Haniel, was involved as a director in Rheinische Stahlwerke. He, too, lost his fortune, blaming the failure on the dishonesty and incompetence of his subordinates, and thereafter lived in relatively straitened circumstances. His eldest son, Edgar Haniel von Haimhausen, abandoned business and became an accomplished German diplomat (and was one of the members of the German delegation to Versailles in 1919).

The young Franz Haniel's caution about the GHH was not altogether misplaced. When war broke out in August 1870 and the financial markets were disrupted, the company—less than a few months old—was unable to make an interest payment and almost went bankrupt. The company survived by credits from family members, with no major bank credits (except 26,202 thalers from the Sparcasse Sterkrade).[3] It would have been hard in late 1870 to predict that GHH would become one of the great names in German industrial and engineering history.

Steel Technology

The formation of the new company Gutehoffnungshütte, under the guidance of Franz Haniel's eldest surviving son, Hugo, came at a time of great technical advance and equally great economic and financial uncertainty (there is a link between the two phenomena). This was the combination that destroyed the fortunes of the Max branch of the Haniel dynasty in the Rheinische Stahlwerke. In terms of technology, the critical development was the replacement of wrought iron by steel. The Bessemer process (blowing air from below through a container of molten metal, burning off carbon in a very short time) had been introduced in 1856; and the Siemens Martin open-hearth method, in which waste gases were used to heat air and fuel, in 1864. But both techniques took more than a decade to have any real impact on production, and both required high-grade, nonphosphoric ores. Neu Oberhausen was constructed between 1868 and 1872 as a Bessemer plant. Lueg then constructed his first Siemens-Martin oven in 1879 at Neu Oberhausen, and used the resulting steel to make rolled wire.

In the 1860s and 1870s the center of the Ruhr iron and steel industry was shifting farther west of the Rhine, to the area where

11. *GHH Martin Works*

COURTESY OF THE RHEINISCHES INDUSTRIE-MUSEUM, OBERHAUSEN

the Haniels had established their business empire. One motive was greater proximity to ores or to places to which they could be cheaply transported.[4] Geographic location thus gave the Haniels a considerable advantage.

Both the German and French industries were at this stage quite vulnerable because they lacked access to high-grade ores, while the Bessemer and Siemens-Martin innovations were pushing down prices on international markets.[5] Prices and output thus fell simultaneously in the 1870s. The price of steel rails fell from 303 Marks per ton in 1873–74 to 147 Marks per ton in 1877–78. Pig-iron production at the GHH rose between 1867 and 1872 (see Figure 9), then fell until 1875. The first year in which the GHH produced serious quantities of Bessemer steel (5,167 tons) was 1872–73; the quantities rose until 1875–76, then fell abruptly to 1,839 tons in 1881–82. Thereafter the output of Bessemer steel fell off sharply and ceased altogether after 1890 as the GHH moved entirely to Martin steel.

The new company quickly made substantial losses because of the sharp fall in prices. For 1872–73 there had been a profit of 1,787,178 Marks, for 1873–74 of 450,000 Marks, but for 1874–75 a loss of 1,488,654 Marks, and the heavy losses continued until 1879. The company had to borrow extensively, but managed to finance part of the loss through a bond issue (which was placed almost entirely with the shareholders, who thus needed to raise additional money themselves). From 1873 through 1875 this bond issue was supposed to bring in 12 million Marks, though in fact it raised only an additional 10 million. In 1878 the GHH finances were restructured, with a reduction of the original capital from 10 million thalers, or 30 million Marks, to 6 million Marks, which was now denominated in "A" shares, while the bonds were converted into 12 million "B" shares. (These were eventually converted into "A" shares, after the company became much more successful, between 1898 and 1901).[6] The heirs of Franz and Gerhard Haniel had to swallow a considerable loss on their capital investment. The financial problems set the stage for a substantial tension between the owners and the managers: the owners were worried about the extent of their losses, while the managers argued that the only way out of the misery was to make large investments, using if necessary the new joint-stock banks that were emerging as prominent features of the German business landscape. At the same time, the management remained very conscious of the owners' view that the GHH was an "old family association" that needed to avoid the "help of the bankers" and did not want to be "delivered into the hands" of the stock market.[7]

The debate about the cost of the new technology was indicative of the extreme sensitivity of the company's owners at this financially strained time to any kind of new financial burden. The management, on the other hand, now separated from ownership, had a clearly different agenda, and liked the technology that it believed strengthened its own hand. The GHH managing board thus consistently wanted expansion, and complained that it was not proceeding quickly enough. This would be the only way of getting lower production costs and becoming competitive in prices. The Bessemer work had not been enlarged, so there was insufficient steel produced; there was a shortage of steam in the rolling mill Neu Oberhausen; and the older Oberhausen plant had not been expanded enough to allow a wireworks. Lueg wanted to introduce the direct conversion method, by which heated steel was formed into hot blocks, as at Phönix and Rheinische Stahlwerke, thus avoiding the inefficient and costly reheating of cold steel. He was a great proponent of the move to Martin steel. In December 1880 he wrote to Hugo Haniel: "In order to reduce our costs for producing rails, it seems to be necessary, apart from the Thomas conversion process, to convert the pig iron direct at the blast furnace, and to avoid the forging of steel blocks but instead to roll these hot into rails at double length." But he added: "Such projects will have to be deferred because of the current opinion on the supervisory board, where every financing causes the greatest difficulties."[8]

In 1879 a crucial technical breakthrough came, which transformed the position of the German and French steel industry: the availability of the Gilchrist-Thomas process for processing phosphoric ores, such as those of Lorraine or Sweden (which previously had ruined the linings of the Bessemer converters). In 1879 Rheinische Stahlwerke (Ruhrort-Meiderich) and Hoerder Bergwerks- und Hüttenverein (Hoerde, Westphalia) bought the rights for Germany (but not for the occupied territories of Alsace and Lorraine) to the Gilchrist-Thomas process, which made possible the use of phosphoric ores from Lorraine. Wendel bought the rights first for German Lorraine, then for the French areas.

Initially the GHH rejected the idea of trying to acquire the right to use the Gilchrist-Thomas process. This stance seems to have proceeded from the rather conservative attitudes of the owners, and especially of Hugo Haniel, who at first was very hesitant.[9] But the GHH did introduce the process in 1882. The patent rights were in fact ludicrously inexpensive. And Gilchrist-Thomas formed the basis of an initial expansion of the GHH's business, until the company made the transition to the electric Siemens-Martin process.

The Haniels worried constantly about their ability to control the management. The chairman of the supervisory board, Hugo Haniel, talked about "the cancer of keeping on incapable officials for years." In 1884 a long-serving works manager of Neu Oberhausen was dismissed for not paying enough attention to cost calculations. A company report in early 1884 stated: "The works managers are not to be held responsible for the unfavorable result."[10]

At this point a clash developed between different generations of

Haniels. Hugo Haniel, born in 1810, and thus already an old man, had in effect long been the heir apparent to the patriarchal figure of Franz Haniel after the early death of his older brother, Eduard. He had consolidated his family position through his marriage to Bertha, the only daughter of Gerhard Haniel. In 1845 he held power of attorney for the GHH's antecedent company, Jacobi, Haniel & Huyssen, and in 1858 he had taken on the direction of the Oberhausen coal mine. On the death of Franz Haniel in 1868, it was he who took over the family business and played the central role in the conversion into a joint-stock company. He played a major role in industrial politics in the 1870s, in putting together cartels, as well as in the politics of demanding tariff protection for iron and steel products. Like his father, he sent his memoranda on the subject to the government and expected that Berlin would listen. In the family, he was challenged by his nephew, Eduard James Haniel, the second son of Max Haniel. The new Haniel business leader had studied in England, where the anglophilia already expressed in his baptismal name blossomed. In 1876 he, too, married into the family, taking as his wife his second cousin Henriette, the youngest daughter of Carl Haniel. He was much more of a conspicuous consumer than his uncle.[11] He had an extensive riding stable, and eventually, when he left active business, he bought a large estate in Haimhausen, to the north of Munich.

Alphons Haniel, the largest shareholder (along with his brother's widow), was unhappy with the status quo and with Hugo Haniel's leadership. In November 1880, at the beginning of a long letter, he listed the substantial bank debts of the GHH (to the Essener Creditanstalt, the Duisburg-Ruhrorter Bank, the Disconto Gesellschaft, Schaaffhausen, and Sal. Oppenheim), which amounted to 1,696,150 Marks in a total indebtedness of 6,806,069 Marks. He added: "The majority of the supervisory board believes the situation of the GHH to be so endangered that the withdrawal of bank or other credit, which is always a possibility, could bring the firm to collapse, as was the case with Krupp, so that the "A" and "B" shares would be worthless. With such enormous debts as these we have every reason to be frightened. The dangerous time of September 1870, when we could not find the sum of 250,000 Marks to make the semiannual interest payment, shows how quickly and suddenly great enterprises can plunge into bankruptcy without adequate working capital."[12] It is possible to see different interests in the two Haniel branches: the Gerhard line of the family as big shareholders but with little input into business decisions were more worried about excessive expansion.

In 1880 Hugo Haniel reported that within the supervisory board there was a "substantial disagreement . . . in the assessment of the question of new construction, that is, regarding its usefulness in maintaining competitiveness." His nephew, Eduard James Haniel, at the general meeting of the company in December proposed a program that would involve stopping new building, reducing debt, and resuming payment of greater dividends. Hugo Haniel argued that such a retrenchment would be disastrous: "a program that renounced new construction would be the same as destruction." But he was himself quite cautious: "With the present overproduction in iron and steel and the quick change of industrial conditions, it is just as essential to avoid unsure and costly experiments as it is to cultivate truly proven improvements, if the firm is to survive. The new financial situation is due to our efforts at maintaining competitiveness, while many larger ironworks have already collapsed."[13]

Hugo Haniel also complained about "the unbearable pressure of the wretched bank credits" and called for a major belt-tightening program. "If in the light of our current financial position in overcoming the most severe crisis, which has already demanded such a great sacrifice, we do not want to lag behind our best-managed competitors, we will need to observe the greatest economy as well as the most perfect manufacture, and use all the opportunities of price changes as well as the ceaseless search for profitable orders in order to achieve once more and maintain our considerable industrial position."[14] The general suspicion of banks was shared by other big steel families, such as the Krupps and the Stumms, and after 1895 the dependence of the steel business on banks was generally reduced.[15]

The competition that Haniel feared, and the source of substantial innovation in steelmaking, were the nonfamily joint-stock companies, with their larger financial capacity. Technically, tilting converters allowed a substantial increase in the size of the Bessemer plants. In particular the Hoerder Verein borrowed money, and also repeatedly raised its share capital. This strategy occasionally produced major financial distress that required substantial bank rescue packages.[16] Such a financial formula, however, brought high rates of growth. These were enterprises that seemed to go well beyond the possibilities of the family firm.

Rescue through Cartels

One obvious reaction to the price decline of the 1870s, the industrialists' demand for tariff protection, had led to the new Bismarckian tariff law of 1879, which came into effect at the beginning of 1880. The GHH had played a part in the lobbying effort that led to the government's abandonment of its previous free-trade position in presenting the industrial argument. Lueg took a strong position in this debate. But the tariff actually solved little for the GHH, as it rapidly appeared that the problem lay as much with competition within Germany as in competition from abroad, from Britain or elsewhere. Other big firms that threatened the GHH actually had a similar family background. It was the big increase in production from the Wendel and Stumm companies that threatened the GHH's production of steel rails in the early 1880s.

Hugo Haniel's cautious path was blocked, and in 1880 he was replaced as supervisory board chairman by the representative of a younger, critical generation of owners. His successor, Eduard James Haniel, wanted above all to pay out a higher dividend in 1880–81; but he seems to have yielded quickly to persuasion, and in fact the company followed a direction largely in accordance with the management's conviction of the need to expand. Instead of a million-Marks dividend, there was only half a million. The sudden conversion of E. J. Haniel to the management's point of view at first appears puzzling. Thanks to the new harmony, the enterprise could continue to expand. In Neu Oberhausen the steel mill and the wireworks were expanded, and then a new boiler facility was constructed. E. J. Haniel worried about the continuing soft prices. He tried to block export orders at less than 105 Marks, "or else all our efforts to obtain external orders for rails will be fruitless because of the low prices of our competitors."[17] But without a basic minimum of orders, it would be unprofitable to work the rolling mills.

Hugo Haniel, though no longer a member of the supervisory board, continued to press the managers to observe and learn from the competition. He asked the managing board "to get on friendly terms with truthful and businesslike competitors," so that the costs of the competitors might be calculated. He wanted Lueg to research "the detailed internal costs of all competitive Rhenish-Westphalian works."[18]

Ultimately the solution preferred by the Haniels, and by many other German steel owners, because it preserved their autonomy while protecting their income, was the cartel.[19] The cartel explains E. J. Haniel's change of mind, and hence the new harmony of owners and managers. It provided an institutional answer to the problems raised by the creation of the two boards in the 1870 law. Owners became obsessed by price questions and the implications of fluctuating prices for their income flows: cartels allowed them to have more of the security of the *rentier.* The GHH came to think of cartels as an "idea whose time is thoroughly ripe."[20] In fact, though, most cartels created in the 1880s did not last very long, and competition remained potentially destabilizing.

In 1882–83 discussions about a cartel for railroad ties began. Hugo Haniel noted: "If we are not to be more and more pushed out from our old position, which was equal to the foremost German works, we must not lag behind anyone in caution and energy, but must produce outstanding products at the lowest cost. Then we will achieve again that position in the industry which we occupied with honor for decades." In December 1882 prices for iron rods were reduced again. In 1883–84 the GHH complained about "a mutual underbidding of prices for export to below cost levels."[21] In that year 27 percent of rails went for the export market. But here again, cartelization offered a way out, this time on an international level. In 1884 the International Rail Cartel (Internationale Schienen-Gemeinschaft) was established.

In 1885 the GHH welcomed moves to a tinplate convention in order to "stop the terrible price dumping." It also welcomed the idea of a general convention on rolled products.[22] In 1886 the producers reached an agreement on thin sheet, and in 1887 on the more general Rhenish Westphalian Iron Rod Convention and the General German Rolling Mill Association. Lueg, in recognition of his major role in pushing for greater industrial organization, became the first president of this association. The fourteen largest rolling mills now had a common sales organization *(Syndikat).*

The GHH management expressed its satisfaction with the development of cartels and syndicates, which offered a way out of an otherwise irreconcilable conflict with the owners of the company. Its 1889–90 report stated: "Without this equilibrating activity of the associations, price increases as well as reductions would have been more severe, as is shown by developments in other products."[23] The report also mentioned "appropriate" and "satisfactory" prices.

On the other hand, the GHH management complained about increased wages at the end of the 1880s, and about the effect of the new Bismarckian welfare laws: "The social laws, however beneficial in themselves, have the bad effect that workers feel entitled to report sick for the smallest injuries that they previously would not have noticed."[24] The company preferred its own paternalism to that imposed by the German empire. Lueg reacted to the 1883 law by establishing a works insurance company, and later created an analogous pension insurance company. The GHH also built new homes for workers, as Wilhelm Lueg had done. When Carl Lueg was given the title "Geheimer Kommerzienrat," or privy commercial councillor, in 1897, the Prussian trade minister's citation stated that under his leadership the GHH had expanded and now employed more than 8,000 workers, "for whose welfare he cares in a paternal way, so that unrest and work stoppages do not occur."

The company returned to innovation as a way out of difficulties. In 1884 discussions of a block train were revived, and a second process of rail and ties production began. The Martin works was to be expanded from two to four furnaces. The managing board wrote in 1885: "nothing would worse affect the enterprise than if the management was too slow in reaching the conclusion that equipment from former times is no longer in a competitive state."[25]

E. J. Haniel, who had initially been skeptical about suggestions to invest more and to reduce the GHH's dividend, now asserted that he was convinced that investment would be useful, but that it would not be "equitable" for the shareholders, in particular for the owners of the converted bonds: "You presume that the ordinary shareholder should bear new and perhaps impossible burdens." He was fully aware of the need to protect the GHH from stagnation. But one of his objections was that the time horizon of the proposed investment was too long: if it took six years to complete the extension of the works, "there might be new technology in blast furnace and steel," which would paralyze the works once more. Accordingly, in the general meeting of December 1885 he initially proposed a bond issue; but this would entail "onerous conditions," and in the end the meeting agreed to renounce a dividend for 1885–86 in order to finance new investment. E. J. Haniel repeatedly complained about the divisions on the supervisory board about the financing and worried that this was a "miserable business."[26] In 1884–85 the GHH constructed a rolling mill for beams with an average width of 650 millimeters, and in 1892–93 a new universal train.

For the year 1886–87, a dividend of only 2.5 percent was paid, but 7.5 percent was paid in 1887–88 and 10 percent for 1888–89. The cartel had restored prosperity to the German family business, and thereby family happiness.[27] By the late 1880s the management was becoming cautiously optimistic. In December 1887 it reported: "It is to be hoped that only in this way a long-lasting improvement of our commercial conditions can be made possible, and thus the prospect of an adequate yield on the substantial capital invested in our plant."[28]

The GHH was involved not just in steelmaking but also in complex engineering projects (based in the Sterkrade works)—in particular the construction of bridges, with 6 bridges over the Rhine built during the nineteenth century, bridges over the Vistula at Thorn (Torun) and Fordon, and 140 bridges for the Gotthard railway in Switzerland. The railway station hall in Frankfurt, with its grand canopy (1887), was a GHH product, as was the large Frankfurt hall for airships, a sort of predecessor of the Frankfurt airport (1911). The GHH Sterkrade also constructed the major Chinese dock at Qingdao (1905).

Continuous expansion accounted for part of the normalization of business expectations in the last decades of the nineteenth century. The possibility of business failures, which had loomed so large in the 1870s, now seemed much more remote. Instead a belief in "ever upward and ever onward" entrenched itself firmly. In 1935 the general director of the GHH, Paul Reusch, wrote in a historical reflection on his company: "Twenty-five years ago, when we celebrated our hundredth anniversary, the GHH could look back on a shining history and on generally uninterrupted growth. There seemed to be no boundaries to subsequent development."[29] This was a business world that had become much more confident and even self-satisfied, and felt very comfortable with the German em-

12. *GHH-constructed dock at Qingdao*
COURTESY OF THE RHEINISCHES INDUSTRIE-MUSEUM, OBERHAUSEN

pire. Radical choices about new technologies of the kind that Franz Haniel had faced were no longer needed.

Nevertheless, in business and in politics, some people began to feel that the limits of the existing possibilities had been reached. In politics, that logic meant going beyond the nation-state and developing an empire (in that prognoses of the future involved the domination of the world by a limited number of large states). In business life, the equivalent of the turn to empire was to expand the business model beyond the pursuit of a core technology. By the beginning of the twentieth century, new technologies—especially connected with transport—were opening up.

The essence of the success model of the last decades of the nineteenth century was that the owners could trust the managers to take the firm along a course of steady expansion. By the beginning of the twentieth century, some managers wanted to do more than just that; and that demand raised once more the problematic character of the link between ownership and management in a large and complicated enterprise. Thus within a few years of creating a giant stock company to apply a new technology for tubemaking (in 1890), the Mannesmann brothers were cast out of the firm by bankers and shareholders, who complained that the brothers had valued the patent too highly. Two brothers moved to America, while Max Mannesmann stayed in Germany and bombarded the management with countless letters: "His constant objections, criticisms, suggestions, and countersuggestions, in short everything, points to his trying to regain active influence in a management from which he was removed against his will . . . There is almost no day on which Herr MM does not honor us with one or more letters . . . It is disturbing the smooth course of business."[30]

In the GHH, by contrast, the owners had survived and retained their influence. They had now identified their business with a particular focus, a steel and engineering group that was differentiated from the bigger mass steel producers. This was a modern business in a way that half a century earlier Franz Haniel's creations had definitely not been. And modernity now appeared as *the* German characteristic.

Chapter 5

French Companies in Two Countries

With M. de Wendel the House was a family in a company, and without M. de Wendel the House must be a company in a family.

1870 family council

AFTER 1870 the Wendel enterprise was plunged into a crisis that was personal, national, and also technological. The patriarch died, and his sons were imprisoned in a German fortress as prisoners of war; the territories on which all the Wendel mines and ironworks were situated were seized by the new German empire; and the technology of iron gave way to steel. The new order of Europe as established by the 1871 Treaty of Frankfurt could be epitomized as Germany and steel. These two new dynamic forces were linked, and many Frenchmen saw the new German domination as that of a technically and scientifically advanced system over an older and mellower culture that emphasized its rural roots. The French cliché held that the new Europe was a product of Krupp and of the Prussian schoolmaster. The new German style of business also produced innovation at the level of business organization, with a move to coordination and market dominance through syndicates and cartels.

At the beginning of the twentieth century a relative of the Wendel family, Henri Grandet,[1] undertook a systematic comparison of French and German business practices, and of the different forms in which the state intervened in business life. Being a French patriot, he argued that the French development was significantly more logical and balanced: "France presents a model of industry that is moderately and rationally developed; Germany, in contrast, is perhaps the country where the metallurgic industry expanded at the most abrupt and exaggerated rate."[2] Later generations would interpret this kind of statement as a characteristic product of French Malthusianism (the deliberate choice of lower growth) and hence a cause of economic retardation in which French business failed to develop to the extent required by the national cause.

Grandet should have been in a fine position to judge the comparative merits of working in France and Germany, for the Wendels developed two separate companies on the two sides of the new border in Lorraine. These companies needed to observe different commercial laws. And they represented different forms of company, although both were established as companies under French law: the older type of company, with unlimited liability, was chosen in the German territory, while a newer form of joint-stock company was established as the Wendel instrument in France.

Death of a Patriarch

The shocks unfolded with great rapidity. Within a few months of the death of Charles de Wendel, on 15 April 1870, war broke out between France and Prussia. The Prussian cavalry arrived at Stiring on 6 August, and a pitched battle occurred in the railroad station. Charles had two sons (Henri and Robert) and a daughter. Both Henri and Robert fought in the war, and were captured and interned by the Prussians, so that the enterprise was apparently left headless. As in the previous age of military and political upheaval, an elderly woman played a crucial role in preserving the family venture. The company was directed in this critical period by Charles's mother, the widow of François de Wendel, Joséphine de Fischer de Dicourt, who was widowed, was now childless and blind, and had been treated with contempt by her son. She had had fourteen grandchildren, of whom nine were still living in 1870 and formed the basis for dynastic continuation.

Charles de Wendel himself had always been worried about setting the nominal capitalization of the company too high, lest an excessively large payout be expected by his large clan in settlement of their legal claims at his death. A month before his death—perhaps he felt it was imminent—he argued once more against increasing the notional capitalization of the company, and instead tried to provide for a larger depreciation allowance, as a consequence of the low prices for metals prevailing in the wake of the 1860 Anglo-French commercial treaty (Cobden-Chevalier). In addition, he believed that the sum that was devoted to maintenance payments to his elderly mother would be used better if it were diverted to the financing of productive investments in the company:

> The depreciation of the factories should follow the lowering of the price of iron. It is enough to maintain the firm's capital, increased by the assets of the widow Madame de Wendel, at the amount that it was at the time of the establishment of the deed of partnership, or 26,912,750 francs. Raising the capital above this amount would expose us to setbacks by giving it a value that could one day be unattainable. What we have been able to do, what we will continue to do, with some exceptions, was or will be done from a perspective that I will quit only if *constrained and forced.*
>
> I had thought, as I still do, that the additional contributions of my mother, assets that the agreement designates as a reserve (appropriately in my opinion), should pay for these constructions, which I consider only to be expenses to maintain the productive value of the capital. If this is no longer the opinion of our advisers, and I have to meet with them again about this topic, the value of the converted factories should be reduced by the value of the larger factories that are replacing them. When it comes to the liquidation of the firm, the factories will be sold for the price that we can get for them; all the expenses incurred will be presented, and nothing will have been withheld. If this price rises above my expectations, all the better! But I hope that it does not fall below; to prevent that will be the focus of my constant efforts.[3]

In fact Charles's stipulations ignored the origin of most of the financing that had underpinned the rapid expansion of the past two decades. It was Madame Joséphine who, for instance, had put in over 1.5 million francs in order to build a new coking furnace at Heischbach in 1856, and continued to pay to cover the amortization of these coking works.[4]

Eleven days after the death of Charles de Wendel, the family met to decide how to continue the enterprise as a single unit, and to transform it into a "company held by a family" instead of by an irascible and suspicious patriarch. This was not a regular family meeting—there is no evidence of such occurrences at this time—but rather the formal meeting of the family council provided for by the Civil Code to regulate family affairs in unexpected or difficult circumstances. The record of the debate stated:

> To sum up these observations, it follows that with M. de Wendel the House was a family in a company, and without M. de Wendel the House must be a company in a family. It is evident that M. de Wendel, the principal author of the great achievements of the factories, could not pursue any line of conduct other than one that followed from his principles. "As a natural proxy of my mother, I have built her fortune twice; I don't doubt that any of her children, out of the same respect for her, and gratitude to me, will readily accept what I have done and what I will do. I hope that after I am gone my children and our heirs will be able to obtain the fortune that is written on the books of our House."
>
> In this agreement M. de Wendel administered from the viewpoint of a good father of the family and very rarely saw himself as an industrial manager. He intended to leave his family an industrial fortune that was the exact representation of still available assets. For him the company was created only to concentrate in one hand the administration of shared affairs, in order to prevent the divisions that could occur with the opening presented by inheritance to Madame de Wendel.
>
> His prudence was thus very wise and practical when his coheirs were still only, so to speak, the young ones soon to be called to obtain a significant inheritance. But for the last thirteen years that they have been waiting they grown into mature men, who are in a hurry to be the owners of a fortune. We can understand, therefore, their impatience, and the cooling of their feelings toward the family benefactor. In these conditions the prudence of M. de Wendel will become increasingly difficult; at one given moment it will even become impossible.
>
> He himself, in his last appraisal of the affairs that he left in writing, explicitly recognized that it may be necessary, following the advice of the counsel to the House, to provide some modi-

> fications to the contracts, not altering the agreement, but leaving to his successors the care of thoroughly examining the necessity of certain reforms. This necessity was demonstrated to them by the conferences, where the accordance of affairs and people was discussed at length.
>
> The form of the contracts has thus been decided, but they should be made by the successors of M. de Wendel only in a way that is in accordance with his own principles during his lifetime. Thus the fundamental difference that exists between the old administration and the new administration is that the old one, like every father of the family who only works for himself and his own, increases his assets only with spending that is immediately productive. Whereas the new administration, like companies that work with everyone's money, will be managed in a result-oriented way, and raise its capital with the goal of providing profits that will be divided only afterward. But if the new management is wise it will follow this course of action until the rise in earnings justifies the rise in the capitalization.[5]

To succeed, the new company would have to find an institutionalized way of forcing saving and economy on members of the growing dynastic group, and in this way would make a long-term bet on the future. But that future looked very precarious because of the political uncertainty produced by the Franco-Prussian War.

The Lost Provinces

Though the Wendel works in the Saar basin and then in Hayange and Moyeuvre had been quickly seized by German troops after the outbreak of the war, their long-term status was unclear. Hayange and Moyeuvre lay in the far west of the area that could plausibly be claimed by the new Germany on linguistic grounds (which at first provided the main German argument about a territorial reordering in Lorraine). Bismarck had already anticipated a final settlement when, on 21 August 1870, he persuaded the king of Prussia at the field headquarters in Pont-à-Mousson to agree to the transfer of five arrondissements in Lorraine to the Alsace government as a preliminary to German annexation. But the precise line of the frontier was not clearly set even at the time of the Treaty of Frankfurt

(May 1871), and at the peace negotiations the German empire set out a range of alternatives for French acceptance. France could either have less territory around the strategically important Alsatian fortress of Belfort or it would lose a strip of land to the west of Thionville. The French Assembly chose the latter. The inhabitants of the areas concerned lobbied vigorously to stay in France; but businesses in Germany that would be affected by the outcome of the treaty endorsed the French demands. Iron industrialists in the Saar, for instance, in February 1871 sent a petition to Bismarck's office asking for the cession of ore fields around Thionville, but not of the modern Wendel works at Hayange and Moyeuvre, which they feared would provide them with too much competition.

French industrialists tried to affect German decisions by direct interventions. Baron Théodore de Gargan traveled to Berlin in April 1871 and tried to persuade Bismarck, his chief of staff, Helmuth von Moltke, and the highly influential Prussian minister of commerce, Rudolf Delbrück, that the Wendel works would be "useless to Germany" and that the territory had no strategic significance, an argument that Moltke accepted. But the German lobbying (especially from the Saar) probably convinced the Prussian authorities that there was something rather valuable about a modern ironworks. Delbrück noted about the Saar proposal: "Of course after the decisions already made there can be no question of supporting this demand to leave the westernmost works in the valley of Hayange as well as the ironworks at Moyeuvre outside the German frontiers."[6]

Meanwhile the Wendels in France tried to convince the new prime minister, Adolphe Thiers, that the loss of the ironworks of Lorraine would be a serious blow; but Thiers was not persuaded, and appeared to be hostile to the family business and to the regional economy of Lorraine: "The fine productions of M. de Wendel transported the entire iron industry to the east; this is not natural and will not last. The prosperity of this industry has therefore been exaggerated; nonetheless, the Germans wanted a part in it; we gave it to them." He told the French parliament: "There will always be iron throughout France that is as good as in Sweden, and the prosperity of the east's metallurgic industry is a complete illusion that will not last forever."[7]

Thus the final boundary put the Wendel works in Hayange and

Moyeuvre, as well as Stiring-Wendel, in Germany. In these circumstances company law could be a weapon to protect the family interests. On 3 December 1871 a company *en commandite* was created, Les Petits-Fils de François de Wendel et Cie. (PFFW), with a capitalization of 30 million francs ($5.7 million). Under French law, such a company was managed by its *gérants* (managing partners), who had almost unlimited power but also unlimited liability—for a steel company in the 1870s, a risky proposition. Its first *gérants* were Théodore de Gargan and Henri and Robert de Wendel. As part of a strategy to preserve a French company in Germany, in an obviously precarious situation, its corporate structure was intended to stop individual shareholders from making difficulties and to place business decisions firmly in the hands of the three managers. Retrospectively, Grandet concluded: "In order to preserve for the company this previous advantage that could have disappeared by the parceling out of the shares, the regulations stipulated that each share could not have more than one sole representative designated by the co-owners of the share . . . The best comparison that we can think of, from this point of view, in contrast with joint-stock companies, is that of an absolute or nearly absolute monarchy with respect to a parliamentary republic."[8] The managers would be their own Sun King. The Wendel family projected their vision of Franco-German differences onto their analysis of management styles. The German government could easily declare war, while the French Republic had to consult two fractious and recalcitrant parliamentary bodies, the Chamber of Deputies and the Senate, before making such a move. The PFFW, by imitating the German monarchical or absolutist model, assured for itself greater room for business maneuver and avoided French indecisiveness.

The Treaty of Frankfurt required the inhabitants of the ceded territories to choose their nationality. Men of the age of military service were not permitted to stay in occupied Lorraine if they chose French citizenship. Gargan and Robert de Wendel chose French citizenship, while Henri remained in Hayange (and thus in Germany).

A German Company

The managers of PFFW emphasized its financial solidity, especially in contrast with German steel companies, which were expanding rapidly and energetically in the *Gründerzeit* of the early 1870s. "The strong position of the firm is known: it is completely independent with respect to banks, and we never even see bills circulating with the firm's corporate signature." This was radically different from the experience of almost all German companies at the time. "Nothing is more instructive in that respect than the reviews of the balance sheets that are published in Germany and that, when read, allow one to verify that a number of companies, which appear to be flourishing, are in reality in a poor financial state."[9] This verdict was shared by a later German commentator, Max Schlenker, who wrote that the reason the stock market crash of 1873 was not so destructive in Lorraine as in the rest of Germany was that there was far less "speculative rage." This phenomenon Schlenker attributed explicitly to family ownership, where "the economic situation was not so secure as to invite greater extension of activity."[10] This verdict on the 1870s was substantially correct (see the discussion of GHH problems in Chapter 4).

There was a moment's hesitation, at the beginning of the era of German rule, when the stock-exchange boom showed finance capitalism in its most alluring light. The production of the Wendel works had shot up from 68,000 tons of iron in 1870 and only 20,000 tons in 1871 to 158,000 tons in 1873.[11] In March 1873 the PFFW discussed a proposal by a group of German and Austrian banks to buy a substantial stake in the companies while leaving the family a narrow formal control, with six out of eleven seats on the *conseil d'administration.* The family rejected the proposal less on the basis of economic rationality than on the basis of ancestral piety and the grand idea of France. "Is it fitting to abandon in this way the tombs of our ancestors? Is it very honorable in the end to leave this country, where we have been the most esteemed representatives of the Catholic and French elements?"[12]

The need for greater capital arose out of the technical transformation of metalmaking: every German company at this time faced exactly the same problem, and its financial implications often tore families apart (as witness the problems of the Haniels in the 1870s). Wendel had already employed the Bessemer process since its development in the 1850s, but it had not been suitable for use with the phosphoric low-grade *(minette)* iron ores found in most of Lorraine (with the exception of the spectacular iron mountain at Audun-le-Tiche). Now the availability of the Gilchrist-Thomas process made possible the emergence of a really large-scale metallurgy. In consequence, Wendel abandoned the production of a large range of miscellaneous iron products used by a primarily rural society: nails, horseshoes, plowshares. Moyeuvre and Hayange were rescued by the Gilchrist-Thomas process, for which Wendel bought the rights in Lorraine (for 980,000 Marks, or $232,000). Hayange started to produce steel by this method in 1881. A new sheet mill was constructed at Jamailles.

PFFW could also develop the extraction of the phosphoric *minette* ore near Hayange. In 1872 it extracted 322,000 tons, but by 1880 the amount rose to 440,000. By the 1880s a good deal of Lorraine *minette* was being shipped to the rapidly growing Ruhr steel industry, and German-owned firms were also rapidly pushing forward in Lorraine. The Rombacher Hüttenwerke moved into the Orne valley with iron-ore mines at Saint-Paul (Moeuvre) and Rosselange. The economics of location depended on the cost of transport and on the changing proportions of iron ore and coking coal that needed to be shipped. In the 1880s the Wendels tried to block proposals to make the Moselle navigable, a move that would have greatly reduced the cost of water transport and produced advantages for the Ruhr. By 1905, however, they accepted such a scheme: in the meantime the German railroad had adopted a system of freight tariffs that was highly advantageous to Ruhr producers shipping ore from Lorraine. The Wendel position was at both points in time exactly the reverse of the Ruhr producers, who initially had been great advocates of Moselle canalization because it would bring them cheaper iron ore, but by the end of the century, with technical progress that reduced the quantity of coal needed in steel production, feared that canalization would favor Lorraine at their expense.[13]

In 1892 a renewed proposal by German companies to buy out the Wendels aroused a wave of French nationalist polemic. One Lorraine priest, for instance, noted: "Such a sale is in no way morally desirable, since, as conservatives and Christians, the Wendels have a duty of honor."[14] In the event, nothing came of the proposal, and Wendel continued to make large-scale investments in order to modernize and increase the size of their works. In 1897 a new rolling mill was added in Hayange.

The French orientation of the Wendel enterprises obviously

reflected the views and political choices of the owners, but it also had a commercial logic and advantage. Working with French (or at least non-German) managers and engineers, and with a Catholic and non-German workforce, the company developed a strong internal sense of solidarity that made for harmonious labor relations. At Hayange in 1914, of the five works directors, three were from Luxembourg, one from Sweden, and one from France. None were German speakers. From the 1890s the works began to recruit Italians as a way of keeping Germans out, and the owners emphasized the importance of a Catholic faith. By 1898–99, 17 percent of the workforce at Hayange and 26 percent at Moyeuvre was Italian, and these proportions continued to rise until 1910. By 1905 only 38 percent of the population of Moyeuvre and 44 percent at Hayange had been born in Lorraine. The inflow of immigrant workers, and the Catholic and anti-German feeling of solidarity that prevailed in the Wendel works in western Lorraine, were reflected in very low rates of unionization (less than 5 percent before the First World War).[15] The enterprise was motivated and driven by anti-German and pro-Catholic feeling, which produced what modern analysts might term its distinctive "corporate culture."

Farther east, in the Saar basin, the Wendel interests were more vulnerable to the powerful German competition. PFFW developed the Petite-Rosselle coal field near Stiring; but the ore there was suitable for heating, not for coke-smelting. The situation of the Stiring ironworks looked increasingly unfavorable, and in general Saar ironworks turned to Ruhr coal for coking use. In the general business-cycle downturn of the 1870s, the Wendel production of iron rails fell off, and in 1877 the company temporarily closed the blast furnaces at Stiring. Stiring never fully recovered, and in the 1890s iron production there stopped altogether.

The unsuitability of Saar coal forced the Wendel works to look to the Ruhr or to Belgian coal to supply its coking needs. In 1874 PFFW bought a participation in a Belgian cokery, and in 1900 it bought a mine producing high-grade coking coal at Hamm, in Westphalia. In 1907, under the leadership of a new generation, and in particular of Charles de Wendel (grandson of the Charles described above), who favored an American-style expansion of capacity, PFFW added yet another mine, Glückauf, near Aachen; and in 1908, a majority stake in the very large Dutch mine of Oranje-

Nassau, whose nonmining holdings in the late twentieth century would form one of the major bases of the poststeel development of the Wendel enterprises. PFFW also bought several French mines.

These acquisitions were financed in part through a bond issue, managed by the giant of the German universal banks, Deutsche Bank: again, a break with the usually conservative financing traditions of the Maison de Wendel.[16] The coupon of the loan was 4.5 percent, which looked slightly higher than interest rates in France, but the issuing costs were significantly lower through German banks.

By this time, PFFW was greatly concerned about competition from the large German steel companies. It had joined the German steel syndicate, the Stahlwerksverband, established in 1904, which gave significant advantages to "mixed works" with blast furnaces and rolling mills. Prices and quotas of "A" products were carefully controlled because these were easily standardized products: semifinished steel: ingots, sheet bars, billets; and the standardized railroad equipment. On the other hand, regulation of output of the less standardized "B" products—merchant bars, rolled wire, steel plate, pipes and tubes, and cast and forged pieces—was much harder. The steel syndicate thus presented considerable advantages to works that processed their steel into more finished products, and a race to acquire finishing works began. In 1908 Wendel had the fourth-largest share of quotas in the Stahlwerksverband, well behind the largest, Phönix, as well as Krupp and Thyssen. At this time Hayange produced 345,000 tons of B products and 280,000 of A products. The Wendel production was 55 percent of that of Thyssen.[17] After this, a tremendous expansion of "B" products began: in 1911–12, when the attempt to regulate "B" products finally collapsed, "A" production was 32 percent higher than in 1905–06, but "B" production had risen by 124 percent. For 1912–13 Wendel had a quota in the Stahlwerksverband of 346,000 tons ("A" products), but six German works had larger quotas.[18] The Wendel position was clearly slipping.

Being a German company built on anti-German sentiment had a clear business logic. But, equally clearly, it would be an obstacle at a time when the German steel industry as a whole was engaged in a race for scale and size. French nationalist sentiment was not the only impediment; radical change was needed to keep up with such large and fast-growing companies as Thyssen and Phönix. This sort of change was incompatible with the Wendels' notion of corporate governance, and the unlimited liability of the *sociétés en commandites* (which limited both willingness and ability to expand by borrowing). There was by now a strong sense that forty years of being part of the German Reich was quite enough.

A French Company

In 1906–07, Wendel produced 907,000 tons of cast iron and 815,000 tons of steel, with two-thirds of this amount coming from PFFW in Germany. The remainder of the Wendel production came from an initiative to save the iron industry of French Lorraine after the Treaty of Frankfurt. Together with the director of the Pont-à-Mousson ironworks, the Wendels tried to demonstrate that the *minette* ore field extended farther into France than had been generally thought. There was also a technical issue: in German-occupied Lorraine the ore could be easily extracted from the surface, whereas in France the ore seams sloped deep into the ground. Mining proved to be very difficult because of the presence of water, which flooded shafts and caused them to collapse. But after the mid-1870s the technical problem was overcome and ore production increased greatly. For the whole French department of Meurthe-et-Moselle, the extraction of iron ore rose from 976,000 tons in 1875 to 6,399,000 tons in 1905 and 19,813,000 tons in 1913, by which time it accounted for 91 percent of all French ore production (though the figures were slightly less than the ore production of German Lorraine).[19] Indeed, by the beginning of the new century, the major German steel industrialists were beginning to cast envious eyes at the big new discoveries of ore in the Longwy-Briey basin.

Hayange was very close to the new French frontier. The Wendels were tempted by the idea of a French works producing products for the French market, but the Gilchrist-Thomas patent for using lime slag and then a basic lining of the converter in the working phosphoric ores had been bought by Henri Schneider for the department of Meurthe-et-Moselle. The great rival dynasty had thus secured what might be an unanswerable technical superiority, given that the fundamental problem of Lorraine lay in the phosphoric content of the *minette*. The English clerk Sidney Gilchrist Thomas, who with his cousin had secured the patent, had originally approached Schneider and offered a patent for France for his process, explaining that "one of the leading French firms has also seen our results and has proposed to enter into negotiation. I am however hopeful that because of their predominant position and their reputation, your factories should be able to be among the first to adopt my methods in France." It turned out that Thomas had already sold the French rights to a Belgian company, but had reserved the Meurthe-et-Moselle for a separate agreement.[20] Schneider immediately left for England to visit the Middlesborough works, where the process could be seen, and agreed at once to a contract. The attraction of the deal was that a big new government program of railroad and infrastructure construction (the Freycinet plan) was being launched, and the availability of guaranteed public orders set off a general speculative boom in France, with an unusually large number of company formations.[21] The eventual contract concluded by Schneider involved a payment of 45,000 francs ($8,600) plus a one-franc-per-ton payment for each ton of steel or cast iron from Meurthe-et-Moselle, as well as a conventional penalty if the works had not been established by 1881.

By this stage many of the largest continental works were engaging in a desperate struggle to secure the rights to use the Gilchrist-Thomas process.[22] The Wendels thus negotiated with Schneider Creusot; Henri de Wendel was a friend of Henri Schneider, and rather more astute than Schneider at business politics. He had been on the supervisory board *(conseil de surveillance)* of the Le Creusot works since 1877. In October 1879 he wrote to Schneider that he had just returned from a trip to Germany, to see the Thomas process applied at the Hoerder Verein works, and that he wanted to establish a Thomas-process steel mill in the French department of Meurthe-et-Moselle, at Joeuf. He argued that Schneider should not try to establish a Thomas works at Villerupt: "Your trip to Villerupt caused a great deal of emotion in the country. Several of our associates demonstrated their repugnance to creating a participation in Joeuf if you install yourself in this country."[23] Wendel himself went to England to negotiate about the rights to the Thomas process.

Wendel had, as the *gérant* Théodore de Gargan pointed out, only one substantial card in dealing with the Schneiders: the Thomas process had not been completely perfected in Britain, and Wendel's knowledge of the way that the Hoerder Verein had adopted the technology gave his firm a certain edge. The practical application of Gilchrist-Thomas was by no means simple. The Aciéries de Longwy, for instance, which had hired the technical director from Le Creusot, Charles Walrand, one of the greatest French steel-making experts, still found that it could not produce steel rails of sufficient quality to satisfy the Paris-Lyon-Marseille railroad company.[24] In addition, construction of a works was held up by the inability to produce in France the right kind of brick for the furnace lining. Schneider wrote to Gargan: "I am going to ask this of you, because you are more advanced than we are." And Wendel boasted to Schneider: "I am returning to Germany. The Thomas process is handled with more care there than in England; the results will also be better."[25] Wendel derived a distinct technological advantage from its existence as a German company.

At first the negotiations between the two great figures of France's eastern iron industry took place through the intermediary of the banking house Demachy et Seillière, which had become a major financial influence in the development of iron and steel. Demachy was the chairman of the Schneider supervisory board. His bank's international business also included loans to the Krupps of Essen in the 1850s and 1860s. The Seillières had originally financed both Wendels and Schneiders, and seemed an ideal financial marriage broker. By the First World War, Demachy had become simply the house bank of the Wendel companies.

In fact the financial marriage went along with some human marriages, and marriage strategy became one of the most obvious routes of preserving the family.[26] The Wendels did not generally marry into other iron families, and there was no liaison with the most obvious choice, the Schneiders, who viewed the Wendels with a reciprocated suspicion, until the 1930s. The Wendels had been an aristocratic family since the eighteenth century, and marriage to aristocrats (whose emotional consequences were the subject of a weepy but tremendously popular novel of 1882, Georges Ohnet's *Maître de forges*)[27] was a commonplace for Wendels. Female Wendels married into the families of Comminges de Guitaut, du Coëtlosquet, Corbel de Vaulserre, de Gramedo, Larochefoucauld, de la Panouse, de Maillé, de Mitry, de Montaigu, de Montalembert, de Montremy, de Noailles, Rohan, de Soucy. The marriage of Pauline de Wendel (daughter of Victor-François, the eldest son of

François de Wendel) to the vicomte Albert de Curel produced the writer and novelist François de Curel (1854–1928), who later stated that he would have been an ironmaster but for being banned from Lorraine by the German government in 1877, and instead became a famous poet and author. One of the rare business marriages (but to a titled businessman) was of Renée de Wendel to Baron Jean Seillière in the 1930s, which cemented the long business relation with the Seillières.

The main advocate of a new Wendel company in France was the younger Théodore de Gargan, who wrote a long memorandum in 1876 explaining why the economic development of the east of France required a French rail factory. "The Compagnie de l'Est does not actually have more rail factories in its network. We will be the only industrialists in the east taking advantage of both minerals and coal; this will allow us to deliver marketable iron to the eastern industry at prices below those of any other establishment. Finally, we will be able to bring back to France all or part of our worker population in Lorraine."[28] Traditional Wendel paternalism thus also played a role in the decision to build a new French factory and participate in the company creation mania of 1879–1881 that accompanied the Freycinet plan.

Thus the two great rival iron dynasties of Schneider and de Wendel in 1880 launched a share company, Wendel et Cie. SA. In a *société anonyme*, unlike a *société en commandite*, the company's owners had limited liability, and the directors could engage in ventures without endangering their own wealth or that of their families. The object of the new company was to build a steel and rail factory in France at Joeuf, on the river Orne. Early in the 1870s the Wendels had built houses at Joeuf in order to house their Moyeuvre workers who did not want to take German citizenship, so there was a ready pool of labor. The shares of the new company were very concentrated: the Demachy bank had one of nine shares, while the Wendels and Schneiders four each. The company name implied a stronger Wendel presence than was evident from the minority share of the ownership, and Wendelien dominance was also evident in the location of the new works. Joeuf was only a few kilometers away from Moyeuvre, but on the French side of the border, and in fact it was mostly managed from a central bureau in the German works of PFFW. The management was also highly personalized (in contrast to the German works, where there was a managerial hierarchy in place): at the beginning of the twentieth century, "apart from Monsieur Flacon, and three or four supervisors who are former foremen, there is no one between Messieurs de Wendel and the workers."[29] Henri and Robert de Wendel shared an office but had a quite rigid division of labor: Henri dealt with technical and Robert with administrative and commercial matters.[30]

The Joeuf site was linked to the Moyeuvre works (and to the German rail system, which was needed for the import of coking coal) by a private railroad line. By comparison, the rail connection to the French network was underdeveloped: in 1895, as an incredulous report from the Crédit Lyonnais noted, there was a branch line from the Conflans-Briey track that ended at Homécourt, two or three kilometers from Joeuf, and the rest of the transfer of goods had to be carried out by means of pulleys.[31] Coal for heating was taken from the Wendel-owned Rosselle mine (in German Lorraine), and coking coal from the Ruhr. After 1892 such coal imports became more expensive because of the new tariff imposed by the Méline law. But fourteen-fifteenths of the coking coal still came from the Ruhr, and Joeuf became a pioneer works in the recycling of exhaust gases from the blast furnaces in heating as a substitute for coal.

Completed in 1887, the Joeuf works by 1900 had reached a daily production of 380–400 tons, or an annual production of 30,000 tons of rails, 8,000 tons of girders, 24,000 tons of wire, and 52,000 tons of cast pieces (blooms and billets). There were then six blast furnaces in all, standing in a line; by 1914 there were eight. A report commissioned by the Crédit Lyonnais with the objective of examining the relative capacities of the major French Lorraine producers concluded in 1900: "The manufacturing is of a superior quality, and the management among the most noteworthy from the different commercial, administrative, and technical points of view. Even though the factory is not new, Joeuf will be one of the most formidable competitors that the two new [rival] steelworks of Homécourt and Neuves-Maisons will meet."[32] Two years later a follow-up report sounded less enthusiastic, even though it still commended the personal involvement of Robert and Henri de Wendel, exceptional in terms of "probity, technical knowledge, and business zeal": "In general, the factory can be considered as well equipped, and better in this regard than the old factories of the Meurthe and Moselle. But if compared with Homécourt and Neuves-Maisons, whose equipment is entirely new and which have more space, the conditions are less favorable, especially for the casting of bars."[33]

Wendel et Cie. SA also generated intense controversy within the French business community, which cast its competitive feelings in a political mold. The Joeuf site held the monopoly for Thomas steel for fifteen years as a subconcession from the major German concessionaires, the Hoerder Verein and Rheinische Stahlwerke. Not surprisingly, Wendel was reluctant to share the concession with other Lorraine ironmasters. In consequence, the Aciéries de Longwy of the Adelsward and Labbé families had to build its works in the Meuse, and buy a Thomas license from the Belgian group of Rocour and in addition elect Robert de Wendel to its board. Wendel also refused to sell a license to the Forges de Montataire, and threatened the Pompey works with legal action if the latter used a Walrand process that the Wendel enterprise regarded as too close to the Thomas patent.[34] One highly visible result was that the Paris Eiffel Tower, built by Pompey, was in cast iron and not in steel. Some authors consequently blame French economic backwardness on the hardheadedness and hardheartedness of the Wendels: in the 1880s there were sixty Thomas converters in France, but only two were in the Meurthe-et-Moselle, the area most suited to the production of steel in a process using phosphoric ores. Put in the context of the importance of Lorraine ore (with its phosphoric content) and of the Franco-German rivalry, this situation looked very serious. In 1914 French Lorraine was producing less steel than German Lorraine, and in smaller and more antiquated works (with twenty-seven works on the German side, but forty-two in France).[35] One historian concluded that the Wendel expansion in Lorraine was made "perhaps unconsciously, at the expense of French national interest."[36]

Thomas steel in 1890 accounted for 60 percent of German production, and only 42 percent of that of France. Whether the Wendelien focus on the Gilchrist-Thomas process, stemming from the mineral characteristics of the Lorraine fields, was technically and economically beneficial is a topic of continuing controversy. Thomas steel generally had a poorer reputation (reflected in its lower price). It smelt of sulfur. British shipyards banned its use.[37] In the 1930s the Wendels still needed to reassure purchasers that the Thomas rails they produced broke less frequently than rails produced by the Martin process. They worked hard to try to correct some of the obvious problems. The adoption of mixers developed in the United States in 1892 was a partial solution, allowing steel to be mixed and homogenized to ensure constant quality before reprocessing. The German Hoerder Verein had been the first European work to employ this process, as it had been the first in Thomas steelmaking.

The move to mass production of Thomas steel, above all for rails, also invited organizational and marketing changes. Here, too, the Wendels frequently applied German techniques, with which they were familiar from their activities in the German empire. In 1884 they created a cartel on the German model (the *comptoir des rails*), with a quota of 20,000 tons in an overall amount of 115,000 tons; and this was the basis on which France participated in a short-lived international rail cartel (1888–1891).

By 1907 the Joeuf works employed 2,407 workers. Most were Frenchmen from occupied Lorraine who wanted to remain in France, though some also came from the Loire valley. Later the Wendels recruited large numbers of Italians for Joeuf, who (as in neighboring but imperial German Hayange and Moyeuvre) had the advantage of being Catholic and non-German. Most of the Italians, however, worked in ore mining, and the manufacture of steel remained mostly in the hands of French natives. Wendels developed ore mining much less than the rival companies of Marine (Homécourt), Auboué, or Pont-à-Mousson, with the consequence that it had a rather lower proportion of immigrant employees.

The Frenchness of Wendel operations fitted well into a historic and wide-ranging strategy of paternalism. As in previous Wendel towns, there was a careful program of housing construction—justified in part by the argument that it was necessary to preserve the good "morality" of workers by adequate housing, and to ensure that clerical and managerial employees participated in the morally stabilizing ownership of "property." The workers were also relatively well paid. As patriarchal owners, Wendels built hospitals (at Moyeuvre in 1874, Hayange in 1899, and Petite-Rosselle in 1902), which provided subsidized medical care. In France, the Joeuf workers participated in an old-age pension plan from 1894 (in the German facto-

13. *Madame Henri de Wendel with her sons Humbert, François, and Maurice, posing for the windows of the Hayange church*
COURTESY OF THE WENDEL ARCHIVE, ARCHIVES NATIONALES, PARIS

ries there were the state-run Bismarckian insurance schemes for accident, old age, and sickness). The Wendels also constructed and paid for private Catholic schools, although after 1904 the Marian brothers were forbidden to teach in France. In 1906 the Fonds Henri de Wendel was established to help victims of accidents and to support maternity services. As previously in Stiring, the Wendels constructed churches as a cement of Catholic religiosity. Before the Joeuf steelworks were even completed, its owners had built a large chapel on the Génibois hill in Joeuf, which was replaced in 1910 by a large church, Notre-Dame de Franchepré. In 1884, on the German side of the frontier, a very ornate church was built in the main square of Hayange, with stained-glass windows depicting the patrons in pious poses.

The value of the paternalist strategy was evident after 1905, when violent labor unrest erupted in other Lorraine steel mills. François de Wendel started a political career based on his ability to manage industrial problems. He successfully bought off a corrupt labor

14. *The Wendel chateau of Brouchetières in Joeuf, 2002*

union leader, Paul Everard, who had been the major organizer of the strikes of 1905. The sociologist Georges Hottenger, a disciple of the conservative Le Play (the upholder of single-heir inheritance in the middle of the century), provided a glowing eulogy to the uniqueness of the Wendelien world. "Joeuf obeyed a traditional patronal leadership, thanks to which industry had the range of institutions that were given life by the personal ascendancy of the directors and were subsidized by their liberality, and which allowed the works to retain and make prosperous the working population."[38] But paternalism was also politically controversial, and descriptions by the Wendel bosses of the metalworker as a "big child" and the owner as the "father of his workers" were widely felt to be condescending and insulting.[39]

The insult was certainly rubbed in by the dynasty's seigneurial manner of life. The Wendels built spectacular new residences in Joeuf, since they could not live in Hayange and retain French citizenship. Henri de Wendel wanted a chateau for his sons in France: the first (Franchepré) was constructed, on a wooded hill overlooking the Orne and the steelworks of Joeuf, around 1890 by the architect Albert Jasson. It had walls a meter thick and more than thirty rooms. After he married, Maurice de Wendel built a smaller chateau on the same hill (Brouchetières).[40] Guy de Wendel also built a chateau in the German style at Hayange in 1904–05 (Tournebride).

Henri continued to live in Hayange, but his three sons (François, Humbert, and Maurice) were born in Paris, in order to avoid German citizenship, between 1874 and 1879. But it was easy to cross the frontier and move between Joeuf and Moyeuvre, and even on to Hayange, on uncontrolled trails through the forest. And the children were educated in France, as Frenchmen.

The Wendels and Politics

The division of Lorraine by the Treaty of Frankfurt had made clear how important politics were to the Wendel business. On both sides of the border, the energetic defense of Frenchness was an integral part of the making of a distinct Wendelian corporate culture. One way of making their culture very visible was participation in parliamentary politics, so that elections could be turned into a sort of company rally and a celebration of the unity (in a political sense) of masters, management, and men. (Such orchestrated displays of unity took place elsewhere in imperial Germany, notably in the Saar, where Karl Ferdinand Stumm also secured election to the Reichstag.)[41] In 1881 Henri was elected to the Reichstag for the electoral district of Thionville-Boulay, as an independent and *protestataire* (that is, pro-Lorraine) candidate. He remained a deputy until 1887, though he never took his seat in the Berlin assembly. There was also a business interest: already in the 1870s, Henri de Wendel had taken part in the discussions of the iron committee that had recommended that Bismarck adopt a protective tariff on iron and steel products.[42]

On the French side, Robert de Wendel played a prominent part in French business politics. He was elected president of the Comité des Forges in 1898, despite an initial reluctance. He feared a discussion of the national issue, and another steelmaker, Emile Henry of Pont-à-Mousson, noted: "It seems that the candidacy of M. de Wendel to the presidency has been much discussed, not because of his personality, but because of his double role in France and in Lorraine; there was something shocking in that." This was obviously more than a merely symbolic issue. French producers were worried about the way in which marketing power might be used in neighboring countries. The issue arose especially in relation to cartels: Robert was also president of the Lothringisch-Luxem-

Élections du 28 Octobre 1884
POUR LE REICHSTAG

CANDIDAT
pour les arrondissements de Thionville et de Boulay.

M. Henri de WENDEL
Maître de Forges à Hayange.
DÉPUTÉ SORTANT.

15. *Ballot paper for Henri de Wendel in the Reichstag election*
COURTESY OF THE WENDEL ARCHIVE, ARCHIVES NATIONALES, PARIS

burgisches Comptoir für den Verkauf von Roheisen, in other words of a competing German organization.[43]

In 1903 Robert de Wendel died, and in 1906, Henri de Wendel. The proximate deaths of the two patriarchs left the firm in the hands of a new generation without much preparation for a transition. In the next generation there were thirty-three great-grandchildren of François de Wendel, with inevitably varying conceptions of how the Wendelian tradition might be modernized.

The natural growth of the different branches of the family meant that there was now no single obvious candidate to function as a new patriarch. Henri's oldest son, François de Wendel, eventually emerged as the leader of the family. He had studied in Paris at the School of Mines. In 1903, on the death of Robert de Wendel, he had become (with Charles, the son of Robert) a *gérant* of PFFW. François and Charles were supposed to share the technical portfolio that had been run by Henri.[44] In 1906 François's younger brother Humbert also became a *gérant*. The three sons of Henri acted as a close team throughout their lives, regularly sitting with one another all day in the offices and then sharing their evening meals.

Humbert managed the steel mills, and Maurice was interested in public relations and in the social provisions of the Wendel enterprises. Humbert also managed relations with the German steel cartel (Stahlwerksverband). In later life the brothers attributed their exceptional closeness to their constant problems with the German authorities when they wanted to do anything on the German side of the frontier. Humbert later stated: "My brothers and I were authorized to visit Lorraine only a few weeks each year. This stringency of the German administration appeared to compromise our future in the family management; it provided a disposition that loved independence more than orders with a sufficient reason to direct its choice toward careers that left more room for a cult of oneself."[45]

At this stage, a major family quarrel erupted. Originally Charles had seemed to take control of the German interests of the family. But he had a violent temperament (he was described as "a violent man, a bitter man") and also a passion for modernizing. A later internal memorandum on the company's management structure merely emphasized "his special [bad] temper, to which we need not return."[46] From 1897 to 1902 he had worked in the United States in the heart of the steel industry at Pittsburgh. On his return he wanted to create the most modern plant in Europe, at the Pâtural works in Hayange, which opened in 1908 with four blast furnaces on a U.S. model, tipping wagons, and a central gas station as an additional supply of energy.[47] He dismissed older workers and tried to employ American managers. He was also rather impatient with the traditionally fiercely anti-German Wendelian house style. When obstructed, he repeatedly threatened to resign. The other *gérants* grew increasingly disconcerted by the obvious breach with the family way of behaving.

Charles, who was resident in Hayange in German Lorraine, had been given a medical discharge from the obligation to serve in the German army, and in 1905 had chosen German nationality in order to preserve the family interests in the empire. In 1907 he was elected to the German Reichstag, to the seat previously occupied by Henri. It is a reflection of the continuing effectiveness of the Wendel patriarchy that he won almost every vote in the company town of Hayange. Charles is chiefly remembered in German constitutional and parliamentary history as being the first German parliamentarian recorded as having said "shit" in the Reichstag, while pleading for the Polish case against the Germans. But the German government found his peculiarity preferable to having a Catholic Center Party deputy for the constituency, and the German governor of Alsace, Johann Friedrich von Zeppelin-Aschhausen, in 1911 threatened not to renew the German residency permits of François and Humbert if Charles was excluded from the company. Despite, or perhaps because, of this threat, on 6 February 1911, a few weeks after the residency permits had been renewed, the general assembly of shareholders voted to exclude Charles. Charles, who was supported by his mother and his sister, successfully took legal action. In 1914 he agreed to resign, receiving a large financial settlement and retaining three of ninety-four shares. He retired to the exceedingly opulent neo-Renaissance chateau built by his parents between 1898 and 1902 at Orfrasière, in the Touraine, and still inhabited by his mother.[48]

Charles's younger brother, Guy, maintained his position and in the 1920s became mayor of Hayange. But he also gambled heavily and lost a great deal of money, was increasingly marginalized in the enterprise, and resorted to rather ineffective tactics (such as arriving late at business meetings) to demonstrate his independence as he slid into the life of a foppish dandy. Eventually, after large losses on Paris real estate, he was obliged to resign his position as *gérant* in 1933.

François de Wendel wrote of the February 1911 meeting in his diary: "It is difficult in spite of everything! . . . It is an execution . . . and the condemned is one of our own. Our old company register had never seen anything so deplorable to insert."[49] In contrast to Charles, he staked his future on French politics, and regarded French patriotism as the glue that could stick a divided family back together.

From a very early age, François had wanted to go into politics. In 1906 he had stood as a candidate for the Chamber of Deputies for the Briey district of the north of the Meurthe-et-Moselle, against the sitting deputy, Albert Lebrun, whom the ironmasters had previously viewed as an able exponent of their interests. Wendel's enemies accused him of being too subject to clerical influence, and he was humiliatingly defeated. In 1910 he stood again, creating a chamber of commerce in Briey as a way of mobilizing political support. Now, with the 1905 separation of church and state receding into memory, Wendel moved away from clericalism and emphasized his accommodation with the principles of the Republic. He also used his influence in Paris, so that the leading figures of the Democratic Left Party, Aristide Briand and Alexandre Millerand, pushed Lebrun to stand for another district, in Longwy. Nevertheless François de Wendel was narrowly but painfully defeated by a margin of 3,827 votes to 3,506. He demonstrated the solidity of paternalism in politics in Joeuf, where 85 percent of the votes were cast for him, and he attracted a substantial support in the small towns and in the countryside. But he did badly in all the steel towns apart from Joeuf, in part because the other owners deeply distrusted him and used their paternalist influences to back his rival. In Briey he received 36 percent of the vote, and in Auboué only 22 percent.[50] At this time another steel industrialist, Camille Cavalier, who was openly contemptuous of what he sneeringly termed "the noble steelworks," wrote: "I very much fear that this man, who, by his name, his position, could reach a very great and high station, and would only have to let events follow their own course for that, is tormented by what Voltaire called the little ambition . . . it is rather painful, in any case dangerous."[51]

In April 1914 François de Wendel finally became a member of the Chamber of Deputies for the constituency of Briey-Sud (in a department soon to be occupied by the invading German armies). From then on, his political career overshadowed his business operations. He became the archetype of the political businessman, to an extent that hurt his own reputation and perhaps also that of his business. His political activity generated a powerful myth in French life about the power of money in politics, of how the Third Republic had been captured by sectional interests.[52] This myth raised to a fever pitch the issue of the relationship of steel and the state. The House of Wendel had built a business tradition by elevating French patriotism to a high moral position that—infused with traditionalist Catholicism—then defined its corporate culture. It was in consequence highly vulnerable to the accusation that the company had interests that ran counter to those of the Catholic faith, but above all to those of France.

Chapter 6

An Italian Joint-Stock Company

We should be confident that the present conditions of crisis will disappear . . . and allow the financial consolidation and amortization of the company.

G. E. Falck, 1909

For Italy at the turn of the century, the new power of banks was a powerful political but also business reality. It unleashed a new organizational potential, and Italians saw a new age of the *grande balzo*, or great leap. This was the moment that corporate capitalism really came to Italy. Joint-stock companies, permitted since 1882, were now being put together by banks. They could transform the industrial economy, and in particular enable large-scale steelmaking to supplant the old small-scale production of the Alpine valleys.

Already in the mid-nineteenth century, the Falcks had proposed daring answers to the problems posed by industrial backwardness—in particular by building the Malavedo works. Giorgio Enrico Falck's major response to the new geography of the Italian steel industry was to formulate a Lombard answer to the large-scale coastal works being built in the 1900s. He proposed to develop a modern and very large steelworks in the Milan area, at Sesto San Giovanni, a new industrial area to the north of the city, where other new large factories were being constructed by Breda, Ercole Marelli, and the Officine Sestesi Valsecchi Abramo.[1] For this he needed the help of the Banca Commerciale Italiana (BCI), the new German-style universal bank directed by Otto Joel and Federico Weil, and the great rival of Credito Italiano, which had also played a prominent role in the creation of a company (Quartiere Industriale Nord Milano) for the development of Sesto San Giovanni as a way of shifting industry out of the center of Milan. Falck himself joined the board of another property development company, the Società Anonima Milano, in 1905.[2]

For Falck, the attraction of Milan over a coastal site or the traditional iron-producing centers of the Alpine valleys lay not in any resource advantage (there was no coal or ore close at hand), but rather in the proximity to a major market and also in the network of skills that were believed to be available around the Lombard capital. Since the mid-nineteenth century, the Society for the Encouragement of Arts and Sciences had promoted technical education of workers. Many of the great Milanese entrepreneurs emerged out of this society. Falck himself became involved in its work, and from 1929 to 1937 sat on its board.[3]

The year 1906 marked the near peak of an intense speculative bubble, in which the banks were promoting a large number of new companies, many of which turned out to be worthless.[4] Falck certainly saw a unique opportunity to raise money for what must have been a long-considered enterprise. Before taking the final steps, Falck embarked on another technical trip to Belgium and Germany. He inspected steel mills at Burbach, Cockerill-Seraing, Charleroi, and Ougrée. In September 1905 he noted: "I hope not to diminish Dongo, but to revitalize it by bringing it together with strength."[5]

On 26 January 1906, in the buildings of the Banca Commerciale, opposite the great theater of La Scala in Milan, the Società Anonima Acciaierie e Ferriere Lombarde (AFL) was established with capital of 6 million liras ($1.1 million), divided into 30,000 shares. Its president was Angelo Migliavacca, and Falck was vice president with special responsibility for the construction of steel plants (which had become his expertise). The major financing of the creation came from the BCI, which initially exercised a substantial influence over the company, with several representatives on the board, including an engineer (Emilio Tansini) who could provide detailed technical evaluations of new projects.

In a sense, the new company was a merger of Falck's operations with the Vobarno works controlled by Alfredo d'Amico and the

Dongo firm of Rubini & Co. Vobarno was a major producer of steel forms and tubes. Dongo and the Rubinis had an association with the Falck family that dated from the 1830s, and had become above all an important producer of steel plate. Nevertheless, it was more or less predictable from the outset that there would be tensions among the founders that would lead to a struggle for control. Falck had little to contribute by way of capital. But the more the technical imperative behind the merger was emphasized, and the more the emphasis was placed on expansion and market power, the greater would be the influence of Giorgio Enrico Falck.

The site chosen for the new works was Sesto San Giovanni, because of its proximity to the major customers and because the railroad line from Milan to Monza gave easier access to imported German, Belgian, Luxembourg, and Swiss coking coal, semifinished products, and scrap. It was also a site intensely promoted by the BCI. The company as a whole would be seen as a large integrated steelworks, an impression that was calculated to play a major part in the new surge in industrial activity in Italy, identified by Alexander Gerschenkron as the breakthrough moment in Italian industrialization.[6] Four Siemens-Martin furnaces with a capacity of between 30 and 35 tons were to be constructed to plans by the Dortmund engineering office of Lackner. The first furnace was fired in 1908, the second in 1910. By 1909, Sesto San Giovanni produced 39,000 tons of steel, or over 4 percent of Italian steel production, and by 1914 84,000 tons, or over 9 percent.

But the new firm was immediately hit by a plethora of start-up difficulties, and then by a new and general Italian industrial crisis of 1907. AFL's annual report for 1906–07 identified two major problems: "disputes, provoked by slow and inadequate railroad connections," and "serious disruption from workers continually agitated by strikes."[7] The third annual report (1907–08) spoke of the general crisis of all branches of industry, and the reduction of demand for metal products, at a time when the firm was committed to a very extensive investment campaign.[8] There was intensified competition from German products.[9] The banks no longer loved bold initiatives, and were quite embarrassed by the laxity of the boom years.[10] One of the appointees of the BCI on the board of AFL, Ferdinando Adamoli, wrote of "the great disorder" in the administration, and that the accounting was in danger of "a complete shipwreck."[11] This echoed more general banking concerns about the financial health of the steel business in Italy, into which they had previously poured funds with gay abandon. The president of the Banca Commerciale, for instance, wrote a letter to the director general of the Banca d'Italia, Bonaldo Stringher, in which he described the Italian ironmasters as having "a common characteristic, megalomania and improvidence."[12]

This was also a decade of exceptionally violent labor unrest in northern Italy. Adamoli highlighted the labor problem: "As it seems, the technical sides of the new factories are very good. But the workers are a serious problem, and even Signor Falck does not conceal his worries in this regard. The immediate proximity of important metalworking and engineering plants leads to shortages of labor, and life in this area is very expensive, which has its effects on the level of wages."[13] There was indeed skilled labor in Milan, but the flood of new enterprise meant that it became scarce; the new employers were in competition with one another, and workers could with impunity be militant in their quest for better pay and conditions. The AFL report of 1908–09 emphasized the difficulties of beginning with no skilled workforce. In fact Milan was not as well supplied with skilled workers as the founders of AFL had supposed, and the company eventually had to build housing in order to encourage workers to move from the traditional centers on Lake Como. "We had to begin the operation of our plant at Sesto San Giovanni and accept all the inconveniences of operating an important steelworks in a place where there had been nothing except bare soil, where there were no similar works and thus no working traditions, where we had to create the workforce from scratch. Thus there was no existing development, and no support from an adequate and trained local workforce."[14] But in fact the works were quite profitable until they were hit by a drop in demand in the second half of 1908.

The Vobarno works as well as Sesto S. G. required a substantial investment, greatly exceeding the limited amount of capital that had been raised at the outset in 1906. Falck himself explained in July 1906: "Today the capital of 6 million liras is no longer adequate."[15] From 1906 to 1909 another 5.5 million liras were required. One way of raising the money would have been to engage in another merger, and there were talks with the large steel producer Ilva already in 1906: the beginning of a conflictual industrial flirtation that continued on and off for the next ninety years, but always ended more off than on. In 1908 there were again discussions about another steelmaker, the Ferriere Italiane, taking a 25 percent stake.

Falck explained that he hoped for bank help in raising capital. He told the AFL administrative council: "The transaction was completed with the decisive support of the Banca Commerciale."[16] In practice the most obvious solution was indeed bank credit, raised in part from the BCI and in part from the Banca Feltrinelli; the Feltrinellis were an important Milanese business dynasty that would work closely with the Falcks through several generations. At an early stage the BCI had raised an additional million liras of capital. But the banks were pressing for discussions with other iron- and steelmakers in order to bring financial relief. There were bills drawn on major consumers of iron—in particular the Società Ferrovia Mediterraneo—that might prompt new cooperation and capital participation. On 2 September 1909 a member of the AFL board close to the BCI, Francesco Rodolfo Queirazza, explained that "the financial position is serious and worrying. Even if the need for money can be met through the issue of bonds, the demand for a mortgage security for the bonds will exceed the credit of the society and make subsequent negotiations very hard."[17]

The BCI wrote, probably to the general director of the Bastogi railroad company, in an attempt to establish a significant industrial liaison for AFL:

> The administrative council is composed of people who have the right knowledge from a technical point of view, and the presence of Queirazza and of one of our representatives (engineer Tansini) will be in any case a brake on the revival of expansionist ambitions of further industrial growth. With this, the needs of the enterprise will remain within the limits set by the current finance plan, that is, a need for 5.5 million liras, of which 5 million will be consolidated, and 500,000 will come from short-term debt.[18]

Giorgio Enrico Falck, however, did not want the BCI to push him into the arms of the big coastal steel producers, and he sought additional funds to keep AFL independent. In 1909 Falck reported:

"With these resources, it would be possible to win two more years of tranquility. We should be confident that the present conditions of crisis will disappear by this time, and allow the financial consolidation and amortization of the company."[19]

The BCI now gave very detailed instructions on how AFL should conduct its reporting: a sort of instant course in good management (of a kind that it had utterly neglected in the years before 1907). In June 1908 the BCI's credit committee specified that AFL should keep a daily record of payments and deliveries, that all the branches should keep accounts in the same form as those of the principal works in Sesto San Giovanni, and that the directorate should have an overall view of the business of the firm: "One should make a memorandum or collection of documents about the contracts with suppliers, and their bids, for the use of the general director and the managing administrator, in order to ensure that each is informed about the business transaction of the other, which may not be the case otherwise in the absence of the one or the other."[20]

Banks in general seem to have blamed business, and especially heavy industry, for the misfortunes of 1907. The BCI in 1909 was determined to halt what it viewed as Falck's frenetic and dangerous overexpansion, and it instructed its representatives on the administrative council of AFL to apply the brakes. An agreement with the BCI and the other banks stabilized the financial situation for a two-year period. Falck continued to press for expansion, however, and in 1911 demanded the construction of the third furnace at Sesto.[21]

This was also a time of renewed labor disturbances, with a strike in Sesto and tensions in Vobarno. The director general of AFL, Alfredo d'Amico, proposed to grant a wage increase of 10 to 15 percent because of the "danger of a strike."[22] But he immediately became enmeshed in a bitter personal dispute with Falck. Falck took a much harder line: "he referred to a disturbance that spread among all the workers in the ironworks. Concessions would create a bad precedent, especially since Falck was negotiating with other employers in order to establish a league to resist the workers' demands." In November 1910 Falck complained that "the workers show signs of revolt. In Sesto there is obstruction, in which work is slowed down, in order to demand an increase in the piece rate. Meetings of business owners have already occurred, and will continue to be held in order to organize a collective defense. But in the meantime we can do nothing but wait."[23] The AFL works were closed down for a substantial time.[24]

There seems to have been a much more general and increasingly personal animosity between the two directors of the firm. In 1910 Falck had attacked d'Amico's purchasing policy, "especially as concerned the rails intended for Vobarno, which had been made by the general director in an incautious way, without consulting him, for scrap prices were falling. Signor Falck added that he could not accept administrative methods that went counter to the interests of the company."[25] At the end of the dispute, in 1911, d'Amico was limited to the supervision of the two works at Vobarno and Dongo, and Falck became AFL's director general. He received not only a salary of 40,000 liras ($7,700) but also 6 percent of the company's profits in excess of 550,000 liras.[26] By now he was in practice the master of the new company; but he wanted to secure his position by a new merger with a smaller company (not one of the giants that the BCI would have preferred).

In 1911 AFL took over Ferriera Milano, an important Milanese manufacturer of seamless steel tubes, and a wide range of steel profiles. The transaction required AFL to raise its own capital to 8.7 million liras ($1.7 million). The director of Ferriera Milano, Ludovico Goisis, became a close and exceptionally loyal collaborator of Falck's. Though not a member of the Falck family, Goisis played the same role of irreplaceable confidant that the Luegs and Reuschs had for the Haniels (and for which there is no equivalent in the Wendel history). From 1 January 1911 Giorgio Enrico Falck had the exclusive management of AFL.

During this time of renewed general economic setback, Falck spoke of "permanent conditions of crisis."[27] But despite all the unfavorable developments, including the idle furnaces at Dongo and Sesto, Falck characteristically proposed a new program of investments, including a new tubing plant in Milan. Falck noted: "As to the financial side, we can be assured, but the same cannot be said for the commercial side, because of the long-standing crisis and the reduction of sales as a result of fallen demand."[28] In particular, he was worried by the effect on Italian prices of German dumping of steel products, and by the big German push to form *Konzerne*, or combines. In 1913 Falck's old associate Redaelli even proposed a solution to the international competitive struggle in the form of joining

Mannesmann in a consortium, thus making concentration international. Mannesmann at this time was investing heavily in Italy and beginning to make tubes using an electrical steel process; AFL had begun to emerge as a major competitor in the narrower tube sector, with prices slightly below those of the Mannesmann products.[29] Falck himself was one of the most vigorous figures in Italian industry denouncing German competition and demanding some sort of government protection.

In 1911 the Italian steel industry did indeed develop a cartel-like structure of its own. Falck's prominent role was rewarded by a relatively large share of the sales quota calculated by the Consorzio Siderurgico: 10.1 percent, compared with 7.7 percent for Ilva and 17.7 percent for the Società Ferriere Italiane.[30] Falck also engaged in a major cost-cutting program. In June 1912 he reduced employment at all the AFL plants: Dongo, Vobarno, Sesto, Milano. He noted: "Certainly, this will mean hardship for the workforce, but it is necessary to go ahead with due prudence."[31]

It was at precisely this moment of crisis that Falck developed the strategy that would characterize his leadership of the Italian steel business: concentration on the use of scrap rather than imported iron ore as the basis for a new type of steel business. In a sense it was a reversion to the practices of the microindustry around Lake Como at the beginning of the nineteenth century. The success of the strategy allowed some reduction in the outstanding debt even before the First World War, in the course of which inflation largely wiped out much of Italian industry's debt. AFL's bank debt reached a maximum of 5.6 million liras in 1912; by 1914 it was just over 4 million liras. In 1913 there were 800 workers employed at Sesto San Giovanni, with a capacity of 80,000 tons in annual production. At Dongo 500 workers produced primarily sheet steel, with a capacity of 25,000 tons. Ferriera di Porta Romana in Milan had 400 workers and 25,000 tons' capacity. The steel production of the company had doubled from 40,000 to 80,000 tons over six years. In June 1914 the Milan works began to produce seamless tubes that could compete with those produced by Mannesmann.

Falck had made a strategic gamble on continued expansion. The economic setbacks of 1907 and 1912 were tests that, if repeated, might well have destroyed the new venture. But the First World War, and Italy's engagement, brought a new era of expansion.

Anyone who had worked with banks in the years immediately before and after 1907 would have been skeptical about their influence on industry: first they had pushed for fast expansion, and then they had hit the brake pedal hard and destructively.[32] Indeed, after 1907 a substantial discussion developed about the harm done to the Italian economy by the German-style universal banking system. But 1907 saw a much milder setback in industrial production than that of the 1890s, when iron production in Italy had fallen by half between 1890 and 1896, or the severe crisis of 1900–01, when pig-iron production declined by a third. From 1905 to 1907 Italian pig-iron output fell from 143,000 tons to 112,000 tons (or 22 percent). The fact that steel production actually rose over this period indicates that this was a crisis of adjustment in production technology for more traditional works. But the crash of 1907 produced a profound crisis for prices, industrial management, and the newfound enthusiasm for bank-led industrialization. The stock market remained very depressed.[33]

From 1912 Falck consciously began to work much less with banks, and instead began to build up a network of private individuals who would work with his firm and supply capital: in particular the Rubini family, and then also the Feltrinellis and Luranis. Like the adoption of scrap as a primary source, this appears to have been an instance of the adaptation of nineteenth-century strategies: Irene Rubini would have felt quite familiar with the technique. Using networks instead of banks allowed Falck to stay largely untouched by the interwar catastrophes that overwhelmed Italian banks and the industries they managed. The rapid liberation of Falck interests and of AFL from bank oversight would have been unthinkable without the First World War, and without the strategy that Falck adopted in order to satisfy the hunger of the Italian armaments industry for metals.

At first the war produced a shortage of scrap metal and of coking coal as imports from Switzerland and Germany fell off. In December 1914, with Italy still at peace, G. E. Falck noted: "The future is bleak, because of the possibility of needing to stop production this winter on account of a lack of raw materials."[34] At the same time, military demand for metal products increased even before Italy's entry into the war. Falck in 1916 considered buying a bankrupt steelworks, Barelli, as well as the Milan works of Redaelli. In May

1918 AFL discussed the purchase of a shareholding in an engineering works, Franco Tosi, thus making a step in the direction of vertical integration with steel consumers. The company also acquired some small strategic participations in other significant steel companies: at the end of 1919 it held 2.71 percent of the shares of Terni (the large new steel company in central Italy) and 0.415 percent of the shares of Ilva.[35]

But it was quickly clear in wartime Italy that the major bottleneck in steel production was the energy supply. The most important breakthrough of the wartime years was the beginning of Falck's involvement in hydroelectric production, financed through a high level of wartime profits (AFL profits rose from 508,278 liras, or $95,900, in 1913–14 to 2,939,098 liras, or $464,312, in 1917–18). The administrative board first debated the issue on 23 June 1916. In view of the general energy shortage in Italy, a government decree of September 1916 (the Bonomi decree) gave favorable treatment to enterprises that would construct their own generators, networks, and distribution systems.[36] At the end of 1916 AFL decided to construct a hydroelectric generating plant at Boffetto, in the Valtellina. AFL reported that it had used its own resources for the initial investments but "could not exclude" a later need for external support.[37] The construction was delayed by difficulty in shipping material from England for the power lines in the San Marco valley. In its 1917–18 report AFL also complained about delays in payment from the Italian government, whose subsidy was in fact central to the whole operation. The hydroelectric plant and the power lines were eventually completed by the end of 1919. In 1918 Falck had an additional contract to use water power from the Ligio and Boggia, but eventually abandoned this possibility as postwar demand collapsed.[38]

The use of hydroelectric power became a continuing strength of the company in the interwar period. At first AFL justified its investments by the high price of imported coal.[39] Later the firm used its successes in the electric production of steel to argue that Italy could have an autonomous steel industry without large-scale imports of foreign ore.

The immediate postwar period was also characterized by a revival of the bitter labor conflicts that had paralyzed the company before the war. One solution was to build more housing in order to secure a stable workforce. The company also established a huge dormitory with washing and canteen facilities for single workers. A vision based on a powerful sense of company paternalism and an ethic of social responsibility looked like a way of binding a reliable workforce: the Falcks now made the same calculations, and the same provisions, as the nineteenth-century Wendels and Haniels. But the First World War was precisely the moment when such paternalism was castigated as reactionary by a highly radical labor movement all across the European continent.

PART THREE

The Age of Organizationalism

In the first part of the twentieth century, the balance between owner and corporation (or between family and manager) tipped decidedly in favor of the corporation and the manager. Management became more powerful; technocracy blossomed. Ownership became subject to more and more state regulatory initiatives and controls. Organized labor tried to promote a new program, challenging the decisionmaking authority of owners. Monetary disorder made long-term strategies of business development in the private sector very precarious. On the other hand, family life also became harder, and the expansion of the state and its claims affected the way in which family property could be transferred across generations.

The easiest and most obvious way of understanding this development is the one spelled out by Alfred Chandler, as a response to the internal logic of bigness and of business expansion ("scale and scope").[1] Large business required large-scale organization. The restructuring and reshaping of management along modern lines did not, however, occur in a political vacuum. The concentration of power evident in large-scale business organization quickly brought a demand for control or regulation. Attacks on business power became greater with the spread of democratic politics and mass politicization, especially in the aftermath of the mobilization of society for twentieth-century war. Business owners in consequence were frightened and felt a need to shape their environment. They responded to the accusation of influence with bold attempts to shape political outcomes through public opinion, elite policymakers, and public policy. Much of the new organizational drive in the end amounted to a shift away from technical innovation and toward rent-seeking and attempts to capture politics.

Business dynasties became a powerful symbol in the battle for the political control of business. Modernizers painted the family as an obstacle to growth and a relic of a feudal age. The notion of "family business" frequently became the scapegoat for a generalized economic and political discontent. Especially in France, the idea that the family firm caused national backwardness became firmly entrenched. Mussolini's regime took up some of these slogans in its promotion of a new corporatism; as did some of the planners of the

Weimar Republic. If the family and its ownership structure was dysfunctional, it seemed logical that the state should take measures to discourage this form of capitalism.

The extreme politicization of business life and of the family firm became very obvious after the First World War, but the origins of the development can be traced to before the conflict. One focus was taxes, especially taxes on the transmission of property across generations. Inheritance tax began to be widely discussed in the early twentieth century, when demands for redistribution in the name of social justice and fiscal demands resulting from the armaments buildup coincided. France had a long tradition of low taxation, the *centième denier* of the ancien régime. The rate was 1.25 percent until 1901, but then some element of progressivity was introduced (the rate could rise as high as 2.5 percent for direct descendants, and 20.5 percent for nonrelated persons). In 1907 the government proposed a much more extensive tax, but this plan was not realized until the First World War. Some German states, notably the Hanseatic states and Baden, had long had a moderate tax (the Baden tax provided for rates of 3 to 4 percent for inheritance by siblings and their offspring), but the tax burden in Prussia was substantially lighter, and inheritance by direct descendants was untaxed. The creation of the German imperial inheritance tax in 1906, which allowed states to impose taxes on direct descendants, and the discussion of a widening of tax brackets in 1908 caused major political tensions and in the end contributed to the collapse of the Bülow government in 1909. In Italy the nineteenth-century level of inheritance tax was similarly low, 0.55 percent for direct descendants, 2.2 percent for spouses, 5.5 percent for siblings, and 11 percent for nonrelatives.

Only with the First World War did rates of inheritance tax increase dramatically. France had a tax of this kind from 1917, with a strong pro-natality emphasis: estates with no children were taxed at up to 39 percent, while those with one child had a rate of 21 percent and those with three children only 7.50 percent. Germany in 1919 introduced a generalized system of death duties. There was a general estate tax of up to 5 percent, with an additional inheritance tax to be paid by particular classes of inheritor: in the 1919 version the rate for linear descendants ranged from 4 to 20 percent, and for nonrelated legatees from 15 to 70 percent. These rates were substantially reduced in 1923 (when descendants were taxed at between 2 and 10 percent and nonrelatives at 14 to 70 percent) but increased again in 1925. Italy experimented with a tax on the German model, but this was lifted under Mussolini for direct descendants, spouses, siblings, uncles and aunts, and nephews and nieces.

The Second World War brought a new round of tax increases. France and Germany had a relatively low rate, with a maximum of 15 percent in the late 1950s for inheritance in the direct line. In the 1950s Italy imposed taxes of between 1 and 35 percent on the estate, with additional taxes for inheritance by those not in the direct line (spouses would pay one to 35 percent, nieces or nephews 5 to 70 percent). The new fiscal environment might have been expected to destroy family capitalism. In Britain after the Second World War, death duties and other legal charges dramatically altered the character of ownership and eroded family firms.[2] The mystery of how the phenomenon of family capitalism survived in continental Europe will be explored in a later section.

There were other threats to family businesses besides fiscal ones. With longer-established families, increased distance from the founder generation brought a greater range of contacts (more social capital), but less family coherence. In addition, in a world that was becoming ever more political, the temptation to enter politics and directly affect the political process (if only to alter the business environment) also increased.

Some comparisons:

Wendel, 1929: 1,629,000 tons of steel and 34,000 workers (48 tons per worker)

GHH, 1929: 1,066,000 tons of steel and 32,895 workers (32 tons per worker) (the GHH AG was by this time a major engineering firm, and only a small proportion of its workforce was engaged in steel production)

AFL (Falck), 1929–30: 210,000 tons of rolled steel and 8,202 workers (26 tons per worker) [illegible] reduced in 19[illegible] [illegible] descendants were taxed at between [illegible] percent and [illegible] percent [illegible] percent [illegible] [illegible] [illegible] from [illegible]. But this was [illegible] for direct descendants, siblings, uncles and aunts, and nephews and nieces.

[illegible] Second World War [illegible] a new round of tax increases. France and Germany [illegible] relatively low rates with a maximum [illegible] percent in the late [illegible] for [illegible] in the direct line. In [illegible] taxes of [illegible] percent [illegible] rate, [illegible] taxes for inheritance [illegible] not in the direct line [illegible] would pay [illegible] percent [illegible]. The [illegible] fiscal [illegible] might have [illegible] expected to destroy family capitalism. [illegible] after the Second World [illegible] death [illegible] charges [illegible] dramatically [illegible] the [illegible] family firms [illegible] of family capitalism survived in [illegible] commercial [illegible].

There were other threats to family businesses besides [illegible] taxes. [illegible] families, [illegible] and distance from the [illegible] regardless of [illegible] from [illegible] social [illegible]. In addition, [illegible] that [illegible] the temptation to [illegible] political [illegible] the [illegible] increased.

Chapter 7

The Politician as Businessman

Wendel signifies France.

François de Wendel, 1918

THE EARLY TWENTIETH-CENTURY François de Wendel remains the best-known member of the family, because of the political controversies that surrounded him rather than because of his business career.[1] His considerable personal self-assurance, perhaps even arrogance, added to the ferocity of contemporary and subsequent debates. The other steel barons of France hated his easy assumption of preeminence. Strange myths circulated about him. In 1934 *Fortune* magazine portrayed him as "a modern Pooh-Bah; his connections and directorships would fill this page . . . Yet for all the illustriousness of this remarkable man, the newspapers of France never mention his name. He does not like publicity."[2] In fact there was a considerable amount of publicity, but much of it was unflattering. The journalist Gustave Téry, for instance, wrote that he was "a great devil with red hair, so thin, so slender, that he looked as if he himself had been through a rolling mill. In vain he assumes the impertinence of a grand seigneur: he protests with timidity, responds with embarrassment, and frequently reaches with his hand for his tie as if he were trying to free his neck from an invisible rope."[3]

In a trilogy of post–Second World War novels, *Les grandes familles*, based loosely on the Rothschild and Wendel dynasties, and originally written for the Communist newspaper *L'Humanité*, the popular writer Maurice Druon presented a patriarch, Noël Schoudler, who humiliated his son when the latter had ideas about expanding and modernizing too quickly, and destroyed the son when the company needed to raise capital. In this family, the members hated each other and despised each other's abilities, but they were "bound by the same chain of riches." In this parable about the dire effects of French family capitalism, it was "l'augmentation du capital" that made a firm and a family vulnerable.[4] Schoudler was an obvious amalgam of Schneider and Wendel. Druon was not just making Communist propaganda, but reflecting what was even a semiofficial view. As early as 1919, for instance, the Ministry of Commerce published a study arguing that the family structure of capitalism had weakened France in its long struggle with Germany.[5]

François de Wendel was ubiquitous in interwar French politics. He had become a deputy to the French Chamber for the Meurthe-et-Moselle in 1914, and was reelected regularly until in 1932 he moved to the Senate seat vacated by the election of Albert Lebrun as president of the Republic. His cousin Guy de Wendel was also a politician, a member of the General Council of the Moselle until 1927, when he entered the French Senate.

The Wendel influence was not confined to, or indeed primarily expressed through, representative parliamentary politics. François de Wendel also played a great role in interest politics. He was president of the Comité des Forges, which was massively demonized as the sinister interest group of heavy industry, although Wendel privately insisted that the institution's unpopularity derived from the personality of Robert Pinot, its formidable secretary general, and not from his own actions. Wendel was also a regent of the Banque de France from 1913 until 1936, when the Popular Front government reformed the bank and cast out the old oligarchs. Since there were 200 private shareholders of the bank before the nationalization, it was this institution that gave rise to the left-wing slogan of the "200 Families" that allegedly controlled France's fortunes. The Wendels, with the two political cousins, appeared to offer a prime example of the malign influence of money. Old-style patriarchalism alienated reformist and leftist Catholics, who saw the political activity of François de Wendel as destructive of the chances of a socially engaged Catholicism. He was attacked by the left-wing Catholic

16. *François de Wendel, 1874–1949*
COURTESY OF THE WENDEL ARCHIVE, PARIS

journal *Esprit* more vigorously than by the Socialist or Communist press, and after the Second World War was cast into the cold by the new Christian Democratic party, the Mouvement Républicain Populaire.

Much of the discussion of nation, interest, and sabotage in interwar France followed from the heightened nationalism that accompanied and followed from the enormous military, political, social, and economic mobilization of the First World War. It brought with it a strong rhetoric of betrayal and treachery. Steel formed the backbone of the early twentieth-century vision of the nation. François de Wendel himself sometimes explained how steel had been central to the war. In 1919, for instance, he told the Chamber of Deputies commission of inquiry that "from the metallurgical point of view, this war was a war of Martin steel. We had at the beginning of the war 150 Martin furnaces. We finished the war with 225. It is these 225 Martin furnaces which allowed us to win the war."[6]

The First World War

François de Wendel's political and business career was framed by two periods of war and by the German occupation and administration of the family business. Even as the great powers began partial mobilizations, on 30 July 1914, the Wendels planned to close their factories, located on the borders of France and the German empire, because of the imminent likelihood of military action. On the evening of that day, François, Humbert, and Maurice left Hayange in Germany and drove by car to Paris. And in fact on 2 August, before any declaration of war, Saxon soldiers raided the French works of Wendel et Cie. at Joeuf and destroyed the post office and telephone system. The Wendels moved to inland France, and most male members of the family entered government or military service. Humbert was sent in 1915 to London to liaise with the British government over the supply of arms to the front; and Maurice and Guy were in active service.

The works in imperial Germany, at Hayange and Moyeuvre, were left under their loyal management, but on 26 November 1914 the Germans passed legislation authorizing the sequestration of enemy property, and at Hayange the military-imposed administrator, Bergassessor von Skal, replaced the manager left by the Wendels, Robert Pastor. During this sequestration the private Saar steel firm of Röchling struggled with the Bavarian state over who should control the Wendel works: in both the First and Second World Wars, Röchling wanted to extend its activity into Lorraine. The steel production of the Wendel works fell off dramatically, from a prewar level of 775,000 tons to 250,000 tons in 1915. Under German control the workforce was augmented by Russian prisoners of war from the summer of 1915, and in June 1916 a direct military administration was imposed. During 1918, after the Russian collapse and the conclusion of the humiliating peace treaty of Brest-Litovsk, as the German government looked forward to a reordering of *Mitteleuropa*, and also as it looked for new ways of raising money, it put the Wendel industrial holdings up for sale. A liquidator had been imposed on the factories in August 1917, and on 2 September

17. *Return of the Wendels to Hayange, November 1918*

COURTESY OF THE WENDEL ARCHIVE, ARCHIVES NATIONALES, PARIS

1918 the auction began. But this last-ditch German effort at privatization of confiscated assets was overshadowed by the rapid German military collapse, and there was no realistic bidding.

There was some physical damage in Hayange and Moyeuvre, with repeated aerial bombardment after July 1915. Particularly in 1917 and 1918 there were frequent raids.[7] The Joeuf works, on the other hand, were scarcely used by the Germans, and the factory installations were systematically destroyed. After the war the French made a monument of the wrecking ball used in the German demolition.

After the armistice of 11 November 1918, as in other parts of the German empire, workers' and soldiers' councils took over the factories. But unlike in Germany, the councils handed the works over to the French directors under Robert Pastor on 14 November, six days before the arrival of American and eight days before the arrival of French troops. The latter day, 22 November, marked a celebration of French patriotism, with an address by François de Wendel: "I clearly see, and I am glad, that today's demonstration is not only acclaiming the representatives of an old firm from Lorraine but also the representatives of the idea of France. It is because—the liquidators of our firm have said it often enough—Wendel signifies France that our firm is today the object of an ovation that moves me so deeply."[8]

The two companies, PFFW and Wendel & Cie. (the Joeuf works), continued as separate companies, though Wendel & Cie. was now entirely owned by PFFW. The capitalization of PFFW was raised from 30 million to 60 million francs ($3.5 million) in 1920, and to 117,180,000 ($6.2 million) in 1923; that of Wendel & Cie. was raised from 9 million to 24 million francs ($0.9 million) in 1925 and to 80 million ($3.1 million) in 1929. In 1924 PFFW was transformed into a company *en commandite en actions*, or joint-stock partnership, since the number of owners (all family members) was increasing quite dramatically (by 1926 there were sixty-nine), and the simple *commandite* form was thus no longer appropriate.[9] The family members were now represented in a supervisory board, an institution that had little function except to choose *gérants:* in the 1920s it was at first composed of Maurice de Wendel, Emmanuel de Mitry (François de Wendel's son-in-law), and François de Curel, the last to represent the descendants of the Gargan line. It seems to have had little reason to intervene or to oppose the *gérants*, who were also of course family members: the three brothers François, Humbert, and Maurice.

Politics and the Wendels

The display of social and national solidarity of November 1918 in which workers had demonstrated in support of the French owners was short-lived. The enterprises were hit by the postwar slump of 1920, with a fall in orders and a surge in unemployment. Social tension correspondingly increased, and labor was quickly radicalized. The Wendel family became an object not of veneration but of vituperation.

Part of the discussion of the links between politics and business that now flared up and concentrated on the Wendels centered upon the issue of the "abominable venality of the French press," which was castigated in a famous polemic published by the Communist newspaper *L'Humanité* in the mid-1920s, and then as a book in 1931 (and based on the secret reports of a tsarist agent, Arthur Raffalovich, who had bribed the French newspapers in the early 1900s).[10] Financial corruption had in fact been a theme in literature and in popular political discussion at least since Maupassant's *Bel ami.* The accusation was that "interests" manipulated political events and formed political opinions in order to extract financial advantage. François de Wendel seemed a prime example of the nexus between business, the press, and the political world, in that he exercised his political influence in some part through his control of newspapers. From 1906 he had subsidized *L'Echo de Lorraine.* In 1901 his father had put 100,000 francs into *Le Journal des débats* as part of a capital increase for the paper, and in 1913 he and his brother and mother extended their investment. With a circulation of 20,000–25,000, the newspaper, like most French political journals, made a regular loss, a fact that never really worried the owners. Wendel had it distributed free to all the teachers in his electoral district. The newspaper's director, Etienne de Nalèche, became a close friend of Wendel but was never simply a voice for Wendel's opinions. Wendel felt that he was too sympathetic to Aristide Briand's pacific and allegedly pro-German foreign policy, and was outraged by the "inadmissible" financial articles of the journalist Maroni, who was paid for his views by the banking house of Lazard. In 1926 Wendel actually dismissed Nalèche, who saved his own position only by removing the offending Maroni; and Wendel then raised extra money for the newspaper from the banking house of Rothschild, which was sympathetic to his views on financial and economic issues. In 1929 he also was involved in the purchase of *Le Temps,* which he wanted to manage discreetly, and to preserve as a moderate and neutral newspaper, in order to exercise a more subtle form of political influence. He never had sole control over that paper.

The major controversies around François de Wendel involved his role in the First World War; his attack on the center-left coalition of Edouard Herriot (the *cartel des gauches*) in 1924–1926; his support of the conservative nationalist Lorrainer Raymond Poincaré, which provoked an intense discussion about the power of money (*le mur d'argent,* "the wall of money") in politics; and, finally, his position during the Second World War. The most important attacks claimed that Wendel had sold France's true interest. During the First World War, conspiracy theories had flourished as politicians and generals liberally used charges of inadequate prosecution of the war effort, and a willingness to compromise France's sacred national interest, in the day-to-day intrigues of Third Republic politics. After the war the political atmosphere remained poisoned.

The wartime "affairs" of 1914–1918 in particular demonstrate the way in which myth overtook reality when it came to the political assessment of the Wendels and their influence. The "affaire de Briey" developed from a wartime discussion. In a series of 1916 articles in the Catholic newspaper *Le Correspondent*, a parliamentary deputy and lawyer, Fernand Engerand, emphasized the importance of steel produced in Briey to Germany's economic war effort. (In fact, as the historian Jean-Noël Jeanneney has shown, the Briey industries produced no iron or steel during the war; but German business did indeed desperately want to annex the area in order to establish a postwar industrial supremacy in Europe.) Engerand went on to suggest that France should engage in an artillery or aerial bombardment of the principal industrial sites in Briey. During the same period the left-wing newspaper *L'Oeuvre* began a campaign suggesting that powerful interests in the Comité des Forges were keeping steel prices high. After the war Wendel's critics, above all the Socialist deputy Edouard Barthe, accused him of having blocked the destruction by the French military of the steelworks in Briey, thus contributing greatly to the capacity of Germany to produce munitions.[11]

François de Wendel always sternly tried to rebut these accusations. It does indeed seem that the reason the Wendel works behind the German lines survived relatively intact is that the destruction of factories by precision artillery attacks or aerial bombardment was simply too difficult given the technology of the First World War. The military leadership had decided that it could not invest in the new equipment that would be needed to aim an accurate artillery bombardment at a site 45 kilometers away. In February 1917 General Robert Nivelle had explained that the Lorraine ore mines were not vulnerable or appropriate military targets. In January 1918 General Philippe Pétain had declared that he did not have the means to attack industrial targets. But there were a quite substantial number of air attacks, although these were rather ineffective, and the amounts of explosive delivered were small. For part of 1916, French aviators had indeed been asked not to attack the Wendel works in Hayange and Moyeuvre, but after December 1916 these works were explicitly included in lists of suitable targets, and the most damaging raids occurred in 1917 and 1918.

Wendel was also accused of having blocked plans to take over the Thyssen properties in Normandy at Caen, in an effort to stop Germans from taking retaliatory action against the Wendel works in Germany and in the occupied areas. Again, the implication was that he had obstructed the full development of the war economy. But in fact the German authorities were in the end eager to sell off Wendel assets and were oblivious of any protection that might have been offered to Thyssen.

In 1919 a parliamentary commission of inquiry heard the details of accusations that blamed Wendel specifically. But none of these claims about a Wendelian conspiracy were ever substantiated or corroborated. General Maurice Sarrail claimed that in 1914 there were notices posted in the French language on the doors of some industrial establishments (including Wendel) that they should not be touched in military actions. In the Chamber of Deputies debate of 31 January 1919, Fernand Engerand told a story about a memorandum to the French General Staff urging the bombardment of steelworks, but that it had been received by an unnamed "ironmaster" attached to the staff; the insinuation was that this sinister ironmaster had then destroyed or lost the document in order to protect his property. Engerand made the "ironmaster" appear more mysterious by adding that "his name was quite un-French" and that he seemed to have a "strange immunity."[12]

The Chamber deputy Barthe also raised the case of articles in 1916 in *Le Temps* by the journalist Max Hoschiller explaining that the destruction of the Briey industrial sites would not substantially weaken Germany, articles that had been encouraged by the Comité des Forges. In the Chamber debates of 24 and 31 January 1919 François de Wendel began by denying that the Comité had a publicity fund. He then moved on to the specific charges and concluded categorically: "I did not intervene in the issue of the bombardments of the mines of the Briey valley. I contented myself, while supplying a few useful indications, with saying that that there was no reason to spare our factories in Hayange and Moyeuvre, located in Alsace-Lorraine, which I knew were to be exploited by the Germans." He told the Chamber of Deputies that he would not deserve its estimation if he "had intervened by reasons of the interests that I possessed on the Lorraine frontier in order—as has been claimed—to stop an offensive in the Briey valley or to block the bombing of mines. Quite to the contrary, I would say that I myself brought the plans of the mines and factories to show what were the strategic points for bombardment."[13] The 1919 inquiry heard about a Second Lieutenant Lejeune, an engineer employed by Wendel, who in 1917 had formulated bombing targets that included many railway stations (as transportation hubs), but not industrial sites. Again, there was a logic to this position, in that it was indeed in 1918 the inadequacy of transport and the inability to move troops and supplies quickly that led to the disintegration of the German positions on the Western Front.[14]

In 1938, when in the face of the Nazi challenge the idea that the rich might be betraying and selling France surfaced again in a very potent form, a letter purporting to be from François de Wendel was published. It was dated 7 May 1916 and asked for an appointment at the general headquarters to discuss the aerial bombardment of "our annexed factories in Hayange (Meurthe-et-Moselle)."[15] It said that the Wendel works in Joeuf had already been bombed and asked why de Wendel factories, rather than German-owned works, should be targeted. As Jeanneney pointed out, this alleged letter contains an elementary error that François de Wendel almost certainly would never have made, in that Hayange is not in the department Meurthe-et-Moselle (it is in the Moselle). The letter was in all likelihood a forgery concocted in order to sustain the by now very elaborate conspiracy theories. By the end of 1938 a veteran of the Briey controversy, Henri de Kerillis, was attacking de Wendel as "a prominent German feudalist" who had "played a decisive role in the capitulation of Munich" when France had given in to Hitler's pressure.[16]

The second large political debate concerned Wendel's role in the politics of the *cartel des gauches* from 1924 to 1926, during a period of acute financial destabilization in France. Both as a politician and as a regent of the Banque de France, Wendel developed a ferocious criticism of the budget deficits of the government, which he blamed for the speculative pressure against the franc. He also made little secret of his admiration for Benito Mussolini, and wanted a strong man of the right to assume power in France.[17] When Herriot's center-left administration was replaced, without elections, by the nationalist cabinet of François's fellow Lorrainer Raymond Poincaré, the left argued that financial interests (the *mur d'argent*) had blocked Herriot. Poincaré was indeed for some time a close political ally, but when he was actually in power he ignored Wendel's views on many themes, including the economically crucial issue of the appropriate exchange rate for the stabilization of the French franc.

In the 1930s François de Wendel continued to champion Mussolini, especially in the aftermath of the Italian invasion of Abyssinia. But there is a logic, perhaps even a convincing one, to his argument that the noisy French (and British) reaction to the Italian dictator was driving him into the arms of France's true enemy, Germany.

Finally, the most absurd of all the political accusations portrayed François de Wendel as a betrayer of France during the Second World War. François de Wendel never deviated from his profound hostility to Germany, and the Nazi seizure of power only confirmed his view about the true character of Germans. Unlike most of the French right, he had no hesitation in the end in preferring an alliance with Stalin's Soviet Union to compromise with Hitler's Germany. In June 1939 he announced that he hoped for the success of a diplomatic approach to the Soviet Union, "whatever the feelings that one might hold toward the government of Mr. Stalin."[18] With the German attack in May 1940, he fled to the Wendel chateau in the Touraine. He refused to go to Vichy for the vote of *pleins pouvoirs* to Marshal Pétain on 9–10 July. (His cousin Guy, on the other hand, participated in the Senate vote that ended the Third Republic and replaced it by the "Etat français.")

Wendel became increasingly powerless during the conflict. The Comité des Forges, one of the bastions of his power, was dissolved by a decree of 9 November 1940, and in place of previous interest organizations the Vichy regime established a new network of corporate organizations. He felt disillusioned about the French press and refused to support *Le Temps* any longer, since it had in his eyes simply become a tool of government propaganda. In November 1940 he also explained that he saw no point in continuing to pay subsidies to the *Journal des débats*. He was not permitted to visit Lorraine, and he refused German offers to involve him in the industrialization of German-occupied Russia, even though one of the offers the Germans made involved the release of his son, Henri, who was interned in a prisoner-of-war camp. The steelworks were expropriated, and the Hayange and Moyeuvre works were eventually integrated into the "Hermann Göring Werke."

After the Liberation, Wendel was again demonized by most of the new politicians. The Communist newspaper *L'Humanité* claimed that he had signed a voluntary agreement with Göring. *La Voix de l'Est* stated that he was member number 13 of the fascist Croix de Feu and that the Wendels had for three centuries practiced infamous treason. Wendel had certainly thought that both the Croix de Feu and the parallel fascist movement of Jacques Doriot might play some useful role in French politics, and he met Doriot; but his support went no further.[19] His old, more centrist Catholic political allies began to move away from him. In particular, the influential Louis Marin in the late 1930s made a point of denouncing "the constant and dominating intervention of financial and banking elements in French politics."[20] After the Liberation Marin made a political pact with the new Catholic political movement and, finding Wendel an embarrassment, kept him off all electoral lists. A jury under René Cassin, vice president of the government, declared that François de Wendel was ineligible for election to the new parliament, since he had voted power to Pétain on 10 July 1940. This charge was obviously false, and Cassin was later obliged to retract the decision and apologize, but everybody wanted to believe in the lack of patriotism of the steel dynasties.

François de Wendel became increasingly disenchanted with politics. The high point of his influence had been in the mid-1920s, but it had called forth a new crescendo of public vilification. In the 1932 legislative elections, all of France shifted to the left, with a victory of the center-left coalition under Herriot, and in his own constituency of Meurthe-et-Moselle, Wendel had barely defeated the challenge of an attractive and rhetorically gifted left-wing Catholic, Philippe Serre. When a seat in the prestigious but politically less important Senate became vacant upon Albert Lebrun's election as president, Wendel ran for his seat and won handily. In the subsequent election for the Chamber of Deputies, though, Serre beat the Wendel-supported candidate. The controversies of the 1930s only increased Wendel's sense of isolation. After the formation of the Popular Front government in 1936 and the big surge in labor union power, he came to the conclusion that "it is in the course of nature that old trees lose their branches, but it is still sad to see them fall."[21]

A Business Rationale for Politics

When François de Wendel was criticized by his brothers or by other members of the family for his extensive political involvement, he tried to explain that it was good for business. It is possible to see the validity of this point in a number of cases. His implacable hostility to Germany and to German economic reconstruction was largely emotional, and came out of extended experience of the humiliations imposed by the German administration in prewar Lorraine. But it did have a business logic, in that—as before the First World War—the Wendel works needed access to a secure supply of coking coal. It did not need to come from the Ruhr valley. Indeed Wendel disagreed with Foch and Poincaré when they presented the case for French control of the Ruhr basin or substantial territories on the right bank of the Rhine. France could renounce the Ruhr if it maintained with all the force it could muster its claims to control the left bank of the Rhine. In December 1923 Wendel invested 100 million francs ($5.2 million) in the Friedrich Heinrich coal mine in the county of Moers (which was practically next door to the Haniel Rheinpreussen mine), which would supply four-fifths of the Wendel demand for coking coal. François de Wendel wrote: "It is clear that we would not risk an equal amount in this affair if we were not hoping to see the French flag wave again for a long time over the left bank of the Rhine. In any case, we will have done what we could to make it wave there."[22]

This control of the left bank was threatened by the policy of Aristide Briand, the foreign minister of the *cartel des gauches.* Briand was the architect of all the most serious plans for European pacification in the 1920s. François de Wendel, who had begged rather ignominiously for Briand's help in an early stage of his political career, when he wanted to obtain the Chamber of Deputies seat for Briey, now regarded Briand as a fool and a traitor to French interests. When Briand died, in March 1932, Wendel had himself excused from the Chamber of Deputies so as not to have to participate in a unanimous resolution that Briand had "served his country well."[23]

The bitter campaign against Briand did little good for either France or the interests of the Wendels. Wendel's biographer Jean-

Noël Jeanneney concluded that it was rarely "that his status as a member of parliament added much to the effectiveness of his steps taken for the defense of his establishments or his corporation."[24] On the contrary, the degree of political attention that François de Wendel attracted was almost certainly a disadvantage for the company. Indeed Wendel sometimes explained that politics was luxury, for which he was quite happy to pay. He told the Radical politician and newspaper editor Joseph Caillaux: "Not having any racing stables, and not playing baccarat, I can afford myself the luxury of an independent opinion."[25]

The most striking case in which Wendel's political position appeared to contradict the strategic interests of his company was the one in which Wendel's political influence had been most apparent and successful, and which precipitated the denunciation by the left of the power of the "200 Families": the struggle against inflationary fiscal policies in the mid-1920s, and in particular the demand for a revaluation of the franc. Wendel justified a higher valuation in terms of a defense of the interests of small savers, the petite bourgeoisie: a rise in the value of the franc would be for "the greatest good of the most serious elements of our population and, we should also say, of the honor of the country in relation to its neighbors [that is, postinflationary Germany] who do not do what is required by justice." In the newspaper article in *La Nation* in which Wendel set out his defense of saving and savers, he also addressed the obvious argument that a revaluation of the franc would hurt French industrial export interests, which might be thought to wish to preserve "the relatively favorable situation created for export, for our trade, and for our industry by the depreciation of our currency." But he went on to argue that such advantages were illusory: "It is enough to follow the movement of the indices to notice that, because of the increase in our bulk and retail prices, if the franc lowers, the bonus on export that our products benefit from is fatally destined to disappear. We can hope that this phenomenon happens as slowly as possible. We cannot believe that it will not come about."[26]

In fact the demand of François de Wendel and Baron Rothschild to let the inflow of capital push up the franc was frustrated by the actions of the governor of the Banque de France, Emile Moreau, who from December 1926 bought foreign exchange, and thus prevented a rise in the exchange rate. Moreau eventually convinced

18. *Propaganda against the "200 Families"*

Poincaré of the merits of a stabilization in which the franc would be held at a relatively low level in relation to the British pound; and the powerlessness of Wendel and Rothschild was revealed.[27]

François de Wendel was clearly convinced of the intellectual case for a hard currency, and he retained this conviction through the long misery of France's depression in the 1930s. Indeed he broke his usual public silence in 1935 to make a passionate and even flamboyant speech to the general congress of the major part of the right, the Fédération Républicaine, at Nice in 1935. The historian Julian Jackson describes the performance as "notorious."[28] The speech praised the virtue of austerity and fiscal deflation, demanding constraints on French public spending that did not immediately tally with the interests of a large producer of standardized steel products.

Malthusianism

The political criticism of Wendel sometimes extended to a general attack on his company, and on family business in general, as a prime example of a certain French "Malthusianism." The reluctance to invest for fear of losing control of the company was in this interpretation responsible for France's relatively low level of investment, and in general for its economic backwardness.[29]

On the face of it, there was no lack of technical knowledge at the company or among its owners and managers. François de Wendel, like his defeated prewar rival Charles, was consistently interested in the American steel experience. Like his cousin Guy, as a young man he made a short trip to the United States (in 1901), and in the 1920s and 1930s he was keen to send engineers on technical trips across the Atlantic. He was above all interested in coal-mining technology, and in the late 1920s he applied electricity to the transport of underground coal, first in the German works at Hamm, and then (in 1931) at Petite-Rosselle in Lorraine.

The company also began to develop international links, above all through a trading company in the Netherlands, created in 1924, which also controlled the mine holdings acquired at Oranje-Nassau on the eve of the First World War: the N.V. Import en Export Maatschappij Oranje-Nassau.[30]

After the First World War, the steel industry in the annexed part of Lorraine formerly in the German empire and now transferred back to France was completely restructured. PFFW was the only substantial French-owned enterprise at the outset; the formerly German-owned businesses were expropriated by the French state as part of the reparations process and sold to business groups in France (as well as Belgium and Luxembourg) for a total of 536 million francs ($90 million).[31] But such a purchase was not possible without massive financial support, and the major French and Belgian banks therefore played a prominent part in the transfer of Lorraine industry to French ownership. The transaction brought a very heterogeneous group of owners, including some of the major French automobile producers, into Lorraine. Wendel played some part in buying new steelworks, but he did so in a consortium with Schneider and the Luxembourg company Arbed: in particular it took part in the creation of the Société Minière des Terre-Rouges in 1921, with a capitalization of 20 million francs, which owned the former Gelsenkirchen works in Audun-le-Tiche. The consortium also held a small participation in a parallel company, Société Métallurgique des Terres-Rouges, which took over Gelsenkirchen Bergwerks AG, near Aachen.[32]

Some sort of new investment in steel was inevitable in postwar Lorraine, in part because of technical opportunities, but more because of the wartime devastation. In the case of the Wendel works, Joeuf had been devastated, and required a complete reconstruction. In Hayange, four blast furnaces were rebuilt, two with a capacity of 300 tons (which was relatively high for the 1920s). At Saint-Jacques, the triple rolling mills were electrified.

In general, however, the company was reluctant simply to substitute capital and technology for labor. Instead the Wendel enterprises continued the prewar practice of recruiting foreign labor, primarily Italians, but from 1924 also Poles (who were also Catholic), and then in the 1930s Algerians. In 1930 there were 4,600 Italians, 3,100 Poles, 700 Luxembourgeois, and a few hundred Algerians working in the iron industry in the Fensch and Orne valleys.[33] In general, a strategy was evolved of decreasing costs by using immigrant labor rather than by investing in more modern technology.

In 1926, at the height of François de Wendel's political influence and power (and at the time when he was pressing for a revaluation of the franc that would clearly be damaging to the interests of French manufacturing and exporting industry), he intervened most clearly and directly to urge caution on his business in regard to investment plans. The Thomas technology remained fundamentally unchanged until after the Second World War. Although some Lorraine steelworks built electric furnaces (at Micheville, Homécourt, Réhon, Neuves-Maisons, Longwy-Bas, Thionville, Uckange), there were none in the Wendel plants.

Some of the equipment was indeed antiquated. After an accident in 1930, the director of the works in reported: "We think that by 1 January 1933 we will own two [gas bellows] for blast-furnaces and that the Mulhouse [steam bellows] will no longer have to run . . . One possible cause of accidents, which seems even more important to us than the Naeyer closing system, is the deterioration of the equipment. Our boilers have been in use since 1885. The recently broken GH 10 boilers were installed in 1875 at Stiring-Wendel and then in 1885 at Hayange."[34]

François de Wendel also repeatedly made it clear that he considered himself bound to a particular course by the character of past investments. Thus, for instance, he wrote in 1921 to the management of the Fenderie works: "I should also note that we already own three Potter gas generators, without distributors or agitators, and that for this reason we can temporarily avoid the cost of the Morgan gas generator of currently 435,000 francs by preserving the old Lencauchez gas generators for our oven, and by using three of the five Potter gas generators already stationed there. I would take this information into account, which obliges us so to speak to stay on the track to which we have committed ourselves, only if the steelworks that have actually used the Morgan gas generators, and not only the manufacturers, celebrated the merits of the new equipment."[35]

Problems caused by antiquated equipment emerged in Joeuf as well. Blast furnace No. 7, for instance, had been constructed in 1907, and was in quite poor condition by the mid-1920s. In 1921 a discussion began about the best way of renovating the blast furnaces, but it was only in 1930 that a decision was reached to start a new construction.

In 1927, after a visit to the Joeuf plant, François de Wendel laid out his view that American-style furnaces would require too much additional investment:

> If the American furnaces offer an advantage because of the labor economy that they provide and the secure fastening of the blast furnace mouth that offers an advantage for the maintenance of pressure in the gas ducts, we should not lose sight of the fact that the difficulty with these machines always lies in the mechanism for their supply. They require full-length silos, and that is something that cannot be implemented everywhere, and at Joeuf even

less than at Moyeuvre, where the presence of coke ovens directly feeding the furnaces enables one to foresee a diminution in the capacity of the silos.[36]

He was worried about additional expenditure:

We have examined the plans of the new furnaces . . . [From] the advance projects that I saw, it follows that the establishment of two furnaces with skips, on the site of the old boilers, appears possible and even presents certain benefits. But there is an objection to the very large supplementary cost entailed by the shifting of the bundle of ducts that pass from under the rails behind the furnace bellows. The figure of 10 million was put forward, and I am the first to recognize that if the construction of two furnaces should, by the adoption of this project, cost 40 million in place of 30, we need to hesitate greatly before agreeing upon a program entailing equally large supplementary expenses."[37]

The management wanted four trains in the new furnace, while Wendel thought that two would be enough.

There were plenty of bad experiences with new technology in interwar Lorraine, enough to justify Wendel's caution. The specialty steel producer Société des Aciéries Electriques d'Ugine-Uckange used an electrical process to remove phosphorus and sulfur, but was financially destroyed by the depression. The Société Lorraine Minière et Métallurgique de Thionville built an electric Thomas mill to supply the automobile industry, but in 1933 was obliged to dismiss three-quarters of its workforce and went into receivership. The comte de Saintignon and his nephew Amidieu de Clos developed a new process (the Basset process) for the direct reduction of ore in a rotating furnace, which wasted millions of francs in investments. François de Wendel had rejected this process, it later proved rightly, as a fad.[38]

In interwar Lorraine it was the cautious, not the bold, who survived. The Wendel works were of course also badly hit by the Great Depression, but they weathered it. The production of cast iron at Hayange, Moyeuvre, and Joeuf fell from 1,664,000 tons in 1929 to 934,000 in 1932, and the steel output from 1,629,000 to 919,000. The workforce was reduced between 1930 and 1935 from 34,000 to

23,000.[39] Wendel managed to take the strain by selling in late 1932 a large part of the Dutch assets associated with the Oranje-Nassau mine. The most obvious reason for survival was the highly cautious financial management of the company. In 1924–25 the Schneider group had sold its shares in Wendel et Cie. in exchange for shares in the Luxembourg steel producer Arbed, with the result that the Wendel family now controlled both PFFW and Wendel et Cie., with the latter reorganized as a subsidiary of PFFW. There was some borrowing associated with this transaction, financed through a 7 percent 100-million-franc ($3.9 million) bond issue managed by a syndicate headed by the Banque de l'Union Parisienne. In 1928 the firm guaranteed a hard currency loan (20 million Swiss francs, or $3.8 million) to the German mine Friedrich Heinrich at Moers.[40] By this time the Wendels controlled a quite extensive group of holdings: mines (Crepin-Nord, Thivencelles, La Clarence), special ironworks (Forges Tréfileries et Pointereis de Creil), a metals trading company (Etablissement Nozal), and a prospecting company (Compagnie Métallurgique et Minière Franc-Marocaine). Here again, François de Wendel consistently blocked schemes for expansion and urged financial caution. He wrote, for instance, to the director of the German mine: "I know very well that it is better, if one undertakes a program, to realize it quickly and employ all the necessary means immediately; but we are still working out the gains that might be expected, and that is where the demonstration that you claim to have made about the necessity of executing your program immediately is incomplete."[41]

In the wake of the banking crises and financial crises that characterized the depression of the 1930s, the Wendels reasserted their traditional hostility to banks and bank credit. They felt especially vulnerable because of the increased role of banks in controlling much of the competing industry in formerly German Lorraine. Sometimes the family blamed "politics" for the whole economic malaise. Thus Maurice de Wendel noted in 1936:

> I do not believe in the recommended banking dependence, and I believe that the biggest flaw of the financial methods for some years has resulted above all from an often imprudent distribution of credit, an imprudent distribution in which politics had too

> large a part. The financial catastrophes are due to swindles in which political figures found themselves involved, and resulted in the mingling of an equal disapproval for all business, serious or not, good or bad, and we have stopped differentiating with sufficient care between people and companies.[42]

There may well again have been a strong case in the particular context for suspicion of bankers, in an era in which banks were extremely unstable. Like prudence in investment decisions, financial conservatism was eminently defensible in the circumstances of interwar France. The presence of bankers in some instances by itself was a cause of weakness: the Peugeot family business experienced a severe crisis in 1930 largely because two bankers who had been added to the board in order to reorganize the company's finances themselves went bankrupt.[43] In Maurice Druon's fictional account, it was the link with a mysterious foreign financier (based on Ivar Kreuger, the Swedish match king, who killed himself in 1932) that brought down the Schoudler enterprises; but the Wendels avoided such an engagement and such a collapse.

With some recovery in the economy in the late 1930s, the company's management again pressed for expansion, but François de Wendel again was skeptical. He thought that it was better simply to operate the furnaces at full capacity around the clock, even though doing so greatly increased costs because of the wear on the converters. In 1938 he wrote:

> I do not know what the future will bring, but I would be surprised if we were able always to count on selling our product in the favorable conditions of today, which evidently permit the Joeuf works to claim, with a certain semblance of logic, that there is every advantage in principle of running the works at an intensive pace, since the profit showing on sales assures sufficient returns to compensate for the increase in the prices of maintaining the furnace that results from the forced pace.[44]

François de Wendel also rejected the idea of using the controversial Bedaux method for rationalizing and improving labor efficiency through the measurement and control of worker inputs, on account of the high management charges levied by the Bedaux company:

> We shouldn't hope to trust everything to Bedaux; it is an excellent recorder of effort; but it is not a judge of the method of management. The director of the mine remains the animator and the one who should organize the system of management; Bedaux offers him the means of perfecting the organization of his mine. When a mine has been well organized, when, thanks to an active supervision, idle time is reduced as much as possible, one can make a call to Bedaux, who will be the man for the 5 or 10 percent permanent savings . . . It is therefore important to balance the raised rates requested by Bedaux and the benefits that can be taken from his system, in evaluating the suitability of using his engineers.[45]

The managers of the Wendel works were conscious of the conservative business climate and of its costs. The leading metallurgical expert of the Wendel company, Paul Piérard, in 1939 discussed the possibility of a move into stainless steels but came to the conclusion: "The manufacturing . . . would require a complete change in the mentality of the staff and employees, and at all levels the anxiety about the quality of all prices should take the place of the notion of tonnage and the price of output."[46] When in the face of an imminent military threat the Armaments Ministry in November 1939 asked for the production of high-quality steel, Wendel turned it down. The consultant engineer in the ministry, Henri Malcor, was to play a major role in the postwar reconstruction of the French steel industry, and it is unlikely that he forgot his dealings with Wendels in the last years of the Third Republic. A last chance: in the spring of 1940, when the state of metallurgical preparedness was obviously an issue of national importance, Wendel again turned down a government request to produce specialty steel. At this point Piérard noted in a letter to François de Wendel: "If we have sound reasons for declining all manufacturing of so-called specialty steel, it would be useful to show a certain willingness as long as it concerns soft steel like silicon-manganese."[47] It is not surprising that many observers came to the conclusion that the inertness of management was part of a general malaise. A technological reticence that had made business sense in the environment of the late 1920s looked like national vulnerability and even national sabotage by 1939–40.

War Again

On 16 June 1940 advancing German troops reached the Wendel works, and the second military and economic occupation of Lorraine in the twentieth century began. With the defeat of France and the German occupation, the works passed under German management, who wanted to increase production quickly in order to sustain the German armaments economy. In July François and Humbert de Wendel secured a permit to travel to Hayange, and on 12 July the Saar businessman Hermann Röchling met them in Hayange and presented them with an authorization signed by Hermann Göring to take over the works. The Wendels were expelled from Lorraine with forty-eight hours' notice, and on 16 July all the non-Lorraine personnel of French nationality were also expelled. Female members of the Wendel family in Paris, Lyons, and Charente later organized elaborate support systems for the expelled population of Lorraine: Madame Maurice de Wendel in the Union Lorraine (Paris), her daughter Mademoiselle Ségolène de Wendel (the daughter of Maurice) in Lyons with the Union Lorraine and the Red Cross, and another daughter, Baronne Jean Seillière, in Charente with the Centre Social Mosellan. Ségolène was imprisoned by the Germans in 1943.

Over the British radio the Wendel brothers heard the (incorrect) report that their Joeuf works had been sold to the German state in exchange for 50 million Marks' worth of Vereinigte Stahlwerke shares.[48] A memorandum of November 1940 sent from the managers in Hayange to the *gérants* explained:

> The mines have been placed under the technical, administrative, and commercial control of the General Commissar and his colleagues; the companies assure the exploitation of the iron mines belonging to them, under their full financial responsibility. To this end, they are defraying all the expenses, subject to all of their rights to war damage compensation and insofar as the advances on these indemnities would be granted to them by the

> French government, as well as the expenses of exploitation: salaries, wages, material for compensation, equipment . . . Against this the companies freely dispose of the amount coming from the sale of minerals, but the mines commit themselves to constantly maintaining, in a blocked account, an amount equal to one month's salary and wages. The deliveries made in France are payable in French francs and in a French bank under the account of the General Commissar, who in turn will pay the sum total of the account on the mine. The deliveries to foreign countries will be paid in the same manner, after the transfer of amounts coming from the sale of minerals.[49]

The German government proposed, as in the First World War, to sell off the captured works in territory that was to be annexed to the Reich. In 1941 it reached an agreement with the Vichy regime on the "Unfreezing of German Occupation Assets," and there was a flurry of activity as German companies such as the Schorch-Werke Rheydt and the Süddeutsche Drahtindustrie Mannheim tried to buy the confiscated assets.[50] In practice, however, the German ministries largely excluded private companies, and the Hayange works were incorporated into the state-owned steel and engineering complex "Hermann Göring Werke" in March 1941. One month later the German Economics Ministry noted that a final decision on the allocation of the ore fields would be made only after the conclusion of the war, and that Germany was more interested for the moment in access to the ore fields than in the exploitation of the iron- and steelworks of Lorraine.[51]

This attitude reflected the relatively poor technical state of the French industry. During the Second World War the Germans accused the French businesses of having underinvested and neglected their works. There had been, the German complaint went, no substantial investment since the attempted increase in production (under German occupation) during the First World War: "the maintenance of the factories in the same state that the French found them twenty-two years ago is the proof that the matter of economic assimilation was considered after all to be insoluble; the French barely pursued the modernization projects under way that they found in Lorraine."[52] The German engineers, however, also neglected the maintenance of the steel mills and blamed the results on the French and their uncooperative character. For instance, during the firing of the No. 3 blast furnace in Moyeuvre they added material from the top of the converter, and then after the slag solidified needed to use dynamite to remove the calcification. In the Pâtural mill at Hayange, they also used dynamite to remove calcite accumulations and thus damaged the furnace.[53] They were more interested in the potential to produce vanadium from the Lorraine ore (which required very high temperatures and tended to destroy converters), and tended to regard steel as a by-product.[54]

When the priorities changed somewhat in the plans of Munitions Minister Albert Speer for the mobilization of Europe's economic potential, and the German authorities wanted to move production back to France, the French engineers sent to Germany were indeed impressed by the superior technical state of the works. One Wendel engineer reported: "One is struck by the value of the engineers of construction companies such as Gutehoffnungshütte, Demag, Schloemann, Lurgi; their level, their knowledge of the whole world, makes one a little despondent about ever succeeding in competing with such companies in France."[55]

Joeuf was a particular case. As in the First World War, the occupiers made no serious attempt to use the works for the production of iron and steel. The equipment of Joeuf was largely dismantled in late 1942; intended for use in the construction of new steel mills in Russian territories occupied by the German army, it was packed up in forty-two railroad cars. An initial postwar assessment of the damage done in Joeuf was devastating: "Terrible impression of this plant stopped four years ago and stripped of its essential equipment . . . We think that it will be necessary to revise the plan for the reestablishment of the blast furnace at Joeuf."[56] In May 1945 the cost of replacing the missing parts was estimated at 20 million francs, and of repairing the damages at 25 million.[57]

France and French industry had been devastated by war for the second time in thirty years. How could a more satisfactory reconstruction than that of the 1920s be achieved? Many in France now believed that such a project required the transfer of industry to public or state authority, since the principle of family ownership had so signally failed to benefit or even protect France.

Chapter 8

A Family Concern

A very good man . . . the only danger is that he will become too big.

Franz Haniel about Paul Reusch

The twentieth century put heavy strains on the idea of the family and on the family firm. Obviously some of these strains were general German or European developments and not confined to the specific history of the Haniels: increased generational conflict, the shocks of wartime mortality, altered expectations about family existence, distrust of cousin marriage, and a new preference for individualism. These trends had their effects on corporate management and on the form of enterprises. For the Haniels, as the distance in time from the founding patriarch increased, the family expanded and developed a range of artistic and cultural interests quite distinct from the day-to-day concerns of steel and mechanical engineering. Cousin marriage, which had been a vital underpinning of nineteenth-century wealth-preservation strategies, became unfashionable after the First World War. Family firms became more vulnerable.

The Haniels in short followed one part of the classical Buddenbrooks trajectory, away from entrepreneurship and toward culture and patronage. But the shift did not involve any economic decline. The Haniels also started to intermarry with the aristocracy and the military elite of imperial Germany. In the first half of the nineteenth century, marriages had occurred within a bourgeois elite. After 1870 the joint-stock company allowed social ostentation and dissipation without threatening the core of family business. The Kaiserreich enhanced social mobility and a rapprochement with a different sort of elite. Hunting, pistol-shooting, horseracing, art collecting, even bohemianism, became fashionable business pursuits.[1] One family member, for instance, Julius Haniel's younger daughter, Elsa, married not one but two aristocrats: first the owner of a Mecklenburg estate, Fritz von Michael, and after his death Count Franz von Waldersee. She developed an interest in the dissident nonchurch Protestantism of Johannes Müller and paid for the creation of a large retreat center at Schloss Elmau, near Garmisch. Gerhard von Haniel-Niethammer became a painter and studied after 1908 with the leading German impressionist Lovis Corinth; after the First World War he moved to France. There were more Haniels who indulged their tastes for horses (Richard Haniel, Julius Haniel's only son, had a well-known "Stall Haniel" before the First World War) and for big houses. John Haniel had a magnificent estate at Landonvillers, near Metz, and was frequently invited by his neighbor, Kaiser Wilhelm II, who every May stayed in nearby Urville. Eventually John was ennobled. Haniels were moving away from strictly business interests, not least because there were too many of them for all to be involved in the management of a family firm.

On top of all these purely and characteristically familiar strains came the costs of increased taxation, then the monetary and political instability that accompanied the First World War, and the ensuing German experiments with democracy and then with dictatorship.

In addition, there were technical developments that required quick business responses, though this was much less the case in the first half of the twentieth century, when there was surprisingly little change in European steelmaking technology, than in the second half of the century, when the technological imperative for corporate change became much clearer. But the challenges of bigness and diversification were constants throughout the century. It is on this basis that Alfred D. (du Pont) Chandler came to a striking but misleading characterization of the role of German families in early twentieth-century business life. The Krupps, Klöckners, Flicks, and

Haniels in his view now played a much-reduced role because "they managed a larger number of companies with a greater variety of activities than did leading American industrial families such as the du Ponts and Mertons."[2] In fact the German dynasties remained quite powerful, but they realized that they needed to diversify in order to distribute or reduce risk.

The consequence of these circumstances was that the history of the family business became fundamentally a history of organizational response to both the changing character of ownership and the dynamics of the market. As a result the history of the Haniel businesses in the first half of the twentieth century is much less a history of the Haniel family involvement than of the activities of two very powerful and influential general managers, Paul Reusch in the GHH and Johann Welker in Franz Haniel & Cie. GmbH (FHC). As the branding of a corporation became an essential part of business strategy, the business established a new corporate identity quite distinct from the tradition of the family enterprise. In developing a new image, the GHH emphasized its engineering skills and its global markets rather than its ownership. The rather lavish commemorative histories of the time barely mention the Haniel family except as a feature of a distant past. Corporate culture meant technology, not family. It was only after the Second World War that the family again asserted itself and intervened as the economic and industrial structure of Germany was being recast.

Paul Reusch and the GHH

The making of the new brand of corporation in Germany was often the result of the actions of powerful and charismatic general managers, rather than owners. Franz Haniel commented of Paul Reusch that he was "a very good man . . . the only danger is that he will become too big."[3] Reusch came from Swabia and had worked as a metallurgical engineer, at first in the Habsburg empire, in Tyrol, Budapest, and Vitkovice, and then as the director of a Krupp ironworks at Mülheim.[4] After the retirement of Carl Lueg as general manager of the GHH at the end of 1903, there was an unsatisfactory interlude of a year when a scion of one of the founding dynasties, Hugo Jacobi, succeeded him; another director, Gottfried Ziegler, did little from 1905 to 1909. And then came Reusch. As GHH gen-

19. *Paul Reusch, 1868–1956*

COURTESY OF FRANZ HANIEL & CIE. GMBH, DUISBURG-RUHRORT

eral manager, Reusch immediately set about transforming the GHH into a *Konzern:* an integrated empire of vertically linked companies that stretched from the traditional Haniel focus in coal mining, iron, and water transportation into steel processing, shipbuilding, mechanical engineering, and the production of machine tools. In the course of this enlargement he also shifted the geographic focus to southern Germany (whose industrial landscape he knew very well) for mechanical engineering, and to coastal locations for the major new shipbuilding business.

This development of the GHH into a widely diversified business, which required guidance and management from the center, but not tight control, was not driven by any big development in technology. The technology of steelmaking and mining had been completely transformed in the third quarter of the nineteenth century. Thereafter companies grew larger but applied the same basic processes: Siemens-Martin and Bessemer for steelmaking and, where necessary, the Gilchrist-Thomas process for phosphoric ores.

The new push was initially an organizational response to the increased organization and cartelization of German heavy industry, in particular to the practices of the Rhenish-Westphalian Coal Syndicate, and then the Steelworks Association (Stahlwerksverband) which at first covered only very standardized products, so-called

"A" products, semifinished steel, railroad material, and structural steel, where there could be little differentiation and prices were hence easy to set. When the Steelworks Association was renewed in 1907, so-called "B" products (rolled iron, merchant bars, wire, steel plate, forged and cast piece steel), whose prices could not be easily set as there were too many gradations of quality, were subject to syndicalization. The cartel now set production quotas. Since cartels limited sales on the domestic market, any attempt to expand would require the purchase of new plants and the negotiation of new production quotas, or the increased utilization of products within the company for further manufacturing, or an export offensive. Most companies chose some combination of all three strategies, but all raised difficulties for a family firm. On the eve of the First World War the GHH was not one of the largest giants of the German steel industry; indeed it had a smaller share of the German steel market than the Wendels.[5] In 1912–13 it had only the eighth largest quota in the Steelworks Association, while Wendel was in seventh position.[6] The choice to move more into finished products and engineering unambiguously derived from the firm's tradition (in 1803 and 1806 the St. Antoni and Gute Hoffnung ironworks had started to supply parts for steam engines, and this engagement soon evolved into the Sterkrade engineering works). By the beginning of the twentieth century vertical integration had evolved into a powerful business imperative.

The push toward *Konzern*-building became much greater with the monetary disequilibria of the First World War and postwar inflation and then hyperinflation. Since for long periods real interest rates were negative, access to finance from banks or the central bank could be a way of building business empires very quickly. Such was the model offered by Reusch's great rival, the most prominent and indeed most notorious business man of the inflation era, Hugo Stinnes.[7] The availability of cheap finance also offered apparently attractive inducements to older firms to surrender their independence.

Dramatic changes in labor relations also affected the choice of business strategy. In the first decade of the twentieth century, greatly increased radicalization offered a profound challenge to the firm's traditional and paternalist approach. Then, during the First World War, military conscription changed the composition of the

20. *Prisoners of war at GHH, First World War*

COURTESY OF FRANZ HANIEL & CIE. GMBH, DUISBURG-RUHRORT

workforce. The Gelsenkirchen works of the GHH, for instance, lost half of its workforce to military service and from 1914 began to employ women in the thick-wire department. Sterkrade, which was converted almost entirely to munitions production, eventually employed 3,000 workers. Beginning in March 1915 the rolling mills in Neu Oberhausen and the iron foundry in Oberhausen employed prisoners of war (POWs), whose presence was advertised by a notice: "From next week prisoners of war will be employed in our works. We are confident that our staff and workers will take the attitude appropriate to a German to our imprisoned foes, and that they will avoid not only any confidences, but also any insults or mocking. Every contact that is not strictly related to business is to be avoided. Particularly we warn against any assistance to flight, by giving clothes, money, or food. Violations will be punished with imprisonment of up to three years." By 1917–18 the Oberhausen mills employed 950 German males, 180 German females, 32 recruited Belgians, 25 Greeks, and 360 POWs (including 142 Frenchmen,

123 Russians and Ukrainians, 41 British, 32 Portuguese, 13 Italians, and 9 Belgians). From 1917 civilian prisoners were also employed in the coal mines and in the Sterkrade munitions works.[8]

After the war the revolutionary wave of labor radicalism encouraged a strategy of widely dispersed production instead of concentration in a few core plants. For the GHH, the *Konzern*-building phase occurred in a relatively short fifteen-year period of exceptional political and economic instability, between Reusch's appointment as general director in 1909 and the end of the German inflation (November 1923). Reusch followed a well-articulated philosophy: he sought majority participations (that is, at least 51 percent) in the firms that were brought into the concern, but he was prepared to leave a fair measure of management autonomy and even welcomed the idea of some limited form of competition between different parts of the GHH empire. Such autonomy fitted well with the overall idea of spreading risk more widely.

The Vertical Empire

The reorganization of business life provoked something of a crisis in the family firm tradition that still dominated a large part of even the German heavy industrial landscape. Many of the firms that Reusch took into the GHH were themselves family firms that had reached the end of their expansive capability. They had adapted reasonably successfully to many of the business dictates of the late nineteenth century, which pointed in the direction of professionalized management and away from tight family control; but they could not deal with the uncertainties and vicissitudes of the major variations in relative prices and the sudden collapsing and opening of new markets, and then a new cycle of collapse during the war and the inflation. There are obvious analogies with the Italian creation of joint-stock companies such as the AFL at this time, which likewise took into an encompassing embrace previously independent family firms.

The early twentieth century led to a great culling of the stock of German family businesses. Dealing with these firms and their owners obviously required a degree of negotiating and psychological finesse, by means of which proud owner-managers were to be converted into managers of parts of the large overall GHH structure.

As a result the categories of owner and salaried manager became rather blurred. Some of the old owners were happy with this outcome; others were extremely resistant. In such cases the transformation usually occurred by means of several cautious steps.

In 1910–1912 the GHH bought a family-owned wire producer, Drahtwerk Boecker & Comp., a limited partnership *(Kommanditgesellschaft)* owned by several families. Initially the GHH signed a contract with Hermann Boecker for a nine-year period in which the GHH would supply Boecker, and in return the owners of Boecker were to be compensated in line with the dividends paid out by the GHH. Over the next two years the shares of Boecker were sold in stages to the GHH, and Hermann Boecker became a deputy member of the GHH management board.

Other GHH purchases were drawn out over a much longer time. In 1911 the tinplate-producing Altenhundemer Walz- und Hammerwerk GmbH, which was half owned by Hugo Schmitz of Hagen, expressed interest in some kind of association with a producer of basic iron and steel products in order to secure its supply of iron and to stabilize prices. At the time the full sale went through, in 1918, the GHH explained: "The ambition of the larger works has already for some years gone in the direction of finished production. We, too, are not blind to that necessity."[9] A wire factory in Osnabrück, owned by the Witte and Kämper families, but in the form of a joint-stock company, had started an ambitious rationalization and expansion program in 1912 that required a large bond issue. In 1914 the GHH secured a contract to supply up to 18,000 tons of raw rolled wire to Osnabrück. The company expanded further during the war and in 1919 was finally sold to the GHH.

Taking over existing businesses was not the only way of expanding, although it was certainly the easiest. An alternative was to build new sectors from scratch, in some cases in cooperation with other large German companies with particular technical specializations. Reusch was a driving force in the foundation of the shipyard Deutsche Werft in the last months of the First World War (June 1918). To a large measure this expansion into ship construction was driven simply by the wish to secure sales of the product of the existing Sterkrade bridge-building and engineering plant—particularly when the peace settlement would obviously bring completely altered circumstances on the German and international markets. But the Deutsche Werft clearly created an initial engagement in a branch of business, and further investment would be needed in order to follow up the opportunities. Thus, for instance, shipbuilding involved a large-scale consumption of rivets, which the GHH did not produce before 1918. From 1919 to 1924 Reusch consequently bought up in gradual stages the Westphalian rivetworks (Nietenfabrik) Ludwig Möhling, owned by four brothers Möhling. The relationship began as a lease, with an option to purchase, which was eventually taken up.

The most significant geographic extension of the GHH was, however, not to the seacoast, but into the mechanical engineering businesses of southern Germany, and occurred after the First World War. This push may have been driven by Reusch's Swabian background and interests, though it is striking that a substantial number of Haniels had begun to move to Bavaria, and especially to Munich and to the upper Isar valley, to the south of Munich. There was also a much more obvious political reason: after 1919 and especially with the Ruhr occupation of 1923, works in the Rhineland were directly threatened by France. By the late summer of 1923, Reusch and Haniels were terrified that the German government was on the point of collapse and that it would hand over the keys to German industry to France. In a nervous letter, Reusch told August Haniel (the chairman of the supervisory board from 1916 to 1921 and the son of Alphons Haniel, from the Gerhard Haniel family line): "The developments of the last weeks have caused me many worried hours . . . Stresemann is the chancellor of capitulation. The chancellor speaks, and his social democratic ministers act and will soon force him to deal directly with France. With the present political orientation of the current cabinet the outcome of the negotiations can only be unfavorable . . . If the present cabinet capitulates to the French, it must be reckoned that French ownership will be forced on the enterprises lying in the occupied area."[10] Consequently, the GHH was reorganized (November 1923) with the Gutehoffnungshütte Oberhausen AG controlling works in the occupied area, while a Gutehoffnungshütte Aktienverein acted as a holding company for a much more geographically and also technologically dispersed group of companies.[11]

The first object of Reusch's move on the southern front was the

Eisenfabrik Nürnberg AG vorm. J. Tafel & Co., a family firm established by the Tafels, but with a large shareholding by Theodor von Cramer-Klett (of the engineering firm Maschinenfabrik Augsburg-Nürnberg AG, or MAN). It produced steel rods from scrap, but found it difficult in the postwar period to secure a reliable supply of coal. In 1919 the GHH took over the company and placed Bavarian members of the Haniel family on the supervisory board. Its manager, Lambert Jessen, became a key figure in Reusch's extension of the GHH into southern Germany.

In 1920 the GHH participated in a capital increase of the Fritz Neumeyer AG, a Munich engineering works whose products ranged from cables and detonators to sewing machines.

The Maschinenfabrik Esslingen, one of the oldest and most significant Württemberg engineering companies, had begun as a locomotive building company in 1846 with a state participation. After the war it faced a serious capital shortage, and the capital increase of 1920 provided an opportunity for the GHH to become involved. The GHH also bought up stock on the exchange, and by May 1923 owned over 50 percent of the company, while a Dutch GHH subsidiary, the N. V. Rollo, held another 25 percent. The company's managers explained the takeover in the following terms: "the public's propensity to purchase industrial products has receded."[12]

The most dramatic (and often-narrated) GHH takeover in southern Germany involved a prolonged struggle with the Haniels' rival on the Ruhr, Hugo Stinnes.[13] The object of this clash of corporate titans was a family firm that was itself built out of mergers: the Maschinenfabrik Augsburg, run since the 1840s by the Buz family, and a Nuremberg enterprise created also in the 1840s and incorporated in 1873 as the Maschinenbau-Actiengesellschaft Nürnberg (or MAN). MAN had been built up into a major enterprise by Theodor Cramer, a relative of its founder, Johann Friedrich Klett, who added the Klett name to his own. When he died in 1884, his son (also Theodor Cramer-Klett) had little interest in a direct business involvement and turned to artistic patronage, hunting, and some involvement in beer-brewing in Hohenaschau, along with the management of a picturesque railroad branch line from Prien, on the Chiemsee, to Aschau. In short, the son was a catastrophic businessman. Under a dynamic general manager, Anton Rieppel, however, the enterprise did very well, and in 1898 merged to produce a company that would eventually be called the Maschinenfabrik Augsburg-Nürnberg AG (also MAN). It manufactured the first diesel engine. Heinrich Buz, from the Augsburg family, was the first general director.

After the war MAN tried to forge a strategic alliance with a major heavy industrial producer. Rieppel thought that an isolated secondary producer, even a very dynamic one, could not achieve a sustainable position. In 1920 he became convinced that the best chance of a rescue would come from the most dynamic of German inflation-era businessmen, Hugo Stinnes. Stinnes had just formed the gigantic Rhein-Elbe Union between his Deutsch-Luxemburgische Bergwerks- und Hütten AG and the Gelsenkirchener Bergwerke AG (18 August 1920) and was set to expand further (and to threaten the GHH's position). Rieppel justified his stance by a contrast of Reusch and Stinnes: "Stinnes differs from Reusch only in his manners and customs. He is cleverer, clearer in his goals, and emphasizes his power less and tries to convince of the necessity of his proposals and intentions."[14]

At a meeting of the supervisory board of Eisenwerk Nürnberg, which had been an important supplier to MAN, Reusch and Karl Haniel told Cramer-Klett (whom they recognized as the weak link in the MAN armor) that they regretted the negotiations with Stinnes and would like the GHH to move to a closer relation with MAN. This initiative would obviously involve going behind the back of the powerful MAN general director, Rieppel. Gerald Feldman characterized Reusch's approach in the following way: "Reusch was not the romantic type. He approached his prize with threats and won it by entering through the back door."[15]

Reusch visited Cramer-Klett in September 1920 and tried to lure him with a vision of stable prices and stable supplies in an age of obvious uncertainty. At the same time, he warned Cramer-Klett of the perils of working with Stinnes:

> Because of the large rise in raw material and semifinished costs, heavy industry is currently in a substantially better position than manufacturing industry. Almost the entire engineering industry in particular is in great difficulties because of the exceptional increase in the value of its inventories. The consequence is that if in the present conditions an engineering firm fuses with a steel

> company or makes a community of interest, the engineering partner will necessarily make out worse, since current conditions will necessarily be taken into account in setting the price for the merger. I personally, were I a representative of manufacturing industry, would never undertake a marriage with heavy industry in the present times, in which the profits would be merged for all times or for a substantial period. It will also one day be the other way round, and manufacturing will be in a better position than heavy industry.[16]

On the basis of this approach, Cramer-Klett gradually worked out conditions for a sale that would lead the GHH to take a one-third stake in MAN. While these negotiations were taking place, banks began to buy MAN shares, and Lambert Jessen, who had persuaded Reusch to visit Cramer-Klett in the first place, reported that Rieppel was encouraging Stinnes to launch a raid.

In October 1920 the MAN directors had three alternatives. The most limited was to concentrate on the core south German business and to sell a plant in Duisburg to Rheinstahl; the more radical options involved *Konzern*-building through a link with either Stinnes (who appeared to be more predatory and less family oriented) or the GHH. But Cramer-Klett, who was very worried that he might be outmaneuvered by the north German giants, quickly moved on his own initiative, fearing that Stinnes was behind the big bank purchase of MAN shares—a supposition that Oscar Schlitter of Deutsche Bank and Franz Urbig of the Disconto-Gesellschaft rejected. On 24 October 1920 Cramer-Klett met Reusch in Frankfurt and offered to sell a large quantity of shares to the Haniels, a move that would allow him and the Haniels to dominate the MAN supervisory board, and then agree on the liaison with the GHH. The attraction of the Haniels lay in their character as a family business.

Some of the bankers—notably Urbig—warned MAN that it was getting a poor deal, and on 7 November Cramer-Klett again met with Reusch, this time at Reusch's Württemberg estate at Katharinenhof, and agreed to an arrangement that included the sale of the Duisburg works to Rheinstahl and a higher price to be paid by the GHH for the stock.

The arrangement remained controversial. At the general meeting of MAN on 15 December 1920, which was required for the constitution of a new supervisory board including Reusch, Karl Haniel, and the Swiss financier Carl Winkler, there was a substantial attack by a shareholder linked to the Stinnes interest, who protested that Rieppel was not present to defend an alternative vision of the future of MAN. Reusch was quite aware that he had outmaneuvered Stinnes in what he saw unambiguously as a struggle for power within German industry. He now wrote to Jessen: "Stinnes is well informed about the power relations and will draw his conclusions."[17]

At the beginning of 1921, now controlling 36 percent of the capital of MAN, the GHH set about reducing the influence of Winkler and of the American financiers behind him and his plan. Reusch wrote to Jessen: "I see that without ownership of the majority of the share capital that influence on the management is not to be achieved which would be needed to push the management in the right direction."[18]

The MAN statutes did not allow one shareholder to vote more than 500 shares in a general meeting, so the GHH distributed its shares among its affiliates in order to exercise control. In southern Germany, the new ownership was often interpreted as a victory of the big over the small, and of the north over the south. Cramer-Klett himself was rapidly disillusioned about his new and rather short-lived friendship with Reusch, and was obviously quite unsuited to be a managerial cog in the giant GHH machine. In November 1921 he wrote a bitter and provocative but influential article in the *Münchener Zeitung* with the title "The Line of the River Main as an Industrial Demarcation" ("Die industrielle Mainlinie"):

> Under all circumstances, however, the big difference between north and south German industry has become clearly evident as a result of the close association of the two works. This difference, as well as the circumstance that the more powerful sister in the north has taken such very different principles, creates a regret that is deeper because over the last fifty years development has made Germany into an industrial state. It cannot be a matter of indifference for us Germans that such a powerful factor in our national life has quite different views from the rest of the German people.[19]

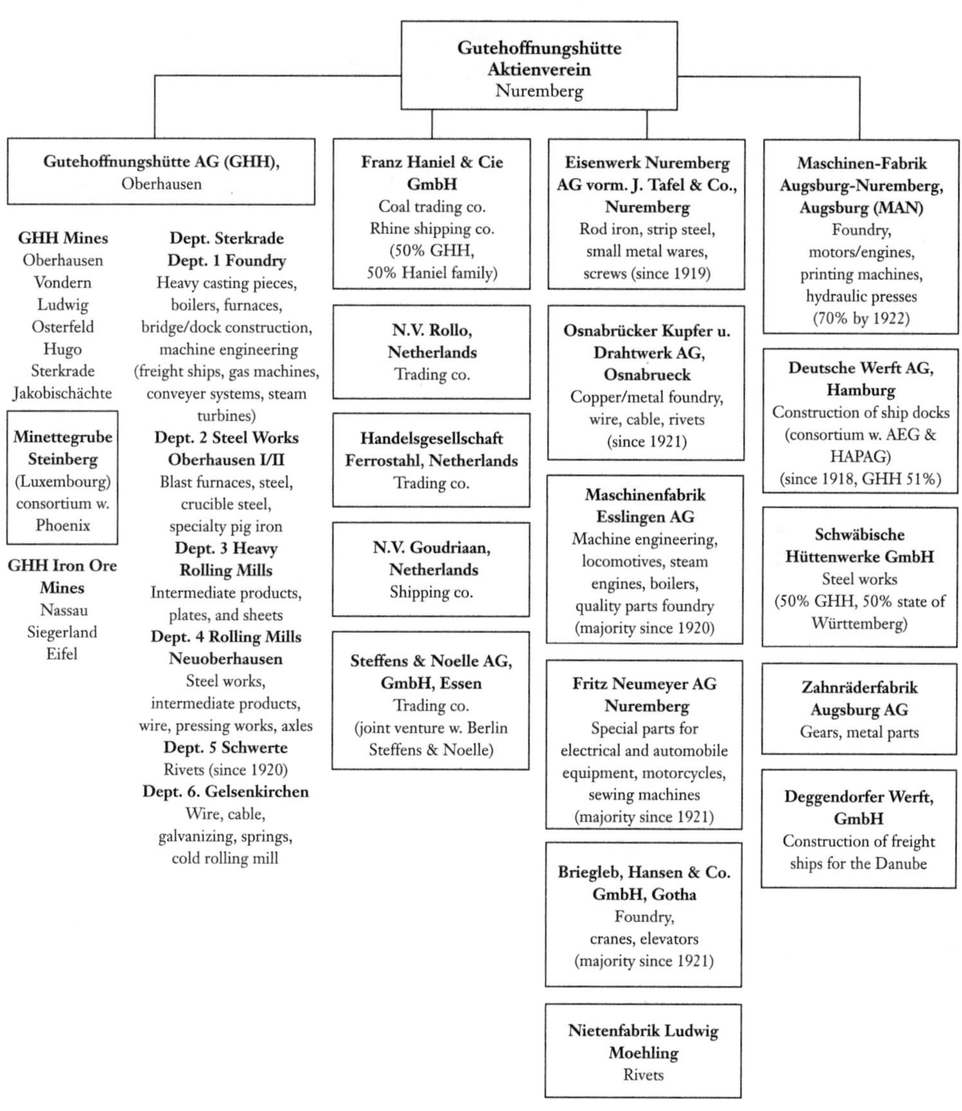

21. *The GHH Konzern in the 1920s*

SOURCE: ARNOLD TROSS, DER AUFBAU DER EISEN- UND EISENVERARBEITENDEN INDUSTRIE-KONZERNE DEUTSCHLANDS [BERLIN: J. SPRINGER, 1923], PP. 48–57; HAROLD WIXFORTH, BANKEN UND SCHWERINDUSTRIE IN DER WEIMARER REPUBLIK [COLOGNE: BÖHLAU, 1995], PP. 124–170

The first attempt to delineate systematically who would produce which product within the *Konzern* occurred in March 1921. MAN, for instance, agreed that it would no longer build high-pressure piston compressors, which would be produced only in Esslingen.[20] From October 1921 there were regular *Konzern* meetings, usually held in a new and opulent meeting center (modestly called the Werksgasthaus) in Oberhausen. The first meeting was intended to end overlapping activities of sales representatives.[21] Karl Haniel as the chairman of the supervisory board (from 1921 to 1944) regularly attended these meetings, along with Reusch. A basic principle was laid out in 1922 that the works that formed part of the *Konzern* should buy where conditions were best, but if similar offers were made they should make purchases within the *Konzern*. If a plant received an inquiry that it could not supply, it should pass on the request to the *Konzern* office in Sterkrade.[22] Also in 1922 an office for the establishment of norms throughout the *Konzern* was established in Nuremberg.

In fact the major parts of the *Konzern* sold relatively little to other parts of the GHH, and the proportions actually declined. Thus in 1924 the GHH AG sold 7.2 percent of its production to other parts of the GHH Aktienverein, and in 1926 6.0 percent. MAN sold 3.3 percent and 2.0 percent.[23]

One major function of the *Konzern* was to allow the central management to make comparative judgments about financial performance. A standardized system of reporting was established as early as December 1921. By the late 1920s, Reusch was treating the general meetings of *Konzern* managers as a sort of grading exercise. Looking back on the results of 1928, for instance, he complained that sales per employee had not risen sufficiently. Only in two works (MAN-Augsburg and Eisenwerk Nürnberg) had sales risen by more than the cost of living. The engineering shop in Cannstatt (a subsidiary of the Maschinenfabrik Esslingen) and the old GHH works in Sterkrade, on the other hand, were pilloried as having had the worst results.[24]

Internationalization

Reusch's ambitions were not limited simply to making the GHH a powerful enterprise across the whole of the German industrial landscape, from the North Sea to the Alps. The new orientation of business also involved an internationalization, again in two waves. Before the First World War, the main worry of Reusch and the GHH, as well as of the other large German iron producers, was to get access to raw materials. This involved at first an expansion in Lorraine (part of the German empire) in 1906–07, with iron mines near the Luxembourg border (a jointly owned operation with Phönix, the Konzession Gustav Wiesner). In 1912 the GHH began preparations to build an ironworks nearby, at Monhofen, near Diedenhofen (Thionville). But the search for ore to feed the German iron and steel industry also went to North Africa, Brazil, and, in Europe, to Sweden and Normandy. In France, at a time of a sharp deterioration of international relations, in 1911 the GHH bought four-fifths of the capital of the Société des Mines de Fer de Barbery, a mining company to the south of Caen, and established the Société des Mines de Fer d'Urville, which was operated through a holding company that soon afterward acquired 70 percent of the share capital of Société des Mines de Fer de la Basse-Normandie.

After the war, Germany's assets in France were sequestered as part of the reparations settlement. The major interest of the GHH was now less to secure raw materials than to find sales outlets for a period in which business was unlikely to grow as quickly as it had before the war. Contacts in neutral countries, above all in the Netherlands and in Switzerland, also appeared to offer some protection against the political turbulence of postwar Germany, as well as against higher rates of corporate taxation. The most important GHH acquisitions were in the Netherlands. The first was a Dutch trading company bought by the GHH in 1920, the N. V. Goederntransport Maatschappij Rollo, of Dordrecht. Its main office was moved to The Hague, and after 1923 it became a central holding company for the GHH's foreign assets, since they were threatened in the aftermath of the French occupation of the Ruhr. Anxious to find new markets, in 1921 the GHH acquired part of N. V. Algemeene Ijzer- en Staal-Maatschappij "Ferrostaal," which had been founded as a collaborative venture between the German Metallgesellschaft and a company in The Hague. There were three GHH representatives on its supervisory board, including Paul Reusch and Karl Haniel. This was a trading company, whose aim was to represent the GHH as a sales organization all over the world; it formed a substantive rival to the Rhine shipping activities of FHC.

The attentions of the GHH were not focused entirely on Europe. The previously lucrative Asian market was affected by the civil war in China, but the GHH wanted to expand sales in the Western Hemisphere. In 1925 the GHH debated establishing an office in the United States, less in order to secure U.S. markets than to arrange the financing for orders from Central and South America.[25]

Reusch's empire had been largely consolidated during the volatile and unstable years of the German inflation and hyperinflation. But other corporate developments of that era had been even faster and bigger. In particular, Reusch saw his business style as a contrast to that of Hugo Stinnes, undoubtedly the best-known German businessman of the inflation period. It would have been possible to expand more quickly on the basis of companies buying companies that then took a holding in the parent company, and thereby provided further possibilities for expansion (*Verschachtelung*, the principle that underlay the creation of twentieth-century Italian "capitalism without capital"). For Reusch, such a financing strategy was inherently unstable, and he felt vindicated by the collapse of the Stinnes business empire after Hugo Stinnes' unexpected death in 1924. Reusch in fact tried to avoid debt even at the height of the hyperinflation, when the attraction of debt with highly negative real interest rates might have been overpowering for any ordinarily ambitious business executive. But he was obviously aware of the possibility or even likelihood of a sudden and dramatic credit crunch that would follow any attempt at stabilization. Thus in September 1923 he reported to August Haniel on his precautions: "Obtaining money was difficult, but up to now was possible. There is for the moment no worry about the existence of the *Konzern* works. Most of them managed up to now with no debt. The few that were obliged to take up debt in order to pay the increased wages and salaries stand on strong foundations. In order to reduce expenditure, I have ordered a reduction of work, despite the high level of orders."[26]

When the inflation ended, many less conservatively managed enterprises were vulnerable, and offered an opportunity for new GHH expansion. Several more business partnerships expanded

GHH's reach: for instance, an agreement in 1927 with Carl Linde Eismaschinen demarcated the distribution of refrigeration equipment between the GHH's Esslingen works, which would concentrate on industrial equipment, and Linde, which would deal more with small-scale and domestic applications.[27]

But even under Reusch's more conservative methods, once the inflation was over the issue remained how to raise the new capital required for business expansion. At the end of 1923, with stabilization of the Mark imminent, the GHH asked Deutsche Bank for hard-currency loans: £50,000 and $100,000.[28]

After the currency stabilization, GHH production increased rapidly, with a considerable amount of new investment. In the business year 1927–28, for the first time in its history, it produced more than a million tons of pig iron. The order books continued to expand until March 1930, when much of German industry was already in recession.[29] In the older Oberhausen works, the three blast furnaces without modern diagonal lifts were demolished. In 1925 new ventilation machines improved the supply of oxygen, and from 1926 the furnace gases were processed through a new clearing system for reuse in heating. Beginning in 1927 the slag was used in cement production. Output per manhour in the Oberhausen ironworks rose from 0.125 ton (1913–14) to 0.162 (1927–28), and in the rolling mill from 0.057 ton to 0.071 over the same period.[30] But these increases lagged behind wage rises, and both managers and workers easily assumed that the pay levels were determined by politics rather than by market pressures.

Most of the financing of the late 1920s improvements was self-financed. There was, however, a relatively modest $10 million bond issue in 1925, placed in the United States through two of the banks that were most active in developing central European business, Lee Higginson and Harriman. In 1931–32 long-term debt amounted to a relatively small share (33.8 percent) of the company's capital.[31]

As in the prewar era, the GHH saw a link between domestic cartelization and its ability to supply foreign markets. In 1924 the former steel cartel was reconstituted as the Rohstahlgemeinschaft. From 1925 cartel regulations applied to "A" products and wire but also to "B" products: rods, sheets, and pipes. For the engineering products of the GHH, foreign markets were vital. The Sterkrade engineering works built bridges for Argentina, China, and Peru, and floating docks for Bordeaux, Rouen, and the Yugoslav navy, as well as for the reequipment of Belgian and French canals. A substantial part of the GHH sales went into exports: 34 percent in 1925–26, falling with the German domestic recovery to 25 percent in 1927–28, but rising steeply again with the onset of the depression, to 49 percent in 1930–31. The GHH responded to the logic of these figures in cartel politics, struggling to reduce the rebates given by steel producers to steel-consuming German exporters in order to retain the internal cost advantages of a substantial level of vertical integration.

The international environment generated a constant pressure on costs. Thus there was no major poststabilization return to profitability; but neither was there a major financial crisis of the type that destroyed Stinnes and required a major reorganization of Krupp in 1925 and, among other steel producers, prompted the creation of the Vereinigte Stahlwerke in 1926 (by the Rheinelbe-Union, Thyssen, Phönix, and Rheinstahl).[32] In part, the explanation lies in the more diversified character of the GHH concern. But the GHH still felt financially vulnerable. In November 1928 the GHH, along with other Rhenish-Westphalian works, imposed a lockout after the unions demanded a general increase of 15 pfennigs per hour; an arbitration award allowing a 6-pfennig increase was imposed as a binding decree by the Reich labor minister.

Since the economic conditions for business activity were increasingly being set by political decisions, Reusch came to the conclusion that businessmen would have to become more political in order to survive. He took a quite common view to its logical conclusion. In fact one way of understanding the peculiarities of the Weimar economy is as a struggle for rents in which businesses were likely to divert their attention from looking for technical innovation to pursuing innovation in rent-seeking strategies. They became political rather than technical entrepreneurs. Paul Reusch had made himself into a major political figure in the struggle against government interventions in the labor market, and had formulated the slogan: "Leave Business Alone for Once!"[33]

The Family and the Business

Even as he made the GHH into a national and indeed international *Konzern*, Reusch preserved the GHH as a family enterprise, controlled by the Haniel family. The continuing family ownership inevitably involved quite considerable strains and tensions, whose resolution required the building of strategic alliances between the management (Reusch) and particular members of an increasingly large and dispersed family. Reusch worked closely, and exceptionally harmoniously, first with Franz Haniel, then with August Haniel, and finally with Karl Haniel. All of these three leading family members trusted Reusch completely, even if they had doubts about specific parts of the Reusch strategy. Such collaboration might be expected to have been very problematical, since Reusch had an imperious temperament and did not conceive of himself as anyone's employee, let alone steward.

While Franz Haniel (the grandson of the first Franz Haniel, and the son of Hugo) was alive, it was impossible for the GHH to manage its own distribution, since there was a completely parallel Haniel company (FHC) that managed predominantly waterborne coal transportation. In February 1916 Reusch suggested to Franz Haniel that FHC should work with the Vereinigte Frankfurter Rheedereien GmbH and in this way develop a closer association with the GHH. But the reorganization came only after Franz Haniel's death (16 June 1916), when the young Alfred Haniel returned to Germany from a military career (on the front and then in the control of the Belgian coal industry). He pushed for the reorganization of the Haniel enterprises along the lines suggested by Reusch.

The new company, FHC GmbH, was established with a nominal capital of one million Marks, of which the GHH took 42 percent, and the three Haniel-owned collieries (developed by the first Franz Haniel) the rest: Gewerkschaft Rheinpreussen, 25 percent; Gewerkschaft Zollverein, 20.5 percent; and the Gewerkschaft Neumühl, 12 percent, with 0.5 percent held by Dr. Franz Haniel. This company leased the facilities of both the old FHC and the Vereinigte Frankfurter Rheedereien GmbH. There was thus a shareholding association between the GHH and the Haniel trading company, but the new FHC retained a substantial independence, unlike all the other previously family-controlled firms that the GHH was taking over in its push for expansion. FHC representatives as well as members of the Haniel family attended all the *Konzern* meetings, but FHC was not listed as part of the *Konzern*, and its results were treated separately.[34] This degree of separation of the GHH and FHC laid the foundation for later trouble.

The Haniel family members that Reusch liked and dealt with were in general even more conservative than he. In 1921 August Haniel had worried that the new creation was too dependent on the personality of Reusch. The extension of the enterprise and its southern German expansion would be in danger of a "disintegration," "when the leading forces are one day no longer at the rudder."[35] Reusch replied confidently: "On the contrary, I am of the opinion that our connections that we sought with finished product producers will bring great advantages to the main work. Cyclical fluctuations will appear much less important to us than to other works, because the finishing factories secure sales for our production to a much greater extent than for any other rival firm."[36] This statement is a neat explanation of the theory of risk dispersion for a family holding company, and it almost certainly had its desired effect in satisfying August Haniel's anxiety. If the family could be secure about adequately diversified investments, financed on a solid basis, it would not be so dependent on the business genius of Reusch.

With Karl Haniel the relationship was even more pleasant. At the beginning of each new year, they exchanged cordial greetings. Early on in their relationship, at the end of 1922, Karl Haniel wrote to Reusch: "But I believe that we both do not require many words, we understand each other as it is, and we are yoked by the same understanding and the same goal of the good of the work that has been entrusted to us, and of the welfare of the whole."[37] Reusch still needed to ensure that Karl Haniel remained cheerful. The best way of doing this was to keep up regular supplies of fine wine (in part from vineyards on the GHH's own estates), which provided an effective lubricant of a business and a personal relationship.

Karl Haniel also gave advice and encouragement to Reusch. In June 1926, for instance, he wrote to congratulate the manager on a trip to the United States, since "I am convinced that your trip will be useful for the mutual understanding of two such economically dynamic nations."[38] Reusch also saw that he needed to encourage and shape the attitudes of a younger generation of Haniels. Thus, twelve years after Paul Reusch's U.S. visit, his own son, Hermann, who was by now a member of the managing board of the GHH, wrote about the appropriate education of Karl Haniel's son Klaus. But Hermann was skeptical about the potential benefits of a U.S. trip, noting that the United States had nothing to teach about mining, and that the language spoken would not be useful either. "Klaus should not imagine that he will learn perfect English in America. A terrible dialect is spoken there, which it is better not to acquire, unless one has previously secured a good pronunciation in England."[39]

Karl Haniel remained substantially in the shadows, though he took a prominent public role as a representative of heavy industry. He had spent a large part of his early life as a Prussian civil servant, and in 1914 moved into the occupation regime for Belgium as president of the civil administration of Hennegau (Mons). In 1917 he became the chief administrator of Wallonia. With the end of the war he left the civil service and devoted himself to Haniel business interests and to public representation. In 1928 he became chairman of the Industrieclub in Düsseldorf, which held regular meetings at the Parkhotel to which prominent or interesting speakers were invited. He was present at the most famous or infamous of these sessions, that of 26 January 1932, when the Nazi leader Adolf Hitler gave a two-and-a-half-hour-long exposition of a carefully tailored version of Nazi ideology; but the introduction was made by the mayor of Düsseldorf and a rapturous commentary presented by Fritz Thyssen.[40] Karl Haniel's souvenir of the meeting was a letter from Hitler politely declining an invitation to a more intimate dinner. A subsequent speech, which might have been almost as significant, by former chancellor Franz von Papen, was scheduled for 2 February 1933 but was canceled "because of an alternative commitment of the lecturer" (he had just become vice-chancellor in the Hitler cabinet).

In February 1922 Reusch had used a *Konzernsitzung* to set out his philosophy of management. "As long as he was at the head of the GHH, and in this he had the agreement of Herr Haniel, who has since recently been chairman of the supervisory board of the GHH, the view would prevail that the associated enterprises could generally go their own way but must also keep the larger association in view. The slogan should be: March Separately but Fight Together."[41]

But a younger generation in the family wanted an even more dynamic management, and wanted to go further in consolidation into concerns and trusts. For the innovators, Stinnes appeared to be a more attractive role model than the excessively conservative

Reusch. The major Young Turk, in constant rebellion against his elders, was Werner Carp. He was the son of Eduard Carp, a successful lawyer and judge in Duisburg and then Düsseldorf, who had married Alma Haniel, the daughter of Friedrich Wilhelm Haniel. Werner Carp was born in 1886 and had married into a prominent Catholic political family, the Windthorsts (Ludwig Windthorst, the father of Werner's bride, Elsa, had been Bismarck's great opponent in the *Kulturkampf*). He became a director of the Darmstädter Bank at an early age, before leaving to go into the family business. In addition to his own, quite separate firm of specialty steels, he became in 1923 the chairman of the *Vorstand* (executive board) of the Haniel family mines, Rheinpreussen and Neumühl, which held a substantial participation in FHC. His principal ally within the family also had a banking background: Theodor Böninger, from an old-established Duisburg business and banking dynasty, who had also married a Haniel (a daughter of Franz Haniel). Werner Carp in 1924 wrote to Theodor Böninger and urged that they both get elected to the supervisory board of the GHH. He outlined the family politics of the issue: Böninger had already once been regarded as a candidate for a board position, but had been rejected because of his links with the rival steel firm Phönix. Carp, too, regarded himself as marginalized, and suggested that the way of overcoming the perception of a division in the family between GHH interests and Phönix interests was for the Carp-Böninger wing to establish an influence over the GHH:

> To the outside the story is told that the Haniel family is split into two camps, and I believe there cannot be a more suitable action on your part than to end this talk by electing both of us to the supervisory board of the GHH. This is a prestige question, for my father was for thirty years on this board. Apart from these reasons, which are partly emotional, we also believe that it would be economically better for both works, as well as for the prestige and the influence of the family to the outside, if the representation of people led to the documentation of a unanimous cooperation of the family.[42]

The tensions had already begun in the postwar and inflation years. Böninger and Alfred Haniel had been worried that the Socialists might nationalize coal mines, and had sounded out the influential Cologne banker, Robert Pferdmenges, about the possibility of a sale while it was still possible. Pferdmenges immediately mobilized a wide range of banking and industrial contacts, including Georg Solmssen of the Disconto-Gesellschaft Bank, and Wilhelm Beukenberg of Phönix. It soon became clear that Phönix was highly interested in such a purchase. Initially it was proposed to sell the coal shares for cash: partly Marks, and partly (in view of the already evident deterioration of the Mark on the foreign-exchange markets) in Dutch guilders. At this stage Carp moved into the negotiations and made the smart suggestion of a sale not for cash but for Phönix shares, which would link Haniels and the GHH with one of the most dynamic (but also most risky) business expansions of postwar Germany. Solmssen was irritated by Carp's intervention, and the Cologne metal trader Otto Wolff, who also held Phönix shares, did not want to see Haniels move into Phönix.[43] They tried to block the transaction, but it had become clear that Carp represented a way to bring Haniels into a bigger business picture that went well beyond the scale that Paul Reusch could imagine. Carp in return felt frustrated by Reusch's conservatism and hesitance, and by what he saw as an unseemly alliance with bankers (who had generally been treated with disdain in the Haniel family tradition).

As a result of the sale of the Zeche Zollverein mine, Carp and other members of the Haniel family acquired Phönix shares: in 1921 they had 9.72 million Marks of 100-million-Mark shares, while Deutsche Bank controlled another 9.54 million Marks (which could be bought up), and the hostile Otto Wolff had 21.11 million Marks. By 1925 the Haniels had doubled their share to around a fifth of Phönix, and had reached an agreement with Wolff on voting their shares as a bloc (a so-called *Poolvertrag*). Carp had become the chairman of the supervisory board of Phönix. But the Phönix works at Ruhrort clearly might benefit from cooperation with neighboring works: Rheinstahl was close by, at Meiderich, and the GHH was not that far away, in Oberhausen and Sterkrade. Carp thus took part in the negotiations of 1925 that led to the 1926 creation of the Vereinigte Stahlwerke, in which both Rheinstahl and Phönix participated.[44] But Phönix held only a quarter of the capital of the new steel trust, and in the late 1920s Friedrich Flick moved in and acquired a large stake in Gelsenkirchener Bergwerks AG, but also a holding of just under a fifth in Phönix. Carp at first complained bitterly that he had insufficient influence over the business policy of the Vereinigte Stahlwerke, and in 1927 resigned from its supervisory board, although he returned in 1928. He tried to form a new entity on the basis of the old Phönix company, which he tentatively called Stahlwerke Niederrhein, in order to keep some power position. But the only convincing way that Carp could have preserved his position was by taking the GHH into the Vereinigte Stahlwerke, and this was a strategy that Paul Reusch was determined to oppose. After 1924 Carp (who in 1925 owned 1,497 of the total of 80,000 GHH shares) thus tried to buy up more GHH shares in order to control the company, and to build a strategic alliance with the Thyssen works and with Vereinigte Stahlwerke. But it was hard to buy up large numbers of GHH shares directly, as there was no anonymous market on which the family-owned shares could be traded.

Reusch had always worried about the effects of Germany's profound social and political changes on the wealth of the family members and on their ability to keep their shareholdings: in the first days of 1919, shortly after the end of the empire and before the elections to the National Assembly, he had already sent family members a letter offering to buy GHH shares if high rates of taxation forced owners to sell.[45] Reusch saw quite clearly the link between instability in the shareholding and a danger to managerial control of the company. He now responded by proposing strict guidelines on how sales of family shares should be managed: they must first be offered to the GHH, which would find suitable purchasers. This procedure survived even through the painful and problematical period of the Great Depression. It provided the key for Reusch to control the company. A memorandum of 1935 showed that of the 80 million RM ($10.1 million) nominal capital of the GHH, over the previous five years, 4,732,000 RM nominal capital had been traded through the intermediation of the GHH, and 3,669,000 directly between shareholders or through external mediation. The document concluded: "Despite all previous changes of ownership, the nature of the GHH as a family firm has in essence not been shaken."[46]

Carp, frustrated in his plans to buy up the GHH and integrate it into a much larger steel trust, took a new tack in the midst of the world depression. The massive destruction of value gave new opportunity to people who wanted to undertake a fundamental restructuring of companies. In April 1930 he asked the shareholders of the GHH to make an exchange of shares with the Vereinigte Stahlwerke that would bring the company into the steel trust. It was easier now for Carp to work through the more limited Haniel trading company than to renew his attempt to buy up a dominant position in GHH stock. He thought he could use FHC and its trading network as a way of dictating terms to Reusch. The GHH had only a minority shareholding in FHC (unlike in other GHH acquisitions) and thus could not directly control the enterprise. On the other hand, the mines Rheinpreussen and Neumühl, which Carp dominated, had a powerful vote on the board of FHC. In late 1930 the general manager of FHC, Johann Welker, spoke with Carp, who was seething with anger about Reusch: "Why is Herr Reusch acting in such a hostile way? Why doesn't he want to talk with me? One can't really break up Haniel!"[47] Welker reported that Carp "would never again undertake any action concerning the sale of GHH shares, since the family did not want it. He was not thinking of that any more. The family must know what it was doing, and with that the business was settled as far as he was concerned."[48] Reusch had proposed a valuation of the assets of FHC and then a transfer to the GHH: the GHH intended "to secure for itself its share in the capital of Franz Haniel & Cie. GmbH for every possible case, so that it would not have to deal with the eventuality that a majority was in the hands of strangers and that thus the influence of the GHH would be ended completely."[49] An agreement would be needed in order to prevent any future challenge from Carp.

Reusch felt increasingly worried about the possible threat posed by FHC: "he no longer felt comfortable as a minority owner of Franz Haniel, and he could not risk that the GHH might run the danger of suffering adverse consequences from this minority participation."[50] In particular, Reusch feared that Carp was going to use his mine interests to extend the coal ownership of the steel trust Vereinigte Stahlwerke.[51] Carp then proposed his own version of a compromise, in which the GHH would be given a right to buy the FHC assets "in the case that the economic power over the enterprise of a shareowner went into new hands," and thus threatened the GHH, which had always had a competitive advantage because of its ownership of highly productive coal mines.[52]

Reusch contemplated a counterattack, in which he might try to break up FHC and thus destroy the power of Carp and the threat posed by the steel trust to the GHH.[53] In 1932 he wrote to Edgar Haniel von Haimhausen: "In consideration of the present distress of the German people and the catastrophic situation of German industry, I have refrained—for the moment—in pressing the interests of the GHH in this case in the most ruthless way, as it would have been my damned duty, and I hope that it will still be possible in the not-too-distant future to reach an agreement that is acceptable to the GHH."[54] Reusch's scaled-down pressure was eventually sufficient, and FHC was brought under control.

On 2 April 1932 the FHC statutes were altered, at an extraordinary general meeting, in order to reassure the GHH that it would not be threatened by FHC, and that FHC would not undertake any action against the GHH. The new agreement gave the GHH a 50 percent vote in all accounting and cartel issues, as well as "measures of every kind that affect the existence or the extent of the enterprise or the basis of its business activity, as well as all commercial measures that go beyond the sphere of normal business."[55] Karl Haniel immediately wrote to Reusch to congratulate him on his victory over Carp: "I must say that I am greatly relieved. I would like to congratulate you personally on having got your way in the interest of the GHH, after so many unpleasant negotiations."[56]

This was not the end of Carp's plans to create a major new German conglomerate. The circumstances of the depression and the banking crisis were favorable for such an exercise, providing that funds were available. The banks in particular were eager to sell their holdings of industrial assets, but also their own shares. Deutsche Bank asked Carp whether the Haniels might be prepared to buy 250,000 shares, which were trading at a deep discount while the official stock exchanges were closed. Welker immediately informed Reusch of the proposal, to which he appended a skeptical comment: "I see the thing in this way: if the crisis gets worse, then the new shares are largely a waste of money. But if there is a way out of this crisis, then the Deutsche Bank will doubtless have good returns once more, and the purchase of such shares would not be a bad business proposition."[57]

Carp also continued to plan for control of Reusch's company. In 1933 he was angling to replace Karl Haniel on the board of the GHH, probably because he detected that Karl Haniel was in some financial embarrassment and would need to sell some of his shareholding in the GHH. Welker reported that Carp had tried to give assurances that he would not humiliate Karl Haniel, who was seen, especially after the April 1932 agreement, as a close ally of Reusch. "Herr Carp emphasized again that he is not in any way hostile to K. H. [Karl Haniel], and that he would be quite content that Haniel should not be abandoned but should continue to have a living." But this manner of assurance was obviously in itself intended as a humiliation. Welker advised Carp to continue to occupy important positions in Vereinigte Stahlwerke while he waited for the passage of time to bring changes in the supervisory board of the GHH: "If the conditions should develop so that he would be summoned to the GHH as a successor to Karl Haniel, it would in my opinion make a good impression on public opinion if he gave up all his positions with Vereinigte Stahlwerke and cut off all links with the company."[58]

In 1939, with a new shortage in Germany of raw materials in general, and of coal in particular, the crisis in relations between FHC and the GHH came to a head again. At the beginning of the year a GHH executive noted that the 42 percent shareholding of the GHH in FHC still meant trouble, in that the GHH "had nothing to say, and that must sooner or later lead to a parting of ways . . . Neither in the case of the GHH nor of any other company is it possible for a subsidiary company to have quite different views from the parent enterprise and indeed to fight public battles with the parent."[59] Reusch told Welker that he needed to be sure that Haniel and GHH would "march *pari passu*," and recalled that he had promised that as long as Welker was general manager of FHC he would not allow the GHH to move into business areas serviced by FHC. "It should, however, be taken into account that one day there will be other people in charge of the firms, and that it would be therefore a sensible precaution to put the GHH on the same footing as the mining companies in the ownership structure of FHC."[60] In the end, a reordering of relations between the GHH and FHC occurred only in the completely new circumstances of the postwar world.

Reusch and Politics

Paul Reusch had always been exceptionally active in business politics, above all in the interest associations and lobbying groups that proliferated in imperial Germany; and he became if anything more engaged in the Weimar Republic, with involvement in the Reich Association of German Industry, the Langnamverein (Long Name Association), the Northwest Group of the German Iron and Steel Association, and the Ruhrlade, a group of "Ruhr barons," in which he played a leading role. When he was absent from a meeting of the Ruhrlade, Karl Haniel sent him very detailed reports of what had gone on in his absence.[61] Reusch was also engaged in the creation of a group pressing for constitutional reform in order to overcome the tensions between the central state and the federal states, and in another direct political pressure group, the League for the Renewal of the Reich. During the depression he tried to create a unified party of the German right. He complained that the industrial pressure groups had spent too much time attacking the government, and not enough energy on attacking labor unions.[62] In addition, he represented the German business community on the board of the Bank for International Settlements, which began operating in 1930.

Politics clearly became a major passion, and there was obviously a danger that purely business interests might be neglected; in the French case, François de Wendel certainly fell into this trap. But Reusch never lost sight of a business rationale for his energetic intervention in politics, even when that rationale might make the actual intervention less effective. In the late 1920s he grew increasingly distressed by what he believed to be the effects of government policy on the profitability of the GHH. In early 1929 he told the general meeting of the *Konzern:* "Today the economy and parliaments are under the terror of the trade unions. This condition requires urgent relief. How we can get this cannot yet be seen."[63]

Underlying some of Reusch's policy positions was the competitive situation of the GHH, especially in relation to the Vereinigte Stahlwerke, which Reusch increasingly saw as the major enemy (not least because of its role in his struggles with Werner Carp). In mid-1930, when the Vereinigte Stahlwerke offered the government a big cut in steel prices if a wage reduction were imposed, Reusch and his advisers concluded that the GHH would not benefit as much, as it was less engaged than the Vereinigte Stahlwerke in the production of mass steel products.[64] He thus argued passionately against the proposal.

Reusch followed a clear and consistent line during the later 1920s and in the depression. He resisted state engagement in industry, subsidies, and bailouts, on the basis that these were likely to be asked for by, and granted to, larger firms than the GHH, with a larger political pawprint and consequently an enhanced rent-seeking capacity. "We should not," he wrote, "ask the government for help in carrying out particular transactions, but should keep our attention on securing a healthy economic policy and ensuring that policy measures allow a free and independent business without particular subsidy."[65] In particular, the Vereinigte Stahlwerke, which incurred heavy losses during the depression, would be likely to get favorable state aid. After 1931 the relationship between GHH and the Vereinigte Stahlwerke bore a resemblance to the clash of Falck in Italy with the large integrated steelworks, all of which passed from bank ownership to state control during the depression. Reusch first argued that Vereinigte Stahlwerke plans to get more liberal discounting of bills by the German central bank would lead to unsolid finance of the type that had prevailed during the German inflation.[66] In 1932, when the government proposed a large-scale bailout, Reusch opposed this plan resolutely, and thus actually helped to destroy the chance of building a united political front of heavy industry in the delicate and highly unstable political circumstances of 1932.[67] He was also very sensitive to the danger that a coordinated action by industry might lead to the divulging of GHH processes and secrets to competitors: on these grounds (rather than for any political ideology), he objected to plans for a united German industrial effort to supply equipment to the Soviet Union.[68]

Reusch drew the conclusion that what Germany needed was a profound reorientation of policy, a dismantling of the kind of corporatism that he associated with the inflation and its aftermath, and in business terms with Stinnes and Vereinigte Stahlwerke. He rejected the idea of a devaluation of the German currency on the grounds that it would be effective only once a satisfactory domestic reform program had been put in place: once industrial equipment had been modernized, once the public-sector bureaucracy had been cut back and removed from the domain of party politics, and once Germans saved more.[69] Reusch formulated this argument in broad theoretical terms, but it also coincided with his interpretation of the business interests of the GHH. Like many large German businesses, as well as the banks, the GHH had a substantial part of its debt denominated in foreign currency, mostly dollars rather than Reichsmarks, so that a devaluation of the Reichsmark would have immediately increased GHH liabilities in the midst of the general deflation. The balance-sheet effect would outweigh any gain achieved from increased competitiveness (especially as quotas and tariffs were closing off many export markets).

On at least one occasion, on 19 March 1932, Reusch had an extended (two-hour) conversation with Hitler, on which he sent a report to the influential former central banker Hjalmar Schacht, who by the second half of 1931 had moved very close to the Nazis. Reusch, according to this account, had urged Hitler, if he were to form a government, to appoint experts not just on economic policy but also to the Finance, Foreign, and Interior Ministries: "With regard to these men it is less important whether or not they belong to the National Socialist Party than that they have a professional approach. Hitler agreed with this last thought."[70] Later in the year Reusch wrote to Schacht about his disappointment that the Nazis were working with the Communists.[71]

After 1933 Reusch became much more restrained in his political interventions. The originator of the League for the Renewal of the Reich, Hans Luther, wrote that the organization could be dissolved now that its aims had been accomplished through "the political acts of the German revolution, even though some important things remain to be done." Reusch, on the other hand, just commented to Luther that the improvements in Germany were the result of the economic measures of previous governments (implicitly therefore not of Hitler's regime): "the situation has at least improved in that the relentless economy measures taken over the course of the last years have had an effect, and factories at least do not lose money, even if they do not make profits."[72] And Reusch still complained in the middle of 1933 about the "legal uncertainty" that the Nazi revolution had brought, which blocked the "confidence needed for the recovery of the economy."[73] In late 1934 he told Welker of FHC of his alarm at a decree by the Labor Front (Deutsche Arbeitsfront) that he saw as likely to lead to greater wage demands and pressure for improvement of labor conditions: "This decree was issued without the knowledge of the Reich economics minister and the Reich labor minister. It is worded so that anything can be made of it. Any protest to Schacht [the economics minister] would have no purpose. I would like to tell you more about this in person."[74]

In 1936–37, like most other private steel industrialists, he opposed the creation of a large state steelworks working with low-grade domestic ore, the Reichswerke "Hermann Göring."[75] But the business opposition was easily broken by the state. There are still surviving signs of Reusch's skepticism after the outbreak of the war. Thus on 20 September 1939 he wrote in a letter that "despite the big successes of German arms in the East, I believe that there will be a long war. Only a miracle can in my view produce an early end to the fighting. But I don't believe in miracles, and am hence reckoning on many years of conflict."[76] To say during Hitler's war that one did not believe in miracles could easily be interpreted as treason.

Recovery in the 1930s

Both the GHH and FHC recovered in business terms quite rapidly after the disasters of the depression. Both had been quite confrontational in the their labor relations, and these clashes had formed the business backdrop to much of Reusch's political engagement and in particular his attack on the involvement of government in the arbitration of labor disputes. After a government binding wage arbitration of December 1930, which the employers bitterly contested, on 1 April 1931 FHC shut down the operation of its entire fleet of barges and of most of the tugs on the Rhine. This was the equivalent for the shipping industry of the great Ruhr lockout of 1928, but the dynamics of industrial power had shifted with the Great Depression. The 1931 clash ended with a victory for the employers. The enterprise eventually got around the wage award by leasing forty-five barges from the beginning of October to its captains at a low rental. But by this time business confidence had been dented further by the banking crises of the summer of 1931.

From the depth of the depression in 1932, there was a striking rebound in production, but levels of profitability remained below those of the 1920s.

An old-style conservative, Reusch was not an enthusiast about the new regime of Adolf Hitler, not least because he was now even more removed from political power than he had been in the Weimar Republic.[77] He remained very worried about the loss of the GHH's traditionally important export markets. But many of the GHH's younger managers were more willing to use the opportuni-

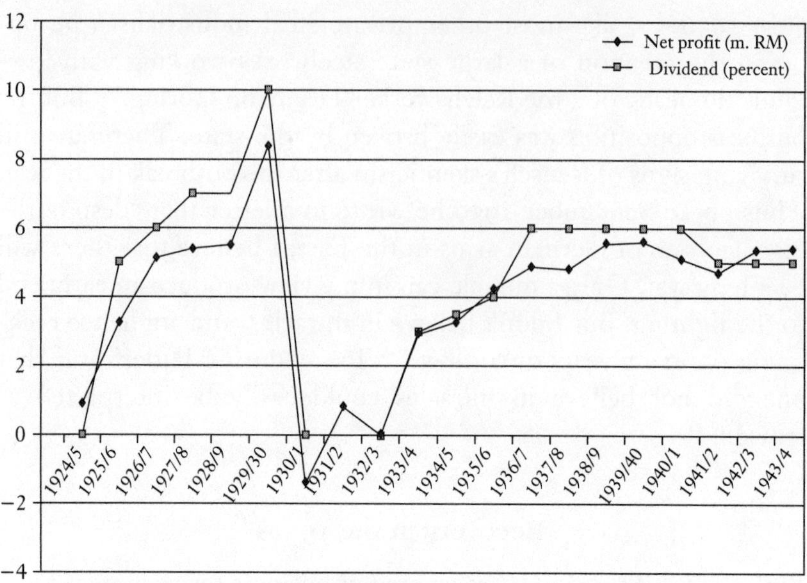

22. *GHH Aktienverein profits and dividends, 1924–1944*

ties offered by the rearmament economy, which brought big engineering orders. From 1933 the GHH participated in one of the central institutions of the new armaments economy: it was one of four commercial firms that joined to create the Metallurgische Forschungsgesellschaft. This entity was central to the camouflaged financing of rearmament in that its signature allowed the Reichsbank to discount bills that would otherwise have been ineligible.

The trading business of FHC recovered much more slowly from the depression than the manufacturing output of the GHH. Despite the economic recovery, the annual reports from the mid-1930s complained continually about the currency and trade controls (which they explained as "constraints imposed by the world economy" in order to avoid any explicit criticism of the Nazi government).[78] Given that the political circumstances had changed dramatically in 1933, an obvious question about any German business is how it responded to, and how it tried to use, the new political environment. In particular, to what extent were firms accomplices or participants in the implementation of the anti-Semitic program of the regime, including its purge of Jewish-owned businesses?

In 1938 FHC reported the initial effects of the *Anschluss* of Austria: "The annexation seems to have negative consequences for the development of our firm, because according to the government at first only Austrian firms should be active in the 'Ostmark,' and new acquisitions or foundations are forbidden or require a permission given only in exceptional cases. We are trying to acquire our old representative, Krum & Co., as the basis for activity in Austria."[79]

In 1938 FHC indeed took over the Viennese trading house, with which it had worked quite closely before the *Anschluss*. Technically, it was not an "aryanization," in that the proprietor, Krum, was not Jewish. But his wife, who played a leading role in the day-to-day operation of the business, was classified by the Nazis as a Jew (she was a baptized Protestant), and Krum had many enemies who denounced him as having been sympathetic to the Austrian Socialists. The Viennese Vermögensverkehrstelle, which handled "aryanizations" and whose authorization was necessary, approved the transaction on 27 September 1938. Krum had pressed repeatedly for Haniel to take over his business; and he had also tried to make it a more attractive proposition by himself taking over a Jewish coal-trading firm, Hirschfeld (since there were considerable doubts about the viability of Krum & Co. by itself). He wrote in pencil a long and moving letter to an FHC manager, Werner Ahlers, pleading for quick help. FHC was especially interested in Krum because it had dealt with Petschek coal from Czechoslovakia and Poland (the Petscheks had a gigantic network of holdings in the Czech, Polish, and German mining industry, which in the course of time the Nazis would seize). Frau Krum was related to the Petscheks, and this relationship had sustained the Krum business in Vienna.[80]

In order to secure the transaction, Ahlers had repeatedly traveled to Berlin, as had managers from the GHH. The Nazi party and parts of the bureaucracy had already in 1936 used the alleged prominence of Jewish representatives of the coal and steel industry as a way of attacking the management of privately owned heavy industry and demanding a greater role for the state. The attack was clearly intended to soften up heavy industry at the same time as the state steel sector was expanding with the Reichswerke "Hermann Göring." In October 1936 the Nazi party's regional economic adviser (a figure who played an important part in "aryanizations") in Essen sent to Hermann Kellermann of the GHH, who was chairman of the supervisory board of the Rhenish-Westphalian coal syndicate, a letter enumerating the supposed "Jewish" agents of German coal firms, including the Prussian state works, Mannesmann, Stumm, Klöckner, and FHC. Ahlers had visited the Economics Ministry in April 1936 and been told to contact a bureau with no name and no door sign, which he believed to be an information service of the Economics Ministry, where he was received by a man with an Austrian accent who swore him to secrecy and then warned him against dealing with Krum & Co.[81]

This was not the only "aryanization" in which FHC was involved. Rhenania was a Mannheim Rhine shipping firm that had been founded in 1908 and quickly taken over by two brothers, Hermann and Jakob Hecht. In 1933, under substantial pressure from the Nazi authorities, Jakob had sold his share of the enterprise to the Bavarian state, and from 1934 the state authorities treated Rhenania as an "aryan" firm. With increased official anti-Semitism, the Bavarian officials who had originally behaved courteously toward Hermann Hecht became much more aggressive. At the supervisory board meeting of 15 February 1938 the Bavarian representative, Fritz Gutleben, announced that "General Director Hermann Hecht has decided after negotiations with the state of Bavaria to retire from the board of management. I intend to respect this wish and to allow the resignation of Herr Hecht with effect from the present day."[82] Gutleben himself, who made no secret of his friendship with and respect for Hecht, resigned at the same time. In June 1938 Welker of Haniel started negotiations with the Bavarian government to buy Rhenania while the Deutsche Bank's Mannheim branch was trying to broker a sale to another Rhine shipper, Fendel. The price agreed between Haniel and the Hechts was 127,000 Reichsmarks and 78,000 Swiss francs; the Hechts were able—characteristically for the time—to transfer almost nothing of the Reichsmark payment out of Germany.[83]

In September 1938 the Hechts wrote to Welker: "as a result of the domestic political circumstances in Germany, we have had to renounce our participation in Rhenania and Express GmbH after a struggle that lasted five and a half years. We also willingly declare that the sale of our firm to you has been conducted with pleasantness, and that you have not sought to exploit our unpleasant and unfavorable situation in terms of a price . . . Our shipping company was a family business, and it was our firm intention to leave it to our heirs. We were devotedly attached to it and worked for it with pleasure."[84] In 1949 Jakob and Hermann Hecht's shares were restored to them, and they controlled over 50 percent of the capital, but Haniel retained a minority share (25 percent), as did the Bavarian state (12.95 percent).[85] The restitution negotiations were quite tense, and the Hechts insisted on the dismissal of the manager whom Haniel had employed, and then quite quickly sold their shares to a Swiss holding company.

The GHH also took over at least one firm in Austria in the wake of the *Anschluss:* the Viennese Vergasungs-Industrie AG. By the time the transaction was completed, Germany was once more on the brink of war. There was only one major GHH acquisition during the war, of the Maschinenfabrik Tarnowitz in 1941, which the GHH ran with very heavy losses.

The Second World War

The controlled economy and the primacy of military orders raised for the GHH the same issues as in the First World War: in particular that of labor scarcity. At first the demand for labor was met by the transfer of workers from nonessential industries oriented to civilian consumption, and by female workers. Already in the last stages of the peacetime armaments boom, the GHH had tried to recruit more women to deal with the problem of labor scarcity. After September 1940 the demand was met largely by forced workers, largely from eastern Europe. The response to wartime labor shortages was thus analogous to that in the First World War. The GHH eventually became by far the largest employer of forced and foreign laborers in the Oberhausen area.[86]

At first most of the workers came from Poland, especially from Upper Silesia, and many were classified as ethnic Germans. But their employment created unrest among the workforce and protests from the party and the secret police, who demanded a harsher treatment. Thus, for instance, in the summer of 1940 the Düsseldorf Gestapo wrote to the GHH mining direction to complain that the Polish workers were paid the same wages as Germans: "German miners, who include many party and SA [Sturmabteilung, or Storm Troopers] members, regard this as a disrespect of their person. They say that on the one hand they are expected to form a working community with the Poles, and use the same washing and changing rooms and sanitary facilities; and on the other hand they are enlightened by the press and the party and its organizations about how Poles are to be regarded, and that any community with them is prohibited and punishable."[87] Many of the Upper Silesian workers quickly tried to return to their homes, complaining of their treatment on the Ruhr.[88]

After this experience with Polish workers, and after the launching of Operation Barbarossa, the GHH recruited a workforce from farther east. *Ostarbeiter* (workers from the Polish Generalgouvernement, Ukraine, Ruthenia, Latvia, and Estonia), forming the largest category, were supposed to be kept in camps surrounded by barbed wire, organized by the German Labor Front, though after July 1942 these security provisions were partially relaxed. Poles from the areas of Poland incorporated into Germany were treated differently, with conditions similar to those imposed on forced laborers from western Europe.

In June 1942 the mining enterprises of the GHH employed 1,217 foreign workers, of whom 112 were men from the Soviet Union and 100 women. At this stage the GHH built a separate camp for Russian men.[89] The Soviet POWs arrived in very poor health. In October 1942, just as the large numbers of Soviet prisoners were beginning to arrive, the GHH noted that 17 workers in the mines had died of general weakness.[90] In March 1945 there were 2,000 Russians in the mines.[91]

The GHH steelmaking plants in Oberhausen employed 2,856 foreign workers in May 1943, of whom 401 were Russian POWs and 384 French POWs.[92] Some of the guidelines issued by the company for the treatment of Soviet POWs had an almost idyllic tone, and spoke of the provision of Russian-language newspapers, entertainments such as games, regular (twice-daily) warm meals, and premiums in the form of cigarettes for good work.[93] But the actual conditions did not live up to these rather utopian intentions.

Each category of foreign worker was treated and remunerated in a different way. The company paid the POW camp administrators 70–75 percent of the German pay rate, plus an additional 10 percent wage tax, but the POWs never received any German money themselves. By contrast, non-POW workers from western Europe and Poles from the Reich were paid the same rates as Germans.

The *Ostarbeiter* were often brought to Germany in groups, and children (under fourteen) were also employed by the GHH for up to twenty-four hours a week. *Ostarbeiter* were paid minimal amounts (10–17 RM a week) until July 1942, and the difference between this rate and a regular wage was paid by the employer as a special "social tax" to the German state. This rate of pay produced poor results, and after July 1942 the amounts actually paid to the *Ostarbeiter* were increased slightly in the interest of increasing productivity.

The food supplied was also carefully differentiated: French and Italian POWs were fed according to the Geneva conventions, and received lower rations than Germans, Poles, or western workers. *Ostarbeiter* and Russian POWs were fed even lower rations.

Since the employers had to provide the accommodation and food, the GHH's calculations show some categories of foreign workers (but not POWs) as costing more than German workers. A postwar calculation also described lower levels of productivity relative to German workers (57 percent of the German level for male *Ostarbeiter*, 81.7 percent for female *Ostarbeiterinnen*, 84.7 percent for French POWs, and 41.7 percent for the Russian POWs).[94] On the other hand, some wartime documents describe elaborate training for some of the female *Ostarbeiterinnen*, after which they reached very high levels of productivity, especially in electrical welding for bridge and boiler construction.[95]

Structures of control in enterprises eroded as the Nazi ideology increasingly permeated German society, and gave lower-level officials in the enterprise opportunities to appeal to the state and the party against their superiors in the enterprise. The controlled economy thus also led to the weakening of the traditional position of management. For the GHH, the apparently well-entrenched supremacy of Paul Reusch as general manager became vulnerable. The "property rights" of the corporate ownership structure, on which Reusch had worked for so long, were now of secondary importance. As in other German corporations, the management was vulnerable to politically motivated attacks. In one south German GHH enterprise, the Kabel- und Metallwerke Neumeyer AG, of Nuremberg, ideological managers launched an initially anonymous attack on Reusch. In March 1941 Reusch received a letter from someone who claimed to have been saved from ruin by a member of the Haniel family. The letter continued: "I am a member of the National Socialist party in a high function and am informed that an action is planned against the GHH 'because its leadership has an attitude that is not in conformity with the aims and vision of the state leadership.'"[96] Reusch removed the leadership of the cableworks in Nuremberg, but the attack continued. He resigned from the board of management of the GHH Oberhausen in the autumn of 1941, and in January 1942 informed supervisory board chairman Karl Haniel that he would resign from the Aktienverein holding company at the annual meeting in March 1943. He also told Economics Minister Walther Funk of his intention.[97] This schedule was not short enough for his opponents, and on 21 February 1942 the party insisted on his immediate resignation. In June 1942 his son, Hermann, was obliged to resign the position on the GHH management board that he had held since 1937.

Other business leaders in the GHH empire were also vulnerable to political and personal attacks. Carp had a wide range of business interests that brought him into the focus of attention. In the 1930s he was not only the chairman of the supervisory board of FHC but was also on the boards of the Albingia Insurance Company, Daimler-Benz, Demag, Deutsche Kabelwerke AG, Kabelwerke Rheydt AG, Harpener Bergbau AG, and the Rheinisch-Westfälische Sprengstoff AG. He also had substantial business dealings with the Netherlands. These raised the attention and interest of the German fiscal authorities, especially because of the way he had managed his affairs since the Great Depression. In 1930 he had given all his foreign assets to his son, Carl Eduard Carp, who later took Dutch nationality, and after discussion with a Swiss asset manager, Pinösch, of the Allgemeine Treuhand AG in Basel, created a Swiss-based fiduciary company, Aeterna. Aeterna had two Dutch accounts, one with the well-known Dutch bank Rhodius Königs, the other with NV Unitas, which was managed by Fentener van Vlissingen. In February 1943 these accounts were blocked by the German authorities in the Netherlands, the infamous currency protection squads (Devisenschutzkommandos). Already in 1942 the occupation authorities had begun an investigation of Hones Staal Maatschappij, the Dutch subsidiary of Carp's private firm, Carp & Hones, Düsseldorf. But Carp believed that the push for the zealous investigation of his family's Dutch business came from Berlin and from the central Foreign Exchange Control Board. The tense relations within the Haniel family played a role even here. The man in charge of investigating the Carp affair was Eugen Grolman, who was a member of the by now quite extended Haniel family, albeit from the Gerhard Haniel rather than the Franz Haniel line.[98] Carp attributed the behavior of the Berlin authorities to a continuation of the vendetta dating from the early 1920s, a "deep-seated family grudge." He managed to get the Dutch assets unblocked through the intervention of a Düsseldorf customs inspector, to whom he gave a loan of 10,000 Reichsmarks.[99]

Carp's family links extended also to the opposition to Hitler, with which, however, he personally had no involvement. Werner Carp's niece Barbara, the daughter of the Weimar foreign minister Julius Curtius, was married to a diplomat, Hans-Bernd von Haeften, one of the leading figures in the July 1944 resistance who connected the German Foreign Ministry with the military. Haeften was the man who told Roland Freisler's People's Court: "My conception of the Führer's role in world history is that he is a great perpetrator of evil." His heroism, and Freisler's sputtering indignation in interrupting him at this point, are captured on a film of the trial.[100] He was hanged on the same evening, 15 August 1944.

The family struggles and the wartime intrigues fascinated the Allied investigators after the war, who were quick to see political connections in the story. The U.S. occupation report on the GHH depicts a struggle in the 1930s between the conservative Reusch and an ambitious and Nazi-sympathizing Carp. Carp "was obsessed by a deep-seated ambition to play a big role as a Ruhr industrialist and as a politician." But ultimately he failed: "Werner Carp did not succeed in uniting, as he intended to do, the Franz Haniel family behind him in opposition to the more stable and more conservative leadership of Director General Paul Reusch with the backing of Karl Haniel." The Allied investigators believed that Carp derived some leverage from links with Hermann Göring, and in particular they excavated a bizarre attempt by Göring to sell the notional German claim to South-West Africa for a relatively modest hard-currency price (£5,000, or about $23,000), in which Carp, who owned a farm in South-West Africa, acted as an intermediary. After the war

Carp was arrested and treated with great suspicion by the U.S. military authorities.[101] To the occupation authorities in the west as well as in the east, dynastic steel magnates looked like part of the old German political problem. The Krupps, Thyssens, Röchlings, and Flicks in particular had achieved a notoriety that could easily be generalized into a reflection on the danger of the power of the dynasts.

Chapter 9

Models of Italian Industrial Development

While I express my gratitude allow me to say that for me the most satisfying sense of such an event lies in the will to express the unity and unanimity with which our great family has always marched toward ever-greater goals. For twenty-five years I have identified myself with this work of construction, to which I have devoted every fire and every passion.

Giorgio Enrico Falck, 1931

In 1926 Giorgio Enrico Falck, speaking in celebration of the twentieth anniversary of his firm, but also as president of the Italian Federation of the Metallurgical Industry, set out what he believed to be the most appropriate model of national industrial development. Italy as a resource-scarce economy should not attempt to create a large-scale industry analogous to that of Belgium, France, or Germany, but should rather develop processes for working scrap metal. Such use was a response not only to Italy's relative dearth of mineral resources and of coking coal, but also to its advantageous access to hydroelectric power for treating scrap metal. The mountain valleys of the early Italian iron industry would thus be at the center of a new technical transformation.[1]

This model stood quite deliberately in opposition to a much more ambitious vision of the industry, which emphasized the necessity of the *ciclo integrale* in a large-scale path of developing a big manufacturing sector, and which ignored the economics of resource scarcity. Oscar Sinigaglia, who played a central role in the development of the state sector, later referred to the slowness of the adoption of such a cycle as the characteristic "Italian problem."[2] In the 1930s the large-scale state steel industry seemed to be competing on unfavorable terms with the private producers, above all with Falck. Sinigaglia designed schemes for autarky behind which the idea of the complete cycle could be realized. An adequate national production of steel could then provide the basis for a modern engineering industry.

The Electrical Reduction of Scrap

AFL produced on the one hand large quantities of coarse steel that could be used for a broad range of products, and on the other hand a wide range of geographically dispersed specialty steel products. At Sesto it operated four electric Siemens-Martin hearths, with a rolling mill producing hot profiles and bars; a second establishment in which there were hot and cold working of tubes and bolts, and a sheet mill; and, in a third works, metal finishing with hot and cold milling, and wire production. At Porta Romana, in Milan, there was a hot rolling mill, producing seamless tubes and wires; at Arcore (Brianza), the cold working of steel wire for netting; at Vobarno (Brescia), cold and hot working of bars and tubes; and at the old site of Dongo, cast iron production and profiles, and a separate tubeworks.

But the main empire-building of the Falcks occurred in relation not to steel but to energy production as the best answer to the cost structure of steel production in Italy. During the First World War AFL had begun hydroelectric production in the Valtelline with the Boffetto works on the river Adda, and in 1922 another plant at Venina was complete. Falck did not just build new power plants: in its quest for a greater presence in this sector, it also bought up existing companies. Thus in 1928 the company acquired the hydroelectric company Alto Magna. At the end of 1928 a generator at Armisa came on line, and in 1931 the Zappello hydroelectric plant in the Valtelline began production. The fifth Valtelline plant, Vedello, was ready in 1933. In the mid-1930s AFL also constructed a hydroelectric works in the Apennines, at Teglia. The number of works became so great that AFL generated far more power than was required for steel production, and started to sell power. In 1930 it concluded an agreement to supply electricity to the state railroad network.[3]

The electrical production of steel from scrap took place in general on a smaller scale than that of the large coastal steel mills working with imported iron ore; in that sense the Falcks anticipated the big Italian success story of the 1960s, the mini-mills. The typical interwar furnace, with a 25-ton capacity, was a quarter the size of the average Martin furnace. In 1925, 12.5 percent of Italian steel was produced electrically, and in 1935 25.2 percent (a very significant proportion when compared with the classic steel industry of Germany, where the respective figures were 2.5 and 2.0). Italians also began to use a Norwegian process (Tysland-Hoile) that allowed the working of pyrites to produce cast iron. Most of the electrically produced steel was of poor quality, and Falck alone had the technologies required to separate out unwanted minerals that reduced the quality of the final product.[4] As a consequence AFL occupied an unusual position in the intense policy debates of the 1920s, and it used its command of a particular technology to present itself as a national champion of a more rational way of doing business. In 1939 Italy had (after Switzerland) the world's second-highest share of steel produced with hydroelectric power: 29.7 percent, as Falck's report proudly pointed out.[5] For Falck, this sort of production appeared to offer an appealing and particularly Italian model of steel development.

The Italian steel industry in the 1920s faced chronic problems. Falling prices hit the large producers in particular, and favored the small but inefficient producers of low-grade products. The larger producers then argued that the result was a national catastrophe requiring government intervention and industrial planning. The high valuation of the lira at the 1927 currency stabilization created an additional difficulty, since it made imported iron and steel products much more competitive. AFL also noted that "the situation of our industry is difficult because of the consequences of revaluation."[6] The revaluation also gave the large coastal works an advantage over the electric steel producers as imported ores became cheaper.

AFL continued to modernize, on the assumption that it had a better cost structure than the larger-scale coastal producers. The continuing investment in hydroelectric equipment required additional financing, and in 1928 AFL agreed upon a capital increase from 40.8 million to 55 million liras ($19.1 million). AFL also continued to acquire other steel firms, notably in 1924 the Società Cantieri Metallurgici Italiani, producing tinplate at Castelmare and, after 1930, at Naples. So it also built up some participation in coastal production.

Some of the expansion was financed through borrowing, but from public-sector institutions rather than the banks—since the major commercial banks were heavily engaged in, and by this time effectively managing, the competing large-scale steel companies. In 1926 AFL took a credit from the Istituto di Credito Imprese Pubblica Utilità. The formerly warm relationship with the Banca Commerciale had now frosted over.

The indebtedness of the large-scale steel industry became a major problem for banks and also for public policy. The threat to bank solvency pushed banks to lend ever-larger amounts to keep their precarious industrial customers afloat, and their own vulnerability thus mounted. It created an implicit liability of the Banca d'Italia and the government, which would not be expected to stand by in the event of a major bank collapse. In April 1921 Bonaldo Stringher of the Banca d'Italia declared with concern: "We always avoided making great concentrations in one area, but things change, and for such matters as shipyard credits, the demands are for ever-larger sums."[7]

The big steel producer Ilva had in 1920 been rescued by the Banca Commerciale (Comit) and the Credito Italiano (Credit) in a highly costly operation, through a newly created Istituto Finanzaria, but its business continued to remain highly problematical, and it is not surprising that its bank/owners looked for some way out. Ilva could not make money by selling plate steel, and had rather high costs and an antiquated plant. Ilva managers frequently explored ways to rescue their company through some form of closer cooperation or even merger with Falck. In July 1928 a proposal to this effect suddenly came from the banks, who were thinking of ways of reducing their own exposure to a troubled firm. At the central committee of the Credito Italiano, the bank's president, Carlo Feltrinelli, who was also a member of the Falck board, "gave details on an exchange of opinions with Falck from AFL about the possibility of combining with Ilva, and he would reserve the right to speak with the committee if the negotiations became more concrete." Two months later the bank heard "that negotiations continue with Falck about a possible combination with Ilva, but that Giuseppe Toeplitz [the head of the Banca Commerciale] was now, in contrast to his previous declarations, against the proposal, insofar as it concerned the Comit."[8] Toeplitz's calculation was that the proposed merger might benefit Ilva and the Credit, but could not help the Comit.

Falck was also keen to maintain the independence of his company. The AFL 1928 annual report began with a defiant statement about the company's "decision not to join the renewed consortium for rolled products, which had been constituted on the basis of the old consortium of which we had been a member."[9] In the following year it recorded: "The small price increase for rolled steel that was achieved with the completion of the consortium (not alas a comprehensive consortium) had a bad effect, as our quota reduction was pronounced, and the reduction in production increased our costs."[10]

Nothing came of the Ilva/Credit initiative, but similar moves were made subsequently as a result of the world economic crisis. The records of the Ilva central committee of management summarize a discussion in October 1930: "Toeplitz reported on a recent conversation with Giorgio Falck, president and member of the managing board of AFL, about the possibility of a union between his and our company." And at the end of June 1931 Toeplitz stated that "the moment had come to inform the committee about the results of the negotiations that he . . . had conducted on behalf of Ilva with Falck and [general manager Ludovico] Goisis for AFL, in order to reach the possibility of making important agreements." The president of Ilva, Arturo Bocciardo, noted that "as soon as it came to the discussion of forming various sales consortia with AFL, he had a pessimistic sense about the negotiations."[11]

AFL continued to invest in order to retain its independence, with the largest Siemens-Martin furnaces in Italy, with a capacity of 90 tons. On 29 November 1930 Giorgio Enrico Falck presented his board with a remarkable account of the business response to economic depression. While the smaller ironworks at Vobarno and Dongo were running on a more or less "adequate" basis, the major plants in Sesto were operating at only 30 to 40 percent of capacity. But Falck concluded, apparently perversely, that the best response would be to undertake further investment, using the firm's extraordinary reserves (7.78 million liras, or $4.1 million) and raising more capital: he wanted an increase in capital to 100 million liras. In fact the market would not support such an increase, and an extraordinary meeting of the shareholders in December agreed to raise the capitalization to 78 million liras and defer the larger increase to a more propitious time.[12] But the investments continued. In 1931 a blooming mill came into operation in Sesto San Giovanni.

The company also sought to avoid bank debt, since it was the banks that seemed most inclined to push AFL into some combination in a move clearly intended more to rescue their own investments than to be of any benefit to AFL. The company's policy was explained by Falck as "a modest but continual dividend."[13]

The strategy of maintaining independence also led AFL to be cautious about state attempts to rationalize the steel industry by the imposition of syndicates. On 19 October 1929 the state's involvement led to the formation of two new institutions, Consorzio Siderurgico Italiano and Unione Siderurgica Italiana. The former was designed to promote rationalization, while the latter would be a selling organization for Italian steel products.[14] At first Falck protested vigorously against the share of production allocated to Ilva, but his resistance was undermined when another big private steelmaker, Fiat, joined the Consorzio a few weeks later. In 1930 Ilva reached an agreement with Falck and another important privately owned steel firm, Breda, on sales quotas for rails. In 1931 Mussolini summoned Vincenzo Ardissone, the director of Ilva, and Falck to Rome in order to find a solution to the dispute between the leading Italian steelmakers. On 31 December 1931 a unilaterally decreed law established compulsory syndicates for thick and thin rolled products and for tinplate: the Consorzio Lamiere Grosse, the Consorzio Lamiere Sottili, and the Consorzio Latta, respectively.[15]

One of Falck's strategies in the face of both bank and governmental pressure to reorganize in a way that might benefit the "national economy" was to emphasize its family quality, by giving a rather extended meaning to the "family." The 1930 report referred for the first time to "the large family of AFL." In the same year Falck began to promote a pioneering social project to reduce industrial accidents. And the next year Goisis, Falck's loyal adviser, or *consigliere*, successfully proposed a change of name so that Falck would appear in the name of the enterprise: Accierierie e Ferriere Lombarde Falck. The rationale given was that the old name AFL had been too anonymous and had led to "confusion" in business correspondence.[16] Now the company would be controlled by a board with

23. *Giorgio Enrico Falck, 1866–1947*

COURTESY OF THE FALCK ARCHIVE, MILAN

eight members, of whom five came from family: Giorgio Enrico, his sons Enrico, Giovanni, and Bruno, and son-in-law Giovanni Devoto. In addition, Ludovico Goisis, Enrico Scalini, and Antonio Feltrinelli were on the board. The central direction remained in the hands of G. E. Falck and Goisis.

The annual report introduced the notion of a new corporate identity with a personal note from the president: "While I express my gratitude allow me to say that for me the most satisfying sense of such an event lies in the will to express the unity and unanimity with which our great family has always marched toward ever greater goals. For twenty-five years I have identified myself with this work of construction, to which I have devoted every fire and every passion." The report also added a fulsome but largely cosmetic tribute to the Duce: "In this way our sense of citizenship, which goes above all personal interest, allows us to see ourselves as not unworthy soldiers in one of the first and most important sectors of the economic front, which our country has formed under the enlightened leadership of the chief of government against every hostile economic influence."[17]

Another way of building family values was to emphasize not only a paternalist ethos of social responsibility but also Catholic tradition. In the early 1920s the company built a large housing complex, the "village," opposite the entrance to the Unione steelworks in Sesto San Giovanni. In 1934 the village was completed by the dedication of a new church, San Giorgio delle Ferriere, which commemorated Saints George and Irene (the patron saints of the patriarch and his wife) as well as Saint Ambrose of Milan. On the right side of the altar stood a relief of Saint Joseph as a worker, cast from Falck steel. Sesto began to look like the Wendel towns of Lorraine, Joeuf, Moyeuvre, and Stiring.

Falck responded to the continuing depression in Italy with renewed attempts to purchase additional plants. As it changed its name, AFL also changed its structure, and the business reorganized itself into divisions: Unione (steel rolling), Concordia (sheet rolling), Vittoria (cold rolling), and Vulcano (cast iron). The board agreed to the expansion of hydroelectric activity and also voted for a bond issue (25 million liras) in order to finance more expansion and to consolidate the short-term bank debt.[18] In 1933 AFL agreed to buy a concession for power plants in Sondrio at Codera and

24. *San Giorgio delle Ferriere, with Falck village in background*
COURTESY OF THE FALCK ARCHIVE, MILAN

Ratti, and in 1934 G. E. Falck proposed the creation of a separate "Servizi Idroelettrici" in the company to handle the continuing expansion into power. In 1935 he bought a plant from the Impianti Industriale Federico Anselmino.[19]

In April 1934 the administrative council discussed further acquisitions that would "in a not distant time bring new riches."[20] In 1934 Ilva and Falck took equal shares in Società Acciaierie e Tubificio di Brescia. AFL thus continued, remarkably and optimistically, a policy of expansion through the worst phases of the world economic crisis. A new electric furnace at Sesto San Giovanni started operations in 1932 with a production of 11,300 tons and by 1934 was making 26,300 tons.[21] By 1934 the predepression level of steel production (210,000 tons) had been reached. It was followed by a dramatically fast expansion financed by capital increases, with the overall output of the steelworks reaching 586,375 tons in 1938.[22]

The rivalry with the large-scale steel producers, now controlled by the state as a response to Italy's latent banking crisis, continued. On 12–13 April 1932 a meeting of the senior managers of Ilva concluded:

> The main competitor of Ilva is Falck, which has practically written off the cost of its investment in steelmaking plant. In addition it has all the advantages of large-scale plant, of the blooming type, without the burden of interest and depreciation. At the moment, Falck has the advantage. Now it is clear that in order to regain industrial preeminence, Ilva will have to reduce its interest and amortization burden considerably. It seems that it is necessary, that one day (even in a distant future) Ilva must be able not only industrially but also financially to seize the advantage of low costs of production, and put pressure on its competitors by price reductions that will force them to incur losses."[23]

In March 1932 Ilva's general director, Francesco Dandolo Rebua, produced a report in which he compared the low returns of Ilva with the profitability of the Falck combination of steel and hydroelectric works. Whereas, he said, Falck had almost completely amortized its capital investments, those of Ilva were being amortized at a rate of only 3.5 percent, and at this rate the investment would take fifty years to be paid off.[24]

Sinigaglia, who joined the main board of the state holding company Sofindit in 1932, when it took control of Ilva, wrote in response to a report on the profitability of the state steel sector: "It is well known, if not provable, that Falck realizes much larger profits than are set out in the accounts, as this is easy for a family enterprise such as his. We know besides that a large part of the electrical investment was made with profits from steel."[25] He saw the state enterprises as fighting a running war with Falck, and urged Ilva to open more plants in order to crush the private-sector competition. In 1932 he wrote to Giorgio Di Veroli, a banker at the Banca Commerciale, "I do not think, as Ardissone [the director of Ilva] seems to imagine, that Falck will prolong the consortium, but instead I think he will go into opposition in order to make a new profit. Also I believe that if Falck really wants a fight, the government would prevent him in the interest of the national economy; but if there is a conflict, the plant in Marghera [near Venice] would be a trump card, and is an important weakness of Ilva, which is leaving Falck with a free field in an important area of steel consumption in the Veneto and eastern Lombardy."[26]

Ilva's managers continued to be optimistic, but they knew that they could succeed only because of the politics of the state's commitment to steel. Agostino Rocca explained: "We can take Falck as a point of comparison. This enterprise has a particular advantage because of its location, as is well known. The conclusive research on this theme has however showed that enterprises with an 'integral cycle' have a better position than companies that work with scrap. On the basis of its organic situation, Ilva has the preconditions that will allow it to dominate the market." Sinigaglia put the point equally dramatically: "I believe that the comparison should rest on the fact that Ilva in the present competitive situation must always SUFFER the competition of Falck, which has significantly lower costs, although Ilva has the advantage of favorable factors, in particular the price of ore from Elba."[27]

On 26 January 1933 the steel syndicate was renewed, with a share for Ilva of 19,937 tons out of a total steel quota of 67,000 tons, and for Falck (the second-largest producer) of 7,980 tons.[28] Mussolini then intervened again, meeting with the major members of the Consorzio Siderurgico on 13 March 1933. He explained that the steelmakers were not responding adequately to the Fascist initiatives for industrial reorganization: "Unfortunately it is a question of one of these circumstances that have recently become quite common, in which the business leaders say that the company can be completely cured if particular measures are taken. I issue the appropriate orders, and things develop worse than they were before."[29]

But how could a private manufacturer be compelled to join a state industry? Ilva manager Arturo Luzzato wrote to Sinigaglia in July 1933: "The reply from Milan [that is, from G. E. Falck] is negative, and I do not know if you yourself wish to attempt to try to approach Falck, and in this case, that is, if Falck would alter his approach, everything that I say would not be relevant, at least for now."[30] In the end, the state steel sector could use the regime's power to cut prices in a managed trade regime.

Falck finally suffered a competitive loss of position only later in the decade, as a result of Italy's turn to autarky, which made access to imported scrap difficult. In 1936 the board noted the effects of increased tariffs, freight rates, and the fiscal burden at a time when product prices were not rising.[31] In 1938 the annual report stated that "the recent provisions of the law adopted by our country, as part of the plan for autarky, have brought our company into a serious situation, in which our business is diminished and risks even further diminution. The plan does not take account of the nature of a large part of our business, which produces pig iron from pyrites and national ore, using hydroelectric power that we have developed since 1916."[32]

There had been an intense debate about autarky within the Italian business community, in which Falck intervened with great vigor. The president of the metallurgical producers' association Federmetal, Arturo Bocciardo, in October 1936 had prepared a memorandum on "Autarky and the Steel Industry," intended to support the regime's policy. G. E. Falck attacked this as being based on "unreal premises":

> Bocciardo bases his calculations on maritime transport without thinking about other production locations more or less independent of the sea, with varied possibilities of importing foreign raw materials. And as to the consumption locations, he does not calculate the transport costs. Apart from that he does not allow for the hard currency required for particular installations and servicing of coke-powered blast furnaces, which depend directly or indirectly on foreign assistance . . . Future events [that is, the outbreak of war] will reveal whether his calculations are appropriate, and the response will depend on real events and not on presumptions.[33]

Falck's conclusion was that the priorities imposed by the state sector were economically damaging.

One other strategy followed by the regime in rescuing state steel producers lay in the encouragement of foreign investment as a way of modernizing. In the later 1930s the foreign investment was heavily politicized, and in practice meant increased contacts with Germany and German industry. In 1937 the GHH proposed to build a new blast furnace for the Ansaldo steelworks.[34]

There was another sort of political intervention, in regional policy (in which, as with the state encouragement of the *ciclo integrale*, there exists a substantial continuity between Fascist and postwar policy). In the later 1930s the government pressed for greater investment in the Alto Adige region (South Tyrol), which it intended to develop as an industrial zone as a counter to German nationalist claims. AFL-Falck responded with the creation of the Acciaierie di Bolzano, which rapidly became a leader in the manufacture of high-quality specialty steels.

Almost every aspect of policy was now presented in a political light. The company continued to invest considerable amounts in social facilities, in part to defuse political attacks or to court political favor. In 1934 Giorgio Enrico Falck was appointed a member of the Italian Senate. In 1938, on an official visit, the secretary-general of the Fascist party, Achille Starace, inspected new workers' housing and a new model school. In 1936 the board voted to congratulate the Duce on his "brilliant victory" by which Italy had acquired an empire. Italy, the resolution went, "now has an empire, on which are focused her projects, her efforts, and her hopes."[35] The orientation toward empire and autarky was costly for the company, however, and engagement in the European war produced a quick disillusionment with the Mussolini regime.

Production fell off after the outbreak of war in June 1940, largely because of shortages of scrap and other raw materials. But the steelworks continued to operate until they were closed down after the fall of Fascism in 1943, the subsequent German occupation of northern Italy, and the creation of a new puppet state for Mussolini, the Repubblica Sociale Italiana. There were now major shortages of coal. In late 1943 sharp price increases provoked a combination of economic and political protest. On 13 December workers in four of the major enterprises working for German military requirements in Milan began a strike. SS Colonel Paul Zimmermann, the officer in charge of the suppression of labor unrest, shut down Falck as an "enemy enterprise." The German military authorities deported ninety-five Falck workers, and fifty-seven others were killed. Some Falck enterprises, in particular the engineering works Franco Tosi, continued to work as "protected enterprises" in the system introduced by Albert Speer in early 1943.[36]

The Second World War, unlike the First, brought few new business opportunities for Falck. It was hard to be optimistic about the future. For Falck, the past twenty years held out clear lessons:

that banks brought industry into a dangerous compromise with the state, and that state-guided industrialism meant gigantism, inefficiency, a waste of national resources. In June 1942 Giorgio Enrico Falck drew up his will: "I do not know whether future events will allow the enterprise to be maintained and developed. Naturally I hope so. In all things, act so as to create honor for its name and mine, which I tried to make esteemed. Above all, be honest and scrupulous and do not be tempted by unclear affairs whose basis is speculation."[37]

PART FOUR

The Age of the Postwar Miracle

Both the reputation of the family firm and its economic prospects reached a nadir in the middle of the twentieth century. The world war on the European continent had led to a discrediting of every aspect of the old society, and to a search for new models of organization, for more technocracy and more bigness. The idea of the plan dominated not just the wartime but also the postwar era. France had a particular obsession with *planisme*, but such initiatives as the European Recovery Program (or Marshall Plan) helped to establish a general idea that planning might transform the whole European business structure. What the historian Charles Maier termed the "politics of productivity" demanded a new relationship with labor, which would be mediated throught the state.[1] For steel and coal, planning was given a European context by the Schuman plan for crossnational integration and the subsequent establishment of the European Coal and Steel Community (ECSC). But paradoxically, despite some interesting initiatives (such as a proposal that Wendel should take over important parts of the German steel industry, including the GHH), all the debate about the European context, and moves to closer political integration, produced no genuinely European firms at this time. The debate about both planning and corporate restructuring thus occurred in a distinctly national context.

For family firms, the transformation was often accompanied by a generational transition. The general and prevailing uncertainty left its mark on family biographies. In the cases examined here, the larger-than-life figures of the interwar period, Giorgio Enrico Falck, François de Wendel, Paul Reusch, Werner Carp, were all old and exhausted in 1945. They passed the business on—and they themselves passed away, in 1947, 1949, 1956, and 1950, respectively. The men of the 1950s, Enrico Falck, Henri de Wendel, Hermann Reusch, and Alfred Haniel, proved to be transitional figures, and it was only in the 1960s and 1970s that a really new generation looked for a liberation from the past and took a new approach to the definition of family traditions.

Chapter 10

A Costly Miracle in Italy

For us there exists not only production, as the liberals claim, or only distribution, as the theorists of socialism wish to affirm, but both; and woe if the productive process is not at the head of the order of preoccupations.

Enrico Falck, 1945

THE YEARS AFTER the Second World War saw a rapid transition of generations in the direction of AFL. The company's founder, Giorgio Enrico Falck, in 1946 resigned from the direction of AFL, in part because as a senator he was felt to have been compromised by association with Fascism. In any case, he was seventy-eight years old, and both he and Enrico Scalini died in 1947. In March 1948 G. E. Falck's son Enrico also resigned from the management of the enterprise, which he had directed for only two years. Like his father, he had decided to spend his time in politics rather than business. The conflicts of the Fascist era had shown how closely intertwined business fortunes were with political decisions, especially in steel. It was highly likely that the state and the idea of planning would be set to work for the benefit of the state steel sector and of its managers.

During the war Enrico Falck had been involved in the Catholic resistance to Fascism in Milan. A group of Catholic intellectuals met in his house, at One via Tamburini, to develop an alternative to liberalism and the planned economy, but also to the obvious failure of the "third way" offered by Fascism and corporatism. In their approach to economics, the Catholic intellectuals took as a basis the idea of a *nuovo ordine economico* as elaborated in late 1943 at the Catholic University by Professors Francesco Vito and Amintore Fanfani. There was also a political dimension. In September 1942 the leaders of the former Partito Popolare of Don Luigi Sturzo and the Movimento Neoguelfo, with which Enrico Falck was associated, in Falck's house established a new political party, the Democrazia Cristiana. Such activities became quite widely known in Milan. Enrico Falck was arrested by the German authorities in January 1945 and held in prison until the liberation.

After the new political ordering, Falck could pursue the new political agenda. In 1948 he was elected senator for the Lecco area. With this, his brothers moved into the management of the company; thus they had taken over the management before his death in 1953. Enrico Falck also participated in the founding of an Association of Christian Entrepreneurs and Managers, the Unione Cristiana Imprenditori Dirigenti.

Enrico Falck devoted his energy increasingly to sketching out a new philosophy of entrepreneurship, or, as he sometimes called it, "technological spiritualism." There was an intense debate in the postwar era about the appropriate ethic of a new society. Falck argued that Catholics (and more generally Christians) should not see profit as immoral, or the good businessman as doomed to failure, because to accept such a cliché would be to condone the social and economic exclusion of Catholics. "We should not be scandalized when an entrepreneur notes that the share company is not a charitable institution. It would be a mistake to believe that the honest manager is bound to fail, or that the business world is the heritage of scoundrels: as if a young man, driven by intelligence and social circumstances to lead a business that depends on people, must lose his quality as a Christian by contact with conventions that are less than honest." But for this vision of good men participating fully in economic and social life, there needed to be an appropriate kind of state. The interventionist state of the Fascist era, in which initiative was crippled because everyone looked to the state to be the prime mover, had been catastrophic. But an appropriately directed state, in which individuals had a sense of participation, could leave businesses as independent entities. "For us there exists not only production, as the liberals claim, or only distribution, as the theorists of socialism wish to affirm, but both; and woe if the productive process is

25. *Enrico Falck, 1899–1953*

COURTESY OF THE FALCK ARCHIVE, MILAN

not at the head of the order of preoccupations. Of all the forms of anarchy the most productive is to drop into the abyss all brilliant constructions of social life and the proposals and programmatic schemes of parties." The essence of Falck's vision lay in the ability of a democratic process in national politics to provide an attractive alternative to claims by workers to manage factories themselves, or to the state to control the productive process directly. "When will it be recognized that for an industrial recovery to occur, the proliferation of organs of control is not possible, and the directing force must be an aristocracy, to use an unpopular but correct phrase, that is purely elected democratically and not indirectly through the acquisition of shares in the company. I believe that it is better to feel some part in a tangible way, not simply of the process of production, but of the instrumental goods [of politics]."[1] Property needed to be adequately controlled by a political process.

In 1948 Giovanni Falck (G. E. Falck's second son) became president and Bruno Falck (the third son) general manager *(amministratore delegato)*. Was this an unentrepreneurial successor generation? The Falcks certainly behaved according to the model of elite families, with widespread interests in charity, in social projects, and in collecting. They sponsored the Ambrosianeum (of which Enrico was a cofounder) as a center of Milanese Catholic culture. Maly Da Zara Falck, the wife of Giovanni, engaged herself in the Pro Juventute movement of Don Gnocchi for relief for war invalids, and above all in the sponsorship of Montessori teaching for children, with a model school in Sesto San Giovanni. Camille Ciceri Falck, the widow of Enrico, supported the Casa del Giovine of Don Abramo Martignoni. Giulia Devoto Falck, G. E. Falck's daughter, established hospitals for the poor, in particular for women and their children (Casa della Madre e del Fanciullo). Both Giovanni and Bruno sponsored projects to reduce the level of industrial accidents. Giovanni was a major collector of modern art, Bruno of historical clocks (the collection is now in the Museum Poldi Pezzoli), and Alberto of books, manuscripts, Meissen porcelain, and Roman glasses.

But the Falck men were also trained and professional engineers; and it could be argued that their noneconomic interests had a purpose in establishing a mission for the company. In the aftermath of the Second World War, as before and after the First World War, labor relations were particularly difficult in the big industrial cities of northern Italy. The Catholic culture that the Falcks promoted was very consciously an answer and an alternative to class conflict. By the 1950s, on the one hand, the Communist leader Pietro Secchia, who had been sent on a special mission to Lombardy by party leader Palmiro Togliatti, referred to Sesto San Giovanni as the Stalingrad of the day, in which the class war was played out;[2] while on

26. *Cardinal Montini visits the Falck Montessori school, 1952*

COURTESY OF THE FALCK ARCHIVE, MILAN

the other side the archbishop of Milan, Cardinal Montini (the future Pope Paul VI), supported the educational and social concept of the firm. Such contacts inevitably produced conspiracy theories of the left in which Montini worked with the Vatican banker Michele Sindona in order to rescue north Italian capitalism.[3] The Falcks certainly saw family business in terms of a wider struggle about the appropriate form of political life—about the placing of limitations on politics, the viability of democracy, and the ability of industry to satisfy the demand for economic growth.

Expansion and the Economic Miracle

The controversy about the postwar future of Italian steel ran along astonishingly similar lines to that fought out in the 1930s, and was indeed conducted by some of the same personalities—and then by their children. The Falcks played a central role, in part because of their political connections, but in part because their enterprise was one of the few indisputably modern private steelworks in an industry that was castigated by modernizers for its technical backwardness. As in France and Britain, the problems of family firms were often held responsible for the state of the industry, and private ownership was thus supposed to be an obstacle to effective large-scale investment and modernization. In October 1945 an economic commission was established with the goals of "increasing industrial productivity" and "removing the economy of the country from the influence of hegemonic groups."[4] As a defensive gesture, Fiat even acknowledged that it might be desirable to nationalize industries that produced public goods (such as water and electrical energy). The new constitution of the Italian Republic then indeed under article 43 provided for the nationalization of companies in cases in which a monopoly prevailed. The case of steel was peculiar, however, because the largest enterprises were already under state control, and there also existed a suspicion of state-dominated industry as a legacy of the Fascist era.

Giovanni Falck in 1946 told an official inquiry that plants with an annual capacity of 150,000 to 200,000 tons (such as that of the large private-sector producers, Falck, Fiat, and Breda) were the strength of the Italian business landscape: "In order to satisfy the Italian requirements eight or ten works, distributed in favorable areas from the standpoint of energy, transport, and the market, would suffice."[5] Oscar Sinigaglia, on the other hand, who had now become the head of the large semimonopolistic state enterprise Finsider, returned with his already well-formulated concept of the integrated cycle in steelmaking as central to the economic development of modern Italy. He produced a systematic indictment of the existing Italian steel industry as "old-fashioned, inappropriate, and senseless plants (with a few laudable exceptions)." It had been dominated not by entrepreneurs, but by stock-exchange speculators.[6] In 1948 he argued: "in the past, very little was actually done by our industries to reduce costs and bring them down to the level of other countries, though this would have been possible despite the shortage of raw materials." He laid out how the Marshall Plan was going to help to realize an agenda that had been set out even before the war. "During the years immediately before the war . . . the conversion of two integrated plants was started and almost completed, and a third brand-new integrated plant was built. These works were to be followed by the modernizing of the plants for processing steel into semifinished steel and finished mass products and into flat steel products, these being the least efficient production sectors, equipped with the most out-of-date machinery. The war not only put an end to this programme but destroyed the most up-to-date plants [in particular Cornigliano] fitted with blast furnaces."[7]

Such proposals formed the basis of a government plan that encompassed the big private-sector producers, Fiat and Falck, the "Programma di investimenti nel settore industriale per il periodo 1948–1952." A large part of this program was realized with funds from the Marshall Plan, which Falck also used to promote new investment. The 1948 accounts of AFL show a credit of 510 million liras ($0.8 million) from the Istituto Mobilare Italiano and 904 million liras from the Eximbank, as well as 974 million liras from the Istituto di Credito per le Imprese di Pubblica Utilità. In 1949 a new plant for seamless tubes at Porta Romana, in Milan, began operations. Fiat and Falck used the opportunity to expand plate production. The Franco Tosi engineering works, which was part of the Falck group, benefited substantially from the new demand for equipment: it obtained licenses from Combustion Engineering for generating boilers, and from Westinghouse for turbines for electricity production.[8] The reduction of prices for steel plate had an obvious benefit for the Italian automobile industry, and especially for the production of Fiat cars.

The high level of new investment continued through the 1950s, with two new electric furnaces (Lectromelt) at the Unione works in 1952, a new production line at Arcore for seamless tubes in 1953, and a new rolling mill at Concordia in 1956 as well as a mill for the production for large-diameter tubes. In 1955 Falck started to produce thin coils (under 650 millimeters) in a semicontinuous process. At first the increase in steel production took place on the basis of modernized Siemens-Martin hearths. The company's overall steel production increased from the 1938 level of 273,000 tons to 601,000 tons in 1959.

A much more radical set of innovations occurred in the 1960s, with a shift to oxygen-based steelmaking processes. The major expansion in steel production took place in 1961, when AFL constructed a new electric steel mill (Concordia) at Sesto San Giovanni, which opened in 1964 with a 140-ton-capacity electric furnace. In 1961 a continuous finishing train was installed at the Unione works in Sesto San Giovanni. In 1966 this was supplemented by a new rolling mill for billets and rods. In 1968 improved facilities for the recycling of waste gases were added. In 1969 the company opened a new plateworks, Assel, at Sesto San Giovanni.

In 1963 Falck began manufacture of ferrochrome at the traditional family site at Dongo, on Lake Como. This factory, like other small works at Vobarno (Brescia) and Novate Mezzola (Sondrio), was highly specialized and was largely supported by grants for regional development from the Italian government.[9] The works at Bolzano were the most modern Alpine steelworks in Europe. Similar regional policy issues pushed the expansion of southern Italian works, with a big increase in investment in 1961 in the Naples works (Società Cantieri Metallurgia Italiani). In 1962 Falck reported proudly that "not one of our works, however small and however peripheral, has been closed down in the postwar era."[10] The level of employment in the core steel business (which was closely monitored by the political system) remained relatively constant through the big expansion. Falck employed 15,000 workers in 1947 and 13,000 in 1970: an indication of a remarkable surge in productivity.

The Falck works continued to use electric-powered steel furnaces. This process held the key to the company's location. As in 1914–1918, the firm had used the wartime period to expand hydroelectric production. In the months before the outbreak of the European war in 1939, some commentators had drawn attention to Italy's power shortage.[11] Falck launched a large new program after 1941. In 1946 there were further capital investments in the hydroelectric plant at Belviso, followed by new plants at Publino (1950) and Ganda (1955). A new departure was the construction in the province of Milan of a thermoelectrical plant at Tavazzano in 1953, in partnership with Edison, the chemical company Montecatini, the Azienda Eletrica Municipale di Milano, and the state petroleum company AGIP. By the mid-1950s the Falcks were operating fifteen power plants. In 1946 AFL-Falck had produced 203 megawatts of electricity, or 2.9 percent of the Italian national output; in 1962 the company was making 381 megawatts (2.5 percent of the Italian production).[12]

Both the expansion in steel capacity and the development of new electricity works (especially Tavazzano) were highly capital intensive. The drive to expand was financed in part by borrowing (mostly from public-sector institutions). In 1961 Falck launched a bond issue of 50 million Swiss francs ($12 million). Like much of the Italian steel industry, Falck depended on a high level of leverage. In the mid-1960s Falck pointed out that Italian steel could finance only 17 percent of its investment from its own resources, while the French industry had paid for 37 percent and the European Economic Community average was 42 percent. The result was that 68 percent of Italian steel investment was financed through long- or medium-term credits (in contrast with 34 percent in France). The amount paid for through short-term credit (10 percent) was twice the European average.[13]

Expansion for Falck required major capital increases, which went beyond merely making an adjustment for the depreciation of the Italian currency: from 290 million to 500 million liras ($0.9 million) in 1947, to 2,000 million ($3.0 million) in 1948, to 4.5 billion ($6.8 million) in 1949. New increases through the 1950s took the firm's capital base to 7.8 billion liras ($12.4 million) in 1953, 12 billion ($19.1 million) in 1956, and 15 billion ($24.0 million) in 1958. In 1962 AFL increased its capitalization to 22 billion liras ($35.5 million) in preparation for 1963, when AFL was quoted for the first time on the Milan stock exchange. This was the point of maximum confidence in the Italian steel business, when there seemed to be almost limitless expansion on the basis of rapid technical modernization.

In the 1960s, the context of this expansion was the institutional framework of the European Economic Community. The European engagement had been part of the political project of Enrico Falck, who had been one of the Italian representatives at the Consultative Assembly of the Council of Europe. But the economics of integration had at first been rather worrying to the north Italian producers of steel from (mostly imported) scrap by the use of an electrical Martin process.

Falck had been concerned about the likely effects of the Treaty of Rome (1957), and complained in particular that Italian industry was disadvantaged by the freight rates, which were set to the advantage of the industrial concentration in northern France and the Ruhr.[14] But the Falck enterprise also presented itself as a model of efficient steelmaking, with high levels of investment required.[15] In the 1960s AFL launched an initiative in internationalization, buying a participation in the Belgian firm Sidérurgie Maritime (Sidmar) in 1962, which operated an integral cycle, and whose location gave access to seaborne imported ores.

The prewar traditions of paternalism continued. AFL-Falck sponsored the establishment of Montessori schools (a particular interest of Maly Da Zara Falck). The construction of workers' housing continued, as part of the first big postwar investments, aimed at solving the major social problem of the day.[16] In 1960 a large new facility, the Villagio Ina-Casa di Brughiero, opened at Sesto San Giovanni. But the paternalism now had a distinctive technical element, as part of the general emphasis on a modernization of Italian society. To honor the memory of Enrico Falck, in 1953 the company sponsored the Centro d'Addestramento E. Falck to train qualified workers.

At the beginning of the 1960s AFL could look back on a remarkable record of growth, innovation, and employment creation; it seemed to be a perfect realization of Enrico Falck's vision of entrepreneurship. The 1961 annual report stated: "But it is appropriate to recognize that the improperly named 'miracle' is the fruit, maturing over a long time, of the working together of the idea, the will, and the works of several generations of Italian workers, and, without question, in the first instance, of the creators and animators of industry."[17] But in the course of the 1960s this ideal came under strain. Could a family that had creatively overcome adversity in depression and war also survive prosperity? Families now had to innovate in order to continue the family business tradition.

Chapter 11

A New Kind of Family Togetherness

Since it is really the last moment in which the family can take its fortunes in hand, it should be possible for all members of the family to put aside special interests and stand behind one representative.

Wolfgang Curtius, 1951

AFTER THE WAR the Ruhr industry was reorganized by the Allies. In particular, the United States was suspicious of big concentrations of industrial power and of the German tradition of *Konzerne*, and many U.S. officials regarded Ruhr industrial power as one of the driving forces behind National Socialism. France, which like most of continental Europe was politically unstable in the immediate postwar period, demanded greater and preferential access to Ruhr coal, which it urgently required for its sweeping program of industrial modernization. The British Labour government regarded the nationalization of steel and coal as an important part of a strategy of planning and modernization. Steel and coal were thus at the center of debates about the postwar order. In the initial Allied vision, family management of the big heavy industrial enterprises constituted the heart of the German problem.

In the 1950s the challenge to the German industrial structure shifted from international pressure and Allied demands to domestic politics. Riding on the wave of demands for a reconstruction of the economic order, labor demanded a greater role in the management of enterprise, especially in the strategically and socially vital coal and steel industries. The result was the representation of labor on supervisory boards (co-determination), and in the longer run a weakening of this particular institution of corporate governance. Both the Allied demand for the breakup of positions of power and the labor demand for co-determination ended up strengthening the role of families in German business. At first sight, this looks like a classic paradox of the unintended consequences of reform legislation. The explanation is simple: both the Allied and the labor demands involved placing restrictions on ownership that would stand in the way of a capital- and market-driven "Anglo-Saxon" version of capitalism. This arrangement left more room for family ownership. A further consequence of the co-determination legislation was that the requirements for steel and coal were consistently greater than for other industries because of the perception that these were core industries. This treatment of a strategic industry made steel and coal less attractive for owners, and in the end played a part in persuading Haniels to get out of this sector quite rapidly, while in other European countries their equivalents remained for rather longer (and lost a great deal of money in the steel crisis of the 1970s and 1980s).

Deconcentration

An important immediate postwar Allied priority was to break up the large German *Konzerne*, and also to separate steel from coal. In November 1947 the U.S. and U.K. authorities created the Deutsche Kohlenbergbau Leitung in Essen as a central planning instance for the coal industry. On 18 November 1948, Law 75 on the Reordering of German Coal Mining and of the German Iron and Steel Industry (Umgestaltung des deutschen Kohlenbergbaus und der deutschen Eisen- und Stahlindustrie) required the liquidation of *Konzerne* "in order to remove the excessive concentration of economic power and the return to health of German economic life."

In addition, for the Allies family businesses like those of the by-now-notorious Krupps and Thyssens were profoundly problematical. Fritz Thyssen had ghostwritten a book, *I Paid Hitler*. The senile and incontinent Gustav Krupp von Bohlen und Halbach and his son, Alfried, were put on trial before the International Military Tribunal at Nuremberg. Despite the clear opposition of Paul Reusch to National Socialism, the GHH did not escape the substantial

Allied criticism of the German industrial order. The investigation of the GHH by the Office of the Military Government of the United States (OMGUS) began with the observation that "the Ruhr with its big family combines is a classical place to study the influences of family complexes on the economic and political destinies of a country." It set out a highly personalized version of the interwar story as a clash between the conservative manager Paul Reusch and the old-style supervisory board chairman Karl Haniel on the one side and the dynamic intriguer Werner Carp on the other. In 1945 Werner Carp himself, who did not see himself as a "real Nazi," was so amazed and indignant when British soldiers arrested him at midnight and interned him that he refused to dress, and was taken away in his pajamas.[1]

The organizational consequence of Allied suspicion of German business practice was a separation and fragmentation, in which the kaleidoscope of German capitalism was shaken and recast. But when the new pattern settled into place, it retained substantial elements from the past. As in Japan, where the large family trusts *(zaibatsu)* were broken up, but where networks of informal contacts quickly reemerged and resembled many of the old structures, German corporations, though broken up, still had ownership structures that encouraged new versions of old combinations. Tackling the issues that arose out of the splitting up of corporations often required an emphasis on informal contacts, such as those that existed above all in family groupings. In this way, decartelization gave a new impetus to the formation of German-style family capitalism (in a strange parallel to the impetus given to Italian family capitalism by Mussolini's attempted reshaping of business organization).

The former GHH was split into four companies: one, a rump Gutehoffnungshütte Aktienverein, had a capitalization of 83.2 million Deutschmarks ($17.9 million) and included only the engineering and manufacturing parts of the old GHH (that is, no steel and no coal).

On 1 March 1947 the steelworks Hüttenwerke Oberhausen AG was established as a separate company under trustees appointed by the military government, and on 1 September 1951 it was turned into an independent company with a capitalization of 104 million Deutschmarks ($22.4 million). On 31 October 1951 the mining companies Neumühl and Rheinpreussen, which had also held 58

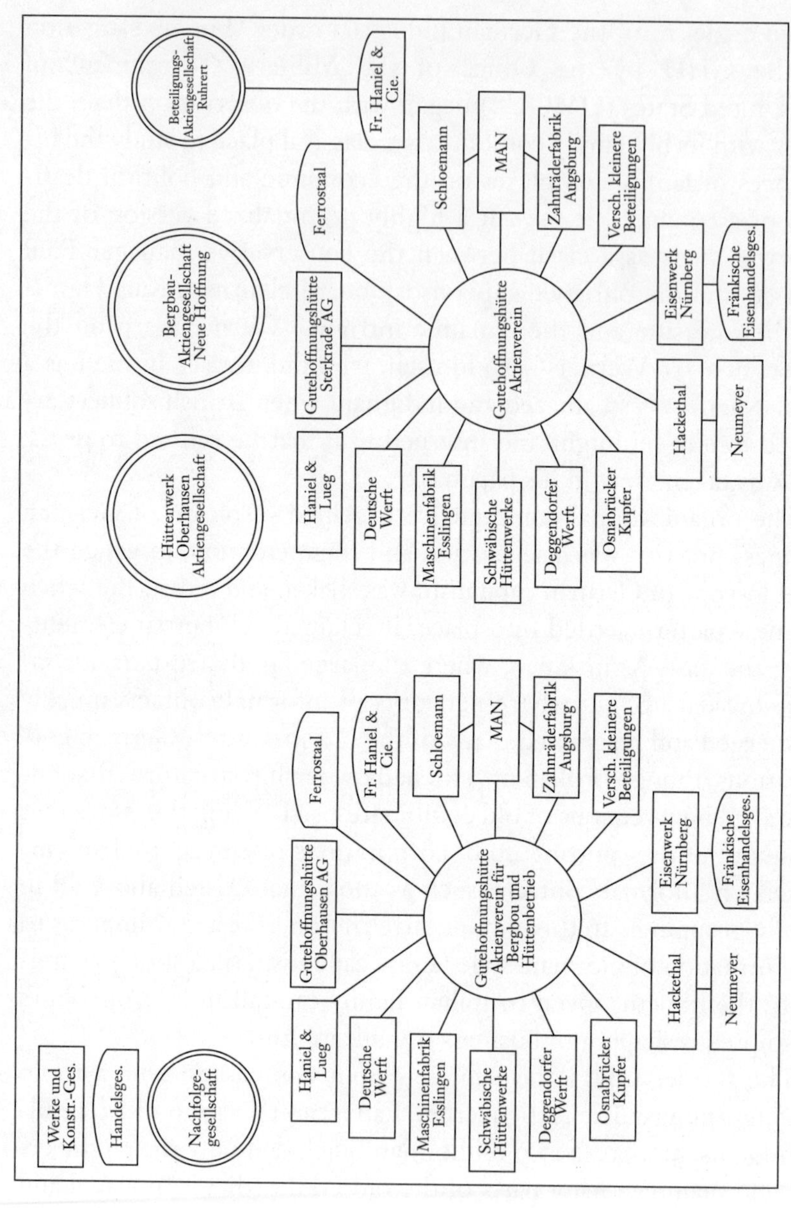

27. *The GHH before and after reorganization, 1953*

percent of FHC shares, were converted into joint-stock companies, Bergbau und Industrie Aktiengesellschaft Neumühl and Rheinpreussen Aktiengesellschaft für Bergbau und Chemie. Through an exchange of shares, their old participations in FHC were now owned directly by shareholders (that is, some members of the Haniel family). On 28 May 1952 the Bergbau Aktiengesellschaft Neue Hoffnung, also with a capitalization of 104 million DM, was created through an order of the Combined Coal Control Group. Finally, the Beteiligungs-Aktiengesellschaft Ruhrort (BAGR), established in 1953 with a capitalization of 5.2 million DM, held the former GHH participation of 42 percent of the stock of FHC.

Reconcentration

The reordering of the German business structure apparently at a stroke destroyed a network of contacts and business relationships, as well as ownership structures. It directly challenged the family network. The different parts of the GHH empire had been locked into long-term agreements to supply one another and to transport one another's goods, often at preferential or long-term rates that did not reflect immediate market fluctuations. The attractions of such a system appeared great, as in the wake of war, monetary turbulence, and shocks such as the Korean war there were obviously a great number of short-term disturbances. The new threats produced a demand for risk minimization, and the activation of old contacts and networks looked like an attractive way of managing an uncertain future. Parts of the system were thus quite quickly reconstituted. In the case of the often quite newly separated Haniel corporations, there still existed many common links. Managers and owners knew and reached out to one another.

FHC still existed as a coal-trading company, but it had lost much of its fleet in the war and was a quite small-scale operation: its overall balance sheet in 1952 amounted to only 115 million DM ($25 million). In April 1952 the Rheinpreussen mine reached an agreement with the Haniel family owners that FHC would conduct shipments and deliveries to its major customers, notably Hoechst, Bayer, and the public-sector railroad corporation (Bundesbahn), as well as to the Wendel company in Lorraine. The 1951–52 report of FHC stated:

> From the recognition that we can still provide valuable services with our varied and long experience in transport and sales organization, the Rheinpreussen Mining Company has made long-term contracts with us for the sale and distribution of solid fuels; similar contracts are being negotiated with the mining company Neue Hoffnung. With the collapse in 1945 we lost valuable participations, as well as advantages from our relationships with other *Konzern* companies, but we believe that in the future we will be able to survive even though we stand on our own.[2]

The most obvious links among companies were provided by common ownership. The core companies for the Haniel family were now FHC and the old coal-mining companies (Rheinpreussen and Neumühl), rather than the dismembered GHH. At the end of 1952 forty-five members of the Haniel family held shares in FHC. The number of family owners rapidly rose, in a remarkably successful adaptation of the family to the new business environment, and also a testimony to the strong demographic growth of the baby-boom years of the Federal Republic. In 1959, 72 Haniel family members owned stock in Rheinpreussen, 34 in Bergbau- und Industrie AG Neumühl, and 99 in FHC (obviously these figures contain some overlaps). By the end of the 1960s, when a distinctive West German model of business life (what Helmut Schmidt later referred to as *Modell Deutschland*) had been securely established and was widely admired, 142 family members owned shares in FHC. The family provided a solid basis for business links in politically turbulent times.

In the past the GHH had been *the* major Haniel vehicle, and this was how Paul Reusch had managed it. Paradoxically, one of the reasons the Haniels managed to retain an influence in the GHH was that their grip was contracting so quickly for economic rather than political reasons and thus appeared to be much less of a political threat. Impoverishment and chaos compelled many family members to sell their shares in the immediate aftermath of the war; Paul Reusch was no longer able to guide family politics; and other major figures of the old days, notably Werner Carp, died. In 1906 descendants of the two Haniel brothers, Franz and Gerhard, had owned 77 percent of the share capital of the GHH. On 1 September 1939 they still owned 65 percent, and this ratio remained largely unchanged through the war, when there were few share transactions: on 8 May 1945, the day of the German surrender, it was 64 percent. But on 15 August 1951 the Haniels owned only 35 percent of the capital of GHH. The New York law firm that represented the GHH in its dealings with the Allied High Commission, Shearman and Sterling and Wright, reported that "the drop from 1945 to 1951 has been due primarily to expenses for estate and property taxes and the necessity of living out of capital. Most of the substantial owners are advanced in years and the prospects are that estate taxes will continue to reduce the holdings." Werner Carp, who owned 6,300,000 Reichsmark nominal shares, had died in 1950, and it was "estimated that more than half of his holding in Company will have to be liquidated in order to satisfy taxes and other debts and expenses." The Shearman Sterling document concluded that

> there is no family foundation or trust or council by which this very diversified group attempts to act as a unit and in fact they do not so act . . . No descendent of a Haniel has been in the management of the business since 1873 and no descendant has active employment with the company except Klaus Haniel, age 34, a great-great-grandson of one of the founders, who is a superintendent of a mine in Geislingen. He owns 264,500 RM [Reichsmark] shares . . . It is respectfully submitted that in no group of the various lines of the Haniel descendants is there any element of control of the company.[3]

The external challenge, the experience of decartelization and deconcentration, mobilized the family to coordinate its activities more closely and to assert itself once more within the GHH. There was also a particularly prominent problem in the management of the GHH, which had become conspicuously and inappropriately politically articulate on a whole range of issues. The GHH's general director, Hermann Reusch, who had been forced out by the Nazis but returned to the company immediately after the war, emerged as a highly vocal and visible opponent of Allied policy and of the new regulations on co-determination in coal mining. In October 1950 Reusch announced his resignation from the iron and steel subcommittee of the Schuman plan committee, since "the Allies take an attitude toward heavy industry that makes me personally see cooperation on an international level as unproductive."[4] Reusch's increasingly intemperate public performances made him a very political and controversial figure, who could no longer appear (as his father had for a long time) to be the embodiment of the company and a guarantee of its survival. On the contrary, he was becoming both a nuisance and a liability.

Not surprisingly, Reusch's prominence antagonized some members of the extended Haniel family. A nephew of Werner Carp, the relatively young Wolfgang Curtius (born in 1910), whose father had been first an economics minister and then one of the last foreign ministers of the Weimar Republic (and had also served on the supervisory board of the GHH), tried to lay out an alternative path. Curtius was in a strong position as the general manager of Rheinpreussen, the coal-mining company that also acted as a holding company of GHH shares. He complained to the manager of the family assets bureau that the GHH had been following a largely independent course of action. He demanded that the family mobilize and assert its collective will in relation to its managers (and especially in relation to Hermann Reusch):

> With regard to the GHH I have the impression that the management has largely lost its ability to control its own fate because of the attitude that it took. But quite independently of all unsettling signs it is in my view absolutely essential that, in setting the right general direction and in making the enormously important decisions about a reordering, the family be widely informed and involved in the discussions. Nobody except the family can really take care of its own interests. I myself am firmly convinced that beyond this for family ownership it is necessary to put together a compact group of highly profitable companies that are not subject to co-determination.[5]

Curtius, who saw himself as a family leader after the death of Curt Haniel, had already turned to Hans Böninger:

> Since it is really the last moment in which the family can take its fortunes in hand, it should be possible for all members of the family to put aside special interests and stand behind one representative . . . Another possibility of stopping the division and dis-

> integration of the GHH *Konzern* is to place members of the family in administrative positions. Necessarily when personal links are ended, egotistical ambitions appear in the management, as was the case of Herr Bruns in the Oberhausen ironworks. The antipathy of the Allies and of the trade unions is in the first place directed against the supervisory board, because they fear a representation of interlocking interests in a bad sense. No one has as yet made any objection against competent work from members of the owning family, if they are properly qualified. The GHH has unfortunately not up to now dealt sympathetically with the applications of younger gentlemen from the family, I am thinking for instance of Klaus Haniel, who already for some time has been promised the position of a mining director in Oberhausen.[6]

The instrument for reasserting the idea of the family would be the corporation that bore the family name, FHC. It could be converted from its post-1917 status as essentially an occasionally fractious subsidiary of the GHH into a holding company on its own terms, although throughout the 1950s and 1960s it remained substantially undercapitalized (this changed only in 1971). The resurrection of FHC as an instrument of family control simply required a break with the principle, accepted at the 2 April 1932 supervisory board meeting, of control of FHC by the GHH.

In 1955 the capitalization of FHC was increased from 10 million to 15 million DM ($3.5 million), and FHC gained control of the Beteiligungs AG Ruhrort (BAGR), since as a joint-stock company it could not participate in the capital increase, 78.74 percent of whose capital it now held. As a result the relationship of the BAGR and FHC was reversed: the BAGR was no longer the holding company of FHC, but the other way around, with the result that the BAGR was superfluous. Finally in 1959 the BAGR was dissolved into FHC, with the result that in 1960 FHC had 4.2 million DM of its own stock, which was sold to its shareholders as part of an increase in the capitalization from 15 million to 30 million DM ($7.2 million). The process of reversed detrustification was now complete, with the exception of a legal postlude. The chief difficulty was that the whole issue of reversed detrustification went beyond German legal competence, and the High Authority of the European Coal and Steel Community in Luxembourg needed to give its consent, since FHC was classed as a coal company and was subject to the new European regulation. The second difficulty was that a number of the relatively small group of outside shareholders in the BAGR (who had been nonfamily owners of GHH stock) brought legal action against FHC and had to be bought out at a higher price than initially offered in 1959.

Almost simultaneously, on 1 October 1959, the old link between coal and iron was restored when the Bergbau AG Neue Hoffnung was merged with the Hüttenwerk Oberhausen AG. The old family companies were being put back together again. But this move to consolidation inevitably raised the question whether the old technologies in the steel industry were still appropriate.

In the 1950s the family began to meet regularly as a group *(Familien Kreis)* in order to discuss and coordinate the legally diversified parts of the family holdings. In October 1953 former members of the supervisory board of Franz Haniel & Cie. founded an "advisory committee" *(Beratender Ausschuss)* to shape strategy regarding the relations of FHC with the BAGR; this new entity included Werner Carp's son Carl Eduard and Alfred Haniel's son-in-law Thuisko von Metzsch, as well as Hermann Reusch.[7] Cultivating a sense of historical continuity was an important part of bringing identity to what had become a quite diverse group. One high point of the reinvigorated family identity was a celebration in September 1956, on the Petersberg near Königswinter, of the 200th anniversary of Frederick the Great's grant allowing the establishment of the Ruhrort Packhaus. History provided an obvious way of bringing a family together. In fact many Haniel family members, who were by now quite distant relatives, met for the first time at this event.

In 1958 family members agreed to register their shares and sell them only through the family office in the Malkastenstrasse in Düsseldorf. The declaration they signed started with a statement of purpose: "In order to strengthen the cohesiveness and to secure the ownership of the family enterprises I promise to . . ."[8]

As the German "economic miracle" unfolded, it became clear that in order to succeed, the associated companies in the Haniel *Konzern* would need to increase their capitalization; but it was also apparent that members of the family would be unable or unwilling to go along with such increases. Hence, the family argued, there was a need to concentrate their interests, selling off units that were either peripheral or too expensive in their demands on investment.

FHC itself was a relatively small trading company, which compared itself—usually unfavorably—with analogous but apparently more vigorous competitors in the Ruhr area: Stinnes, Klöckner, Raab-Karcher, and Thyssen trading.

The problem was that some of the less-desirable enterprises were more or less impossible to sell. One of the first designated candidates for sale was the steamship company Oldenburg-Portugiesische Dampfschiffs-Rhederei (OPDR), which had been partly in the possession of the Haniels since its establishment in 1880, when Hugo Haniel and Friedrich Wilhelm Haniel had acquired 30 of its 185 shares. Since 1951 FHC had been the sole owner of the shipping firm. In 1961 the family and the management reached an agreement to sell. Hermann Reusch explained in 1962 that "the decision to sell the OPDR is not an easy one for me, simply because of the tradition and because the shipping company showed our flag on world markets. But we have thought over everything comprehensively, and are certain that the risk for FHC is too great."[9] But not every decision to divest necessarily generates a sale, as it is sometimes hard to find a purchaser for a business that is judged to be a bad fit or to have a poor future. In the event, the envisaged transaction was accomplished only in 1995, in the context of a major refocusing of the company.

In 1961 the company adopted a divisional structure, although it was still clearly a unitary company. The core of the FHC business was still coal-trading, as conducted by Franz Haniel in the early nineteenth century. Indeed, as then, the circumstances of the postwar world made this a (temporarily) quite lucrative business. In the 1950s FHC derived some of its best profit margins from the importation of U.S. coal, which reached high levels in the wake of the two big international crises of the 1950s, Korea and China. Right at the beginning, when trade was still largely controlled, and there was a temporary shortage of steel plate for the U.S. automobile industry, FHC was part of a barter or compensation deal (a so-called *Lohnveredlungsgeschäft*, in that Germany imported a raw material and exported a semifinished product made in part with the imported commodity), in which coal was exported to Germany in return for plate from a former GHH subsidiary in Essen, Ferrostaal. This was another example of how some business linkages survived the structural breakup of German industry.

In all, between 1951 and 1969 the trade in U.S. coal, which was for a long time regarded as the cash cow of FHC, constituted a trifling 37.4 million DM gross profit. In the 1960s, however, this business (and coal-trading in general) became much less significant. Germany was shifting to petroleum-based energy resources. Coal was still 31 percent of the total FHC business in 1961, but it had fallen to 24.9 percent in 1966 and to 15.4 percent in 1969. This decline was compensated by the increase in trading in heating oil, and also in general shipping business.

Governance in the Family Setting

The reassertion of the family as a potentially managerial group and its claim to a more active role produced considerable turbulence and strain in the relationship with the managers of the family companies. The tensions were exacerbated by the confrontational and unpleasant personality of the leading Haniel figure of the time, Alfred Haniel, the chairman of the supervisory board of FHC from August 1957 to September 1958 (he had previously been deputy chairman). Having as a comparative youngster played an active part in the creation of the new FHC in 1917, he now saw himself as the personification of family tradition. The most contentious issue for Haniel was that labor representation on the supervisory board threatened to make that institution an ineffective expression of the owners' interests, and thus necessitated some institutional reengineering.

Alfred Haniel repeatedly and insistently demanded more rigorous auditing and financial controlling, and did so in an increasingly irascible way. Other family members discussed how he could be made to resign or retire.[10] One of the signs that a family firm is about to dissolve in the wake of hopeless feuding is the eruption of quarrels in semipublic settings and in front of the nonfamily managers. FHC experienced some of these episodes in the late 1950s.

In January 1958 Alfred Haniel had staged a terrible scene at a supervisory board meeting of FHC, when he had demanded greater financial control and discipline. In particular, he demanded approval for a special financial advisory council, which he had already established by unilateral action, and which he saw as an effective alternative to the supervisory board, which in his opinion (as in that of Hermann Reusch) had been made ineffective by the laws re-

28. *Alfred Haniel, 1883–1964*

COURTESY OF FRANZ HANIEL & CIE. GMBH, DUISBURG-RUHRORT

quiring employee representation. A 50 percent co-determination had been established for coal or steel companies *(Montanindustrie)* by the law of 1951 (this regulation was eventually extended to all larger companies, but only in 1976). Hermann Reusch had originally been a proponent of such legislation, seeing it as an alternative to outright socialization, but in the 1950s he turned into one of its most hard-line opponents. Co-determination (like the Allied deconcentration initiative, with which it had originally been linked) was another external intervention that by acting as an irritant in German corporate life in the event actually operated as a stimulant to family ownership to reformulate and reassert its interests. In the first instance, it encouraged steel businesses to look elsewhere in an effort to escape the restrictions upon *Montanindustrie.* The legislature then tried to catch up with them, in 1956 extending the provisions of the 1951 law to the parent companies of *Montanindustrie.* But the flight continued, and in 1967 and 1971 new legislative initiatives delayed companies' exit from co-determination in cases in which the basis of production had changed.[11] For the moment, Alfred Haniel merely tried to find a way of resisting trade-union incursion into the structure of Haniel corporate governance.

The management of FHC pointed out that the supervisory board was not entitled to delegate power in this way to a specially created council. Haniel told them off very sharply, making clear his old-fashioned notion of the prerogative given by ownership: "You are now speaking of things that do not concern your mandate. In my opinion you should have nothing to do with this business. That is the law of companies, and the obligation of the supervisory board, but it is not the right or duty of the managing board."[12] He told one of the employee representatives on the supervisory board: "This has nothing to do with you or your work."

Soon after this and a number of other disputes, Alfred Haniel was replaced as chairman of the supervisory board of FHC by Thuisko von Metzsch, the son-in-law of Alfred Haniel, who had a background in commerce. Metzsch soon formed a sort of triumvirate, with Wolfgang Curtius (who joined the supervisory board in 1962 and remained until 1983, and who had a strong background in the coal business) and Klaus Haniel (who had been trained as a mining engineer and had worked for the GHH). Klaus Haniel was also chairman of the GHH supervisory board from 1961 to 1983. In FHC, Alfred Haniel remained constantly provocative, and it was the initial task of the three "top uncles" *(Ober-Onkels)* (as they were half-affectionately known) to keep him under control.

In April 1960 Alfred Haniel suggested moving into banking activities, the sort of activity that the original Franz Haniel had so decisively rejected in an earlier postwar era.[13] In 1962 he attacked the idea of inland shipping:

> If we draw the inference and make a general formulation, what would in his opinion be needed, the following should be said. "The aggregate of the Haniel businesses that we are directing is stagnating. There are some businesses that are prospering, such as grain storage; but for coal the time is past, and also for much else, like Rhine shipping." The motto "You must actively make what has been inherited from your fathers your own, in order to truly own it" means that we need to take a new path. Because in time there will be more money, he had already made the suggestion of going into the money market.[14]

Fundamentally, this was a quite correct analysis. The conservatism of the *Ober-Onkels* who replaced the volatile Alfred Haniel—and who were characteristic of the business outlook of the first generation of the Bundesrepublik—led them to a much softer variant, in which the separation from traditional businesses would entail a less radical break. Divestment (or "exiting") was a key part in the formulation of a new strategy. At first, however, it was thought of not in this strategic context, but rather as a way of avoiding both the overstretching of capital in a period of dynamic expansion and the difficulty of accessing new capital.

The triumvirate of Klaus Haniel, Curtius, and Metzsch needed to find some way of mobilizing the family interests. The process of shaping policy took place in an institutional setting, a so-called small circle *(Kleiner Kreis)* in which the nonemployee members of the FHC supervisory board met and devised strategies. Reaching out to the family also involved a wider series of initiatives, to increase the sense of inclusiveness: from the 1960s there were regular "youth meetings" of Haniel owners between the ages of eighteen and forty, the first of which took place at the historic Rheinpreussen mine. The need for new ways of binding the family to the firm was obvious, as the family was rapidly expanding. By 1965 there were 150 share owners; by 1971, 199; and by 1981, 216.

Exiting Strategies

The first major divestment by the Haniel family was of the mining company Rheinpreussen, which had moved into an involvement in petroleum. Rheinpreussen was one of the great historical Haniel engagements, and also in the 1950s the initial vehicle for the reassertion of a Haniel family interest because it was a relatively small company. But once the resurrection of the family firm was under way, the assets of Rheinpreussen itself no longer appeared very attractive. By 1959 the family owned less than 70 percent of the capital. The Rheinpreussen company was then sold to the petroleum company Deutsche Erdöl AG through an exchange of shares. The sale of Erdöl shares could then be used at some time in the future to "strengthen the cohesion of the family enterprise," especially if a capital increase for the GHH was considered necessary. Thus the first priority of the family at this point remained the traditional linkage with the GHH.[15] It was with this argument that Alfred Haniel launched his drive to sell Rheinpreussen. The sale had been opposed by the general manager of FHC, Werner Ahlers, who resigned in February 1959 as a result of the traumatic debates that followed from the idea of a sale of a historic participation. Alfred Graf Waldersee, a family member (by marriage) involved in the management of FHC since 1950, also was forced out of the business in May 1959. At the meeting of the advisory committee *(Beratender Ausschuss)* where he announced Ahlers' resignation, Alfred Haniel in a short speech "first stated that those present had heard with satisfaction that in yesterday's discussions Herr Ahlers gave his resignation to Herr von Metzsch and Herr Reusch." Haniel then went on to speak about postwar reconstruction: "Reconstruction of course took place, but in a form in which no one knew what he was doing. The whole financing side was untransparent, and the investments of the company unclear. He could only come to the conclusion that Herr Ahlers managed money in an unbelievably light-headed way." At this point Ahlers got up and declared that he could no longer listen to this tirade of abuse. He left the room and disappeared from the company.[16]

The petroleum interests of Rheinpreussen had been organized separately and were still partly held by FHC. In 1963 FHC attempted to sell this asset, whose main value consisted in an extensive chain of gas stations, to the petroleum company Erdöl, which found the price too high. In 1964–65 Haniel reached an agreement to sell instead to the German subsidiary of British Petroleum, at which point Erdöl intervened with the claim that it had a right of first refusal as a result of the original Rheinpreussen transaction. This sale was then carried out in 1965, at a price of 78 million DM

($11 million) and realizing a profit of 73.4 million DM. The newspaper *Handelsblatt* styled this "the big deal of the Haniels."[17] The sum realized was eventually used to buy a one-third participation in a new chain of cash-and-carry stores, Metro.

There was another, relatively brief, excursion into petroleum as the energy of the future. In 1962 the Haniel trading company in Basel created a joint venture in petroleum-trading and gas stations with Amoco International SA of Geneva, the European subsidiary of the Standard Oil Company of Indiana. But this cooperation was dissolved in 1966, with the company renamed Haniel Handel AG, Basel (and somewhat later Haniel Holding AG).

In the early 1960s Alfred Haniel grew increasingly pessimistic about the prospects for family firms. He wrote to the management of FHC about the bankruptcy of an old Haniel rival, Stinnes: "But these events are just a further link in a long chain of failures of precisely such first-class and well-known firms that bear the label of family firm. Some examples are Borsig, Henschel, Heyl von Herrnsheim, Maffei, Borgward, Schliecker . . . It is certain only that economic downturns will do great damage, now as earlier. I also repeat my earlier conviction, which was meant in a constructive way, that the financing of FHC is not as solid and has not the capital base that would really be needed for such a business."[18]

Such pessimism about family capitalism was inevitably contagious: the family as a business unit survives only when a large number of its members believe in its effectiveness and suitability. When doubts are raised about long-term viability, it is natural to react by demanding higher immediate payouts, which inevitably undermine the investment program. With pessimism on the rise in the early 1960s, many members of the family pressed for higher dividends, and in 1965 the owners' meeting voted for a 10 percent payout. The supervisory board chairman, Thuisko von Metzsch, in the advisory committee *(Beratender Ausschuss)* attacked this view of the dividend policy. FHC had, he said, two responsibilities, and it should not be used as a general "savings bank." First, it needed "to stay healthy and to flourish and continue to pay normal dividends, because in order to maintain a prudent policy some money needed to be left in the business; and second, only in this firm can we cultivate the idea of family cohesiveness in a way that is no longer possible in the GHH or the HOAG [Hüttenwerke Oberhausen AG]."[19]

The GHH and the Transformation of the European Steel Industry

At exactly this moment, a new wave of technical innovation in the steel industry occurred, requiring levels of investment that would be too high for a family business. The issues raised were quite analogous to those that had faced the GHH during the previous great wave of expensive technical change in the steel business, in the 1870s and 1880s. The main technological change of the mid-twentieth century was the almost complete replacement of the Thomas process by oxygen steelmaking (as developed in Austria in the early 1950s, and then taken up in the United States). By 1971 only 7 percent of German steel was made under the Thomas process, while 21 percent still came from Siemens-Martin plants, and 72 percent was oxygen steel.[20] The new technical demands resulted in a wave of consolidation, including some cross-border mergers, in the European steel industry (see below, pages 311–312).

At this time many steelmakers were thinking about the possibilities for reducing their dependence on a high-capital-cost and low-growth industry. Mannesmann, for instance, the German pioneer in seamless tubes, which like Haniel also had a substantial trading and Rhine shipping operation, in the 1960s and 1970s found it necessary to apply portfolio analysis to prospective investments, and to move into automotive parts, automated materials handling, and information processing, before in the 1990s plunging into mobile telephony.[21]

In 1957 the former GHH steelworks, the Hüttenwerke Oberhausen AG, built a new 3.4-meter four-high rolling train with the then most modern technology, designed primarily to produce sheets for GHH steelmaking; but as soon as the early 1960s it became apparent that this investment was insufficient to produce steady returns. In early 1961 the family heard about HOAG plans to build a cold rolling mill. This was exactly the sort of large-scale extension that would require capitalization on a scale not possible for a family enterprise, and Klaus Haniel and Wolfgang Curtius proposed to investigate a possible cooperation with Mannesmann. At first they went through a member of the supervisory board of Mannesmann, Franz Ulrich of Deutsche Bank. In the course of a hunting meeting, still a highly characteristic place for the German business elite to come together, Klaus Haniel and Hermann

Winkhaus (Mannesmann) discussed the possibility of a transaction, and Winkhaus asked the Haniels to leave the "bankers" out of the negotiations.[22] The old suspicions about bankers, dating back to early nineteenth-century experiences, still lingered.

In 1966 the Haniels tried to negotiate some sort of agreement with the Klöckner steelworks, in order to counterbalance a proposed cooperation between Krupp and August Thyssen Hütte (ATH) (which in the event did not materialize until much later). Nothing came of these plans, and instead in 1968 the HOAG was merged with ATH, one of its traditional rivals in Duisburg, with a large capacity in oxygen steelmaking. In the exchange of shares, the Haniel family interests now held 4.8 percent of the capital of ATH. The *Frankfurter Allgemeine Zeitung* commented: "With the motion to merge with the Oberhausen iron- and steelworks there is a new phase after the repair of the damages done by decartelization: the concentration of established steel companies."[23] Most family members agreed to sign a "share restriction and trustee contract," and Klaus Haniel took a position on the managing board of ATH, which he retained for some time as the vestige of the steel tradition of his family. For a time the Rhine shipping business of FHC also benefited from contracts to ship materials for ATH.

At this stage the senior management of the GHH was clearly trying to extricate itself rapidly from any remaining Haniel control in order to take a gamble of expansion. The new orientation was partly a response to a change of generation in the management. Dietrich Wilhelm von Menges in 1966 replaced Hermann Reusch as chairman of the managing board of the GHH. He had had a successful career in the international trading subsidiary of GHH, Ferrostaal. He at once showed that he wanted to introduce a different style, making the GHH more modern and more in tune with a new Federal Republic. In particular, he thought that Reusch had been too moved by consideration of the Haniel position, and not enough by that of the company. In 1966 Reusch had told the supervisory board that he had always seen himself as a "steward" for the Haniel dynasty. Menges later observed that Reusch father and son had lived in symbiosis with the interests of the Haniel family: Hermann Reusch

> derived from this function the right to demand of members of the Haniel family that they hold on to inherited equity stakes,

> and to identify himself in a wide-ranging way with the GHH. This was easier for him because of the substantial minority shareholding he had inherited from his father. From the beginning I saw my position toward the company and the majority shareholders in a different way. The slowly increasing number of independent shareholders alone prevented such an identification with a group. It could also not be expected that the interests of the company and the interests of the ever-increasing number of family members would always be the same.[24]

In particular Menges identified a tradition in the GHH of avoiding any dependence on banks, and came to the conclusion that such a policy was a restraint on growth. In a period of great expansion and need for capital investment, it was unavoidable to go to the stock market and in this to work together with banks. Menges saw banks and their investment and brokering activities as an essential (and highly desirable) part of the new German economic miracle. He noted later, in retrospect: "The gradual transformation of a family-owned firm into a genuinely publicly owned company is a theoretical goal. In turbulent times in the world economy it can lead to power struggles within and outside the companies, which are not in the interest of the share owners or of the people working in the company, and often are also not in the interest of the national economy."[25]

In 1967 the GHH proposed to increase its capitalization, and it was clear that the family could not make such a large financial commitment. The family paid in about 20 million DM in cash and then transferred a further 20 million DM worth of HOAG shares to the GHH (shares that were later to be converted into ATH shares).[26] Menges seized the opportunity to emancipate management from the control of the old owners, telling the family that it was necessary to make "the breakthrough to the capital market."[27]

At this stage the Haniel family still owned 44 percent of the capital of the GHH. Wolfgang Curtius used a social occasion, an equestrian competition in Aachen, to approach a director of the huge Munich insurance company Allianz, Alfred Haase. Klaus Haniel then negotiated with Allianz to sell part of the family's participation in the GHH, while preserving some influence through a "blocking minority" that would require a new legal construction.

The Allianz was attractive because it was not an industrial company—another steel or engineering enterprise—that would try to redirect the course of the GHH. Nor was it perceived as being as fussy or threatening in its intentions as the German great banks. The family owners were in effect trying to make an end run around Menges' plans to ease them gradually out of their position in the GHH, and they (and not Menges) succeeded in preserving their influence for some time. But the final result was the one anticipated by Menges, that the GHH stopped being a family firm.

The initial negotiations took place without consultation of Menges, and there was a red-faced moment of embarrassment at the meeting in Munich when the door opened and an acquaintance of Menges looked in on the discussion, without, however, realizing its full implications.[28] The whole session was filled with great strain: Could the family break free from its historic company and its managerial structure? Klaus Haniel had been so tortured about the possibilities that he had been unable to sleep the night before the Allianz meeting, had then taken too much strong coffee, and at the meeting had been so near collapse that he had to be taken away by a doctor. At the outset of the negotiations with Allianz, Klaus Haniel told his prospective partners that "the proposed transaction makes sense only if the Haniel family keeps a blocking minority and thus its influence in the GHH for as long as possible, at least for a generation, and thus it needs to have the means to participate in future capital increases. A pool agreement among the family members [with a commitment on how votes will be used] will secure the possession of such a long-term minority holding."[29] By July 1970, 165 family shareholders had agreed to the arrangement, by which they retained a nominal capital of 56.25 million DM (a quarter of the 250 million DM, or $68.7 million, capitalization of the GHH). Those family owners who refused, for whatever reason, were bought out; one family member, for instance, was an architect who complained that his design had not been considered seriously in a competition held for a new administrative building for a company that formed part of the GHH *Konzern.* The shares were sold to an Allianz and München Re subsidiary, Regina,[30] on the understanding that Regina and Haniel would each control at least a quarter of the stock of the GHH, and that they would exercise voting rights in coordination as a holding unit. Allianz had bought about 10 percent of the

GHH stock from the Haniels, and acquired a further 15 percent from the market. As part of the transaction, FHC in 1970 also bought substantial packets of GHH shares from minority shareholders MAN and Kabelmetall, and brought these shares into the arrangement with Regina/Allianz. By this stage the Haniel family holding of the GHH was reduced to 27 percent of the stock.

The final stage of the process from the perspective of Wolfgang Curtius was getting both Menges and his designated crown prince out of the management of the GHH: they were to pay the price for having tried to emancipate themselves from the Haniel group. Old-style morality was used to enforce old-style family corporate control. Curtius was able to use Menges' confession of an affair with his secretary, and his intention to divorce his wife, to undermine his position in the firm. As a consequence the Haniel interests were able to secure the appointment of Manfred Lennings as general manager of the GHH. With this choice, there seemed to be a reversion to the idea of general managers whose families were linked to the firm, as in the case of the Luegs or the Reusches: Lennings was the son of an interwar GHH manager, Wilhelm Lennings.

In 1974 Regina bought 1.5 million DM of nominal GHH shares and took an option to buy the remainder of the family pool holding. A further capital increase in 1975 brought the large Commerzbank into Regina as a shareholder, so that for the first time since the 1870s the GHH was in practice in the hands of bankers. By this time the family influence had been considerably diluted, and the dilution prompted a further reorganization of the business and discussion about bringing in another bank as an owner of stock. In all, in the capital increases of the GHH undertaken in 1974, 1975, 1977, 1979, and 1982, the Haniel family paid in an additional 8.85 million DM but at the same time sold shares for 9 million DM, so its influence was considerably reduced. By 1982 its share of the GHH's ordinary capital had fallen to 9.6 percent.

During the 1970s, in the aftermath of the oil price shocks, the stock price of the GHH fell. The traditional notion of the *Konzern* also came under attack as not offering sufficient managerial or financial control of the component parts of the group. At a meeting in 1977 of Regina, in practice the new ownership grouping, the criticism was spelled out in the following way: "The GHH board of management, which the *Konzern* supervisory board thinks has the general control, even with the best information sees the subsidiary companies only from the outside and is as a result of the multiplicity of engagements not in a position to reach its own judgment on what should be done. On the other hand, the general GHH board of management through its omnipotence and interventions stunts the initiative of the management of the subsidiary companies."[31] After the second oil shock of 1979, there were further losses. From 1981 to 1983 the largest of the *Konzern* enterprises, MAN, lost 530 million DM ($196 million), and in 1982 the GHH management proposed to subject MAN to direct and tighter control.[32] But this initiative was defeated, and in a reorganization MAN now took over the GHH instead. Thus the GHH became a subsidiary of one of its own former *Konzernfirmen*.

Through this long process of retreat and restructuring, the GHH and the companies affiliated with it retained substantial links with the Haniel family. In the mid-1970s seven family members were employed in the leading management of *Konzern* enterprises. Another twelve family members sat on the supervisory boards of such enterprises.[33]

In 1971 the capitalization of FHC was increased by the payment of an additional 12 million DM, derived principally from the sale of the GHH shares to Allianz. Its capital was doubled in 1974 (to 100 million DM, or $41.7 million) and then again in 1979 (to 200 million DM, or $116 million). Unlike the GHH, in FHC there was a strict principle that no family members should be involved in the management of the company. At the same time as the recapitalization of FHC occurred, its international range was extended. In 1971 the capital of Haniel Holding AG Basel was increased from 8 million to 20 million Swiss francs ($5.2 million) with the intention that it should act as a general holding company for a wider range of foreign participations and enhance a diversification of the company's activities. The path to becoming a diversified management company rather than an industrial corporation (that in practice had lost its sense of direction) went through the foreign holding company, created and expanded in large part because of heightened political and economic uncertainty.

By the mid-1970s in Germany, the confidence of the postwar miracle had largely evaporated. There were substantial new uncertainties, and the question of corporate survival once again became acute. In particular, the Haniel owners began to doubt the economic future of Germany, and to ask whether it was enough simply to be a very big German company in a world that was being increasingly globalized (though that was not a term used at the time). The move to much greater international diversification was in large part a consequence of the rather pessimistic mood of the 1970s, as well as of a way of thinking about the most appropriate way of managing risk. Wolfgang Curtius produced a memoir on family policy ("Familienpolitik") in which he argued that the economic and political uncertainty was now such that the goal of "securing wealth" had a greater priority than the traditional objective of "the joint pursuit of economic objectives." This meant in effect asset management rather than the old style of entrepreneurship. The justification for this new strategy was more political than based on a calculation of business opportunities: it was a product of what was thought to be an escalation of international Cold War tensions and of doubt about the prospects for continental west European societies.

> Developments in Western Europe everywhere show the same tendency: state authority fails in the face of exaggerated social demands. The economic chaos that has been caused by the masses who misuse their freedom now leads them to look for salvation and order in the dictatorship of state socialism or Communism. To the extent that the power of NATO is reduced, the power and influence of Russia over western Europe grows . . . Industrial ownership is affected in the first place by this anticapitalist tendency. Trading and service companies are much less affected. The United States is to a large extent free from ideological influences on its free-market mechanism. Switzerland, too, is in this sense a liberal enclave in Europe.[34]

In order to finance the expansion of Haniel-Basel, which acted as a holding company for the foreign participations, it would be necessary to sell family shares in ATH, and thus finalize a separation of the company from its past in the classic industrial technologies of iron and steel. It was also the reflection of a clear logic of not owning participations in companies in which there could be no establishment of effective control.

From the point of view of the owners, this was a decisive break with the traditions of the company as they had been evolved in the early years of the Federal Republic. It was, in terms of the story of ownership, a youth revolt against the domination of the *Ober-Onkels*, or a version of "1968" taking place within the business dynasty. A nephew of Wolfgang Curtius, Jan von Haeften, suggested taking the family shares in the GHH into a partnership, or *commandite* form, that would progressively sell the GHH participation in order to acquire a more diversified portfolio in FHC. He had at a quite early stage seen that the GHH had little future as a family company, and had declined a seat on its supervisory board. Wolfgang Curtius noted rather bitterly in an unpublished memorandum: "Surprising, how many family members succumbed without much reflection to Jan's charm and skilled salesmanship."[35]

The reinvention of Haniel business also required a new approach to management: the application of clear financial controls, and of rationally articulated criteria for the management of risk and investment. In large part, this new intensified control was possible only because of technical changes, and in particular the availability of computing power for business solutions. The managers of the 1970s also saw themselves as pioneers of a new approach to business. What had been recreated in the 1950s and 1960s was a reembodiment of the traditional German corporation. What evolved in the 1970s was an internationalized business.

Chapter 12

Postwar Reconstruction in France

We risk being considered retrogressives.

François de Wendel, 1946

After the Liberation, French policymakers were determined to learn the lessons from what was now termed the "Malthusian behavior" of the past. They saw their task very explicitly as a national priority. France needed to be rescued from the sins and errors of the past. There was a consensus that the malaise of the late Third Republic should not be resurrected. The attack on Malthusianism involved both a political and an economic aspect, as the French problem lay (according to the now commonplace diagnosis) in the exercise of political power by an "economic feudality" in order to stop economic modernization. Personified, the feudality consisted of Rothschilds and Wendels. The program of the Liberation involved "the eviction of large economic and financial feudalities from the management of the economy; the rational organization of the economy, assuring, with the collaboration of workers, the subordination of private interests to the general interest."[1]

The realization of the program meant in practice a much greater degree of state activism. If private business, dominated by family interests, would not invest by itself, it would have to be made to invest. But should this be done directly through nationalization or by guided and controlled investment? Three critical sectors were nationalized: the railroads, which became the SNCF; electricity, as Electricité de France; and the coal industry. The banks were also partially nationalized, and the remainder of the financial sector subjected to state guidance.

There was in the event no nationalization of French steel. But the "might have been" of the postwar period continued to play a major part in the politics of steel until a full nationalization was indeed carried out in the late 1970s and the 1980s. Steel figured prominently in the national investment plans, and steel owners and managers were frightened of appearing to be laggards or saboteurs. The result was massive investment and quick expansion. But very rapidly it became apparent that there was a great deal of misinvestment and that the French steel miracle had feet of clay. The government was obsessed with targets of production: in growing more quickly than German steel, and then in warding off the new and threatening Italian challenge to its industrial strategy. Jack Hayward terms the French steel complex one of "industrial patriotism." The French political class saw big steel mills as modern "cathedrals" that gave expression to a "national renewal." Jean Monnet in Gaullist language called for "une politique de grandeur pour l'acier."[2]

Steel thus grew very quickly as part of a comprehensive modernization plan. In the early 1960s *Paris-Match* established a cliché by dubbing Lorraine the Texas of France;[3] but the rapidity of growth, and its uncommercial financing, made the industry very vulnerable. By the mid-1970s Lorraine was in a deep crisis. A new American metaphor now described the Mediterranean coast as a French California, and celebrated the construction of a large integrated steel plant at Fos-sur-Mer, which eventually proved to be a politically well-integrated white elephant.

Meanwhile, those with memories of the Liberation-era conspiracy theories could explain why the steel oligarchs continued to flourish. According to one misinformed but influential account, General Charles de Gaulle was linked dynastically to the Wendels by his wife and to Schneider by his daughter.[4] Another wartime hero, General Leclerc, who after fighting in Africa had led the Second Armored Division to liberate Paris in August 1944, was in fact married to a member of the Wendel family, and his real name was Philippe de Hautecloque.

The Monnet Plan

In the immediate aftermath of the war, there was an intense discussion of nationalization as a way of raising production. The old Colbertist tradition of a state-guided economy was augmented by admiration for the achievements of Soviet planning. There was an additional moral aspect of this question, a biblical conversion of swords into plowshares: as the left-wing Force Ouvrière argued, "what had made war should now serve peace."[5] Not surprisingly, such proposals aroused the vigorous disapproval of the traditional steel industry, including the Wendels. In May 1945 there were 126 shareholders of the Société Les Petits-Fils de François de Wendel et Cie., all direct descendants of the nineteenth-century François de Wendel, who tried to defend their interests in the face of the attack of the modernizers.[6] The old steel producers raised legal issues, related to the status of their holding of mining rights, and concrete political and economic objections. Unlike the railroads, in which there was one network, or coal or electricity, in which there were standardized products, steel involved both standardization and specialization, with highly differentiated products. But in order to make the case for the technical peculiarity of the steel industry convincing, the steel producers had to move away from a simple dependence on the mass production of Thomas steel. Thus the Wendel company argued:

> Raising the question of the nationalization of an industry that is called on to provide a significant amount of equipment would have the immediate effect of cutting off all its credit and of rendering illusory the realization and even the startup of programs as set by the [Monnet] Plan . . . The nationalization of steel would pose serious questions for the life of the industries that are connected with it, given the practical impossibility of limiting the repercussions in the metalworking industries: this explains why the British Labour government has practically given up this program.[7]

This type of argument eventually convinced the government. Steel was designated a key sector in the First Modernization Plan of 1946, usually known as the Monnet plan. The plan scaled down some of the most inflated ambitions of the immediate postwar era, which had been based on figures for French production of between 12 and 15 million tons of steel (the 1929 figure had been around 10 million). These original plans had been supported by the Communist party and left-wing trade unionists. In the revised version as implemented by Jean Monnet, the figure of 10 million would be reached in 1950, with an increase to 15 million only by mid-decade. No new steel converter with a capacity of less than 30 tons was to be constructed in France. And there could be no government subsidy of any work using converters of less than 20-ton capacity. From 1947, the introduction of oxygen-enriched air into the converter as a way of removing impurities ensured a little longer life for the Thomas process (it became entirely obsolete with the widespread use of oxygen production only in the 1960s).

The symbol of modernization became the continuous-strip rolling mill, which was required in order to deal with predictions about an increased demand for sheet and thin-plate steel, in particular to satisfy the demands of the automobile industry. This was a technique first employed in the United States in 1923, in which a slab of steel was reheated and rolled continuously between different stands so as to produce a strip that could be either coiled or cut into sheets. The process offered significant savings over hot mill processing, in terms of both metal lost in the production of tin plate (around 40 percent) and thermal energy (around 60 percent).[8] How many such large-scale mills there should be in France and where they should be located became the subject of a political compromise. The planners had originally decided to build one continuous rolling mill in the Nord (as part of the company that eventually became Usinor), where proximity to the seacoast assured better access to imported ore, and thus less dependence on Ruhr coal. Usinor adopted the specifications and scales of U.S. plants from the 1920s, a choice that later proved controversial and attracted new complaints about French backwardness.

The Wendels, though the largest steel producers in France, were not represented on the Plan Commission for steel, formed in March 1946 in order to draw up a modernization plan (neither, in a reflection of the mood of the times, were their great rivals, the Schneiders). They interpreted the plan for establishing Usinor as an attack on Wendel, as well as on Lorraine. But as the steel plan evolved, the Wendel works played a crucial part which ensured that the east of France would also get a continuous-strip mill. The Plan Commission explained:

> The Wendel establishments as a whole constitute perhaps the most important example of a rationalization effort realized through the factories of a single firm, assuring to this business a nearly constant position in all branches of iron production. The development of the power of modern tools makes the pursuit of such an approach impossible if it is not accompanied by a constant and increasing growth of the firm's entire capacity. The Wendel establishments would not be able to keep their traditional methods by producing under capacity . . . The Commission does not consider such a possibility, and the program that it is proposing for this factory group is only partially based on that which was agreed by the Wendel establishments. Hayange will receive the continuous-sheet mill for the east and will preserve its sheetmetal manufacturing. The Joeuf Moyeuvre group, profoundly modernized, will keep its former orientation.[9]

But the commission also proposed to close some works: Joeuf, Saint-Jacques, and Messempré. The idea of closing works immediately ran into predictable and substantial resistance from the producers.

Wendels replied that big new capacity was not necessarily more productive than the older, smaller, and dispersed units: "We are obliged to recognize that the increase in capacity of our furnaces, which we have been working at vigorously since 1906, has not led to the expected results and that the blast furnaces of 5.25 meters height have not produced better results than our furnaces of 3.50 meters." The plan, they argued, had "an arbitrary character." Instead Wendel suggested piecemeal improvements, based largely on payments from German reparations and on the prospect of better access to German coking coal.[10]

It was not just the state and its bureaucrats who felt that the Wendel traditions were resistant and that the Wendel works were in need of dramatic and radical modernization; the internal reports of the Crédit Lyonnais also painted a rather dismal picture of the technical state of the plant. The bank concluded that the plants strung out around Hayange in the narrow valley of the Fensch were terribly antiquated: "The works have the advantage of being situated on the iron ore, but they are all in all old. The blast furnaces have an average capacity and would benefit from being grouped, although a furnace of 500 tons' capacity is being built and a more powerful one will later be installed. The Thomas converters have a very feeble capacity, although the cost of production is among the lowest—even, as François Paschal, the son of the director general and an engineer at Joeuf, claims, the lowest in France, which seems paradoxical. The Saint-Jacques sheet mill, worked mostly by steam engines, is also old." The overall conclusion was that the works of the PFFW were well supplied with ore but "too old to allow competition to be sustained with works whose geographic position is less favorable, such as [the rival Lorraine producers] Homécourt, Rombas, and Hagondange."[11]

In fact François de Wendel in private was much more explicit about the need for only a very limited and partial reconstruction than he was prepared to be in public when confronting either the planners or the bankers. Thus in May 1946 he explained his thoughts on the future of the Pâtural plant in Hayange:

> If things depended solely on me, I would rebuild almost as it was . . . I would strive, by reducing to a minimum the modifications brought to the previous construction, to build this furnace as quickly and as economically as possible. But it is important to remember that our projects will have to be approved by the Professional Office of the Steel Industry and that if we do not adopt a crucible diameter of 5.250 meters, we risk being considered retrogressives.[12]

Wendel's emphasis on gradualism inevitably looked like a prime example of the worst and most pessimistic side of interwar entrepreneurial Malthusianism. François de Wendel complained to the president of the Nancy Chamber of Commerce in January 1947 that the plan commission's proposals for a major expansion of French steel were "both dishonest and foolish."[13] In March 1947 Humbert de Wendel caught on to the spirit of the age, which demanded large-scale investment, and proposed a new strip mill, easily the largest single investment of the PFFW, at a cost of 6 billion francs ($22 million). The new policy was to be driven by the availability of investment resources: "It is unquestionable that these conditions of credit, which bear upon one-half of the order, are advantageous, since they allow for buying a completely modern material in conditions impossible to find in France . . . Given these numbers, we all agree about setting aside the go-it-alone solution."[14] In effect this was a surrender to the new spirit of Monnet and Marshall, though Wendel said little about how he proposed to undertake the financing.

But it was also a way of preserving industrial influence. Such a large-scale investment could be financed by creating a new company, in which Wendel either would not participate or would have only a minority stake. Instead the Wendels proposed bringing all their existing holdings into the new steel giant in eastern France, becoming a sort of national champion, which for that reason might be expected to appeal to French policymakers:

> By creating a new business, in which we are bringing our industrial and mining assets from the Fensch valley and the mines and factories of Moyeuvre to the Wendel Company, we are meeting the objectives of the Plan . . . The unity of the Plan cannot be achieved unless the Wendel Company maintains its prewar position in relation to the rest of the steel industry, and accordingly its realization does not require the concentration of steel production as foreseen in the draft of the modernization plan.[15]

Wendel clearly feared the consequences of being left out of the plan, and realized that the way to save the firm was to emphasize its national importance. Without the presence of Wendel, the plan commission would need to go elsewhere to find the new capital. The Wendels discreetly painted an American bogey from whom the French planners were supposed to recoil: "this new business will need a major contribution . . . since there will be a reduced [financial] participation of the other businesses, the best solution would be the participation of an American group and in default a call to the French public."[16]

The traditional Lorraine businesses thus made their proposal for the consolidation of the steel sector as an alternative to nationalization. Their new industrial strategy eventually resulted in the creation of a single Lorraine company to operate a continuous-strip mill: Sollac (Société Lorraine de Laminage Continu). It involved nine companies, most notably the three Wendel companies, the Forges de Gueugnon (with an open-hearth plant and an electric steel furnace), PFFW (eighteen blast furnaces, an open-hearth plant, and two Thomas steel plants), and Wendel et Cie. (nine blast furnaces and a basic Thomas plant). The other Lorraine producers were Aciéries de Rombas (twelve blast furnaces); the Union de Consommateurs de Produits Métallurgiques et Industriels, at Hagondange; Société des Aciéries de Longwy, with a major plant in Thionville involving four blast furnaces and three electric furnaces; and the Compagnie des Forges et Aciéries de la Marine et d'Homécourt, with seven blast furnaces. Two non-Lorraine producers were also involved, as consumers of the products of Sollac: Société Anonyme des Forges et Aciéries de Dilling (in the Saar); and J. J. Carnaud et Forges de Basse-Indre (tin plate processors, who clearly represented an important customer for the products of the Lorraine mill). The company was created in December 1948 and started production on 23 December 1949. Its core was the newly constructed continuous-strip mill close to Hayange, at Sérémange.

The financing in effect came largely from the state; if the private steel businesses had had sufficient capital to modernize, they undoubtedly would have rejected the ideas of the planners.[17] François Bloch-Lainé in 1948 justified funding for the creation of Sollac as in the interest of the state.[18] Sollac set a figure of 16 billion francs ($31 million) credit that would be required for the new rolling mill. Again, its representative set out the bogey of foreign competition in his proposal to the plan authorities: "Foreign competitors are following close on the heels of French iron metallurgy. French industry will not survive unless it modernizes."[19]

A large share of the counterpart funds from the Marshall Plan was channeled into steel. Sollac and Usinor in the north accounted for 35 percent of the credits given by the equipment modernization fund, and for 90 percent in 1949, 94 percent in 1950, and 82 percent in 1951.[20] The Marshall Plan funds allocated to purchase equipment for the new works at Sérémange and Ebrange came to $449,360,000 (up to June 1949). Additional public support came as the old supply problem of Lorraine was solved through the canalization of the Moselle, so that coking coal could be brought cheaply. The French railroad system, which had been largely neglected until the 1930s, also received substantial state investment.

There were much more ambitious initiatives: from the German side, Konrad Adenauer and his major financial adviser, Robert Pferdmenges, proposed a scheme to save Ruhr industry from dismantling by asking French companies to take controlling stakes in the major steel businesses. Under this scheme Wendel would acquire a 50 percent stake in three major German steel producers: Klöckner, Vereinigte Stahlwerke, and the GHH. But when Pferdmenges approached Wendel in November 1947, he got a sharp and negative reply.[21] Obviously, it is interesting to speculate what might have happened to the development of integrated businesses in Europe had Wendel been more receptive to the German proposal. As it was, steel remained a national industry. In 1951 Humbert de Wendel, together with the director of the Knuttange steelworks, led the opposition of the Lorraine steel industry to Europe-wide planning.[22]

François de Wendel died, disillusioned, in Paris on 12 January 1949. He had three daughters, but his only son, Henri, who now stepped into his father's position in the family firm, had as a result of a car accident a badly damaged throat that made him practically unable to speak in public. He was generally regarded as timid and ineffective, a man broken by the force of his father's character.

Expansion

The issue of outdated equipment in the Wendel works remained a central topic of discussion and criticism. A continuous mill ordered from the United States was installed at Joeuf in 1952, and the blooming mill at Saint-Jacques (Hayange) was electrified in the early 1950s. In the same period Wendel planned four new blast furnaces to replace older works in the Orne valley. There was also extensive construction of workers' housing.[23]

The Wendels now undertook major investments to complement Sollac, of which it owned just under half. This effort required some rationalization of the existing structure, and in 1951 PFFW and Wendel et Cie. merged to form a joint-stock corporation as a holding group, De Wendel SA. An entity named PFFW remained as a private holding company in order to maintain the family influence. From 1953 the shares were quoted on the Paris stock exchange. The company took up some of the slogans of the age about the need for large quantities of investment. In 1952 Henri de Wendel wrote: "this new equipment should turn out to be a really modern ensemble; therefore we should not make the firm's traditional mistakes, and instead should profit from experience gained and the improvements achieved elsewhere."[24] There were many visits by Wendel engineers to U.S. steel sites. Like English iron manufacture at the beginning of the nineteenth century, or American plants in the vision of Charles de Wendel at the beginning of the twentieth century, the American model provided a template of modernization for French industry. But characteristically the Wendels also tried to use the American example to teach France a certain prudence and conservatism in regard to the complete reinventing of the steel business. The sole survivor from the old generation, Maurice de Wendel, remembered his brother's caution in 1952: "Monsieur François de Wendel was always reminding [us] that the Americans [we] encountered in our youth used to say that before creating new equipment, one must start by pushing [the equipment] already possessed to its maximum output."[25]

However, looking to the United States in the 1950s may have been inappropriate, for this was the era when the U.S. steel industry was becoming quite conservative and was reluctant to adopt the new process of the oxygen top-blown converter introduced in 1952 in Austria by the Alpine-Montangesellschaft. U.S. companies were also slower than German and Japanese producers (many of them with family links) to take up continuous casting in the postwar era. The exceptional slowness to innovate suggests that the rationale for conservatism may have had an economic and financial component that was at least as powerful as cultural conservatism. U.S. Steel, for instance, which was particularly sluggish in adopting the technology of oxygen steel, had its chairman of the finance committee, an accountant, explain in 1967: "A good open hearth shop with half its economic life can't be scrapped. You wait until you cross the economic line." Another U.S. commentator generalized for the steel industry that "there's an attitude . . . that says: if it worked last year, it will work this year."[26] This kind of reasoning, if made by a French steelmaker, would undoubtedly have been cited by critics of French business interests as examples of malign Malthusianism, whereas in fact they simply reflected the reality of business calculation.

The era of Wendelien paternalism, with its small cosmos of social harmony, ended with the turn to industrial gigantism. By 1960 Wendel was producing 2,760,000 tons of crude steel. The company now made very new sorts of arguments in order to justify the state's involvement. It mobilized the employment and political interests of Lorraine. Gigantism itself was sometimes also presented as a response to the new German challenge: *Le Figaro* for instance in 1956 in a gloriously mixed metaphor referred to a "steel fever on the other side of the Rhine in which France should not let herself be outpaced."[27] In the new climate, appeals for funds from the state could be justified as a way of buying off social discontent and instability. Steel employers thus no longer had any interest in maintaining the old Wendelien image of harmony and solidarity. The steel industry in general was plagued with poor labor relations in the postwar era: there were bitter national strikes in 1947, 1948, and 1950. Unlike the wave of labor unrest after the First World War, this upsurge of conflict hit the Wendel works particularly hard; the old-style paternalism became a frequent target. But Henri de Wendel continued to see himself as a traditional steel magnate, and as late as the early 1970s he was still defending the almost exclusive concentration of his enterprise on steel investments: "it's our job, and we believe in it," he said.[28]

As before the First World War, the company responded to the demand for labor created by expansion by importing workers. The new foreign workers no longer came from Italy, but from Algeria. At Sollac in 1955, 1,500 of the workforce of 3,000 was Algerian, and there were more than 500 Algerians in the Hayange works and more than 250 in Moyeuvre.[29]

The large-scale investments of the era of gigantism were financed by credit—in part from the state, but mostly from the banking system. Even with private banking credits, however, the banks first sought the approval of the Banque de France for their loans, and in this sense the credits received an official guarantee.[30] All French industrial finance was essentially directed from the Treasury, which set itself up as the heart of a new style of development and modernization. In the first French modernization plan (1946–1952), the largest share of credit had come from the state. The implicit state guarantee established by the events of the late 1940s, however, then made it possible for the French steel producers to turn to the private sector for credit. In 1953 the industry collectively established a Groupement de l'Industrie Sidérurgique, whose major function was to place bonds for steel investments with the private sector. By 1956 public-sector investment was less than 15 percent, and in 1960 only 4 percent. Bonds constituted 3 percent of the investment in the first government steel plan, and 25 percent in the second (1953–1956).

For Wendel, of the 19.6 billion francs ($47.6 million) invested over the initial period of industrial modernization (1950–1952), 11.1 billion came from self-financing, 2.6 billion from increased capitalization as part of the 1951 restructuring, and 3.7 billion from long-term loans from the state (Fonds de Développement Economique et Sociale). All this brought a rapid dilution of family influence. Since the family could not raise the capital needed for the increase provided for in 1951, shares in the now public company were sold over the stock exchange. Later in the 1950s, profits would no longer sustain investment for expansion. In 1954 there was a bond issue, and also a medium-term credit from the Crédit Suisse and the Société de Banque Suisse. In 1955 Wendel borrowed $1.2 million from the European Coal and Steel Community High Authority. In 1957 the company increased its capital by 10 billion francs. But over the years 1955–1958 the company reported 38.6 billion francs ($77.9 million) in investment, of which 37.9 was self-financed. By 1958 the bank debt of 1954 had been paid off.[31]

Throughout this period of expansion, the company found it hard to establish profitability. The French government, in defiance of the agreements establishing the European Coal and Steel Community, fixed steel prices at the request of the steel-consuming industries (chiefly automobiles), which maintained an effective lobby. The steel industrialists consequently mounted constant complaints about the artificially low prices in France. In 1954 the president of Wendel, Emmanuel de Mitry (the son-in-law of the late François de Wendel), told the annual general meeting of the company:

> The policy of blocking prices, followed in a rigid way by our governments, has placed French steel in an arbitrary position of inferiority, not only in relation to the other steel producers in the

> Community, but also with respect to our large competitors from third countries. This situation is all the more serious since it has the ineluctable result of slowing down, even in a period of favorable conjuncture, the modernization of factories and the renovation of plant, and, in a period of conjunctural recession, of hindering French steel from keeping up with the competition of producers from other countries.[32]

The next year he complained that a 4 percent permitted increase was not enough:

> This very moderate increase still leaves the price of Thomas steel in France at a level far below that of the same steel in other countries in the [European Coal and Steel] Community, notably in Belgium and Luxembourg. The effects of this increase in prices on our industries has already been partially absorbed by the increase in the price of fuel destined for the steel industry. If new burdens were to encumber our costs of production, the result would be not only an imbalance in our financial accounts but also serious consequences for the fulfillment of our investment plan.[33]

In fact the steel industry simply continued to borrow in order to make up the shortfall caused by the fixed-price regime.

By the mid-1950s the overall indebtedness of the French steel industry was over half the receipts. The ratio fell slightly in the favorable environment of the second half of the decade, but then rose once more with some large-scale investment projects. From 1961 the share price of the major steel companies collapsed: Sollac's northern French rival, Usinor, fell to about a third of its original value, and Wendel to a quarter.

The price of public investment in steel had been political guidance, which affected such issues as location and size. The initial justification of political support for the Lorraine continuous-strip mill lay in an argument about the desirability of preserving employment in a structurally weak region. In the 1960s a critical concern of the French government was no longer the east, but the south, with chronically high levels of unemployment and Socialist administrations at odds with Paris. There were also resource constraints. In the 1960s it was clear that access to imported ore was crucial, and

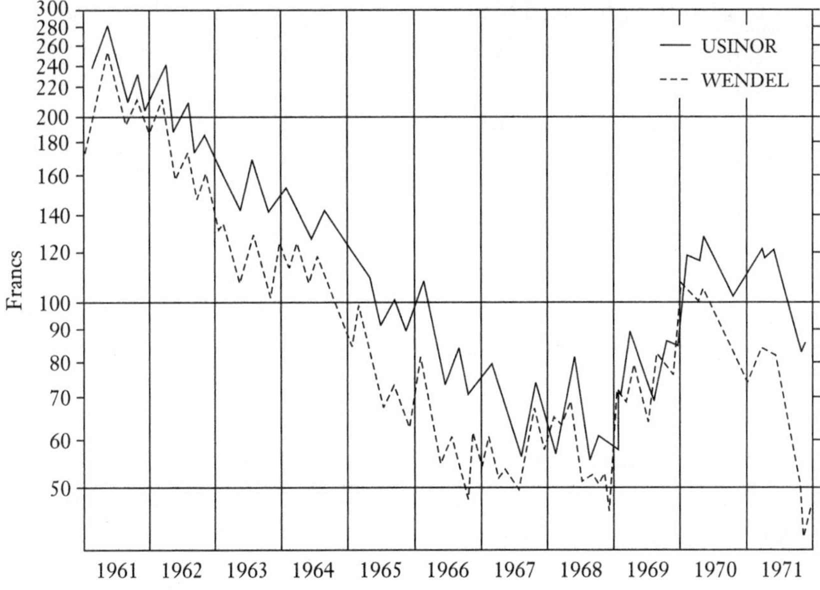

29. *Share prices of major French steel companies, 1961–1971*

ADAPTED FROM *LE MONDE*, 14–15 NOVEMBER 1971, P. 19

there were worried calculations that the Lorraine ore base would be exhausted within thirty or forty years. Usinor built a large facility at Dunkirk, which came into use in 1963. As Dunkirk opened, the French government created a study group to look at a second new steel plant for France. Its chairman was Louis Dherse, the director general of Sollac, who came from a background in the nationalized industries, the SNCF and then Electricité de France.[34] Sollac was also pressed by the state to move beyond its Lorraine base and invest in a large coastal strip mill: it would have preferred a site in Normandy near Le Havre, but the government pushed a Mediterranean site, Fos-sur-Mer, as part of a strategy of regional development. The Rhone delta was portrayed as a new California.[35] Sollac now became part of Solmer (Société Lorraine et Méditerranéenne de Laminage Continu), 47.5 percent of which was owned by the Wendel group, and 47.5 percent by Usinor, with a 5 percent Thyssen participation.

One additional consideration that moved the French government to increase the pressure on Wendel was the European setting of the mid-1960s, and in particular the large-scale restructuring of steel holdings that emanated from neighboring Germany. Hoesch and Dortmund Hörder Hüttenunion merged with the Dutch group Hoogovens to create the largest steel group in Europe, with an output of over 10 million tons of crude steel. But the biggest and most aggressive force in remaking the German steel industry was Thyssen. Its dynamic chief executive, Hans Günther Sohl, suggested an interlinking of shareholdings between Thyssen and Wendel to create a European steel group that would eclipse even Hoesch in size and might stand up to U.S. Steel. But Wendel rejected the proposal. At a later stage Jacques Ferry, the head of the professional organization of the French steel industry, tried to elicit a capital participation by Thyssen in Solmer. For tax reasons the German group wanted a minimum of 30 percent in the holding, but the French government refused to allow a foreign participation over 20 percent.[36] Consequently, the negotiations broke down and another chance for a nonnational and European solution to the French steel industry was lost.

The French government responded to the Europe-wide discussion of the appropriate size of business enterprise by trying to force the concentration of French enterprise. In 1965 the fiscal conditions for takeovers in France were relaxed, and in 1967 the French state permitted shares to be deposited in lieu of tax, thus extending the possibilities of government control. In 1967 the government also legislated a new form of company, the "common interest group" *(groupement d'intérêt commun)*, designed to facilitate large-scale mergers. One initial French step to steel rationalization was the merger of Usinor with Lorraine-Escaut, in which Wendel had an indirect holding that controlled a quarter of the issued capital.

Wendel itself needed to act in response to the new agenda of the French state. For a long time it had resisted industrial concentration on the grounds that it would mean an inevitable dilution of control: this was the old argument of the family firm. For instance, in 1966 the Société Générale in an internal memorandum after the merger of Lorraine-Escaut with Usinor noted: "In contrast, the issue of the merger Wendel-Sidélor was not raised and would only have been a project that Wendel would refuse to carry out, wishing to maintain the control of a company on which the family character remains imprinted."[37] By 1968, however, Wendel could hold out no longer, and it launched a merger between Sidélor and the Société Mosellane de Sidérurgie, which produced Wendel-Sidélor, with the

Table 1 Indebtedness of French steel industry, 1965–1976 (billion FF and $U.S.)

	Overall (FF)	Overall ($U.S.)	Public sector (FF)	Public sector ($U.S.)
1965	8.1	1.7	1.3	0.3
1970	10.5	1.9	3.4	0.6
1975	28.4	6.3	5.5	1.2
1976	33.0	6.7	7.0	1.4

Source: "Les conditions du plan acier," *Le Monde*, 19 April 1977.

aim of building a modern oxygen steelmaking plant at Gandrange. Wendel held 50 percent of the stock. The new company in 1969 accounted for an output of 7.88 million tons of crude steel, or 35 percent of French national production (just slightly ahead of Usinor).[38]

The French steelmakers now presented themselves as the embodiment of a disinterested general or national good. With this kind of argument, power passed from owners to the representatives of organized interests. In 1966 the leading representative of the steel industry, Jacques Ferry, tried to explain that the steel leaders had "abandoned every personal interest." They agreed to a steel plan (the Plan Professionel of 1966), which the minister of finance, Michel Debré, explained and tried to defend as neither nationalization nor dirigisme. Ferry emphasized that the plan was the outcome of "the industry's own effort toward unity." Its goal was declared to be "the establishment or reinforcement where they already exist of a small number of firms or groups of international size."[39]

There was a brief moment of heady success in the late 1960s, when steel prices rose worldwide, French steelmaking capacity was fully used, and share prices made a brief recovery; but this was a fundamentally inflationary boom, which soon collapsed. It provoked a new wave of activist state involvement in investment, whose urgency was increased by the news that the French share of European steel production had fallen in the late 1960s (largely because of Italian expansion). This thinking took the form of an emphasis on, indeed an obsession with, aggregate figures about crude steel output. Twelve billion francs ($2.6 billion) was put into Fos between 1966 and 1975. The new plant was supposed to produce 7 million tons of steel a year. The overall capacity of French industry of 25.8 million tons in 1970 was supposed to be increased to 35.6 million by 1976.[40] In all, between 1966 and 1976, 7 billion francs of public money was invested in steel through a Fonds de Développement Economique et Social.[41] This obsession with rapid growth in the 1970s was shared by the German GHH and the Falcks in Italy and in both cases led to a loss of focus on the issue of profitability. Nor was the U.S. steel industry immune: Edgar Speer, the chairman of U.S. Steel, as late as 1973 was predicting rapid growth for the industry, and even after the oil crisis he affirmed the virtues of growthmanship as a consequence of extrapolating past trends. "There isn't any question that the American steel industry is going to meet the demands of the economy. I'm not an optimist, I'm an historian. That's history."[42]

The private owners were supposed to contribute to the new wave of investment. Wendel's mostly family stockholders put in 90 million francs ($16 million) of new capital in 1970, and were rewarded almost immediately by a big drop in the share value.

In 1971 the steel firms consequently received a new big government support program, and in 1973 Wendel-Sidélor was reorganized as part of Sacilor (Société Aciéries et Laminoires de Lorraine). Henri de Wendel turned over the presidency of Wendel-Sidélor to the man from the state sector, Louis Dherse. That this was the first time that a nonmember of the Wendel family had controlled the management of a Wendel enterprise made the retreat of the family obvious. Sacilor was controlled by Marine-Wendel, with a 46.7 percent holding, which was itself controlled by a 60 percent holding by Wendel family interests. The Wendel company was pressed to close its older and smaller, more specialized works, again in line with government gigantomania. From 1968 to 1972 it closed twenty blast furnaces, eight steelmaking furnaces, and twenty-seven rolling mills. The expansion of Fos then went hand in hand with cuts in Lorraine, for which the French government did not want to carry any responsibility and which might be blamed instead on the private sector. In 1971 Dherse wrote to the workers of Hayange to announce a layoff of 12,350 over a three- or four-year period "in order to increase profitability," and was immediately denounced for his "injustice" by the bishop of Verdun.[43]

During the 1970s the French steel business completed its modernization (often described as Americanization) by adopting oxygen steelmaking and continuous casting. Such modernization might have been secured on the basis of a private-sector response to economic incentives; but not in France. Given the framework of a state pricing and investment policy, modernization in fact was accompanied by a crisis of profitability and an attack on the legitimacy of the steel business.

The Steel Crisis

In practice, state investment in Solmer was much lower than had been planned, and Sacilor output fell to 6.4 million tons in 1977. The modernization was profoundly incomplete. Less than one-eighth of French steel production in the late 1970s was by continuous casting (compared with 30 percent in Japan). The oil crisis after 1973 and stagflation hit steel demand. Shipbuilding stopped, the production of automobiles fell off. The new Mediterranean shoreside plant of Fos, which had once been the hope for the renewal of French steel, now stood as a half-completed monument to a past age. The one lever that the steel industry could pull was that steel was needed in order to provide high-paying jobs in declining industrial areas such as Lorraine and the Nord. In 1975 the French steelmakers' association tried to raise steel prices throughout Europe by an appeal to article 58 of the ECSC, which referred to action in the face of "manifest crisis." Jacques Ferry, the spokesman for the steelmakers, asked for additional credits.

Meanwhile the losses of Wendel continued to rise, and its share price remained in the doldrums. Despite this, the family pulled off what looked at first like a very successful industrial coup. Taking advantage of low prices in the steel sector, the rival north French steel firm Usinor was attempting to buy up on the Paris stock exchange the shares of a steel holding company, Marine-Firminy. The Marine assets included substantial minority holdings in a packaging company, Carnaud, a stainless-steel manufacturer (Forges de Gueugnon) that proved to be quite valuable; but the major strategic impact of the purchase would have been to give Usinor enough shares in Sacilor to allow Usinor to play a wrecking role in the Lorraine industry. Wendel staged a counterbid, initially opposed by the Marine management, that it financed through the disposal of its almost forgotten mining assets in Germany, the Friedrich Robert and Heinrich Robert Hütten. A new company, Marine-Wendel, with a secure family holding, was launched on the Paris stock exchange in October 1975. The Wendel victory over Usinor in the struggle over Marine-Firminy marked the apparent determination of the family owners to preserve the Lorraine and steel interests, at an outwardly most inauspicious moment.[44]

Also in 1975 the Wendel family company was reorganized as a holding company, Compagnie Lorraine Industrielle et Financière (CLIF), its name chosen to reflect links with Lorraine. The new name also avoided any association with a family that was now supposed to be emblematic of the alleged French problem of insufficient or halfhearted modernization. From the family's perspective, the new holding company was above all an attempt to separate profitable activities from the financial whirlpool of Sacilor and its engagement in Solmer.

In April 1977, in response to industry and labor appeals for assistance to the steel industry, the government launched a national restructuring program, the *plan acier.* Usinor and Sacilor had to deposit shares with a state-controlled bank, the Caisse des Dépots et Consignations. In return it would receive more loans, but would be tightly supervised by French government inspectors. The prime minister, Raymond Barre, explained that this was not a nationalization (as was demanded in the joint program of the left-wing opposition parties): "But the government set aside a solution to nationalization that would have transferred to the state, without resolving them, the problems of iron metallurgy, by making the collectivity support all of their weight, so that the industrial and financial responsibility of the groups would find itself relieved."[45] The industry was already very highly indebted: a total of 33 billion francs ($7 billion) for the industry as a whole, or 104 percent of the 1976 turnover (compared with 45 percent for the United Kingdom and 16 percent for German industry). This indebtedness accounted for around 2 percent of French GNP for the year. It was clear that there was now substantial overcapacity, but the government was extremely sensitive to the politics of layoffs, and wanted the steel industry to take the blame for industrial dismissals.

During the most delicate part of the discussions, the government refused to talk to the dynasts who were still the owners of Sacilor. Some of the Wendels attributed what they interpreted as the hostile stance of the government to the old family dispute with the Schneiders that went back to the nineteenth century, and to the fact that Giscard d'Estaing, the finance minister at a critical stage of the negotiations over steel in the early 1970s and the president of the Republic after 1973, was through his wife (Anne-Aymone de Brantes) close to the Schneider dynasty.[46] Mutual suspicions were rife. The prime minister, Raymond Barre, who conducted most of the negotiations, later complained that he had been duped by the steel men and by the steel federation.[47] The steel men felt in turn that they had become the whipping boys for the failure of government. Indeed, a government official explained at this time: "Jobs must be cut, and we want industry to carry the can. It is the only way to overcome our past mistakes in agreeing to loans for successive capacity increases—as a way of avoiding job cuts that would have accompanied major productivity improvements at existing installations."[48] An initial estimate, in the event grossly understated, envisaged a layoff of 2,500 workers by Sacilor.[49]

At the same time, the steel problem began at last to receive treatment at the European rather than the national level. In May 1977 the EC steel commissioner, Etienne Davignon, set minimum prices on some steel products; but the action was only very partial and was subject to legal challenges. In 1979–80 a second and much more sweeping Davignon Plan used article 58 to impose capacity restrictions on the European steel industry. The output of Sacilor was reduced from 6.3. million tons (1980) to 4.7 million (1983).

Prime Minister Barre rejected what he termed the "neoliberal" solution of bankruptcy, as well as a Socialist style of nationalization. Instead, the steel enterprises were effectively nationalized through the conversion of state-held debt to equity. The existing capital of the big steel companies was reduced—Usinor by 33 percent and Sacilor by 50 percent—prior to an injection of new capital. The creditors transformed loans into shares and accepted a reduction in interest payments on outstanding credits. Some more profitable companies were brought into the big steel companies, so that Dillinger Hütte in the Saar went to Sacilor. Sacilor was pushed to take over a bankrupt Metz firm, Pompey SA.[50] The Industrial Ad-

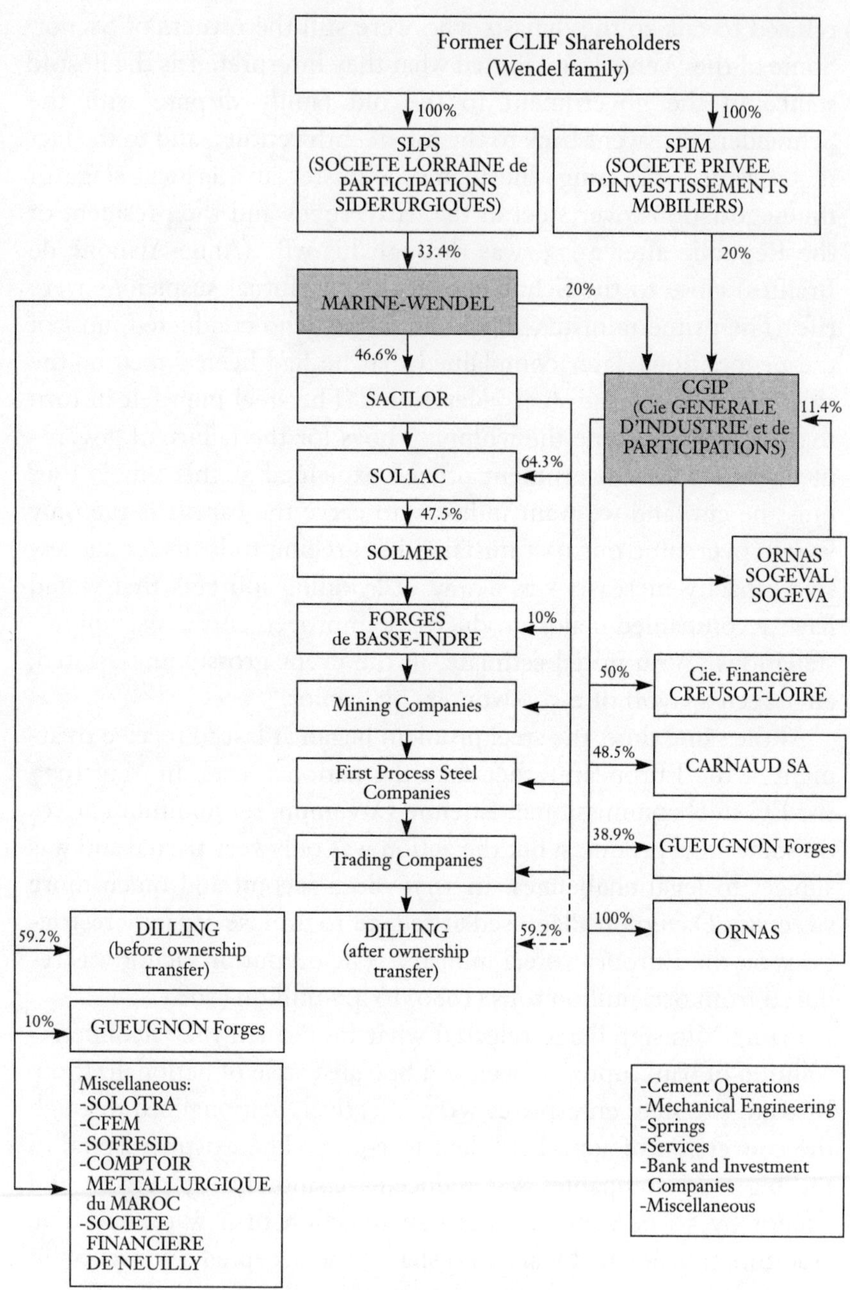

30. *Reorganization of Wendel holdings, 1975*

aptation Fund of 1978 cost 3 billion francs, but in addition the state committed itself to 10 billion over the period 1980–1985 for steel restructuring.

Implementing the Barre solution involved devising a new holding structure for the Wendel interests. The former shareholders of CLIF exchanged their shares for shares in two separate holding companies: Société Lorraine de Participations Sidérurgiques (SLPS), which owned one-third of a quoted company, Marine-Wendel, established to organize the steel interests; and Société Privée d'Investissements Mobiliers (SPIM), which owned a one-fifth stake in another public company, Compagnie Générale d'Industrie et des Participations (CGIP), which held a range of miscellaneous investments such as cement and packaging as well as specialty steel forges (such as Gueugnon). In order to satisfy the government's demand that the family not be released altogether from its steel commitments, the steel holding company Marine-Wendel also took a 20 percent stake in the potentially more profitable CGIP.

The restructuring measures were accompanied by big layoffs that hit Lorraine particularly hard, with the social costs largely paid by the French state (another 7 billion francs, not included in the original figures for the Barre plan).[51] In early 1979 Lorraine was swept by a tide of industrial violence, with strikes and the imprisonment of managers by workers occupying factories. In the Nord, policemen were wounded by rifle fire from striking steelworkers. The 1979 restructuring was followed almost immediately by the second oil price shocks and by recession in the industrial world. More closures and redundancies were required. The number of employees at Sacilor fell from 44,700 at the end of 1977 to 24,400 in 1980.[52]

In 1982 the new Socialist government launched a new steel program, with another 6,000 layoffs at Sacilor. In 1987 the government merged Usinor Aciers and Solmer with Sollac.

By this time the history of French steel had ceased to be the history of the Wendels. But the two stories were still linked at the level of symbolism. In the surge of worker unrest over the new restructuring of the late 1970s and early 1980s, the Wendels still appeared as the enemy, even though they had ceased to be the owners of Lorraine steel. In 1984 there was a new explosion of social unrest in Lorraine as the Socialist government undertook another restructuring of steel. On 3 April 1984 radical steelworkers in Joeuf burned tires in front of the abandoned Wendel chateau, then returned to the town to demolish the statue of the twentieth-century François de Wendel in front of the *mairie*. It was replaced a few months later, at the instigation of the Communist town government, by a statue in the Socialist Realist style (of the kind that would be demolished five years later all over central Europe) of a half-naked steelworker. At the same time the Square François de Wendel was renamed the Square du fer, CGT, CFDT, CGC.[53]

Given such public feeling against the family, the rebuilding of Wendels as an economic interest required anonymity and discretion. Its major architect, Ernest-Antoine Seillière, explained that "we purposely chose the blandest possible name [that is, Compagnie Générale d'Industrie et des Participations] because the last thing we wanted was to attract attention. At the time, all the old legends, phantoms, and prejudices against the family were still very much alive."[54] France's love affair with technocratically charming acronyms was to be used as a way of muffling what was left of dynastic industry.

The 1970s and 1980s offered a very different challenge for French modernization from that of the postwar era. Instead of a quest for a national agenda in the face of the humiliation of 1940, there was a need to respond to a new level of interconnectedness in the European and the world economy.

PART FIVE

The Age of Globalization

Since the 1970s, business structures in Europe and the world have changed dramatically, and created a new setting for entrepreneurial action. Three important features stand out.

First, this was a period of rapid technical change, in which some of the older technologies of the second industrial revolution became obsolete, and the centers of gravity of classical industries, such as textiles but also steel, shifted away from Europe and North America.

Second, corporations were thought of in a new way. Before this, companies had been seen as quite closely confined to a particular and clearly defined line of business. One German commentary in the early twentieth century categorically stated that the joint-stock corporation "is limited to a defined commercial goal and cannot simply move to quite different fields of economic activity."[1] The response to technological change and to increased economic and financial uncertainty was a push to diversify. Such diversification could clearly lead to uncontrolled and promiscuous empire-building. Diversification made sense if there were gains to be realized from the application of particular synergies: new ways of managing or introducing systems controls (as in the case of Haniel), or backward integration (as with Falck's intensification of involvement in energy as a concomitant of steel technology).

Third, international linkages became more important in a globally connected economy as international trade surged and became a dynamo of growth. Markets could no longer be considered in purely national terms. A company's choice of market affected the kind of growth that might be expected, and such decisions could be tailored in accordance with the capitalization of a particular enterprise. Mature markets would be growing slowly and would require little new investment, while very innovative markets would require large amounts of capital and would present greater risk. Somewhere in the middle, in areas such as pharmaceutical distribution, airport management, and building materials, lay fields of activity that might be suitable for a family firm.

Chapter 13

Wendel Becomes a Conglomerate, French Style

Family governance is very exacting; the least suspicion takes on an unusual amplitude. People do not allow themselves to hide anything. One must always be fastidious in order to be legitimate.

Ernest-Antoine Seillière,
2002

As the steel crisis of the 1970s unfolded, the whole character of France's dirigiste postwar economic management began to unravel. In the first two years of the Mitterrand presidency (1981–1983), a last attempt to assert the old program, using extensive nationalization, collapsed speedily and dramatically. With that fiasco, the system of industrial credit allocation directed by the Treasury, which had provided the basic model for postwar economic management, was undermined. France's external capital account was liberalized, so that the French capital market was no longer cut off from international developments. In the later 1980s an extensive privatization program was launched by a conservative government and was taken even further in the 1990s under a Socialist administration. Some of the characteristics of the old national approach to economic management remained, and the directors of the new private sector were frequently the technocratic products of the *grandes écoles* who had also run the state industries of the past.[1] But France was profoundly changed by the rise of the capital market. By the end of the century an estimated 40 percent of the capitalization of French companies was held by foreigners, and some observers began to describe France as more globalized or more "penetrated" than Germany or the United States.[2]

But the crisis restructuring of the French economy produced a rather odd result in that family firms—regarded as largely obsolescent in the postwar planning euphoria—strengthened themselves, turned effectively to the capital markets, and used complicated ownership systems and multiple vote shares to ward off foreign attacks. Thus the French economy, while apparently globalized, actually remained quite French.

For the Wendel holding company in the late 1970s, continued existence depended on a separation from the traditional steel core business. The remaining steel production would stay with Marine-Wendel, which would hold 20 percent of the stock of a new Compagnie Générale d'Industrie et des Participations (CGIP), in which the nonsteel companies of the Wendel group were linked in a new holding structure. The Marine-Wendel participation occurred at the insistence of the government, which was worried that the lucrative nonsteel side would benefit the family while the steel losses would be socialized at the expense of the French taxpayer. The Wendel family, whose shareholders at this time numbered around 350, would be obliged to agree (unanimously) in a relatively short time frame (six weeks) to an exchange of shares for shares in a new family holding unit, which in turn held shares in the publicly quoted companies Marine-Wendel and CGIP. The family shares in the holding unit were valued according to a different process, as agreed with the French Finance Ministry, in order to reduce some of the tax liability on inheritance that threatened the continuity of family enterprises. The lower price corresponded to a reduced liquidity of the family share of the stock.

The Shareholder-Entrepreneur

The question of succession in family enterprises is always problematical, and the Wendelian tensions in the 1970s arose out of the general crisis of steel, out of the perception that the state was attacking the family, but also out of the fact that there were three obvious and rival dynastic heirs. The leading figures in the 1970s in the Wendel holding companies, Henri de Wendel, Pierre Celier, and Emmanuel de Mitry, all had sons, although all were relatively young, in their thirties. It is possible that the existence of three rival claims to succeed produced a dynastic gridlock that demanded a different kind of solution. But it was also clear that the company needed a new and quite radical vision if it was to survive: it had to remake itself, and it had to internationalize. Ernest-Antoine Seillière was over forty, and a nephew of Pierre Celier. He had been trained in the Ecole Nationale d'Administration (ENA) and at the Kennedy School of Government at Harvard and had worked as a civil servant, but he wanted a different experience and had approached his uncle about playing a part in the business. He began to work for CGIP in 1976, but was quickly recognizable as the crown prince, becoming general manager in 1981 and president in 1986. One of his attractions was that he had spent some time in the United States, and he became the first leading figure in the Wendel business who was not chosen simply because he was the obvious dynastic successor.

He presided over a quick change in the core of the business. The major Marine-Wendel steel company Sacilor was nationalized in 1978 through the transformation of debt into shares. The Dillingen steelworks in the Saar was kept in Marine-Wendel, but was eventually sold in 1985–86, when the exit from steel was complete and Marine-Wendel began to function in a radically new way. At the outset CGIP also had definite links with the old Wendel traditions, in particular in its cement interests (Société Thionvilloise de Ciments and Ciments Portland de Lorraine), since cement could usefully be made out of the slag produced in ironmaking. The cement holdings were initially expanded, as Cedest, but were sold off to a Swiss company in 1994.

At this stage there was a redefinition of the core business. CGIP rapidly expanded into new areas, at first usually on the basis of existing holdings. A metal-packaging producer, Carnaud, had been part of the Wendel holdings. In 1989 it was merged with the British UK MetalBox Packaging Company, with CGIP holding a stake of just over a quarter in the new company (CMB Packaging). CGIP later expanded its stake into a controlling holding, with a share of 32 percent. In 1995 the U.S. producer Crown-Cork and Seal bid for CMB, offering CGIP 20 percent of the merged company, which would become the largest packager in the world. There may have been some hesitance about the dangers of being too international.

The high share price of CMB also offered an attractive profit-taking opportunity. In a return to national roots, CGIP quickly sold half of its holding to buy a French automobile-parts producer, Valeo, from the Italian financier and ex-Fiat manager Carlo de Benedetti.

CGIP had also expanded into the very new (for France) sector of information technology, at the heart of the "new economy" of the *fin de siècle*. In 1982 it bought 27.5 percent of Cap Gemini Sogeti, which had been built up by one of France's leading technology entrepreneurs, Serge Kampf. For a long time this looked like a highly auspicious purchase, a leapfrogging from the technologies of the nineteenth to those of the twenty-first century. Kampf kept his responsibility in the company, so that the CGIP stake (which was later raised to 33.5 percent) could never be used to establish effective economic control. But at first Kampf's continued presence was attractive. There was a successful public flotation on the Paris stock exchange in 1985, and in 1991 Daimler-Benz took part in a capital increase, after which it held a 34 percent stake (with CGIP's holding reduced to 26 percent). This was one of the mistaken investments of Daimler; after its initial success the company entered a period of heavy turbulence and losses from 1992 to 1995.

CGIP took stakes in other unlisted companies, notably BioMerieux and Bureau Veritas. BioMerieux had been founded in 1963 by Alain Mérieux, had developed a specialization in biological diagnostics, and used microbiological testing to become a major player in the agrifood business. In 1994 it extended its range further with the purchase of Transgene from Rhône Poulenc. Wendel sold BioMerieux in 2004. Bureau Veritas had its origins in the Antwerp information bureau for maritime insurers, originally established in 1828. It had developed into a certification company, specializing in quality, health and safety, environmental, and social accountability. A 20 percent holding by CGIP was extended in 1997, and in 2004 the Wendel stake was raised to 66 percent.

Part of the motivation in buying Valeo and in expanding the holding of Bureau Veritas was the lesson provided by the experience of Cap Gemini, namely that minority participations were uncontrollable and potentially dangerous. But the turn to Valeo also involved a retreat from the international stage and a concentration on French production, which could be presented and defended politically in terms of the defense of France's national interest. The purchase of Valeo is described in a case study by Christine Blondel and Ludo van der Heyden as a "return to French industrial roots," and indeed there appears to have been a good deal of old-style French nationalism about the transaction.[3] Commentators spoke about saving the auto-parts producer Valeo from the "claws of Anglo-Saxon predators."[4] The two major French automobile producers, Renault and Peugeot, were worried about the possibility of a big U.S. components producer such as TRW or the General Motors subsidiary Delphi purchasing the works from De Benedetti. Ernest-Antoine Seillière could argue that he knew the company well, as CGIP had owned a minority participation (7 percent) in Valeo from 1986 to 1993.

In 1991 Seillière formulated a new strategy for CGIP as "shareholder-entrepreneur" *(actionnaire-entrepreneur).* In the CGIP annual report of that year he explained:

> We are controlling shareholders; that is, we own the majority of our subsidiaries, alone or together with a partner. For instance, we own the majority of Orange-Nassau [a property company] or Cedest . . . It is precisely this position as a controlling shareholder that is the basis for our attitude as an entrepreneur regarding our subsidiaries. What is it? It consists in being actively involved in the key domains of the group's enterprises: strategy, investments, acquisitions, cessions, organization, choice of key executives, financial decisions, etc. Thanks to a direct contact with the management teams, through our participation in executive committees or boards, we take an active part in the decision-making process.[5]

Making a New Business Personality

Ernest-Antoine Seillière embodied a new type of business personality. The social philosopher Pierre Bourdieu in an influential analysis (with Monique Saint Martin) had tried to argue that the planism and statism of postwar France had created two rival entrepreneurial types: one a traditional dynastic kind, either from the *grandes familles* (for big companies) or from petit-bourgeois origins (for small companies), the other an elite produced by the great schools and the civil service, whose social capital lay in education. This analysis, prepared in 1978, actually was beginning to be obsolescent when it was formulated. To start with, some very large and successful companies were founded by people beginning with nothing (like Carrefour, which started in 1960; or the retail opticians' chain Afflelou, founded by a *pied noir*, or returning Algerian settler community. Bourdieu contrasted two entrepreneurial dispositions, "with on the one hand the private men or, as they like to say, the secret ones who are private bosses, and, on the other, the public men who are the technocratic bosses, the ones who give interviews, appear on television, write articles, and publish books."[6] Seillière clearly fit into both categories: he certainly gave a great many interviews and became a major media personality. His world was a long way from the world of discreet political influence as practiced by François de Wendel. Giscard d'Estaing commented admiringly that Seillière understood that "we live in an overmediatized society."[7]

Some of Seillière's decisions were controversial within the group of family owners. The sale of the stake in the very dynamic Crown-Cork in exchange for a clearly mature industry, producing on high-cost terms in France in a sector affected by Asian competition (and pressed by the big French automobile producers), is an example of a contested purchase. It helped to convince the family that Seillière was clearly an insider: a member of the family. His mother was the daughter of Maurice de Wendel, and his uncle and predecessor as CGIP president was his uncle, Pierre Celier. And, as Seillière occasionally pointed out, the Seillière bank had financed Wendel acquisitions in the early nineteenth century.

Seillière gave *Le Monde* what amounts to a classic statement of the peculiar virtues of family capitalism: "Family governance is very exacting; the least suspicion takes on an unusual amplitude. People do not allow themselves to hide anything. One must always be fastidious in order to be legitimate. This is because this group of shareholders privileges the long term. We are patient during bad years. This is a strength for businesses like Hermès, Peugeot, Michelin, or Wendel. With us, we don't talk dough; we talk projects."[8] He also frequently expressed admiration for the dynamism of the Italian economy, founded on the basis of a large range of family firms that might be held up as a model for France to emulate.[9]

Marine-Wendel, meanwhile, took on a different shape, and directly bought stakes in nonpublic companies, usually in packets of 100 to 500 million francs, with the intention of selling them quickly when they had matured. By the late 1990s it had in effect undergone a complete remaking, in which it turned itself from a steel holding company into a venture-capital business. Its most significant holdings were the pen manufacturer Reynolds (50.7 percent); the pharmaceutical company Stallergenes, which specialized in specific immune-therapy treatments, especially of allergies and asthma (45.1 percent); and the retail optician Afflelou (70 percent). These holdings were held jointly with an investment group, Alpha, established by the Wendels in 1985, in which Marine-Wendel held around 15 percent. It managed funds on behalf of large European and U.S. corporations, including AXA, Altinvest, and the Wellcome Trust.

After it experienced intense competition and disappointing returns, Reynolds, which had been bought by Wendel in 1993, was sold to the U.S. company Newell Rubbermaid in 1999. Alain Afflelou, who in 1997 had sold a majority stake in the company he had founded, bought it back in 2002 (at a favorable price).

Seillière saw himself as "un habitué de la refondation," a master of business-restructuring.[10] Such activity depended on influence. In part influence could simply be established by overwhelming intellectual power and authority, of which Seillière had plenty. Social capital and networking in the French elite were important, and the Wendels had accumulated plenty of social capital. But this was generally not enough: influence really depended on voting rights in companies. And the buildup of influence could be facilitated by the high French tolerance for differentiated ownership and voting shares (that is, shares with multiple or weighted votes). In this way it was possible to "cascade" holdings, using relatively little money for company A to have a preponderant influence on B, which then controlled C, and so on. This is the technique that produced the Italian phenomenon of "capitalism without capital." Its perpetuation depends, first, on a political acceptance of the price of this method of control, namely shareholders' being deprived of voting influence. Second, such control survives on the basis of high hopes for the restructuring gains that might be achieved by masters of the technique. France and Italy by the 1990s developed the largest mutual-fund presences in Europe, and it was the managers of these mutual funds who resigned themselves to effective impotence and a lack of corporate control. The technique started to be threatened when outside money came in and sought short-term results as well as the long-term *refondation* that had now become the mission of some powerful family firms. Major institutional investors such as the U.S. Templeton Fund were attracted by some features of European capitalism, but also wanted to experience management sensitivity to investor interests.

The owners who had to trust the judgment of the *habitués de la refondation* also of course included the family owners. The Wendels were quite active in this regard. They convened by the hundreds in elaborate family meetings, in which colors identified the different branches: red for Wendels, yellow for Gargans, blue for Curels. When cousin marriages occurred within the dynasty, as they still occasionally did even in the late twentieth century, the new wife had to change her badge color to that of her husband's branch. The family also had a powerful voice on the boards of CGIP, where the longtime chairman of the family holding company was Louis-Amédée de Moustier; and of Marine-Wendel, whose chairman was Hubert Leclerc de Hautecloque. They rejected some sorts of business as inappropriate for a family: tobacco, stockings, or ladies' underwear.

The transformation of the business thus depended on generating acceptance among the family, chiefly by endowing the idea of the family firm with a certain mythic quality. Previously, the historic legacy had provided the mythical element. But by the end of the twentieth century France required more modern myths. A large part of the myth that Seillière used to mobilize the family involved internationalism: they were, for instance, impressed that such famous figures as David Rockefeller and Jack Templeton had invested for some years in Wendel. Who one's ancestors were now mattered less than whom one had dinner with in New York. And in transforming rather than merely perpetuating a particular style of business, Seillière made himself into a much more important figure in the story of French capitalism than François de Wendel, in that he really transformed rather than merely perpetuated a particular style of business.

The powerful link between nonexecutive directors and a family management is one of the most problematical issues raised by the developments of the twenty-first century. Ernest-Antoine Seillière had always had close connections to the French political class. He had a degree from the elite ENA, where his classmates included two future prominent Socialist politicians, Lionel Jospin and Jean-Pierre Chévènement. But his political ambitions there were frustrated, in large part because of his name and ancestry. His opponents campaigned against his bid to be president of the student union by portraying him as an aristocrat and the heir of the Wendels. After ENA he worked in the French Foreign Ministry, where for a time he shared an office with his classmate Jospin. He then worked in the private office of the Gaullist leader Jacques Chaban-Delmas (alongside Jacques Delors) and played a role in crafting Chaban's speeches about the transcendence of old-style social conflict and the development of a "nouvelle société." But he was soon disenchanted with politics. Gradually the business world seemed more attractive. His bet on private enterprise seemed vindicated in the 1980s, when the possibility of privatization replaced the prospect of socialization; business, not politics, was the future of France.

But like the interwar patriarch, François de Wendel, Ernest-Antoine Baron Seillière remained highly political as a businessman. He became the head of the French employers' association, which was soon renamed Medef (Mouvement des Entreprises de France) in 1997 when his predecessor, Jean Gandois, was attacked by the major employers for being too acquiescent and conciliatory in the face of the Socialist government's proposal to legislate a thirty-five-hour week. Gandois resigned after a dramatic meeting and stated: "I am a negotiator. What you want is a killer." On that principle, he pushed the candidacy of Seillière as a more confrontational option for French business politics. Seillière rapidly ran true to form, and became a contentious and divisive figure, accused by his opponents of abandoning French traditions and consensus and seeking to introduce confrontational hire-and-fire "Anglo-Saxon" labor relations. He was also a baron, and the heir of the steel industry and the Comité des Forges.[11] He seems to have rather enjoyed his ferocious image. In a volume of tributes to him the Trotskyist leader Alain Krivine supplied a reassuringly hostile and predictable comment: "He made Medef into a political party. His arrogance, his insolence, his 'aristo' and 'provocateur' poses made him into the caricature of a boss. His predecessors were less caricatures. For us, he was a dream opponent, because he had one merit: honesty [about the class conflict]."[12]

It was not just Trotskyists, however, who found it easy to attack a baron. The financial and business press frequently wondered critically whether he was sacrificing the management of his family's companies to his political engagement. The high political profile attracted press and political attention to the performance of his business ventures. In fact he used the same formula *(refondation)* that he had applied to the family business to describe what he wanted for France. Seillière's aggressive reformism looked like an invitation to examine how successful the modernization was in the microcosm of Wendel enterprises. Seillière saw his responsibility at Medef as precisely analogous to his responsibility in getting Wendel out of steel: "I arrived in the steel industry when it collapsed. It was not very difficult for me to assert myself and establish a certain legitimacy, because no one wanted my position. Later I experienced exactly the same situation at Medef."[13]

By the end of the 1990s he appeared to have been highly successful, in business if not in political terms. The story of Wendel in the late twentieth century is one of astonishing success, which lasted as long as the century. Over twenty years Seillière increased the family fortune fivefold.[14] Put another way, from 1978 to 2000 the holdings produced an average annual rate of return of 26 percent. The Wendel holdings reached their peak valuation on the stock market on 3 January 2000. Thereafter a steep decline set in, which clearly reflected markets' radically disillusioned view of venture capital and risk-taking.

A Crisis of French Capitalism

The 1990s appeared to bring a new type of capitalism to France, with large amounts of foreign investment. Large institutional shareholders, notably pension and mutual funds, began to demand a larger role in corporate governance. Privatized former state enterprises expanded quickly, and as it later proved, quite recklessly. When the speculative bubble burst in 2000, and the most dynamic examples of 1990s growth such as Vivendi and Pechiney ran into major difficulties, the new capitalism and its flamboyant bosses seemed completely discredited. France, previously widely regarded as a "poster child" of globalization, now became probably the leading source of critiques of globalization. At the G7 Genoa summit in June 2001, Jacques Chirac gave the protesters' criticism of rapacious "Anglo-Saxon" capitalism a presidential endorsement. France's traditional family capitalism began to look ever more attractive.

But family firms were also clearly badly affected by the crisis of the new capitalism. The Wendel group could also be seen as a victim of the downturn. In 1998, near the height of the dot.com bubble, CGIP bought 30 percent of Trader.com, with the goal of bringing it to the stock exchange for a profitable initial public offering (IPO). But when the stock was launched on the Paris market, on 31 March 2000, it fell 23 percent in one day. The presentation of the IPO was widely criticized: 15.96 percent of the capital was offered for sale, with only 2.26 percent of the voting rights.[15] This was a typical case of a "cascade"; but a reversal of sentiment could also reverse the process of value creation. Seillière's critics, especially in the leftist newspaper *Le Monde*, began to speak of a "cascade des difficultés."[16] The publicity that came from bad business deals was at least in some part also the result of a political struggle, and frequently came from those who opposed Medef's view of the necessity for structural reform of the French economy.

In 2001 major problems appeared to plague Wendel. Valeo was increasingly problematical and was put up for sale (unsuccessfully). The information-technology consultancy Cap Gemini, which had been merged with the consultancy part of the accountancy firm Ernst & Young in 2000, lost a great deal of its value. Its capitalization as judged by the stock market presents a remarkable contrast with the stodgy but consistent performance of Valeo, the auto-parts producer, which had never been the subject of irrational exuberance.

The most obviously catastrophic affair involved the largely domestic French airlines AOM and Air Liberté. The adventure began when the investment group Alpha, which was closely affiliated with Wendel, took an interest in AOM at the end of 1998. At this point it was clear that the future of the airline would depend not just on new investment, but also on management by a company with a success record in international aviation. In early 2000 British Airways decided to sell its controlling stake in AOM and also Air Liberté, which were making heavy losses, and whose only really substantial assets were the rights to valuable takeoff and landing slots at Paris' Orly airport. The role of British Airways could be taken only by another airline. SAirGroup, the parent company of Swissair, wanted to buy the French companies as part of an ambitious and aggressive strategy of building up an ambitious European alliance system and competing with the major American airlines and with British Airways and Lufthansa. But European Union regulations prohibited the sale of an airline to a non-EU company (which Swissair was), so the Swiss needed to look for an EU partner. SAirGroup put new money into the French airlines and took a share of just under half, while Marine-Wendel made a 300-million-franc investment in a newly established holding company, Taitbout Antibes BV (of which it controlled 50.01 percent). Taitbout Antibes in turn took a share of 50.38 percent in AOM. SAirGroup added a secret agreement by which it committed itself to buy the remaining shares after four years, so that there would in effect be almost no downside risk for Marine-Wendel; and Marine-Wendel financed itself through a loan from the Italian Banca Intesa. During 2000 and 2001 the financial position of AOM and Air Liberté worsened, and an estimated 3 billion francs were needed to save the airlines. A fierce controversy opened up about who should put up the new funds required. Wendel believed that this was the responsibility of SAirGroup, but the French government seemed to imply that it was more a responsibility of the immediate investors, namely Wendel. By the autumn of 2001 the crisis (as well as the problems of the Belgian national airline Sabena, also owned by SAirGroup) led to the destruction of Swissair, with the result that the repurchase guarantee became unrealizable.

The airline failures became a subject of intense political debate and anger, a good deal of it directed against the megalomaniacal Swissair planners. But the Socialist French minister of transport, Jean-Claude Gayssot, who had been responsible for the decision to authorize the involvement of the Swiss, publicly blamed Seillière, and urged the laid-off workers to "Go demonstrate at Medef!" The business difficulties clearly offered an opportunity for a political attack on Medef. Seillière responded by saying that Gayssot's attacks were a product of his electoral setbacks.[17]

CGIP and Marine-Wendel were not responsible solely to the

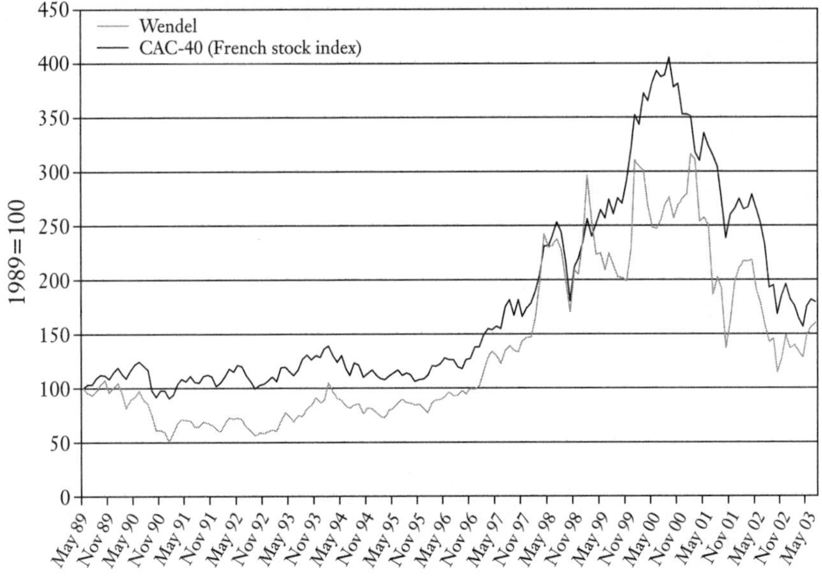

31. *Wendel stock prices, 1989–2003*

family shareholders in the holding companies SLPS and SPIM. There had been outside investors from the beginning, but in the 1990s these investors had much greater influence: investment banks such as Lazard and UBS Warburg, which held 11.1 percent of Marine-Wendel and 9.1 percent of CGIP by 2001, and quite active U.S. investment funds, such as Templeton, which held 3.3 percent and 1.9 percent in shares of the two Wendel companies.[18] With a falling market, "Anglo-Saxon" short-termism began to affect the Wendel self-image. As a whole, the Wendel group traded at a substantial discount to the sum of its parts; in other words, the conglomerate form was believed to detract value.

Outsider shareholders demanded a simplification of the complex holding structure, but in 2001 the family owners blocked a merger of Marine-Wendel and CGIP, as it was unclear how large the liabilities of Marine-Wendel from the Swissair-AOM adventure would turn out to be. At the end of 2001 Seillière announced: "We have heard the market's message that asked us to put ourselves in motion to simplify the group. Restructuring will bring a new shrewdness to investments."[19]

In 2002 Marine-Wendel and CGIP merged as Wendel Investissement, and by 2003 Seillière had evolved a new strategy.

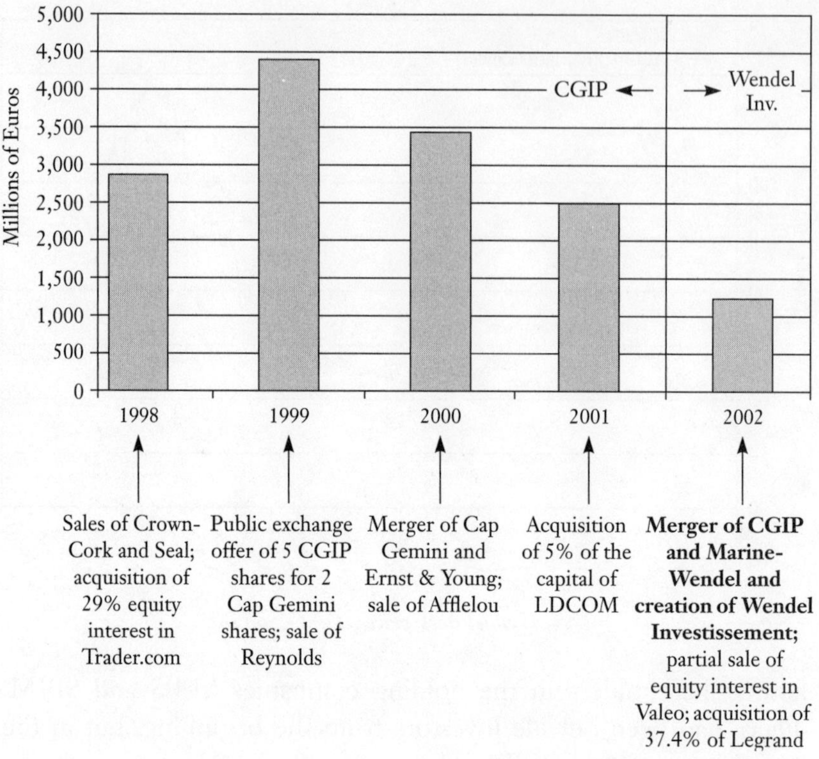

32. *Market capitalization, CGIP/Wendel Investissement, 1998–2002*

The merger involved buying up 500 million Euros of shares at a premium price. The new strategy involved the purchase of significant sums of stock in nonquoted companies (above 100 million Euros) and taking positions of control (with over 34 percent of the capital). The Wendel holding of Bureau Veritas was extended to a complete dominance, and in 2004 Wendel also bought a controlling stake in Editis, the second-largest French publishing group, from another well-known family group, Lagardère, that had come under some financial pressure.

The new company scored a major triumph in 2002 when it joined the American buyout specialist Kohlberg Kravis Roberts in buying the Limoges electrical equipment producer Legrand (Legrand had originally wanted to merge with Schneider, but had been refused permission by the EU competition authorities in Brussels). But the first year's results of Wendel Investissement showed a continued heavy loss, resulting from the need to depreciate 734 million

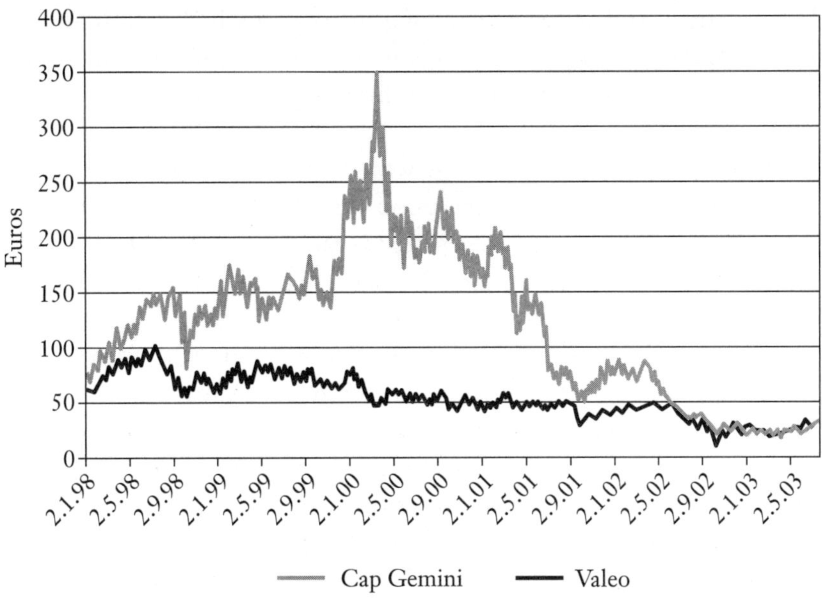

33. *Price charts, Cap Gemini and Valeo, 1998–2003*

Euros on the holding of Cap Gemini Ernst & Young. Valeo, on the other hand, began to demonstrate some signs of recovery.

The new galvanizing myth that had been built up by Seillière relied on a deliberate defiance of traditions in the act of remaking business structures, and on a courting of political unpopularity to show that tough business decisions were indeed being made. In an odd historical echo, this posture recalled that of François de Wendel in the interwar years, and there was indeed at this time a revival of interest in the story of the old steel patriarch. There seemed to be a clear parallel between the man who had incarnated French business at midcentury and his great-nephew. But inevitably this discussion of the role of an individual brought up once more the very old French discussion about families as business managers.

The cost of a family manager is that he is difficult or even impossible to sack even when his decisions are questioned or become problematical. Seillière had taken some strategic gambles that could alternately be described as very courageous or quite risky. He had also always made it clear that he eventually intended to appoint many outside managers, and by the summer of 2002 he had designated a successor, Jean-Bernard Lafonta, who was not part of the

Wendel dynasty.[20] After a very long history in which family members supplied the senior management, Wendel had moved to become a Chandlerian "management firm."

If Seillière had not been a member of the Wendel family, it is doubtful whether the man who was such a remarkable entrepreneurial hero between 1978 and 2000 would still be the president of the family company after the setbacks of 2000–2003. During this period there were purges in private-sector companies (Vivendi) and in public-sector enterprises (Electricité de France, France Telecom) of the iconic, ENA-educated figures who seemed to be responsible for what was seen in retrospect as grandiose overexpansion: Jean-Marie Messier, François Roussely, and Michel Bon. This story reinforces one of the central lessons of the history of the family enterprise: it responds to market conditions in ordinary or expansive times, and thus resembles other enterprises, but is uniquely resilient during downturns because of its ability to mobilize social as well as financial capital. Such resilience is thus a reflection of profound continuity.

The global crisis of corporate governance strengthened the idea of a French (or European) exceptionalism and of family capitalism. More generally, there was a flight of companies from the public market, and a sense that more value was created by companies that did not need to operate in the public glare of the stock market. The new notion that value expanded outside the market was used to redefine the very old concept of the family as the basis for a successful long-term vision of economic growth.

Chapter 14

The Crisis of Italian Steel

When one puts oneself in the hands of the banks, it is a certainty that one will end up being devoured.
Giorgio Falck, 2003

FALCK HAD APPEARED to be one of the great successes of the postwar boom in Italy. By the 1960s, however, some clouds were appearing on the horizon. The first of the cyclical crises that would hit the enterprise came in 1964, with the first operating loss since the immediate postwar years. Profits returned to the nominal levels of the early 1960s only in 1967, then fell back again almost immediately. Italian steel production at this time was surging, because of the entry onto the market of the so-called Bresciani producers with mini-mills. They proved a competitive challenge to other European producers, as for instance the Wendels felt sharply, but also to the established Italian firms.

Falck was especially vulnerable as the long-established AFL strategy of linking steel and electricity came under attack. In 1962 the Italian state largely nationalized the electricity industry, with effect from 4 January 1964, largely in response to the argument that only a coordinated national electrical industrial plan would allow the rapid economic development of the poor Italian south, the *Mezzogiorno*. AFL was allowed to retain its strategically vital power-production facilities only on the grounds that they were part of a group, producing electricity for the steel mills at Sesto San

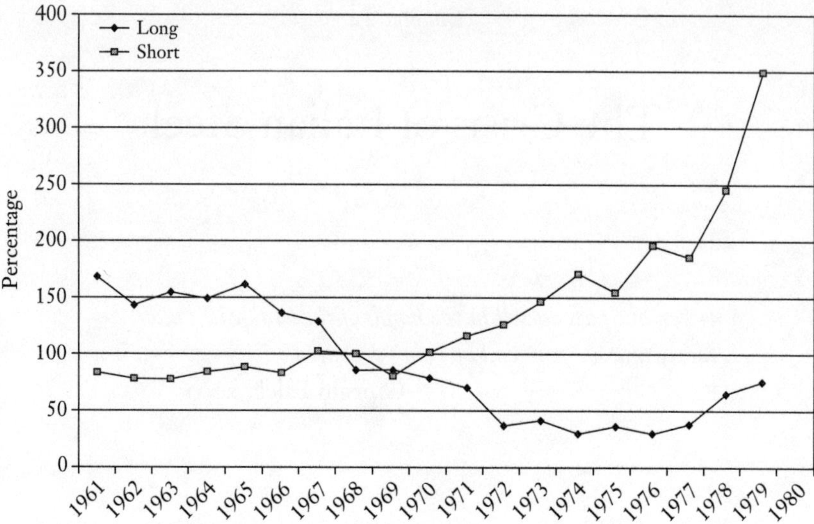

34. *Long- and short-term debt of Falck as a proportion of shareholders' equity, 1961–1980*

Giovanni and elsewhere. The other power plants were transferred to the state electrical company ENEL (Ente Nazionale per l'Energia Elettrica). The result of AFL's defense of its profitable holding in hydroelectric works was to tie the firm to steel for far longer than would be rationally justified: for without the steel, it would lose the electricity. AFL's insistence on defending its electricity works soon became the center of a political controversy. Part of the labor unrest of the late 1960s focused on the electricity holdings of Falck, and after a long strike, on 19 July 1970 the government ordered the transfer of the most important of the Falck hydroelectric plants, at Tavazzano, to ENEL. The loss of elecricity increased the firm's vulnerability in the early and mid-1970s as energy prices rose and Falck no longer had the advantage of being its own major supplier.

In 1968 and 1969 the major AFL-Falck works, especially at Sesto San Giovanni, were affected by the general wave of labor unrest in Italy, in particular the "hot autumn" of 1969. Company reports of the late 1960s complained increasingly about wage increases not matched by productivity increases, and by the shrinking amounts that could be used to pay dividends on shares.

In 1970 a legislative reduction of hours of work increased labor costs at a stroke by 26 percent. The push to labor radicalism was fueled by the heavy dominance of the steel sector by public enterprises, which had no obvious budget restraints, and could borrow more and more as they tried to buy off social discontent. Thus in April 1974 the powerful metalworkers' union FLM (Federazione Lavoratori Metameccanici) reached an agreement with the state holding company Finsider that amounted to a virtually complete surrender of the employers' position. Finsider, equipped with a state guarantee, simply borrowed: in 1974 it financed only 14.2 percent of its investment with its own resources (by contrast, Sacilor in France, which was hardly a model of good financial management either, paid for 33.8 percent and Thyssen in Germany for 48.2 percent).[1] The 1974 wage agreement predictably did not create social peace in Italy: on the contrary, from 1974 into 1977, 2,800 days per 1,000 workers were lost through strikes in the Italian steel industry, compared with 1,163 in Britain and 33 in Germany.[2]

In 1976 Falck closed the Vulcano works and abandoned completely the electrical production of pig iron. In the two major steelworks that remained in Sesto San Giovanni after the closing of Vulcano, there were different patterns of labor militancy. The Concordia works were dominated by the Communist union CIGL (Confederazione Generale Italiana del Lavoro), which maintained a high degree of discipline and control in the plant and tried to make bargains with the management. By contrast, in the Unione plant, the less autocratically run Catholic union affiliated with CISL (Confederazione Italiana Sindicati Lavoratori) was heavily infiltrated by the Red Brigades, and labor relations were much more troubled. Red Brigade terrorists killed a Falck manager, Manfredo Mazzanti, on 28 November 1980.

Falck at this time lost any sense of strategic orientation, and instead of looking at one segment in which it might have dominated the market, competed with Ilva and the other state-run works across the board, in seamless tubes, strip, and plate. It also competed in higher-priced steels. A higher proportion of its output was in specialty steel (41 percent) than for IRI-Finsider (23 percent), although Fiat had a much higher proportion.[3] The extent to which the Italian state could absorb losses in the nationalized enterprises was bound to make this a very one-sided competition. There were consequently big Falck losses, in 1975–76 and again after 1979; and the company needed to borrow large amounts, mostly on the short-term market. From 1970 to 1980 the number of employees was cut from 13,000 to 11,400.

The steel crisis of the 1970s was of course not peculiar to AFL-Falck. Its losses from 1978 to 1980 were large (7 billion liras, or $8.3 million), but looked small in comparison to those of the state sector (IRI-Finsider), which lost 2,437 billion liras ($2,900 million). Even the Bresciani producers lost 59 billion liras.[4] Labor relations in Italy reached a new height of tension after the 1982 "march of the 40,000" on the Fiat works. This spectacular demonstration was occasioned in part by the firm's decision to exit from steel. Fiat, the only other large-scale private Italian steelmaker besides Falck, had sold its steel business, Teksid, in 1981–82 to Finsider after a decade of heavy losses.

The two oil shocks of the 1970s brought a general crisis to European steelmaking, the politics of which made for even greater difficulties for Italy's private-sector steel industry. The discussion was overshadowed by a highly unpleasant and counterproductive economic nationalism. French and German producers blamed the small and efficient mini-mills of the Bresciani producers, which like Falck worked scrap in an electrical process. The Italians in return complained that French and German businesses were distorting the market by selling scrap outside the European Community, where it was worked by producers with lower labor costs, who could then either reexport their semifinished steel products into the EC or drive EC (mostly Italian) producers out of markets in North Africa and the Middle East. The very old Dongo plant of AFL, the largest Italian producer of wrought iron, suffered badly from the competition of such external producers, who in 1982 supplied 60 percent of the Italian market.[5]

The first Italian crisis plan of 1979 responded to this pressure by focusing investment in Finsider, with a large expansion proposed for the works in Cornigliano and Bagnoli. The public sector was still encouraged to expand even as the first European steel plan for restructuring, Davignon I (after the EC Commissioner Etienne Davignon), imposed price ceilings on reinforcement bars (rebars), the largest product of the Bresciani mills. Even in the early 1980s, after a new oil crisis and in the middle of a severe recession with very high interest rates, the Italian Socialist minister for state shareholdings, Gianni De Michelis, proposed new investment schemes for Finsider. By 1982 the state holding company IRI had a debt level that exceeded its total turnover; two-thirds of the IRI debts originated in Finsider.[6]

In 1982 Law 46 provided subsidies for dismantling steel plants, and the government forced the Bresciani producers to cooperate in reducing capacity. Given this reality, there was little alternative for the private sector but to work more closely with the government, and Falck took a leading role in establishing a mixed enterprise (80 percent private, 20 percent public), which was designed to shift bulk production to the coastal site of Cornigliano: Consorzio Genovese Acciai (COGEA). A European Community agreement of 15 April 1983 provided for the closing of four Falck furnaces and a blooming mill. The restructuring agreement was completed in 1984 after problems with the financing of the scheme: the role that was originally to have been taken by the scandal-hit Banca Ambrosiana was eventually taken over by the Banca San Paolo of Brescia. Falck could then conclude some trans-European market sharing agreements on some specialty steel products with Sacilor (the former Wendel company) in 1984.

But COGEA quite quickly collapsed. In its place, a new public-private enterprise was established, the Acciarie di Cornigliano. But Falck (as well as most of the Bresciani) had had its fingers burnt and did not want to get involved in a second round of lossmaking, and the leading role in the new Cornigliano company was taken by a true Bresciani family firm, Riva. Riva had been founded in 1954, in the 1960s became the most dynamic operator of mini-mills in Italy, and in 1971 began to expand outside Italy, with the acquisition of a Spanish subsidiary. Emilio Riva, who held 51 percent of the capital, started to apply the principles of the mini-mill to the modernization of the large state sector and the application of more flexible methods.[7] In 1995 Riva completed its control of the former state steel sector by buying Taranto. Instead of taking over state steelworks, Falck concluded an agreement on sales quotas with another part of the Finsider complex, Ilva, in 1990, which also involved Ilva's taking a stake in Falck.

Falck was in retrospect unlucky in its timing. In the early 1980s, when it started to investigate the issue of private-public partnership in steel, there was no social consensus, and no willingness to see privatization as a route to solving the dilemmas of the Italian steel industry. Disenchanted by COGEA, it lost interest, with the result that it was Riva that transformed Italian steel production.

For Falck, the expansion of capital was accompanied by a reduction in the share of direct family ownership as the family capital was exhausted. In 1947 the proportion of capital owned by the family had been 73.1 percent (other directors, including Goisis and Feltrinelli, had 11.8 percent), but by 1993 the share had shrunk to 32.3 percent, largely through the protracted and costly process of restructuring.[8] By 1999 the joint-stock company Falck Società per Azione (SpA), the successor to AFL-Falck, was 24.29 percent owned by the family group, and 6.3 percent by Mediobanca. (It also held just under 5 percent of its own shares).[9]

In response to the exceptionally heavy financial losses of the mid-1980s, the Falcks sold off assets. In 1984–85 Falck sold its hydroelectric works to Sondel. In October–November 1985 it offered the Sondel shares that it had received in payment for the hydroelectric works to its shareholders. In 1985 the company was reorganized under a holding group (Capogruppo) in which the Techint group gained a major participation. The shrinkage in employment continued, the number of employees falling to 4,800 in 1986. At the same time the company initiated a major capital increase, from 110.6 billion liras to 147.5 billion ($110 million).

After this, retrenchment continued. In 1990 Falck abandoned steel joints and connectors and returned to its origins: AFL now became Ferriere e Fonderie di Dongo. Employment in the core company fell from 5,279 at the beginning of 1990 to 3,155 in 1995. This reorganization took place through an agreement with the state steel sector that had long been Falck's major rival. Indeed the transaction recalled some of the attempts in the 1920s to amalgamate Ilva and AFL.

Under the compact with the state company Ilva, and as part of a recapitalization of Falck in October 1990, Ilva took a 30 percent holding in Falck. Falck sold to Ilva works in Naples and Milan-Arcore. In 1991 Falck was reorganized as a holding company with five companies: Falck Nastri, Falck Lamiere, Trafilerie Vittoria (on the historic Sesto San Giovanni site; this company ceased activity in 1992), Novamet (manufacturing ferrochrome), and Immobiliare Cascina Rubina. In April 1991 it acquired Frontiere Finance Ltd., which it renamed AFI Finance International. With Ecosesta SpA it moved into the environmental protection business.

The deal with Ilva had been made at the end of a brief period of revival in the steel market. AFL-Falck had reported what it called "brilliant" results in 1988–89. But the agreement came apart with a new worldwide recession, and was formally terminated in 1993.

The major alternative to steel envisaged by Falck was at first its traditional focus on electricity production. In the mid-1980s the company began to sell shares in the AFL-Falck hydroelectric works (now grouped in a new company, Sondel) to private shareholders with the help of a consortium of four banks (Efibanca, Interbanca, Centrobanca, Banco Napoli). In 1987, when the transaction was complete, Sondel shares were offered directly to Falck shareholders, so that steel and electricity were now held in separate corporate entities.

The push to diversification and to new sorts of activity in finance and property management caused a great deal of heart-searching among the Falck family. They felt themselves to be industrialists rather than financiers, and continued to surround themselves with pictures of furnaces and of classic industrial activity. Giorgio E. Falck in particular wanted to continue the by now very costly family tradition, but was opposed by the two sons of Enrico Falck, Alberto and Federico (Federico had been trained as a steel engineer, and both were devoted to the traditional activity). At this point a major family quarrel erupted, accentuated by the rather different lifestyles of the cousins: Giorgio was married to an actress, Rosanna Schiaffino, and led a glamorous jet-set existence; while Alberto was a pious and ascetic Catholic. They also embodied different philosophies of management. Giorgio had the traditional suspicion of banks, commenting that "when one puts oneself in the hands of the banks, it is a certainty that one will end up being devoured."[10] By contrast, Alberto thought that the network of contacts that Mediobanca could create among the Milanese business elite, in particular the family's close association with the Pirellis, would provide a stable basis for the restructuring of the family firm in the poststeel age. Crucially for the eventual outcome of the clash and estrangement between Alberto and Giorgio, Giorgio's sister Gioa Marchi, who had participated regularly in capital increases and had become the largest of the family shareholders, supported Alberto.

In 1994, in a last-gasp effort to stay in steel, the Falcks associated themselves with an attempt to run probably the most historic entity of the former state steel enterprises, which were now being privatized; together with other family holding groups, Falck worked with the big German steelmaker Krupp to buy Accai Speciali Terni from IRI. The other Italian groups in this transaction were Tad Fin (the Gruppo Agarini) and Fire Finanzaria (the Gruppo Riva).

The end to the Falck steel connection came quickly after this. On 4 August 1994, Law 481 (frequently known as the "Bresciani law" in that it dismantled the core of Italy's private steel sector) provided for the dismantling, with European Union subsidies, of the plants of Falck Nastri, Falck Lamiere, and Falck Vittoria. After this the company was committed to produce only strip steel of less than 500 millimeters that did not fall under EU regulations. The ground underlying the Bolzano works, which at this time employed 447 workers, was sold for 63 billion liras ($38.8 million) to the province of Bolzano, while the works themselves were sold to another family steel enterprise, Amenduni of Vicenza. In 1996 Falck sold Falck Vobarno and its shares in two metal producers, SIAU and Ferrometalli Safem. The abandoned site at Sesto San Giovanni of the Unione and Concordia plants left a large hole in the center of the town. In 1993 Falck had participated in the North Milan Development Agency, which was 80 percent owned by the Sesto San Giovanni municipal council and 15 percent by Falck. A Japanese architect, Kenzo Tange, who proposed a massive theme park and entertainment center loosely modeled on Disneyland, prepared the first scheme for the redevelopment of the steel site as a model postindustrial site. This proposal was widely ridiculed, and seemed increasingly less attractive with the difficulties encountered by the French Eurodisney park.[11] The Ticino architect Mario Botta then prepared a more sober but also more interesting plan, which preserved the big halls at the center of the old steelworks as sites for cultural projects, surrounded by new residential and commercial development.[12] The major problem remained the cost of the environmental cleanup.

Falck moved into waste management (in a company called Ambiente 2000, run together with Ogden Waste to Energy), energy generation from waste products, and property management. It constructed a large new 20-megawatt waste-to-energy plant at Granarolo dell'Emilia. Through Leonardo holdings, in which it had a 31 percent stake, Falck also owned the company managing the Rome airport, the Aeroporti di Roma. In 2002, as part of a corporate restructuring, 45 percent of the Aeroporti di Roma was sold off, but Leonardo retained a 51.2 percent controlling interest.

Falck also played a major role in the dramatic postprivatization redefinition of Italian capitalism. This part of its history strikingly raised the question of the role of Mediobanca, the bank that had been at the center of the post-1945 reconstruction of Italian family capitalism. In the mid-1990s, with the traditional steel sites abandoned and dismantled, Falck looked very fragile. The Falck group as a whole had employed 8,107 people in 1987, but only 691 in 1996. Its share price continued to languish, and the family's financial means were exhausted. But there was clearly some scope to revalue the individual assets, and in 1996 a Polish-French industrialist with substantial experience in the energy sector bought up on the stock market a holding in the Falck company that eventually amounted to 38.5 percent. Romain Zaleski had started out as a French civil servant but had come to Italy in 1983 as the chief executive officer of Carlo Tassara, a bankrupt Italian steel company in Breno (Brescia) that had been hit by the steel crisis. Initially he represented a supplier of machinery to whom Carlo Tassara had been heavily indebted. Zaleski established a reputation for skillful management of corporate turnarounds (he later liked to say, "I didn't invent the company, only promoted its correct functioning"). By 1989 he had achieved a majority control of the capital of Carlo Tassara.[13] Zaleski then turned to other steelmakers hit by the steel crisis. In the mid-1990s he paid a very low price for the purchase of Falck—less than 1.50 Euros per share. He sold the stock in 2000 with a 300 percent gain. The Falck family had been alarmed from the beginning about the corporate raider, not least because when he initially approached Alberto Falck to say that he had acquired a 5.5 percent stake in the company, he was widely believed already to own around 20 percent of the stock. In addition, Zaleski seemed to have close relations with Fiat, which was trying to diversify and now viewed itself as an antagonist of the Falck company.

In 2000 the major energy producer Montedison, which had grown dramatically after Italian nuclear power plants were mothballed for reasons of environmental safety in 1997, bought an 80 percent stake in Falck with a cash offer of 9 Euros per share as a preliminary to a full merger. The main attraction was the electricity-generation part of the Falck business, in particular the holding of Sondel. But in a

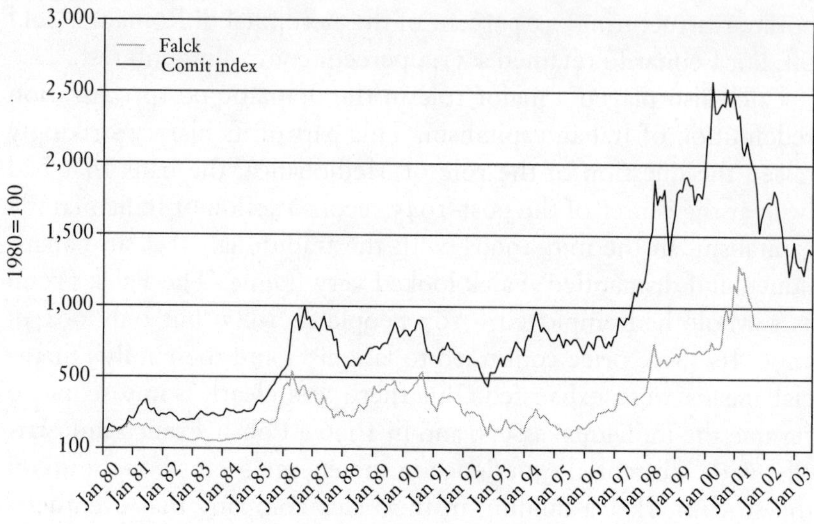

35. *Falck stock prices, 1980–2003*

dramatic shareholders' meeting on 27 February 2001, a minority coalition of shareholders emerged to oppose the acquisition of the remaining 20 percent (with the family keeping a token 0.4 percent stake), and thus blocked the deal. The leading opposition role was taken by Banca di Roma, San Paolo-Imi, the private steelmaker Carlo Tassara (that is, Zaleski), and the Strazzera family. These shareholders abstained on the vote. Only 0.913 percent of the shares were actually voted against the proposal, but the abstainers had 42.688 percent of the voting rights, and the merger was thus blocked under Italian law on corporate governance. The event was widely covered by the Italian press, which treated it as a slap in the face *(schiaffo)* for Montedison, for Mediobanca, which had put together the deal, and in general for old-style Italian family capitalism. The accusation was that the deal greatly overvalued Falck through the proposed exchange of thirty-one Montedison shares for each five Falck shares, making Falck effectively worth 13 Euros per share. The opposition portrayed this as a present to the Falck family.[14] The stock price of Montedison immediately rose, while that of Falck slumped.

One of the reasons Montedison was thought to want to offer such generous terms to the Falcks was that a large shareholding by a reliable and friendly family would resist or block attempts at a hostile takeover, perhaps by foreign companies interested in control

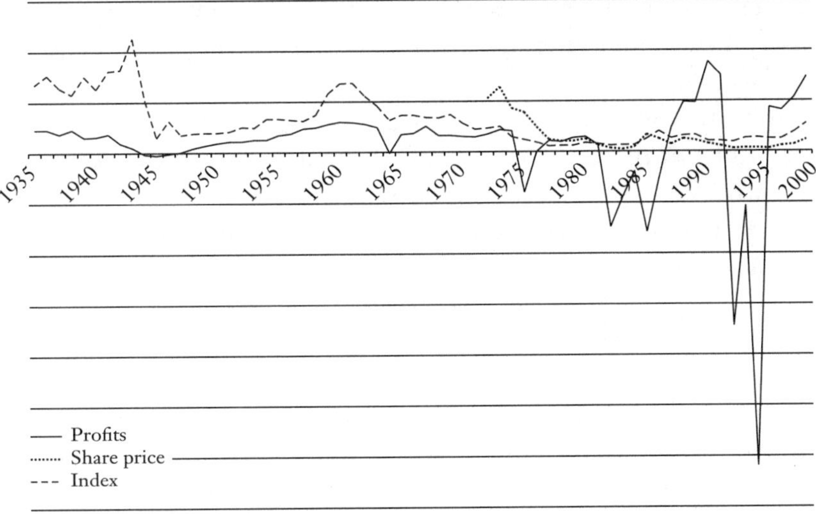

36. *Price-deflated Falck profits and share prices, 1935–2000*

of the Italian energy market. But by the summer of 2001 at least 23 percent of Montedison was controlled by Electricité de France, having bought a substantial part of the share capital from Zaleski, as well as some shares bought through Deutsche Bank.

In May 2002, in an attempt to conclude the final act of the drama, Montedison (now renamed Edison) agreed for 250 million Euros to sell Falck its engineering company Tecnimont and a smaller power-sector engineering firm, and thus reduce its high debt level. But in August 2002 Falck withdrew from the transaction, citing "unfulfilled conditions."[15] What remained of the Falck business empire again appeared to be on the verge of collapse. In October 2002 a shareholders' meeting of Falck SpA merged a number of family-owned financing companies into Falck: Vallemeria SpA, Montrefin Srl (Società a Responsibilità Limitata; limited-liability company), Sinfin Srl, Refin Srl, and Giofin Holding Srl. The subsequent balance-sheet adjustment made it clear just how small Falck had now become.

The episode was a major indicator of the rapidity with which Italian capitalism was transforming itself. For much of the twentieth century, share ownership in Italy had been a way to destroy wealth. After the disastrous two-decades-long experiment in bank-managed industrialization at the beginning of the century, the state had taken control. Families held complicated and intertangled packets of ownership rights, and corporate restructuring was practically impossible.

After the privatization of the main (previously state-owned) Italian banks in the early 1990s, they turned themselves into investment banks and started to criticize the unusual position of Mediobanca. The major role taken by Banca di Roma in the battle over the Montedision buyout of Falck was part of this struggle. Two years after the *schiaffo* of 27 February 2001, the banks directly attacked the Mediobanca way of doing business and forced out Enrico Cuccia's chosen heir in Mediobanca, Vincenzo Maranghi. The *Financial Times* interpreted this public humiliation as signaling "a move away from the kind of backroom deals that have caused foreign investors, in particular, to cast a wary eye on Italy."[16] Everything now became possible, and the national self-sufficiency that previously marked the Italian approach to corporate ownership and governance broke down.

The Falck family stayed in steel longer than the other family enterprises discussed in this volume. Their firm over decades had elaborated a critique of the Italian state's large-scale productivist approach to the steel industry, and it is possible to see the shift after privatization, as Margherita Balconi does, as a victory of a "pre-Fordist" vision.[17] But during the crisis of steel in the 1970s and 1980s, there was no escape from dealing with the state sector and Finsider. The successive attempts to make an arrangement, first in the 1980s with COGEA, then with Ilva, failed. The Riva success indicates that the basic insight, already elaborated much earlier by both Giorgio Enrico and Enrico Falck, that Italian steel could benefit from a private-sector approach was not misguided. But Falck's tenacity in holding to this insight had exacted a heavy price, reflected in decades of substantial losses. The family itself was divided, and as a result of the conflicts between Giorgio (who withdrew from the company) and Alberto and Federico Falck the number of family shareholders shrank from around 30 in the early 1990s to 17 in 2003. In this way the company became a striking symbol not so much of the resilience of Italian family capitalism as of its weaknesses and vulnerabilities.

Chapter 15

German Diversification and Internationalization

The heirs must be proud to belong to the family. But that is a matter of education, and parents are generally not capable of doing this alone.

Hans Willers, 1991

In the late twentieth century, German business practices were transformed and—to use the term currently fashionable—"globalized." The "Americanization of West German Industry," which some analysts such as Volker Berghahn have dated back to the 1950s, was really not very thorough until the 1970s.[1] German business life continued to be dominated by very traditional figures such as Hermann Reusch in the GHH and the banker Hermann Josef Abs.[2] The breakthrough came largely in the 1970s, as a result of the liberalization of capital markets, but also because of German firms' increased experience through either exports or the creation of foreign subsidiaries of international markets. The old German giants such as Siemens, Daimler-Benz, and Bosch relaunched themselves as multinational enterprises, and those that did not, like AEG, perished. The model offered by these examples led other, smaller German firms to consider how they should approach internationalization. Some of the most prominent members of German business dynasties concluded that, as Robert Bosch Jr. put it, in the face of the new challenges of the age, "the family does not fit in any more in large companies."[3] But internationalization was not in fact incompatible with family business principles.

German internationalization was strikingly different from the French experience. France in the 1980s and 1990s globalized with efficiency and brutality, largely by letting foreign capital in as the dirigiste state of the postwar period was dismantled. To many the less densely structured and interlinked "Deutschland AG," with fewer changes in corporate governance, less foreign investment, less of an embrace of capital markets, and remarkably few hostile takeovers, offered a more secure environment. But there was still a globalization of German enterprise. Germany's globalization involved international outreach, a phenomenon that extended not just to the largest but also deep into small and medium enterprises. The internationalization of business was an economic counterpart to the Federal Republic's search for the recreation of Germany not as a nation-state but as a multilateralized political order dependent on a European setting. Indeed it was the vigor and crossnational reach of large and middle-sized German companies that gave the political dynamic its coherence and power. Haniel exemplifies a largely successful development in the German style of globalization.

The modern internationalization of the Haniel business (following similar moves at both ends of the nineteenth century) began in the 1960s, well before the intrafamily debates of the 1970s about the future orientation of business. But the most recent move to internationalize began in response to chance circumstances rather than as a deliberate strategic choice, leaving this new kind of activity semidetached from the rest of Haniel activity. It was also conducted on a very different principle from the rest of the business, which had been driven by a resolve not to participate in enterprises in which there was no control of ownership. But the exercise in diversification soon became so profitable that any objection to the strategy would seem misguided, although it would raise profound issues about corporate governance.

Metro

In 1967, with 78 million Deutschmarks acquired from the sale of the Rheinpreussen gasoline stations, FHC became a partner in a business that responded to the new and increasingly widespread prosperity of the Federal Republic: cash-and-carry discount stores.

It was a shift into the world of consumer goods, away from the heavy industrial products that had characterized most of the history of the Haniel enterprises.

Metro had been founded in 1964 by Otto Beisheim, who set up his first wholesale discount store in Mülheim an der Ruhr. He himself had a controversial, and for a long time quite camouflaged, background. One of his two older brothers had fought in the Spanish Civil War in the Kondor division, while another fought in the SS Totenkopfdivision. Beisheim himself had been a member of the SS Leibstandarte Adolf Hitler; not surprisingly, he shunned journalistic inquiries about his past or indeed his present. He intended Metro as a new sort of enterprise, offering a wide range of goods to retail businesses: small shops, but also the increasingly flourishing restaurant business. Unlike classic wholesalers, Metro did not deliver goods or offer credit, but set out its products in large piles in large-quantity packages in a sort of super-supermarket or hypermarket style. Success required advanced data management of inventory; in the mid-1960s, with the IBM 360 range of computers just being released, this was a considerable innovation, and a break with the traditions of the German wholesale business, which (as with the Haniel coal trade) had liked to focus on just a few products. As Metro developed, a critical role was played by a former IBM executive, Erwin Conradi.

Metro required more capital in order to expand, and in 1967 FHC took a participation of one-third in the Metro C & C Grossmarkt GmbH & Co. KG, Mülheim/Ruhr. The contact with Haniel came about in a rather chance way: the general manager of FHC, Walter Schäfer, happened to belong to the same Mülheim tennis club as Beisheim. Another third of the capital came from the Schmidt-Ruthenbeck family, which supplied the chain of SPAR shops and small supermarkets and thus had solid experience in the food wholesale trade.

This was a controversial investment, as many influential members of the Haniel family were unfamiliar with the business, feared that Beisheim was expanding too quickly and recklessly, and wanted to establish a clear control over companies in which FHC invested. But Beisheim was gripped by his own version of the "family firm bug" and did not want external control by banks or by an outside holding company. The one-third solution was a way of reassuring both FHC and Beisheim when they were joined by a family with retail trading experience such as the Schmidt-Ruthenbecks.

In 1968 Metro expanded internationally, for which it required a further substantial injection of capital; and once again a family group proved to be a more attractive partner than a bank. Haniel encouraged Beisheim to approach a Dutch family group, the van Vlissingens, who had long worked with Haniel in Rhine coal-trading and whose company name reflected its origins: the Steenkolen Handelsvereeniging N. V. Steenkolen established a joint venture with Metro, MAKRO, in which the Metro Group would hold a 40 percent share. MAKRO established wholesale cash-and-carry stores on the Metro model in Belgium and the Netherlands, but also in Britain, Spain, and—very controversially—apartheid South Africa. A mirror image of MAKRO, in which the Dutch would own 40 percent and the original Metro owners 60 percent, was created for other countries (except Germany). In 1971 METRO International started to open stores in France, and then, through the 1970s, in Austria, Denmark, and Italy. In 1998 the dual or parallel structure of MAKRO and METRO was ended when METRO bought out the van Vlissingen interests. By this time Metro was doing business in eighteen countries.

The cash-and-carry concept was soon quite widely imitated in Germany and elsewhere. It stood in a curious relation to traditional retailing business: on the one hand, it offered a cheaper and more convenient way of supplying stores. On the other hand, some retailers complained that in practice retail customers were obtaining membership cards to take advantage of the cash-and-carry discounts. One major attraction of the cash-and-carry stores was that as wholesalers they were not limited by Germany's overly rigid laws on store opening hours, and could be open at convenient times for working customers: the Metro stores did an overwhelming proportion of their business in the evening. By the mid-1990s Metro had 2.8 million customers with club cards in Germany alone. Retail organizations, in particular the Hauptverband des Deutschen Einzelhandels, reacted by taking legal action against Metro. Metro fought a messy and combative rearguard action, which it could string out because each of its stores operated as a separate company with a separate legal personality. Its style of judicial confrontation was widely held to be at odds with the consensual character of West

German society, and inevitably increased the general hostility to Beisheim and his empire. The court cases dragged on until 2000, when all fifty-two were settled.[4]

In the early 1970s the rapid expansion of the cash-and-carry business slowed down. It was a sector that had matured quickly and was ripe for "consolidation." In fact, of the 691 cash-and-carry enterprises in Germany in 1972, half had disappeared by 1986.[5] Metro responded from the second half of the decade by acquiring bona fide retail outlets and in some cases establishing new ones: Primus, Meister, Huma, BLV, Massa AG, and ASKO Deutsche Kaufhaus AG (which controlled a number of important furniture, fashion, and do-it-yourself stores). The most important acquisition was the department-store holding company Kaufhof AG, which was in the hands of the Dresdner and the Commerzbank. In 1981 Metro took a 24.9 percent stake in Kaufhof, the maximum allowed by the German cartel authorities. Only after prolonged legal conflict did the cartel office authorize a majority holding (in 1987). At this stage Kaufhof amounted to about a third of the total business of Metro. By the mid-1990s Kaufhof controlled more than 300 companies, including the important electronics retailers Media-Markt/Saturn and Vobis-Microcomputer.

Metro was a highly innovative company, but it had something of the Wild West about it, and was not subject to close controls by its owners. In the early 1970s some influential Haniel family members began to worry about the pace of Metro's expansion. They complained that Metro was destroying the retail business on whose prosperity it actually depended. Wolfgang Curtius commented in 1971: "In the longer term the reduction of retail trade in numbers and volume is a threat." The business model required a tight control that could easily be lost if the company were internationalized too quickly. In this view, Beisheim needed to have brakes applied. Curtius articulated this feeling:

> It could be that Beisheim in the search for ever new successes goes too far. The already fast-paced tempo of expansion is beginning to be hectic. It is scarcely conceivable that the organization will work with the simultaneous opening of Metro markets in most European countries, or that the selection and training of personnel, as well as purchase, sales, and the control of goods,

> will be carried out with the degree of care that provided the base for the first success of Metro. A consolidation phase is urgently needed. Particularly important is securing a running control of the overall finance.[6]

In particular, family members were worried by the lack of transparency and by the fact that the Haniel family representative, Thuisko von Metzsch, was treating the business relationship with Beisheim as a purely personal matter. Thus the Metro figures were not available to the Haniel family or to the management of FHC.

This was a view of Metro long shared by financial journalists, who complained about the group's untransparent operations and its secrecy. The individual corporate existence of the various Metro stores and the absence of consolidated accounts made any external assessment of the company difficult. In the mid-1980s *Die Zeit* wrote about Metro's attempts to correct its "miserable public image, which apparently bothered no one in the expansion phase."[7] This was also a view held by the senior management of Haniel, who occasionally expressed frustration at their inability to influence a company that Haniel owned in part but did not control. But Hansjörg Hereth, the man behind Metro's controversial legal strategy, was not removed from Metro until 1994, and even after that he continued to enjoy the confidence of Beisheim. In the early 1990s the chief executive of FHC started a discussion about the possible sale of Metro, but was quickly obliged to desist.

Metro's acquisition of a more respectable business profile involved expansion, partly self-generated and partly through takeovers. The growth took place in the context of a new wave of internationalization, both in central and eastern Europe after the collapse of Communism, and in Asia, especially in the giants China and India. In the 1990s Metro became the largest private-sector employer in Poland. By 2003 it was operating 2,300 stores in 26 countries.[8] In 1996 the corporate reform led to the creation of a publicly quoted company.

In the late 1990s there was a race to consolidate and build a position of strength in a European retail market that was seen as analogous to the integrated U.S. market. Metro's bid for European supremacy was to some extent blocked when in 1999 the two large French retailers Carrefour and Promodès carried out a friendly merger that made them the world's second-largest retailer after Wal-Mart. In response to the French challenge, Metro's chief executive, Conradi, tried to negotiate a sale of Metro to Wal-Mart, which would obviously have created a more or less unbeatable transcontinental giant; but in 2000 the proposal collapsed. This humiliation brought an extension of the Haniel hold on Metro. In part because of the Wal-Mart discussions, in part because of his continued micromanagement of day-to-day details, the Metro managers revolted against Conradi, who was by this time chairman of the supervisory board of Metro. He resigned abruptly in 2000 and was replaced by an older member of the Haniel dynasty, Jan von Haeften. When von Haeften retired because of age in 2003, his place on the supervisory board of Metro was taken by the chief executive of FHC, Günther Hülse. Haniel offered a different corporate tradition from the one with which Metro had started out.

There was by now a considerable range of business, from the old-style cash-and-carry activity and hypermarkets to specialty retailing. The focus had been widened. Metro's chief executive, Hans Joachim Körber, said: "The truth is that most large retailers are multi-format groups. The problem is not whether one has too many formats but whether they are all successful."[9] Metro in this way was moving along a development path that had already been taken by other parts of the Haniel Group.

The Management of Systems

One reason the discussion within Haniel of the Metro position was so intense in the 1970s was that it provided quite quickly a major source of returns. By 1974 Metro accounted for just under a third (30.3 percent) of overall FHC revenue, while the traditional areas of heating and petroleum were under a quarter (23.4 percent), and a growing share came from a new branch, pharmaceuticals.[10]

In December 1967, at the same time that FHC was discussing the success of Metro and plans for further investment, the management of FHC reported that it was negotiating with Dresdner Bank for the purchase of an 84.3 percent share of the pharmaceutical wholesaler GEHE & Co. Haniel had already taken a step in this direction in 1961 with the purchase of Lieser-Pharma, a relatively small business. Wholesale and retail pharmacies were carefully separated in

Germany by a legal requirement that retail pharmacies had to be stand-alone units and could not be part of chains. This arrangement actually gave great power to the wholesale side of the business. Eventually FHC accumulated a relatively large number of small pharmaceutical distributors, mostly with only partial ranges of stock, and with nonexistent or only rudimentary inventory management systems. Rationalization and computerization could bring very obvious and quick productivity gains. The key insight—as in the Metro business—lay in seeing commerce as a giant and integrated system that might achieve astonishing improvements in efficiency and scale through the application of new information technology. Indeed it is striking how many of the executives at Haniel in the late twentieth century arrived with a background in systems technology from one firm, IBM Deutschland: Günter Brock and Dieter Schadt in FHC, and Erwin Conradi in Metro.

The purchase of GEHE was finalized only in 1972, and there continued to be a relatively small number of outside shareholders. In 1981 the Dresdner Bank advised against a capital increase, arguing that this would be interpreted in the press as a move by the Haniel interests against the small shareholders. Haniel could have bought out these shareholders relatively easily at an early stage, but the management decided (and convinced the family owners) that some enterprises in the Haniel structure could well be left as joint-stock companies. They might then be used to raise capital that could not be so easily found at the level of the Haniel owners. This technique of expansion through the stock exchange was referred to as "opening on the second level." GEHE, in contrast to Metro, emphasized the importance of control, and by the mid-1990s it accounted for about half of the Haniel profits. Significantly, in 1993 the new chairman of the FHC managing board, Dieter Schadt, came from GEHE, and brought with him a concern for the details of integrating systems as a way of grasping the problems and challenges of a complex group of enterprises.

FHC continued to buy other pharmaceutical wholesalers and add them to GEHE: for example, Rudloff & Waterman, Minden (1982). The rapid GEHE expansion was financed by a capital increase, which reduced the FHC holding from 94 percent to 75 percent (1984) and then to 51 percent (1988). In the 1990s there was a substantial internationalization, with the 1993 purchase of the major French pharmaceutical wholesaler, Office Commercial Pharmaceutique (OCP), which had been badly managed and was in commercial difficulties; of the British AAH in 1994; and of the British Lloyds Chemist in 1997.

During the 1980s GEHE had also acquired some non-pharmaceutical businesses, in particular the office- and warehouse-supplies company KAISER + KRAFT (1985). In a move to focus GEHE on its core business, these new businesses were broken off to form another FHC company, TAKKT AG, in 1998.

The most conspicuous international diversification of the 1970s was the decision to establish a U.S. corporation, Hanamerica, in 1976. Most of the U.S. business that Haniel bought into was focused on retailing, especially in the grocery sector. In 1977 Haniel bought the midwestern grocery chain Scrivner, which expanded further through the purchases of Groce Wearden (Texas) in 1980 and Flickinger in 1984. In 1987 Scrivner added Quinn, in 1989 Gateway Foods, Inc., and in 1993 the upstate New York grocery chain Peter J. Schmitt.

Transportation lent itself even more readily to internationalization; Haniel established a business in New York in 1970, with later extensions to Brazil, Mexico, and South Africa. Transportation fitted well with the old Haniel legacy of Rhine shipping, as well as with FHC's ownership of the steamship company OPDR. Still other historic parts of the Haniel business were modernized to suit late twentieth-century markets: in the late 1980s Haniel began to produce stainless steel from reprocessed secondary material (analogous to the core business of the Falcks), an area where the United States (and Italy) had historically had a technological lead over Germany.[11]

Some diversification, however, went well beyond traditional Haniel activities. In 1972 Haniel moved into the environmental business through the creation of a waste-management company (Westab), at a time when widespread worry about the exhaustion of the world's natural resources had created a new public concern with the environment. In 1976 FHC bought S + I Schlammpresstechnik (sludge treatment), and went on in the 1980s to expand in this area through the acquisition of IHG Duisburg. In 1998 the fire- and water-damage treatment operations that had previously been a part of Haniel Enviro-Service were set up as a separate company, BELFOR.

One of the most important Haniel acquisitions came about not as the result of any strategic search, but from a broker's offer conveyed to the management of FHC in February 1981: the Swiss-based sanitary and professional clothing firm CWS AG. During the 1980s this highly successful business expanded into France and Singapore (1984) and then into the Netherlands and Belgium (1988). It also expanded the range of its activities beyond its initial focus on washable towels and professional clothing: in 1983 it introduced an air-control service for public restrooms; in 1984 it innovated with a "jumbo soap dispenser"; and 1993 brought the hygienic breakthrough of the self-cleaning toilet seat. The CWS business model fits well into the concept of a systems management approach: as in the classic IBM model of the 1960s and 1970s, the key is not to sell products (IBM at this stage did not sell its mainframes) but to establish a long-term service commitment. Thus in 1988 the chairman of the managing board of FHC, Hans Willers, was defining the desirable direction of Haniel business in the following way: "Systems business of all types, partner-based solutions for customers, supported by logistics, are advancing worldwide."[12]

The quite diverse Haniel companies did not have particular synergies and were deliberately not brought completely under a single financial control, although a consolidated balance sheet was prepared. Critics referred to this kind of enterprise as a "conglomerate," a word that by the 1990s had bad connotations in many discussions of management theory. Publicly quoted conglomerates in the 1980s usually traded at a substantial discount to the value of their component businesses if treated as stand-alone enterprises. A recent account of the modern firm concludes that diversification, which otherwise destroys value, may be rational in some specific circumstances: "an example is family-owned firms, especially in countries with poorly developed capital markets." But they are also attractive "if sensitive and subjective information about people and jobs flows more easily within a firm than across firm boundaries." Human capital, or particular skills, thus can be allocated more efficiently in a diversified enterprise. In the Haniel case this was systems technology.[13]

The intentionally loose structure reflected both a diversification strategy and a risk-management approach. There should be no mutual guarantees between the companies, and the form of financing

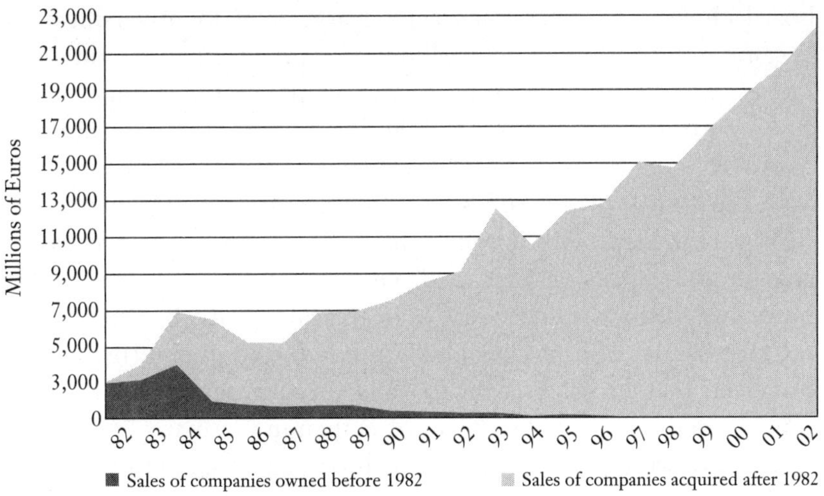

37. *Haniel as a new company in the 1980s and 1990s*

that each unit took was described as "nonrecourse" financing, at first from international venture funds such as Prudential Capital and later from German bank syndicates. This strategy was designed to reassure the owners of FHC about the security of the concern as a whole, and was thus designed to reflect the preferences of owners as well as managers. As the general manager Willers explained to the family meeting in 1990, security was increased "because we can let companies go bankrupt without damaging our reputation in the eyes of the financial community. This is important. In this respect the world has largely changed in the last years."[14]

The logical outcome of the fast-paced developments of the 1980s was reached under Willers' successors as general manager, who returned to a greater emphasis on central guidance or control. In 1995 Haniel changed into a "strategic management holding" company, with the central company functioning not simply as a portfolio manager of an incoherent conglomerate but rather as a definer of strategy. In particular, the subsidiaries had to fit into an overall concept and display common features, in particular market dominance in their respective sectors. The new orientation shifted from simply a concern with systems operations, toward the articulation of a corporate self-image. The great strength of the chairman of the managing board in the later 1990s, Günther Hülse, was his concern about personnel, a responsibility that he retained after he became board chairman. The human-capital argument for diversification became more and more compelling: specific information and techniques, especially in handling relationships with customers, were common to the business as a whole. It thus became more common to envisage the company as a "people business."

In the course of the 1980s and 1990s, FHC had become essentially a new firm, with a commitment to a continuous process of change and expansion that involved a very rapid and unromantic move away from the core areas of historical activity. In 1984, by far the largest part of FHC business was conducted in enterprises that had been bought since 1977. In 1984 there were also for the first time more employees abroad (12,035) than in Germany (7,212). By 2002 there were 39,200 employees abroad and 16,800 in Germany (the latter alone were represented on the supervisory board, in accordance with German company law). Risk was spread internationally, but also across different sorts of activity. Some businesses (such as pharmaceutical trading) were relatively noncyclical, while others were related to investment activity and were highly procyclical. The metalcoating business ELG Haniel (Eisenlegierungen Handelsgesellschaft GmbH, Duisburg, where a 50 percent holding had been purchased in 1983, and the rest bought in 1989) was heavily cyclical, as was the building material business (Haniel Bau-Industrie). Haniel also established a profile for the identification and acquisition of particular sorts of business activity, in particular in areas where there were not very high levels of capital intensity and where, as with CWS or GEHE (which in 2004 was renamed Celesio), there could be an expectation of market dominance.

A major part of managing such expansion involves the selling of businesses that are no longer thought of as central to the group's operations or are performing badly. Some of the most traditional businesses were sold. The mid-1990s was a particularly dramatic period of retrenchment. In the United States, Scrivner and its associated businesses were sold in 1994, for a substantial realized profit, at 1,262 million Deutschmarks ($840 million). In 1995 the OPDR, which had been acquired in the 1920s, was sold, as was a courier-service company, trans-o-flex. The cull was even more dramatic the next year: in 1996 sixty-five companies were "exited" from the Haniel Group, including the pharmaceutical production businesses associated with GEHE, the eco-consulting business, material recycling, iron and steel industry services (and thus the last link with the steel business that had long been at the core of the Haniel vision), and traffic-safety systems. The departure from the traditional businesses, transportation and trading in fuel, was widely seen as a "liberating stroke" severing Haniel from an outdated business model. After taking over Krupp Binnenschiffahrt in 1999, at the beginning of 2000 the whole of the Haniel Reederei was sold.

By 2001 only 21 percent of the business of FHC came from Germany, 36 percent from France, and 26 percent from Great Britain, with non-European countries accounting for 5 percent (they had had a rather higher share before the 1994 sale of Scrivner).

The commitment to a sense of corporate identity was embodied in an ambitious redevelopment of the old headquarters in Duisburg-Ruhrort, with a large new academy for instilling common principles of good management, initiated in 1991. A stunning and modernistic architecture integrated a new internationalism into a setting on the Franz Haniel Platz still dominated by the 1756 Packhaus.

The family remained firmly in control of the holding company FHC, with 502 shareholders in 2002, of whom 3 owned more than 5 percent of the stock, and 21 more than one percent. There is an annual owners' meeting, at which members of a thirty-strong advisory council are elected for five-year terms, who in turn help in selecting eight owners' representatives to the sixteen-seat supervisory board (as stipulated by German law, the others are elected by the German workforce of the Haniel Group).

The same kind of tensions that existed in the nineteenth century—or for that matter in the 1970s—still exist. Any sort of gathering of owners can be contentious, especially in a macroeconomic environment in which there are big and unsettling swings in asset values. In 2001 *Manager Magazine* described how a group of self-consciously "yuppy managers" had demanded a more modern kind of investment, with higher returns: Internet and dot.com companies instead of pharmaceutical retailers and cement and laundry companies. From a perspective of just a few years later, this demand looks quite absurd. The older generation responded to the fractiousness of the young by emphasizing the need for "professional ownership."[15] The idea of responsibility entailed by ownership had also been marked by the creation of a family foundation (Haniel

Stiftung) in 1988 with an initial capital of 10 million Deutschmarks, with the explicit goals of training future entrepreneurs, emphasizing entrepreneurial responsibility for social and environmental issues, and researching the European context of entrepreneurship.

Education and responsibility became shorthand for the interaction of owners and enterprise. The management also now described its function as educating shareholders. No one was more explicit about this than Willers. He told the newspaper *Die Welt am Sonntag:*

> The tendency is logically going in the direction of the separation of ownership from management. This is a better solution than forcing a son to be a successor when he would rather be a physician. In order to secure the future of an enterprise, it is decisive that the spirit of the family, or a particular set of values, should be passed on. The heirs must be proud to belong to the family. But that is a matter of education, and parents are generally not capable of doing this alone. It is the obligation of the management to support the family in talking to younger family members, creating an esprit de corps and enthusiasm for the good and proved traditions of the family.[16]

Willers even proposed a codification of the unwritten rule excluding Haniel family members from the management of FHC, but the proposal was rejected by the family.

But management also faced the temptations offered by the *Zeitgeist*, in particular the demand to create incentives analogous to those offered in the public corporation. Haniel did not provide stock options, with the complex accountancy issues they raise; but from 1996 there was an equivalent in the form of a performance-related security, called an EVA® (economic value added) Certificate, which managers could purchase and which would then tie them into the company's profitability. The EVA® offers a way of taking a stake in the company in a financial as well as a moral sense.[17] It allows a more efficient incentive structure than share options, in which the distance between individual managerial contributions to performance and the overall outcome as judged in the market assessment of the stock price is so great that there is not a specific enough incentive related to actual input.

When a company expands very rapidly, the question arises how to prevent increasingly diverse subsidiaries from getting out of control. One way of retaining control dated back to the nineteenth century: the exclusion of banks and their representatives from the supervisory board, and a refusal to follow the German tradition and deal exclusively with a "Hausbank." The critical instrument for owners to guide (or control or even restrict) the aggressively expansionist management was a set of "covenants," first formulated in 1982: that the capital in plant *(Anlagekapital)* be covered by 125 percent capital or long-term borrowing; that the proportion of capital *(Eigenkapital)* to the overall balance sheet be maintained at around 25 percent; and that the cash flow be sufficient to repay external debt *(Fremdschulden)* over a three-year period. There was also an assumption that a quarter of the aftertax profit should be paid as dividend.

In practice the leverage was for most years substantially less than provided in these guidelines. The *Eigenkapital* quota had risen through the 1960s and 1970s as the firm expanded. In 1960 it had been 17.6 percent, by 1969 it was 25.9 percent, and by 1972 31.0 percent. After 1983, when it stood at 28.8 percent, it fell to 23.9 percent (1987). It then rose to 32 percent (1990) and remained at about this level in the 1990s (in 2002 it was 32 percent). The big expansion of the 1980s was thus financed without extending leverage.

Generally, the investment strategy produced a high rate of return: a calculation of internal rate of return for the period 1981–2002 is 10 percent, a substantially above-average return.

The story of Haniel after the 1970s is one of the continuous remaking of a business world. Until the 1970s, Haniel was a largely traditional enterprise. After the 1970s and 1980s, diversification and internationalization produced a sudden push to modernization. The internationalization of the business corresponds to an internationalization of the family (which was not untypical in the much more mobile and interconnected world of the later twentieth century). This is a much more internationalized (and risk-diversified) business than the other family enterprises examined in this study.

Internationalization requires the replacement of a long-term and quite slow model of development and change in which there is a consistency of vision about the core of the business by one in which the emphasis is on the continuing need for adaptation. This model should also provide a way of avoiding the eruptions of dysfunctional passion within the family—of the kind that occurred in the early nineteenth century, and then again from the late 1950s to the mid-1970s. The idea of managing change—and delegating the search for change to the management of the company—is a way of making discontinuities less stressful and destructive. Innovation and adjustment without tears might be a good slogan to describe this process.

An obvious question to ask in this context is whether the emphasis on continual change and renewal is easier or harder because of a historical legacy. The sense of history was quite paralyzing at some moments in the 1950s and 1960s. Properly used, however, it can inspire a vision of continuity that makes major and sometimes violent short-term structural breaks appear more acceptable and even desirable.

Chapter 16

Family Capitalism and the Exit from Steel

THE LAST TWENTY-FIVE YEARS have been a period of profound transformation of economic and corporate structures throughout the world. The changes are particularly dramatic in the steel industry, where mass production shifted to developing countries, and producers in high-wage countries lost much of their advantage. By 1996 China had overtaken the United States to become the world's largest steel producer. By 2004 the world's largest steel producer was (perhaps surprisingly) still a family firm, but it was the Indian-owned Mittal Steel Company, created out of a merger of Ispat International and LNM Holdings.

It is not just steel that has changed. Internationalization or globalization has forced changes with a rapidity and ruthlessness that were previously usually found mostly in periods of wartime disruption: for instance in the 1790s and 1800s or the 1870s, both of which transformed the Wendel and Haniel stories, or the First World War, which made Falck into a major Italian corporation. Rapid technical change can also destabilize expectations. In these circumstances, it was tempting to write obituaries about old forms of business existence. Two German commentators recently concluded: "The family enterprise is dying. Instead the enterprise as such is being born."[1] But as in previous periods of remodeling in crisis circumstances, the family model had a tenacity and an attraction that would have surprised many observers of the 1960s, who, infected by the *Zeitgeist* of those years, simply concluded that the family was on the way out.

The chronological examination of the three parallel histories has shown how frequently inherently centrifugal families are put back together again by the force of adverse circumstances: by revolutions, wars, attempts to break up industries, or state interventions to strengthen organized labor vis-à-vis employers. Such circumstances might be bad for businesses organized along the lines of an anonymous capital market-driven process of allocating resources, but they are good for associations that have some noneconomic ground for coherence. There is an increased importance given to what can variously be described as human, social, or intangible capital. The family firm is thus curiously shaped and molded by adversity and by its enemies.

A brief comparative overview of the years since the emergence of the crisis of the European steel industry shows some surprising changes in the fortunes of the three enterprise groups considered in this story. At the beginning of the 1970s the Haniel family was beginning to shuffle off its historical association with the steel and then engineering firm GHH. Haniel was much the smallest of the three groups (though the table overstates its growth from 1971 to 2001, in that the 1971 data for FHC exclude the family's separate holding of GHH stock, whose sale was used to increase the FHC capitalization in the 1970s). The first of the three family groups to exit from steel, it was by far the largest at the beginning of the twenty-first century. At the beginning of this era of crisis and adjustment, Wendel was twice as big as Haniel in terms of shareholders' equity; by the beginning of the twenty-first century it was less than one quarter the size. Falck, which was a major enterprise in the Italian corporate landscape in the 1960s and 1970s, but which was easily the latest of the three companies to make the exit from steel (in the mid-1990s), had faded into a niche position and was plagued by family quarrels and legal disputes about failed mergers. Like Wendel, Falck lost substantial amounts in largely ill-judged attempts to diversify into hot technologies in the 1990s: Falck had a bad experience with Speed@Egg N. V., which eventually led to a

Table 2 Shareholders' equity, 1971–2002 (thousand $U.S.)

	1971	2001	2002
Wendel	134,083	328,950	897,593
Haniel	40,633	3,081,354	3,835,784
Falck	61,589	488,927	143,318

Source: Annual statements, converted to dollars at the exchange rate prevailing at the time.

2-million-Euro loss; while Wendel lost large amounts with the information technology of Cap Gemini. Having missed the chances offered by steel privatization in Italy after the late 1980s, it grasped the opportunities of airport privatization. The table summarizes the size of the three firms in terms of shareholders' capital, though the numbers reveal nothing about the extent to which family wealth was lost or gained between 1971 and 2002: Haniel grew, and continued to be wholly owned by the family; while Wendel was for most of this period two publicly traded companies, held in large part by a family group, which were merged in 2002; and in Falck the stake of the family was gradually reduced to 32.3 percent in 1993, with a penumbra of family companies that were merged into Falck SpA in 2002.

The major differences for two family groups between 2001 and 2002 are the result of the corporate turbulence of this time: on the one hand, the substantial increase for Wendel is the consequence of the merger of Marine-Wendel with CGIP to form Wendel Investissement; on the other, the radical diminution of Falck is a consequence of the disposal of assets, often at a loss, and of the mismanaged and ultimately failed merger with Montedison/Edison in 2002. In 2002 the subsidiary deal, in which the engineering company Tecnimont was to have been sold to Falck by Edison SpA, also fell through. Wendel and Falck became exemplary cases for the difficulties of corporate governance in France and Italy.

The most obvious initial conclusion from this story is that steel was a great destroyer of capital in the last third of the twentieth century. The faster the exit from steel, the greater was the potential gain. The Haniel story exemplifies this proposition very clearly. Almost all the growth and the returns came from assets added in the quest for a reorientation: in particular from Metro and GEHE.

The exit from steel was of course a route taken not only by family-owned or -controlled companies. Large joint-stock firms went through similar transitions. U.S. Steel, for instance, in the late 1960s began a cautious diversification, when it bought Armour Chemicals in 1968, and by 1980 the steel division accounted for only half of its assets. In 1982 it undertook a bigger shift toward energy through the purchase of the Marathon Oil Company, and in 1988 59 percent of the revenues of USX (as the company was now called) came from energy.[2] Again, as with the European companies, there was substantial turbulence at the end of the century, and the company was demerged, with the energy interests renamed Marathon Oil and the steel-related business the United States Steel Corporation. Nationalized steel companies, on the other hand, found diversification difficult as employment creation and maintenance generally became their principal *raison d'être* in the eyes of their political masters. Being wedded to old traditions is thus by no means peculiar to family enterprises; political calculations rather than family affairs proved the greater obstacle to adaptation for late twentieth-century companies.

The Haniel Group had a great advantage in not being one of the very largest steel producers, and thus the subject of all the political interventions that went with steel and the social aspects of deindustrialization. Even in the phase of the intense association of Haniel interests with the GHH, the company's managers always emphasized the engineering and nonsteel aspects of the GHH's activities, as well as its difference in scale from Thyssen or Krupp.

Wendel, by contrast, had always been proud of its position as a mass producer of Thomas steel, and had been highly reluctant in the interwar and postwar years to develop specialty steels. Its tradition disposed it to strike a bargain with the French state in its pursuit of industrial gigantism after 1945. It paid a heavy price for the big losses in steel in the 1960s, which continued in the 1970s and began its turnaround only after 1979. So there was a wasted decade. Steel still looked like a regal product, and many of the obvious alternatives would be a derogation from the nobility of steel. In the 1970s the Wendel family still considered the production of women's undergarments to be demeaning. Such attitudes, expressed at the very time that Haniel was moving into bathroom cleanliness, recall ancien-régime attitudes to inappropriate commercial and industrial activities: only ironmaking and glassblowing did not derogate from nobility.

Falck was the unluckiest case. It had the traditions of a specialty steel producer, and its family owners before and after the Second World War had made it their mission to point out the economic irrationality of the big steel producers (state producers after the 1930s) and their quest for maximization of the productivist approach of the *ciclo integrale*. Both Falck and Haniel could have been expected to lay a greater emphasis on being nimble: a sort of "Avis" policy in the sense that Avis once ran a highly successful advertising campaign on the basis of "We're Number Two: We Try Harder."

But in the later 1970s and early 1980s Falck became much more involved in the politics of state-supported steel, and in the state's (and the European Community's) conditions for the financing of steel restructuring. One Italian family producer, the Riva Group, made the transition very effectively and became one of Europe's larger new-technology-based steel producers in the 1990s. By contrast, Falck stumbled, first into and then out of the arms of the power company Montedison/Edison.

The response of business can be thought of in the terms of the model introduced at the beginning of the book: how an enterprise can maintain focus in the face of pressure from politics and financial constraints.

Success depended on the degree to which business was able to avoid being captured by the state. This claim may seem odd, in that at least a century's worth of steel history, since the large-scale turn to tariff protection in the 1880s, was about using the state to promote industrial organization and market-regulating devices such as cartels and shared sales organizations. Most of the history of the steel industry, in every country, was about capturing the state. Nationalism and a tradition of orientation to a national market were especially important in the political context of Lorraine as the site of the struggle between France and Germany, and also in the South Tyrol/Alte Adige. Patriotic sentiment could be used politically to conjure up public support and government money.

In the second half of the twentieth century the process of capture went the other way around, and governments forced businesses in sensitive areas to invest and modernize more than would have been warranted by an assessment of the private interest involved. Especially in the third quarter of the twentieth century, the "golden years" of European recovery, state support meant financing and expansion, and there was a heavy emphasis on overcoming deficits in investment. But it also meant a control on profitability, and thus limits on the possibilities of using internally accumulated resources to discover new markets and processes. The state commitment involved very substantial increases in investment but only in an easily measured form, namely bigness. Technical innovation suffered in the course of a quest for ever-greater size and for the maintenance of employment. Conceptually, the European governments' approach was close to the famous and oft-derided method adopted by the German Democratic Republic as it struggled in a nonprice system to assess the value of television sets produced by its factories, finally using weight as the determining criterion: the heavier, the better. The state's approach to investment in heavy industry derived directly from the widespread midcentury critique of private and especially family firms for having skimped on investment, and thus stunted growth.

The debate centered upon financial constraints and choices. The old maxims of the nineteenth century that Wendel, Haniel, and Falck had all at some time also advocated, the avoidance of excessive levels of external borrowing, were widely ignored in the post-1945 world. But after the 1980s those maxims reasserted their validity. The businesses that found growth problematic had high debt levels. In the inflationary environment of the later 1960s and the 1970s, such a course may have seemed plausible or even attractive, in that there were substantial periods when real interest rates were negative. Even so, there was a considerable drain in debt service. There is clearly a good corporate finance argument for a highly innovative company to increase its leverage, in that the additional returns generated by new productivity are not disbursed among a wider group of shareholders, who would have been needed had the expansion been financed through equity. But innovation was not the reason for the high indebtedness of Wendel or Falck in the 1960s and 1970s; instead the absorption of debt depended on implicit or explicit government guarantees of debt.

The effect of capture by the state is reflected in the different leveraging of corporate balance sheets (see table). The Wendel holding company in 1971 was almost completely unencumbered by

Table 3 Short- and long-term debt as a proportion of shareholders' equity, 1971 (%)

	Long-term debt	Short-term debt
Haniel	18.2	44.9
Wendel (Sacilor)	84.5	78.7
Falck	70.0	116.2

debt; the massive borrowing was incurred by the subsidiary, Sacilor. The nineteenth-century vision was fundamentally right about the loss of control that followed from excessive levels of debt.

The opening of capital markets in the last two decades of the twentieth century provided a new opportunity for innovation in the family firm. The arguments about loss of owner control because of excessive past borrowing had focused on the possibly malign influence of banks (in the nineteenth century or the first half of the twentieth century), or on the problems of state guarantees (in the middle of the twentieth century). The availability of bond market financing and the presence of arms-length investment banks and anonymous capital markets offered a new way of raising money, if the ability to innovate could be demonstrated. The ability to seize the chances offered by the new vigor of capital markets required the reinvention of focus, and a move away from traditional areas of activity. It involved a rethinking of entrepreneurship in the context of the family firm.

Conclusion

Family Entrepreneurship

ENTREPRENEURIAL BEHAVIOR IS crucial to the story of the capitalist dynamic, in which continual reshaping of the business environment and the creation of new opportunities play major roles. Entrepreneurial talent, however, is not necessarily widely distributed. Moreover, talented entrepreneurs are not necessarily or even usually harmonious personalities who work easily with others, including their own families. The happenstance nature of talent is at the heart of the historic issues about the family firm, and constitutes the puzzle that the success of "family capitalism" in continental Europe and many other parts of the world poses for many observers.

The founders of family business dynasties are almost always vigorous and innovative figures, creating new products or markets: François de Wendel, Franz Haniel, and Giorgio Enrico Falck all fall clearly into this category. They created a powerful model that shaped the culture of the family and the enterprise for many generations. On the other hand, for all that their descendants claim that they have entrepreneurship in their genes, such an explanation seems unlikely, and in some cases obviously false. Charles de Wendel was industrious and keen to stop other members of his family from destroying his father's achievement, but he did little more than develop an enterprise in close partnership with his brother-in-law. Franz Haniel's sons were loyal, trustworthy, and hardworking, imbued with all the values and virtues of German Protestantism, and they certainly did not dissipate their father's wealth; but they were not very creative. G. E. Falck's eldest son, Enrico, was much more interested in politics than in the business, where his two younger brothers were much more engaged.

Entrepreneurial vision certainly reappeared in all these families, with François de Wendel's grandsons Henri and Robert in the late nineteenth century and Henri's great-grandson Ernest-Antoine Seillière at the end of the twentieth century. But entrepreneurial characteristics in successor generations can have major drawbacks. In the Haniel dynasty, the most dynamic and charismatic of the twentieth-century figures, Werner Carp, devoted most of his substantial energy to subverting the family firm by attempting to bring it into the enormous steel trust Vereinigte Stahlwerke, which he then hoped to control. A strong entrepreneurial vision is highly individualistic, and may even have a rather demonic quality: it is unlikely to make for peace and harmony in a very extended family. Ignace de Wendel, one of the most technically gifted of the figures explored here, had separated himself from his family and from Lorraine even before the turmoil of the French Revolution. It is easy to see how his monomaniacal, fiery, and sulfurous activities captured the attention and the imagination of the author of *Faust*.

On the other hand, entrepreneurship is required if a business is not to stagnate. Over several generations, as the weight of a historical legacy accumulates, the most obvious course for owners locked in by historical commitment is to cultivate an entrepreneurial management style (from which they may wish organizationally to separate themselves entirely). By the end of the twentieth century, some large family firms, notably the Haniels, began to develop the concept of professional ownership. Some aspects of this idea, notably the long-term interest in building up a skilled and loyal management and workforce, resemble features of the nineteenth-century paternalism found in all the family histories considered here.

The problem of the family firm—how to maintain its focus when poised between the constraints of finance and fatherland—can now be revisited, and the questions asked in the Introduction answered.

They regard the existence of national differences in entrepreneurial behavior, the nature of control by owners over managers, the relationship with the state, the strategic significance of the core industry (steel), and the challenges of crossnational competition (globalization). National differences, which are popularly attributed to intangible differences in supposed national character, in practice amount largely to differences in the legal and regulatory setting. This setting was molded by developments in inheritance law, the law of corporations, and, in the twentieth century, tax law. The joint-stock corporation allowed the development of a professional management detached from the vicissitudes of family life, but in the twentieth century owners frequently responded by reengineering the ownership through nonquoted holding companies. Such strategies ran counter to the state interest in steel, and the new possibilities for control could be realized only through escape to a less politically exposed sector or sectors of economic activity.

By the end of the twentieth century, there were new opportunities for all types of business, and hence a real and novel entrepreneurial challenge. These arose from:

- The relative retreat of the state in European economies.
- The greater activity of capital markets, which freed family businesses from their traditional fear of long-term involvement with and hence dependence on banks. Banks are no longer the major source of business or industrial finance.
- The internationalization of business activity, which added new possibilities for opening up markets, as well as potential new sources of capital.

All three of these considerations enable the family firm to play a greater role than in the past. There is certainly no evidence of the model developed by David Landes and Alfred Chandler that dominated most analysis of this subject in the later twentieth century, in which a one-way street called modernization involves a transition for personalized capitalism to the multidivisional publicly quoted corporation managed by a technocratic managerial elite for whom the question of ownership plays little or no role. The cases studied in this book point in a quite different direction. Falck started out as a joint-stock corporation, the AFL, in which Giorgio Enrico Falck was a gifted technician with little capital of his own. By the 1930s he had turned it into a family business. From the 1870s to the 1950s, the major vehicles of the Wendel and Haniel interests were joint-stock companies; their fortunes revived with a turn after the 1960s or 1970s to different forms of enterprise, nonquoted holding companies (in Germany, the GmbH offered particular advantages). In the early twenty-first century, there is little surprise when even major companies want to "go private." The examples of the retreat from the publicly quoted joint-stock company are not necessarily to be understood as "history reversing itself," but rather as a rational response to better-developed capital markets.

The new situation still involves constraints, but they are different from those of the past. One is that the possibilities of the capital markets are clearly not infinite, and that the private companies will not want to embark on a course that involves too high a capital commitment. They are also freer to choose where they concentrate their activity. Again, this break becomes obvious when we think about how corporations are conceived. Nineteenth-century legislation that enabled the creation of joint-stock companies was very clear that a company existed for a very particular purpose, which needed to be defined in its statutes.

The modern requirements of owners who depend in part on their firms for incomes generate a particular profile of investment. They rule out the extremes of high growth and high investment with no profits (such as characterized much of Japanese industry in the 1980s and much of information-technology industry in the 1990s) or of low growth with stable but low profits (such as is found in most mature consumer markets). The logic of the family firm thus tends to make for a choice of growth industries without very high capital requirements.

The particular advantage of the commitment mechanism that family ownership brings can also be brought to bear most readily in sectors with a particular consumer profile: where there is a core of stable and loyal customers who depend on a relationship. This is the attraction of pharmacy wholesale or professional clothing and laundry services for Haniel, or certification for Wendel, or reusable energy for Falck.

The particular logic of family firms also requires a balancing of risk across different sectors. Again, the idea of diversification is not new: it was actually more pronounced in the era before the joint-stock company, when Franz Haniel invested in coal, iron, and shipbuilding, but also in ceramics and grain trading.

Diversification of risk and the choice of a mixture of cyclical and noncyclical business activities mean abandonment of a core focus, and of the concept of synergy among the different aspects of the undertaking. The move to conglomerate structure is evident in all three corporate transformations examined in this book, even in that of Falck, the last to make the transition out of steel, where there is still a broad range of activity, from renewable energy and biomass to management of the Rome airport.

The business practices of the last quarter of the twentieth century appeared to be very new; the era was often described in the phraseology of Alfred Chandler as a new era in "managerial capitalism." All the firms examined here exhibited the main features of this alleged newness: the rapid acquisition and also divestment or demerging of large numbers of new companies. High-level business managers had to deal suddenly with the prospect of needing to buy into businesses of which they understood very little. The dizzying waves of mergers and acquisitions in the United States, in the "go-go years" of the 1960s described by John Brooks, in the "barbarians at the gate years" of the 1980s, and in the dot.com wave of the late 1990s, were replicated in the United Kingdom; but the first two barely touched continental Europe. On the other hand, the 1990s wave certainly did, and helped to prompt a generalized questioning in Europe of economic institutions: some thought that the new developments vindicated a superior "Anglo-Saxon" model of development, while others believed that the new phenomenon was part of a vicious and destructive process of globalization.

Some sort of historical vision may help us to understand what is involved in this process. For, although from the perspective of continental European developments in most of the twentieth century, this new pattern of corporate instability looked new, in a longer-term horizon it really was not. There is a fascinating connection, indeed, between previous general episodes of globalization and a very volatile market in companies, with large numbers of companies being transferred with considerable rapidity. The late eighteenth century was like this, with the instability increasing because of the French Revolution and the Napoleonic Wars: this was when the Wendel ironworks were sold and sold again, and then reaasembled, and when Franz Haniel and his brother bought the Gutehoffnungshütte. Mid-nineteenth-century Italy and Germany repeated this experience; and both countries had a very high level of corporate instability in the first two decades of the twentieth century. International instability and international markets made ownership much more unstable, but not necessarily at the cost of the concept of family ownership and the principle of the family firm.

Entrepreneurship is still crucial, but it is broken down into smaller segments. Wendel has gone furthest in this direction, with an attempt to define the company less as a traditional business than as a "private equity company." But as the technical focus changes quickly, there is still a need to hold the business together. This search for coherence in an age of change is often captured by those involved in statements that they consider themselves to be engaged in a "people business" rather than in a technical pursuit. The fundamental insight is that the depth of tradition creates a commitment that could not be readily achieved in a young company.

All the groups surveyed in the previous pages emphasize and are proud of the entrepreneurial traditions of their families. In the 1950s all three commissioned biographically oriented *Festschriften* that celebrated the entrepreneur in a family context. The family as a unit of social cohesion was strengthened by the political and social upheavals of the midcentury, and especially by the experience of defeat and occupation common to France, Italy, and Germany.

There are some startling continuities in the histories considered purely as family histories. Wendels had long taken the hands-on approach to management noted by the Crédit Lyonnais in the late nineteenth century. Haniels had already earlier been inclined to leave management to "professionals." Falcks had been technicians who were interested in technical change in iron and steel and cared little for finance, and little for politics.

A branding issue may explain why Wendels and Falcks found it harder to exit from steel. Their family traditions were linked to metal, and their names conjured up images of blast furnaces. Wendel meant not only "France," as the second François de Wendel had put it, but also "steel." Falck's headquarters in the early twenty-first century are still decorated with fiery pictures of blast furnaces, and the male Falcks are trained as engineers. The Haniel history since the nineteenth century had in fact usually been told in terms of output and value created—mostly the iron- and steel-working history of Jacobi, Haniel & Huyssen, later the Gutehoffnungshütte (GHH). In escaping from steel the Haniels could break with the concept of "GHH" and revive the idea of Haniel as a merchant house, trading coal and wine. The original activity of Haniel might even be presented with some plausibility as a late eighteenth-century version of Metro. But there was also simultaneously rebranding in the other company stories: for a time Wendel tried to lose the family link and present itself as an anonymous acronym (CGIP), while Falck eventually abandoned the steel part of the company name (Accierie e Ferrierie Lombarde Falck).

Remaking business is also likely to be successful if the business is able to break out of purely national markets. Much literature on corporate change now deals with the issue of how companies can learn and absorb change. A famous parallel is frequently drawn from evolutionary biology. Titmice in England in the mid-twentieth century learned to peck off the protective foil tops of milk bottles left on British doorsteps, while robins (which previously had been quite successful milk thieves) did not. The explanation is believed to be that robins are individualistic and territorial, while titmice roam in larger groups and thus quickly emulate best practice in other territories.[1] "Flocking" rather than territorial segregation thus pays off.

The national context was a particularly bad way of limiting experience, and a particular way of picking up bad practice. For much of the postwar era, Wendel as a steelmaker was part of a duopoly with the steel producer of the Nord, Usinor. Usinor was seen as the main challenge in a regional race between Lorraine and the Nord. Only quite late did Wendel-Sacilor's chief executive, Louis Dherse, realize that it might be better to look at what Thyssen was doing across the Rhine rather than at Usinor. (In the Third Republic, Wendel had been able to benefit from its experiences on the other side of the frontier, running a German steel company.) At the same time, in the postwar recovery Falck came to see that its main competitor was in the Italian state sector, in the companies associated in Finsider and grouped in IRI. Again, it is hard to think of a less appropriate model for any enterprise than the IRI companies.

There are very obvious early instances of the importance of foreign learning in all the early histories of the companies dealt with in this book: in Ignace de Wendel and then François de Wendel's efforts to find English metallurgists, in Franz Haniel's attempt to learn from James Watt and in his marriage strategy with the Cockerills, in the efforts of both the nineteenth-century Giorgio Enrico Falcks (grandfather and grandson) to apply in Italy the lessons of German and Swiss technology in iron, then in steel, and finally in hydroelectric power. One of the most promising Wendel investments before the First World War was the mine at Oranje-Nassau, which was later the base for a substantial diversification. Haniel expanded through trading companies in the Netherlands and Switzerland in the interwar era. But in the middle and nationalistic years of the twentieth century, learning from abroad was less important than the cultivation of large national markets in large countries such as France, Germany, or Italy (or, for that matter, the United Kingdom). In the 1960s Falcks tried to move into northwestern European steel with the acquisition of a stake in the Belgian steel producer Sidmar. The most striking feature of the Haniel redefinition in the 1980s and 1990s is the scale of business done outside Germany.

"Flocking" can be encouraged by treating the different national companies in a multinational holding as part of the same group and by organizing common educational and other information exchange settings. These strategies were what accompanied Haniel's internationalization, with a "Haniel Akademie" in Ruhrort consciously mixing different national cultures.

The temptation to remain in a particular national context is obviously great for a family enterprise. For companies operating in a French context, there was even in the 1990s a great deal of business nationalism, which insisted on the safeguarding of French enterprises against foreign influences. But such business nationalism results in a greatly decreased ability to learn from outside impulses. The main weakness of the larger family firm is not its approach to finance, as has been suggested by almost every interpretation of the historical trajectory. Insistence on control is not simply "bad" and inimical to growth. Instead the difficulty lies in the family firm's often limited geographical horizon. But this book, which began with businessmen moving frequently across territorial and state boundaries in the dynamic age of the late eighteenth and early nineteenth centuries, suggests that this is a problem that can be overcome.

Appendix

Notes

Acknowledgments

Index

Appendix: Family Trees

Falck Family Tree (simplified)

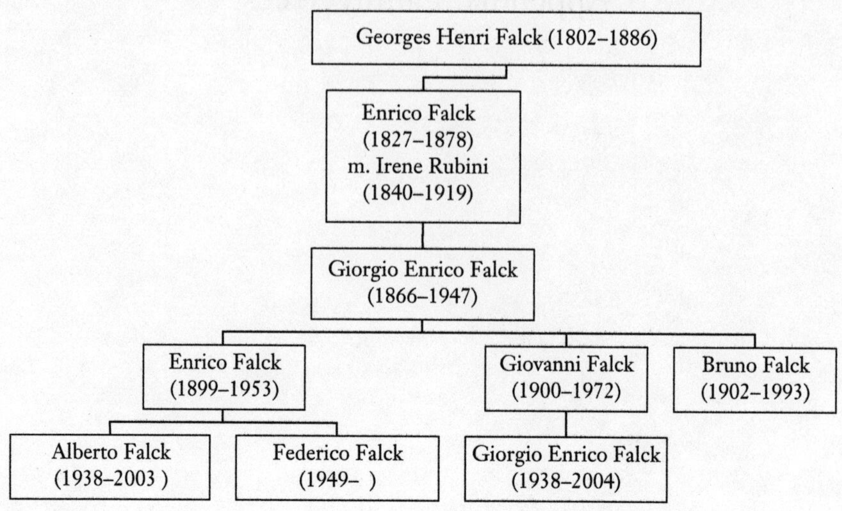

Wendel Family Tree (simplified)

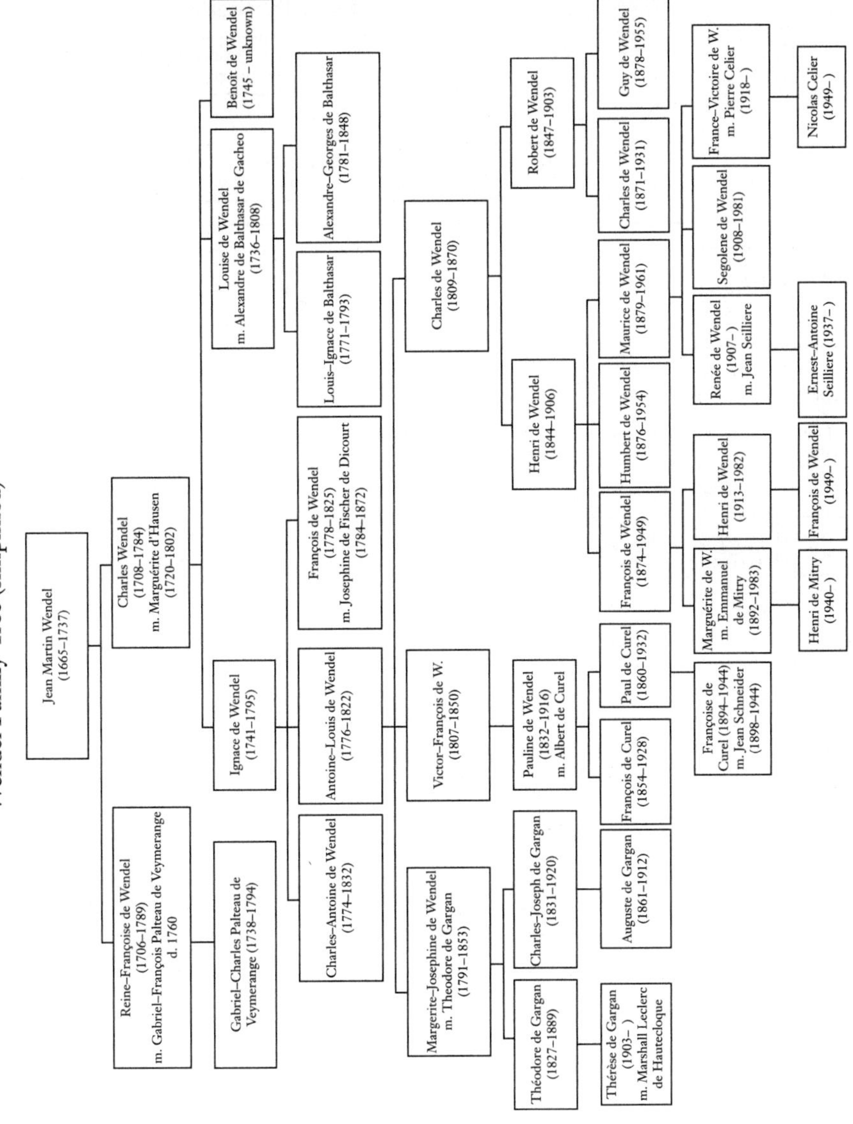

Haniel Family Tree (simplified)

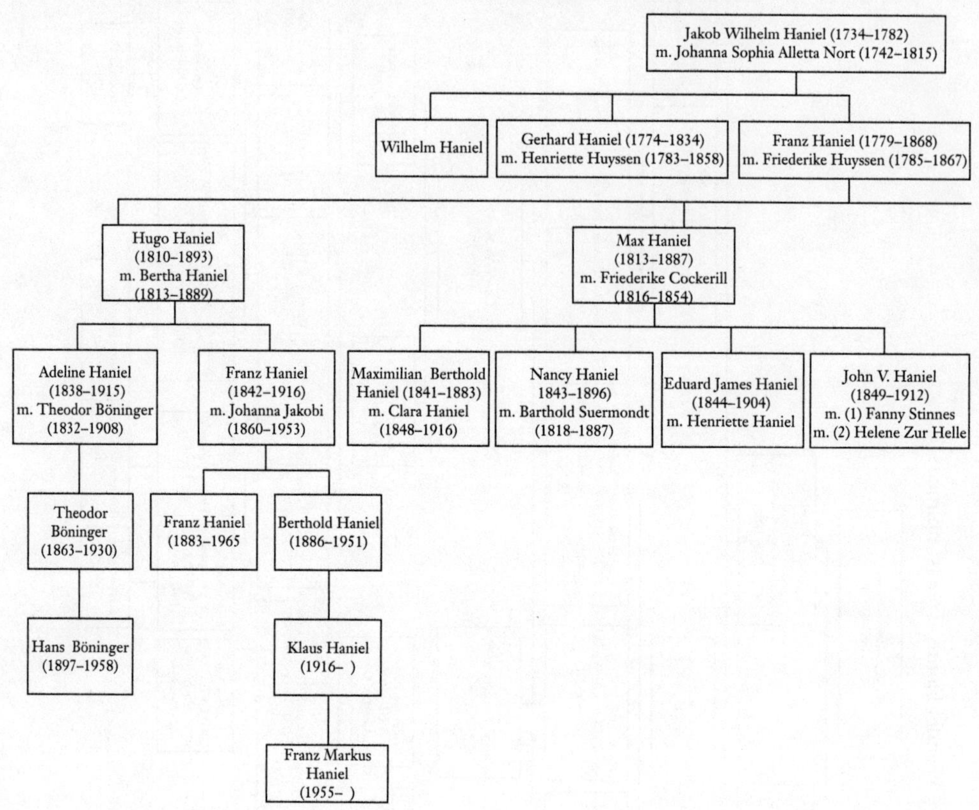

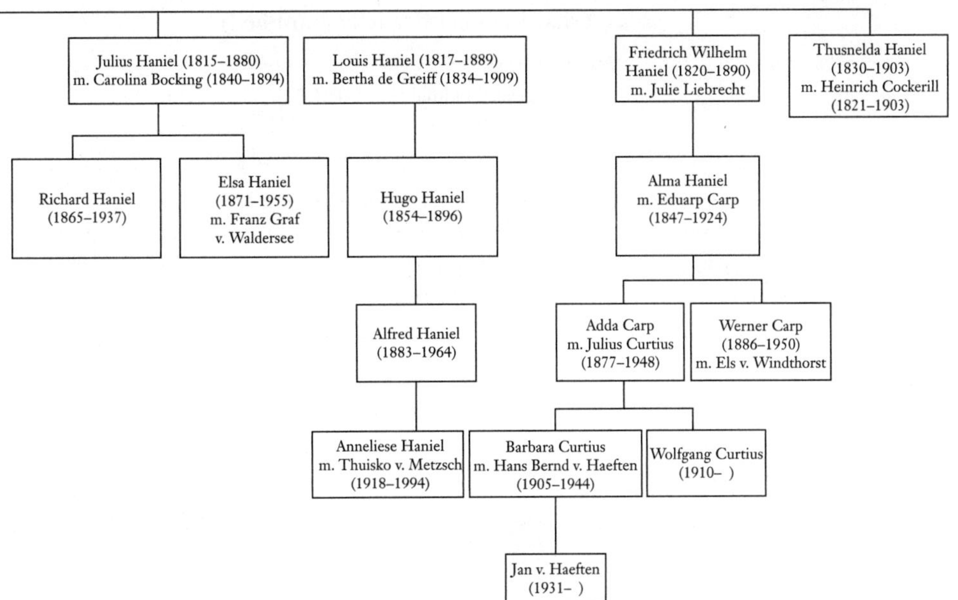
Julius Haniel (1815–1880)
m. Carolina Bocking (1840–1894)
Louis Haniel (1817–1889)
m. Bertha de Greiff (1834–1909)
Friedrich Wilhelm
Haniel (1820–1890)
m. Julie Liebrecht
Thusnelda Haniel
(1830–1903)
m. Heinrich Cockerill
(1821–1903)
Richard Haniel
(1865–1937)
Elsa Haniel
(1871–1955)
m. Franz Graf
v. Waldersee
Hugo Haniel
(1854–1896)
Alma Haniel
m. Eduarp Carp
(1847–1924)
Alfred Haniel
(1883–1964)
Adda Carp
m. Julius Curtius
(1877–1948)
Werner Carp
(1886–1950)
m. Els v. Windthorst
Anneliese Haniel
m. Thuisko v. Metzsch
(1918–1994)
Barbara Curtius
m. Hans Bernd v. Haeften
(1905–1944)
Wolfgang Curtius
(1910–)
Jan v. Haeften
(1931–)

Gerhard Haniel Branch (simplified)

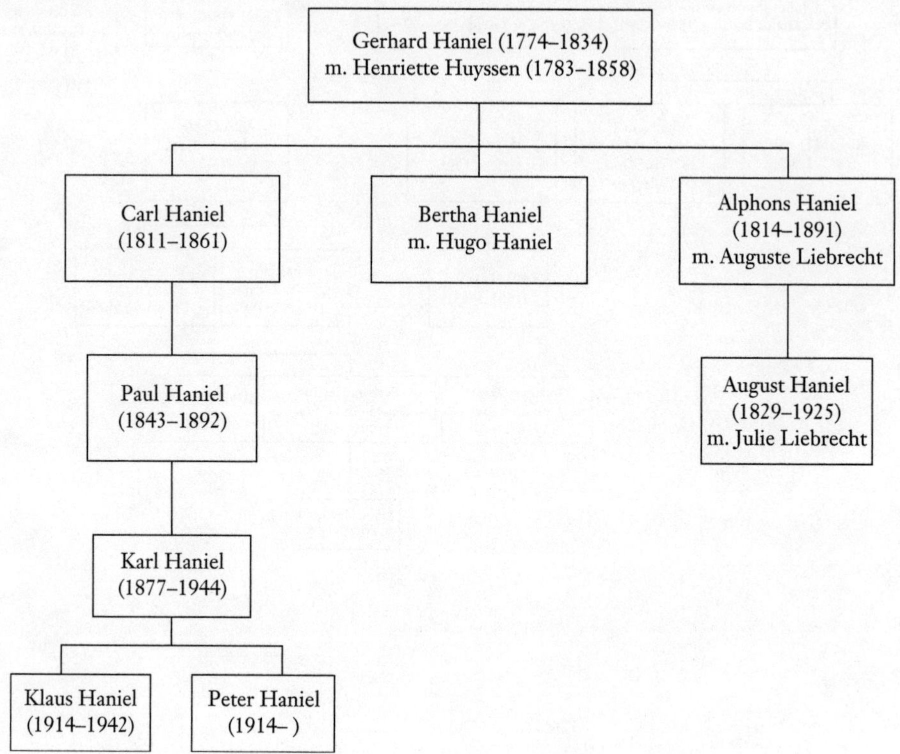

Notes

Introduction

1. For a brief recent overview of the literature, see Andrea Colli, *The History of Family Business, 1850–2000* (Cambridge: Cambridge University Press, 2003).
2. See Raghuram G. Rajan and Luis Zingales, "The Great Reversals: The Politics of Financial Development in the Twentieth Century," *Journal of Financial Economics* 69 (2003), 5–50.
3. See idem, *Saving Capitalism from the Capitalists: Unleashing the Power of Financial Markets to Create Wealth and Spread Democracy* (New York: Crown, 2003).
4. See Rafael La Porta, Florencio Lopez-de-Silanes, Andrei Shleifer, and Robert Vishny, "Law and Finance," *Journal of Political Economy* 101 (1998), 678–709; and Rafael La Porta, Florencio Lopez-de-Silanes, and Andrei Shleifer, "Corporate Ownership around the World," *Journal of Finance* 54 (1999), 471–517.
5. See Weil, Gotshal & Manges LLP, in consultation with the European Association of Securities Dealers and the European Corporate Governance Network, "Comparative Study of Corporate Governance Codes Relevant to the European Union and Its Member States," manuscript, January 2002 (copy in author's possession); also Sandra K. Miller, "Minority Shareholder Oppression in the Private Company in the European Community: A Comparative Analysis of the German, United Kingdom, and French 'Close Corporation Problem,'" *Cornell International Law Journal*, 1997, 381–427.
6. See for instance the session of the 1982 International Economic History Conference in Budapest: Leslie Hannah, ed., *From Family Firm to Professional Management: Structure and Performance of Business Enterprise* (Budapest: Akadémiai Kiadó, 1982).
7. "The Complex Evolution of Family Affairs," *Financial Times*, 3 February 2003, p. 6.
8. Frédéric Lemaître, "La France: Championne du capitalisme familial," *Le Monde*, 18 April 2003.
9. Mara Faccio and Larry H. P. Lang, "The Ultimate Ownership of Western European Corporations," *Journal of Financial Economics* 65 (2002), 393.
10. Colli, *Family Business*, p. 19.
11. See Francis Fukuyama, *Trust: Social Virtues and the Creation of Prosperity* (New York: Free Press, 1995).
12. Lemaître, "La France."
13. See Ronald C. Anderson and David M. Reeb, "Founding Family Ownership

and Firm Performance: Evidence from the S&P 500," *Journal of Finance* 58 (2003), 1301–27.

14. Alfred D. Chandler Jr., *The Visible Hand: The Managerial Revolution in American Business* (Cambridge, Mass.: Belknap Press of Harvard University Press, 1977).

15. David S. Landes, "French Entrepreneurship and Industrial Growth in the Nineteenth Century," *Journal of Economic History* 9 (1949), 45–61. See also Daniel Henri, "Capitalisme familial et gestion industrielle au XIXe siècle," *Revue française de gestion* 70 (September 1988), 141–150; Maurice Lévy-Leboyer, "Le patronat français a-t-il été malthusien?" *Le mouvement social* 88 (1974), 3–50, quotation from p. 5; Auguste Detoeuf, *Propos de O. L. Barenton confiseur* (Paris : Editions du Tambourinaire, 1950), p. 68.

16. Charles P. Kindleberger, *Economic Growth in France and Britain, 1851–1950* (Oxford: Oxford University Press, 1964), p. 115.

17. Robert Pavan, *Strategy and Structure of the Italian Enterprise* (Ann Arbor: University Microfilms, 1973).

18. The concept of Rhineland capitalism as a special path was popularized by Michel Albert, *Capitalism versus Capitalism* (1991), trans. Paul Haviland (London: Whurr, 1993).

19. Alfred D. Chandler Jr., *Scale and Scope: The Dynamics of Industrial Capitalism* (Cambridge, Mass.: Belknap Press of Harvard University Press, 1990), especially pp. 239–240. This interpretation was criticized by Roy Church, "The Family Firm in Industrial Comparison: International Perspectives on Hypothesis and History," in Geoffrey Jones and Mary Rose, eds., *Family Capitalism* (London: Frank Cass, 1993), pp. 17–43. See also William Lazonick, "The Cotton Industry," in Bernard Elbaum and William Lazonick, eds., *The Decline of the British Economy* (Oxford: Oxford University Press, 1986), pp. 18–50.

20. Peter Payne, "Family Business in Britain: An Historical and Analytical Survey," in Akio Okochi and Shigeaki Yasuoka, eds., *Family Business in the Era of Industrial Growth: Its Ownership and Management*, Proceedings of the Fuji International Conference on Business History, 10 (Tokyo: University of Tokyo Press, 1984).

21. Jeffrey Fear, "August Thyssen and German Steel," in Thomas K. McCraw, ed., *Creating Modern Capitalism: How Entrepreneurs, Companies, and Countries Triumphed in Three Industrial Revolutions* (Cambridge, Mass.: Harvard University Press, 1997), pp. 185–226.

22. See Edward S. Herman, *Corporate Control, Corporate Power* (Cambridge: Cambridge University Press, 1981), p. 352.

23. Jack Goody, *The East in West* (Cambridge: Cambridge University Press, 1996), pp. 199, 201.

24. Notably those in Germany directed by Lothar Gall and by Jürgen Kocka.

25. See the model evolved by Yoram Ben-Porath, "The F-Connection: Families, Friends and the Organization of Exchange," *Population Development Review* 6 (1980), 1–30.

26. See Ronald C. Anderson and Daniel M. Reeb, "Who Monitors the Family," Working paper, 2003, http://ssrn.com/abstract=360620.

27. Richard Foster and Sarah Kaplan, *Creative Destruction: Why Companies That*

Are Built to Last Underperform the Market—and How to Successfully Transform Them (London: Currency, 2001).

28. See Oliver Williamson, *Markets and Hierarchies: Analysis and Antitrust Implications* (New York: Free Press, 1975); Masahiko Aoki, Bo Gustafson, and Oliver Williamson, eds., *The Firm as a Nexus of Treaties* (London: Sage, 1990).
29. Tarun Khanna and Krishna Palepu, "Policy Shocks, Market Intermediaries, and Corporate Strategy: The Evolution of Business Groups in Chile and India," *Journal of Economics and Management Strategy* 8, no. 2 (1999), 271–310.
30. See Shigeaki Yasuoka, "Capital Ownership in Family Companies: Japanese Firms Compared with Those in Other Countries," in Okochi and Yasuoka, *Family Business in the Era of Industrial Growth*, pp. 1–32.
31. Knut Borchardt, "Der Unternehmerhaushalt als Wirtschaftsbetrieb," in Tilmann Buddensieg, ed., *Villa Hügel: Das Wohnhaus Krupp in Essen* (Berlin: Siedler, 1994), p. 12.
32. R[ichard] Passow, "Aktiengesellschaften," in Ludwig Elster, Adolf Weber, and Friedrich Wieser, eds., *Handwörterbuch der Staatswissenschaften*, 4th ed., vol. 1 (Jena: G. Fischer, 1923), p. 134.
33. Pierre Bourdieu and Monique de Saint Martin, "Le patronat," *Actes de la recherche en sciences sociales* 20–21 (1978), 27.
34. Denis Woronoff, *L'industrie sidérurgique en France pendant la Révolution et l'Empire* (Paris: Editions de l'Ecole des Hautes Etudes en Sciences Sociales, 1984), pp. 301–302. On the general phenomenon of early nineteenth-century businesswomen, see Bonney Smith, *Women of the Leisure Class: The Bourgeoisie of Northern France in the Nineteenth Century* (Princeton: Princeton University Press, 1981), pp. 34–40; and Anita Göransson, "Gender and Property Rights: Capital, Kin, and Owner Influence in Nineteenth- and Twentieth-Century Sweden," *Business History* 35 (1993), 11–32.
35. Eva Figes, *Patriarchal Attitudes: Women in Society* (London: Faber, 1970), p. 70. See also Janet Thomas, "Women and Capitalism: Oppression or Emancipation? A Review Article," *Comparative Studies in Society and History* 30, no. 3 (1988), 534–549. For a recent interpretation of the role of women in pre-industrial capitalism, see Sheilagh Ogilvie, *A Bitter Living: Women, Markets, and Social Capital in Early Modern Germany* (Oxford: Oxford University Press, 2003).
36. T. C. Banfield, *Industry of the Rhine II: Manufactures* (London: C. Cox, 1848), p. 38.
37. Gerald D. Feldman, *Hugo Stinnes: Biographie eines Industriellen 1870–1924* (Munich: Beck, 1998), p. 851.
38. Yasuoka, "Capital Ownership."
39. "Die Besitzung Hügel bildet einen Theil des Familienvermögens" (from the will of F. A. Krupp, 1898), quoted in Borchardt, "Unternehmerhaushalt," p. 12.
40. Julian Hoppit, *Risk and Failure in English Business, 1700–1800* (Cambridge: Cambridge University Press, 1987).
41. Mark Roe, *Political Determinants of Corporate Governance: Political Context, Corporate Impact* (Oxford: Oxford University Press), p. 6.
42. "Observer" column, *Financial Times*, 12 July 2000, p. 17.
43. The concept was most explicitly developed by Alfred Sauvy, *Histoire*

économique de la France entre les deux guerres, 4 vols. (Paris: Fayard, 1965–1975).

44. Bertrand Gille, *La sidérurgie française au XIXe siècle: Recherches historiques* (Geneva: Droz, 1968), p. 31.
45. W. W. Rostow, *The Stages of Economic Growth: A Non-Communist Manifesto* (Cambridge: Cambridge University Press, 1960), p. 38; Ludwig August Rochau, *Grundsätze der Realpolitik, angewendet auf die staatlichen Zustände Deutschlands* (1869; reprint, Frankfurt am Main: Ullstein, 1972), p. 231.
46. Alexander Gerschenkron, *Economic Backwardness in Historical Perspective: A Book of Essays* (Cambridge, Mass.: Belknap Press of Harvard University Press, 1962). See for a modern critique Hugh Neuburger and Houston Stokes, "German Banks and German Growth, 1883–1913," *Journal of Economic History* 34 (1974), 710–731; Rainer Fremdling and Richard Tilly, "German Banks, German Growth, and Econometric History," *Journal of Economic History* 36 (1976), 416–424; Volker Wellhöner, *Grossbanken und Grossindustrie im Kaiserreich* (Göttingen: Vandenhoeck & Ruprecht, 1989); Harald Wixforth, *Banken und Schwerindustrie in der Weimarer Republik* (Cologne: Böhlau, 1995).
47. Carlo Cattaneo, *Intelligence as a Principle of Public Economy / Del pensero come principio d'economia pubblica* (Lanham, Md.: Lexington, 2002), pp. 72–73.
48. See Carlo G. Lacaita, *L'intelligenza produttiva: Imprenditori, tecnici e operai nella Società d'Incoraggiamento d'Arti e Mestieri di Milano (1838–1988)* (Milan: Electa, 1990).
49. Margherita Balconi, *La siderurgia italiana (1945–1990): Tra controllo publico e incentive del mercato* (Bologna: Il Mulino, 1991), p. 82.
50. The Credito Italiano was founded in Genoa as the Banco di Genova but in 1907 moved its headquarters to Milan.
51. See Douglas Forsyth, *The Crisis of Liberal Italy: Monetary and Financial Policy, 1914–1922* (Cambridge: Cambridge University Press, 1993), pp. 35–36.
52. See Fabio Tamburini, *Un Siciliano a Milano* (Milano: Longanesi, 1992), esp. pp. 30 ff.
53. Quoted in Rajan and Zingales, *Saving Capitalism from the Capitalists*, p. 215.
54. *Financial Times*, 25 January 2003.
55. See also R&S (Mediobanca) paper, "The Italian Stock Exchange from 1928 to January 2003," available at www.mbres.it.

I. The Age of the Individual

1. See for instance the entertaining recent book by Adam Bellow, *In Praise of Nepotism* (New York: Random House, 2003).

1. The Wendels and the French State

1. This is the thesis of a memorable work by Betty Behrens, *The Ancien Regime* (London: Thames and Hudson, 1967). See also Guy Chaussinand-Nogaret, *The French Nobility in the Eighteenth Century: From Feudalism to Enlightenment*, trans. William Doyle (Cambridge: Cambridge University Press, 1985).

2. Given the many different currencies used by the families and firms examined in this book, to make comparisons among countries easier I have converted some currencies into their equivalent value in dollars at the time; and for the eighteenth-century values, I used the silver values given by the Mint Act of 1792. These conversions should be interpreted with caution: an eighteenth-century dollar, for example, was worth substantially more than the U.S. dollar at the beginning of the twenty-first century.
3. Denis Woronoff, *L'industrie sidérurgique en France pendant la Révolution et l'Empire* (Paris: Editions de l'Ecole des Hautes Etudes en Sciences Sociales, 1984), p. 15.
4. René Sédillot, *Deux cents cinquante ans d'industrie en Lorraine: La Maison de Wendel de mil sept cent quatre à nos jours* (Paris: François de Wendel, 1958), p. 41.
5. Ibid., p. 45.
6. Woronoff, *L'industrie sidérurgique*, p. 73.
7. *Fortune*, March 1934, p. 53.
8. There is no consistent equivalent of an arpent, which varied regionally; in most places it was close to an acre. A *corde* was simply a bundle of wood.
9. Sédillot, *Deux cents cinquante ans*, p. 65.
10. Woronoff, *L'industrie sidérurgique*, p. 16; Gabriel Jars, *Voyages métallurgiques ou recherches et observations sur les mines et forges de fer, la fabrication de l'acier*, 3 vols. (Lyons, 1774–1781).
11. Simon Schama, *Citizens: A Chronicle of the French Revolution* (New York: Knopf, 1989), p. 119.
12. Woronoff, *L'industrie sidérurgique*, pp. 357–358.
13. Ibid., p. 17.
14. Pierre Fritsch, *Les Wendel: Rois de l'acier français* (Paris: Robert Laffont, 1976), p. 41.
15. Quoted in Sédillot, *Deux cents cinquante ans*, p. 109.
16. See Laurent Versini, ed., *François-Ignace de Wendel: Essais inédits* (Nancy: Presses Universitaires de Nancy, Editions Serpenoise, 1983).
17. Ibid., pp. 159, 151.
18. See Pierre Hannick, Jean-Claude Muller, and Marcel Bourguignon, eds., *L'ère du fer en Luxembourg (Xve–XIXe siècles): Etudes relatives à l'ancienne sidérurgie et à d'autres industries au Luxembourg* (Luxembourg: Amis de l'Histoire et Institut Archéologique du Luxembourg, 1999), p. 269.
19. Woronoff, *L'industrie sidérurgique*, p. 83.
20. Ibid., pp. 88 ff.
21. Johann Wolfgang von Goethe, *Goethes Werke herausgegeben im Auftrage der Grossherzogin Sophie von Sachsen, Tag- und Jahres-Hefte als Ergänzung meiner sonstigen Bekenntnisse [1749–1806]*, sec. I, vol. 35 (Weimar: H. Böhlau, 1892), pp. 57–59.
22. Quoted in Sédillot, *Deux cents cinquante ans*, p. 122.
23. Quoted in "La psychologie d'un maître de forges français au début du XIXe siècle," *Revue d'histoire de la sidérurgie* 6 (1965), 62.
24. AN, 189 AQ 87, Contract 1030 (le premier brumaire an douze de la République).
25. "La psychologie d'un maître de forges," pp. 63–64.

26. Raymond Dartevelle, ed., *La Banque Seillière-Demachy: Une dynastie familiale au centre du négoce, de la finance et des arts, 1798–1998* (Paris: Perrin, 1999), pp. 98–99.
27. AN, 189 AQ 70, Arrêt rendu le 29 août 1818 par le Cour Royale de Metz qui confirme deux jugements rendus par le Tribunal de Thionville, au profit de François de Wendel.
28. AN, 189 AQ 71, Mémoire de Louis de Wendel (n.d.); and letters of 22 March 1806, 10 June 1811, 9 May 1812.
29. Ibid., Arrêt de la Cour Royale de Metz du 2 janvier 1822 entre Louis de Wendel appelant et François de Wendel intimé.
30. Ibid., Lettre de Louis de Wendel à Charles de Wendel, 31 December 1821.
31. AN, 189 AQ 60, Lettre de M. de Balhasar à Fr. de Wendel, Paris, 21 April 1810.
32. Ibid., Lettre de M. de Balthasar à Monsieur le Premier Président de Serre, conseiller d'Etat membre de la chambre des députés, Quint, 13 January 1817.
33. Bertrand Gille, *La sidérurgie française au XIXe siècle: Recherches historiques* (Geneva: Droz, 1968), p. 111; Woronoff, *L'industrie sidérurgique*, p. 316.
34. Gille, *La sidérurgie française*, p. 17.
35. Ibid., p. 68.
36. Sédillot, *Deux cents cinquante ans*, pp. 162–163.
37. Gille, *La sidérurgie française*, p. 70.
38. Ibid., pp. 71, 72.
39. Quoted in Max Wehmann, "Die Verleihung der Eisenerzbergwerke in Lothringen von 1810 bis 1910," *Stahl und Eisen* 31 (16 November 1911), 1873–80, quotation from p. 1874.
40. See ibid.; and Stefanie van de Kerkhof, "Die Industrialisierung der lothringisch-luxemburgischen Minette-Region," in Toni Pierenkemper, ed., *Die Industrialisierung Europäischer Montanregionen im 19. Jahrhundert* (Stuttgart: Franz Steiner, 2002), pp. 238–239.
41. Jacques Marseille, *Les Wendel, 1704–2004* (Paris: Editions Perrin, 2004), p. 116.
42. See Lloyd Bonfield, "European Family Law," in David I. Kertzer and Marzio Barbagli, eds., *The History of the European Family*, vol. 2: *Family Life in the Long Nineteenth Century, 1789–1913* (New Haven: Yale University Press, 2002), p. 139.
43. Adam Smith, *An Inquiry into the Origins and Causes of the Wealth of Nations*, ed. Edwin Cannan, vol. 1 (Chicago: University of Chicago Press, 1976), pp. 408–409: "The right of primogeniture, however, still continues to be respected, and as of all institutions it is the fittest to support the pride of family distinctions, it is still likely to endure for many centuries. In every other respect, nothing can be more contrary to the real interests of a numerous family, than a right which in order to enrich one, beggars all the rest of the children."
44. AN, 189 AQ 55, Accord de mai 1835.
45. Ibid., Projet de Partage, 15 October 1866.
46. Ibid., Observations sur les compte des membre de la famille de Wendel, 30 June 1867.
47. Dartevelle, *La Banque Seillière-Demachy*, pp. 105–106; also Ernest-Antoine Seillière, "La saga industrielle et financière de trois familles lorraines: Les

Schneider, les Wendel, les Seillière," in *Les Schneider, Le Creusot: Une famille, une entreprise, une ville (1836–1960)* (Paris: Arthème Fayard, 1995), pp. 270–278.

48. Sédillot, *Deux cents cinquante ans*, p. 188.
49. AN, 189 AQ 55, Accord entre les entreprises du Creusot de Fourchambault et d'Hayange pour faire face aux difficultés bancaires nées de la révolution, 27 March 1848.
50. Sédillot, *Deux cents cinquante ans*, p. 193.
51. Corps Législatif, *Débats*, 5 April 1865, pp. 392–393.
52. Frédéric Le Play, *La réforme sociale en France*, vol. 2 (Paris: E. Dentu, 1867), p. 235.
53. Pierre Bourdieu and Monique de Saint Martin, "Le patronat," *Actes de la recherche en sciences sociales* 20–21 (1978), 16, citing M. Battiau, *Les industries textiles de la région Nord-Pas de Calais* (Doctoral thesis, Lille, 1976).
54. Sédillot, *Deux cents cinquante ans*, p. 195.

2. The Pioneer in German History

1. E.g., Gerhard Adelmann, "Führende Unternehmer im Rheinland und in Westfalen 1850–1914," *Rheinische Vierteljahrsblätter* 35 (1971), 338.
2. Michael Knieriem, ed., *Die Herkunft des Friedrich Engels: Briefe aus der Verwandtschaft 1791–1847* (Trier: Karl Marx Haus, 1991), frontispiece and p. 590.
3. Bodo Herzog and Klaus J. Mattheier, eds., *Franz Haniel 1779–1868: Materialien, Dokumente und Untersuchungen zu Leben und Werk des Industriepioniers Franz Haniel* (Bonn: Ludwig Röhrscheid, 1979), p. 13.
4. Hans Spethmann, *Franz Haniel: Sein Leben und seine Werke* (Duisburg-Ruhrort: Privately printed, 1956), p. 15.
5. See Sheilagh Ogilvie, *A Bitter Living: Women, Markets, and Social Capital in Early Modern Germany* (Oxford: Oxford University Press, 2003).
6. Geheimes Staatsarchiv Berlin, Kleve, LV Sec. I, Stadt Ruhrort No. 8, letter from Aletta Haniel to the king of Prussia, 31 March 1800. See also Ursula Köhler-Lutterbeck and Monika Siedentopf, *Frauen im Rheinland: Außergewöhnliche Biographien aus der Mitte Europas* (Cologne: Emons Verlag, 2001), pp. 57–61.
7. Herzog and Mattheier, *Franz Haniel*, p. 22.
8. Ibid., p. 23.
9. Ibid., p. 33.
10. Ibid., p. 35.
11. Ibid., pp. 45–46.
12. Ibid., p. 46.
13. Hans-Josef Joest, *Pionier im Ruhrrevier: Gutehoffnungshütte, Vom ältesten Montan-Unternehmen Deutschlands zum grössten Maschinenbau-Konzern Europas* (Stuttgart: Seewald, 1982), p. 10.
14. Spethmann, *Franz Haniel*, p. 92.
15. Herzog and Mattheier, *Franz Haniel*, p. 53.
16. Ibid., pp. 54–55. Gall gives the price as 12,000 Cleves Reichsthaler for the works and 25,800 for equipment and material: Lothar Gall, *Krupp: Der Aufstieg eines Industrieimperiums* (Berlin: Siedler, 2000), p. 16.

17. Herzog and Mattheier, *Franz Haniel*, p. 56.
18. Ibid., p. 70.
19. See Wolfhard Weber, "Entfaltung der Industriewirtschaft," in Wolfgang Köllmann et al., eds., *Das Ruhrgebiet im Industriezeitalter: Geschichte und Entwicklung* (Düsseldorf: Schwann im Patmos Verlag, 1990), p. 266.
20. Herzog and Mattheier, *Franz Haniel*, p. 57.
21. Ibid., p. 61.
22. Ibid., p. 68.
23. Cited in Angela Redish, *Bimetallism: An Economic and Historical Analysis* (Cambridge: Cambridge University Press, 2000), p. 175.
24. Herzog and Mattheier, *Franz Haniel*, p. 73.
25. Ibid., p. 71.
26. On the early history of the Cockerills see Robert Halleux, *Cockerill: Deux siècles de technologie* (Liège: Perron, 2002), especially pp. 30–43.
27. Spethmann, *Franz Haniel*, p. 207.
28. Ibid., p. 209.
29. Ibid., p. 180.
30. Ibid., pp. 191–192.
31. Ibid., p. 192.
32. Ibid., pp. 292–293.
33. Joachim Huske, *Die Steinkohlenzechen im Ruhrrevier: Daten und Fakten von den Anfängen bis 1986* (Bochum: Deutsches Bergbau-Museum, 1987), pp. 774–776.
34. On the background of politics and Rhineland businessmen, see Jeffry M. Diefendorf, *Businessmen and Politics in the Rhineland, 1789–1834* (Princeton: Princeton University Press, 1980).
35. Spethmann, *Franz Haniel*, p. 213.
36. See Weber, "Entfaltung der Industriewirtschaft," p. 206.
37. Spethmann, *Franz Haniel*, p. 264.
38. *Lebenserinnerungen von Rudolf von Delbrück* (Leipzig: Duncker und Humblot, 1905), pp. 183–184. See also Friedrich Zunkel, *Der rheinisch-westfälischer Unternehmer, 1834–1879: Ein Beitrag zur Geschichte des deutschen Bürgertums im 19. Jahrhundert* (Cologne: Westdeutscher Verlag, 1962), p. 139.
39. Herzog and Mattheier, *Franz Haniel*, p. 101.
40. See Joest, *Pionier im Ruhrrevier*, pp. 37–39.
41. Spethmann, *Franz Haniel*, p. 256.
42. Herzog and Mattheier, *Franz Haniel*, p. 107.
43. Ibid., p. 109.
44. See Walter Schäfer, *Franz Haniel & Cie. GmbH: Ein Fundament aus Tradition und Leistung* (Duisburg-Ruhrort: Franz Haniel & Cie. GmbH, 1987), p. 14.

3. The Industrial Origins of the Falcks

1. See Andrea Colli, *Legami di ferro: Storia del distretto metallurgico e meccanico lecchese tra Otto e Novecento* (Catanzaro: Meridiana libri; Rome: Donzelli, 1999); Giorgio Cortella, *I Badoni e l'industria del ferro nell'800 lecchese* (Milan: F. Angeli, 1988); also Jean-François Bergier, *Pour une histoire des Alpes, Moyen Age et temps modernes* (Aldershot, U.K.: Ashgate, 1997).

2. Armando Frumento, *Imprese lombarde nella storia della siderurgia italiana: Il contributo dei Falck* (Milan: Campi, 1952), p. 45.
3. Ibid., p. 49.
4. Rupert Pichler, *Die Wirtschaft der Lombardei als Teil Österreichs: Wirtschaftspolitik, Aussenhandel und industrielle Interessen 1815–1859* (Berlin: Duncker & Humblot, 1996), pp. 157–161.
5. Frumento, *Imprese lombarde*, p. 62.
6. Ibid., p. 45.
7. Pichler, *Die Wirtschaft der Lombardei*, p. 166.
8. Frumento, *Imprese lombarde*, p. 60.
9. Pichler, *Die Wirtschaft der Lombardei*, p. 208.
10. Frumento, *Imprese lombarde*, p. 77.
11. Ibid., p. 79.
12. Ibid., p. 95.
13. Ibid., p. 95.
14. Ezio Parma, *Dinastie Sestesi* (Milan: MCG, n.d.), pp. 132–133.
15. Letter of 21 September 1862, cited in Frumento, *Imprese lombarde*, pp. 111–112.
16. Ibid., p. 138.
17. Colli, *Legami di ferro*, p. 118.
18. Frumento, *Imprese lombarde*, p. 141.
19. Colli, *Legami di ferro*, pp. 108, 119–120.
20. Frumento, *Imprese lombarde*, p. 165.

II. The Age of the Corporation

1. For instance, R. Passow, "Aktiengesellschaften," in Ludwig Elster, Adolf Weber, and Friedrich Wieser, eds., *Handwörterbuch der Staatswissenschaften*, 4th ed., vol. 1 (Jena: G. Fischer, 1923), p. 136. By contrast, in the GmbH the management was appointed by the general shareholders' meeting.
2. For an authoritative account that demolishes this myth, see Jeremy Edwards and Klaus Fischer, *Banks, Finance and Investment in Germany* (Cambridge: Cambridge University Press, 1994), chap. 3.
3. Max Weber, *Gesamtausgabe*, ed. Knut Borchardt with Cornelia Meyer-Stoll, vol. 5: *Börsenwesen, Schriften und Reden, 1893–1898* (Tübingen: J. C. B. Mohr / Paul Siebeck, 1999), pt. 1, p. 152.
4. Adolf A. Berle Jr. and Gardiner C. Means, *The Modern Corporation and Private Property* (New York: Macmillan, 1932).
5. Thomas R. Navin and Marian V. Sears, "The Rise of a Market for Industrial Securities, 1887–1902," *Business History Review* 29 (June 1955), 106–107.
6. Weber, *Börsenwesen*, pp. 149, 153.
7. Ibid., p. 153.

4. The Gutehoffnungshütte as a Joint-Stock Company

1. RWWA, GHH 3001092/0, Repartition der Aktien [early 1870s].
2. *Gutehoffnungshütte 1908–1929*, vol. 3 (Oberhausen: GHH, 1930), pp. 46–47.
3. A list of creditors of 1 November 1871, RWWA, GHH 3600812, shows the

following sums owed: Louis Haniel, 170,909 thalers; Max Haniel, 90,000; Julius Haniel, 147,863; Friedrich Wilhelm Haniel, 87,885; Hugo Haniel, 248,032; Franz Haniel & Co., 120,083; Alphons Haniel, 93,096.

4. See Wilfried Feldenkirchen, *Die Eisen- und Stahlindustrie des Ruhrgebiets 1879–1914: Wachstum, Finanzierung und Struktur ihrer Grossunternehmen* (Wiesbaden: Franz Steiner, 1982), p. 80.
5. See David S. Landes, *The Unbound Prometheus: Technological Change and Industrial Development in Western Europe from 1750 to the Present* (Cambridge: Cambridge University Press, 1969), pp. 174–178, 256–258.
6. See Volker Wellhöner, *Grossbanken und Grossindustrie im Kaiserreich* (Göttingen: Vandenhoeck & Ruprecht, 1989), pp. 94–95.
7. Helga Junkers, *Entwicklung und Wachstum der Stahl- und Walzwerke Oberhausen und Neu-Oberhausen 1880–1890: Beispiele unternehmerischer Entscheidungen in der GHH* (Doctoral dissertation, Heidelberg, 1970), p. 295.
8. Ibid., p. 179, quoting RWWA, GHH 3001090/5, letter from Lueg to Haniel, 13 December 1880.
9. Ibid., p. 114, citing letter from Hugo Haniel to GHH Vorstand, 6 January 1880.
10. Ibid., p. 145.
11. Haniel archive, Duisburg, HB 444, Theobald Liebrecht, "Notizen zur Geschichte der Familie Haniel," manuscript, 1966.
12. RWWA, GHH 300 1092/12, Alphons Haniel to Hugo Haniel, 4 May 1880; see also Wellhöner, *Grossbanken und Grossindustrie*, pp. 98–99.
13. Junkers, *Entwicklung*, pp. 85–86, 87.
14. Ibid., p. 88.
15. Alfred D. Chandler Jr., *Scale and Scope: The Dynamics of Industrial Capitalism* (Cambridge, Mass.: Belknap Press of Harvard University Press, 1990), p. 495. See also Feldenkirchen, *Die Eisen- und Stahlindustrie.*
16. Junkers, *Entwicklung*, p. 259.
17. Ibid., p. 94.
18. Ibid., p. 146.
19. On cartels see Robert Liefmann, *Cartels, Concerns and Trusts* (London: Methuen, 1932); also Erich Maschke, "Outline of the History of German Cartels from 1873 to 1914," in François Crouzet, ed., *Essays in European Economic History, 1789–1914* (London: Arnold, 1969), pp. 226–258.
20. Junkers, *Entwicklung*, p. 76. See also Feldenkirchen, *Die Eisen- und Stahlindustrie*, p. 95.
21. Junkers, *Entwicklung*, pp. 100, 120.
22. Ibid., pp. 160, 163.
23. Ibid., pp. 215–216.
24. Ibid., p. 234.
25. Ibid., p. 181, quoting E. J. Haniel to Lueg, 5 April 1885.
26. Ibid., pp. 183–184, 211.
27. Ibid., p. 165.
28. Ibid., p. 189.
29. Paul Reusch, preface to Fritz Büchner, *125 Jahre Geschichte der Gutehoffnungshütte* (Oberhausen: GHH, 1935).
30. Horst A. Wessel, *Kontinuität im Wandel: 100 Jahre Mannesmann 1890–1990*

(Düsseldorf: Mannesmann, 1990), p. 74, quoting a letter from Franken to Steinthal, 6 November 1895.

5. French Companies in Two Countries

1. Grandet was the nephew of Madame Henri de Wendel (Berthe de Vauserre); later he became chairman of the banking house Demachy, which acted as a family bank for the Wendels.
2. Henry Grandet, *Monographie d'un établissement métallurgique sis à la fois en France et en Allemagne: Thèse pour le doctorat* (Chartres: Edmond Garnier, 1909), p. 7.
3. AN, 189 AQ 55, Lettre de Charles de Wendel; copie pour M. de Gargan Hayange, 4 March 1870.
4. Ibid., Nouvelle fixation de l'amortissement des fours à Coke Hayange, 6 September 1866.
5. Ibid., Extrait des observations échangées dans la conférence du 26 avril 1870.
6. Eberhard Kolb, "Ökonomische Interessen und politischer Entscheidungsprozess: Zur Aktivität deutscher Wirtschaftskreise und zur Rolle wirtschaftlicher Erwägungen in der Frage von Annexion und Grenzziehung 1870/71," *Vierteljahrschrift für Wirtschafts- und Sozialgeschichte* 60 (1973), 378.
7. Quoted in René Sédillot, *Deux cents cinquante ans d'industrie en Lorraine: La Maison de Wendel de mil sept cent quatre à nos jours* (Paris: François de Wendel, 1958), p. 216.
8. Grandet, *Monographie*, pp. 125–126.
9. Ibid., p. 115.
10. Max Schlenker, "Das Eisenhüttenwesen in Elsass-Lothringen," in Schlenker, ed., *Die wirtschaftliche Entwicklung Elsass-Lothringens 1871–1918* (Frankfurt: Selbstverlag des Elsass-Lothringen-Institutes, 1931), p. 177.
11. Ibid., p. 176.
12. Sédillot, *Deux cents cinquante ans*, p. 224.
13. François Roth, *La Lorraine annexée: Etude sur la présidence de Lorraine dans l'Empire allemand, 1870–1918* (Nancy: Université de Nancy II, 1976), pp. 301–302; Kurt Wiedenfeld, *Ein Jahrhundert rheinischer Montan-Industrie 1815–1915* (Bonn: A. Marcus & E. Webers Verlag, 1916), p. 99. On the Moselle, see Gertrud Milkereit, "Das Projekt der Moselkanalisierung: Ein Problem der westdeutschen Eisen- und Stahlindustrie," *Schriften zur Rheinisch-Westfälischen Wirtschaftsgeschichte* 14 (1967), 111–317; also Markus Nievenstein, *Der Zug nach der Minette: Deutsche Unternehmen in Lothringen 1871–1918* (Bochum: Brockmeyer, 1993), which (characteristically of the German literature) excludes the Wendels from its treatment.
14. Roth, *La Lorraine annexée*, p. 313.
15. Ibid., pp. 335, 366, 369, 403.
16. Ibid., p. 291.
17. Grandet, *Monographie*, pp. 105–106.
18. Gerald D. Feldman, *Iron and Steel in the German Inflation, 1916–1923* (Princeton: Princeton University Press, 1977), table 2, pp. 34–35.

19. See Michael Jared Rust, "Business and Politics in the Third Republic: The Comité des Forges and the French Steel Industry, 1896–1914" (Ph.D. diss., Princeton University, 1974), pp. 25–27.
20. See Claude Beaud, "Schneider, de Wendel et les brevets T," *Cahiers d'histoire* 20 (1975), 364–365.
21. See Charles E. Freedeman, *The Triumph of Corporate Capitalism in France, 1867–1914* (Rochester, N.Y.: University of Rochester Press, 1993), pp. 28–30.
22. See David S. Landes, *The Unbound Prometheus: Technological Change and Industrial Development in Western Europe from 1750 to the Present* (Cambridge: Cambridge University Press, 1969), p. 259, on the race of two German firms to be first to reach Middlesborough.
23. Beaud, "Schneider, de Wendel," p. 371.
24. See Jean-Marie Moine, "Histoire technique d'une innovation: La sidérurgie lorraine et le procédé Thomas 1880–1960," in Paul Wynants, ed., *Mutations de la sidérurgie du XVIe siècle à 1960* (Namur: Facultés Universitaires Notre-Dame de la Paix, 1997), p. 222.
25. Beaud, "Schneider, de Wendel," pp. 370, 371.
26. See Daniel Henri, "Capitalisme familial et gestion industrielle au XIXe siècle," *Revue française de gestion* 70 (September 1988), 141–150; also Jean-Marie Moine, *Les barons de fer: Les maîtres de forges en Lorraine du milieu du XIXe siècle aux années trente: Histoire sociale d'un patronat sidérurgique* (Metz: Editions Serpenoise; Nancy: Presses Universitaires, 1989), p. 146.
27. Georges Ohnet, *Maître de forges* (Paris: Ollendorff, 1882).
28. Raymond Dartevelle, ed., *La Banque Seillière-Demachy: Une dynastie familiale au centre du négoce, de la finance et des arts, 1798–1998* (Paris: Perrin, 1999), p. 117.
29. Crédit Lyonnais archive, Paris, DEFF 59938/1, Report of Crédit Lyonnais, October 1902.
30. AN, 189 AQ 107, Note des Relations de la Gérance des Services Centraux et des Grandes Directions, 4 September 1935.
31. Crédit Lyonnais archive, DEFF 24605, Usines de Joeuf, February 1895.
32. Ibid., Usine de Joeuf, 4 August 1900.
33. Ibid., DEFF 59938/1, Report of Crédit Lyonnais, October 1902.
34. Moine, "Histoire technique," pp. 222–223.
35. Ibid., p. 224.
36. Beaud, "Schneider, de Wendel," p. 376.
37. Ulrich Wengenroth, *Enterprise and Technology: The German and British Steel Industries, 1865–1895*, trans. Sarah Hanbury Tenison (Cambridge: Cambridge University Press, 1994); also, for the Lorraine case, Moine, "Histoire technique."
38. David M. Gordon, "Le libéralisme dans l'empire du fer: François de Wendel et la Lorraine industrielle 1900–1914," *Le mouvement social* 175 (1996), 79–112, esp. p. 99; Georges Hottenger, *Le pays de Briey: Hier et aujourd'hui* (Paris: Berger-Levrault, 1912), pp. 162–177, cited by Gordon, "Le libéralisme," pp. 87–88.
39. *Le Temps*, 1 August 1905, quoted in Gordon, "Le libéralisme," p. 105.
40. Moine, *Les barons de fer*, p. 305.
41. See Margaret Lavinia Anderson, *Practicing Democracy: Elections and Political*

Culture in Imperial Germany (Princeton: Princeton University Press, 2000), pp. 220, 229.
42. Schlenker, "Das Eisenhüttenwesen in Elsass-Lothringen," p. 179.
43. Rust, "Business and Politics," p. 76.
44. Note des Relations de la Gérance des Services Centraux, 4 September 1934.
45. Quoted in Roth, *La Lorraine annexée*, p. 352.
46. Note des Relations de la Gérance des Services Centraux, 4 September 1934.
47. Sédillot, *Deux cents cinquante ans*, p. 276.
48. Yves Guéna, *Les Wendel: Trois siècles d'histoire* (Paris: Editions Perrin, 2004), p. 87.
49. Moine, *Les barons de fer*, p. 149.
50. Gordon, "Le libéralisme," p. 110.
51. Rust, "Business and Politics," p. 327.
52. See Jean-Noël Jeanneney, *L'argent caché: Milieux d'affaires et pouvoirs politiques dans la France du XXe siècle* (Paris: Fayard, 1981).

6. An Italian Joint-Stock Company

1. See Luigi Trezzi, ed., *Sesto San Giovanni, 1880–1921: Economia e società: La trasformazione* (Sesto San Giovanni: Banca di Credito Cooperativo, 1997).
2. Valerio Varini, "L'affermarsi dell'industria moderna nei primi decenni del secolo," in ibid., pp. 70–71.
3. Carlo G. Lacaita, *L'intelligenza produttiva: Imprenditori, tecnici e operai nella Società d'incoraggiamento d'arti e mestieri di Milano (1838–1988)* (Milan: Electa, 1990), p. 323.
4. See Franco Amatori and Andrea Colli, *Impresa e industria in Italia: dall'Unità a oggi* (Venice: Marsilio, 1999), pp. 85–105; Vera Negri Zamagni, *The Economic History of Italy, 1860–1990* (Oxford: Clarendon Press, 1993).
5. Armando Frumento, *Imprese lombarde nella storia della siderurgia italiana: Il contributo dei Falck* (Milan: Campi, 1952), p. 205.
6. Alexander Gerschenkron, "Notes on the Rate of Industrial Growth in Italy, 1881–1913," in *Economic Backwardness in Historical Perspective: A Book of Essays* (Cambridge, Mass.: Belknap Press of Harvard University Press, 1962), pp. 72–89.
7. AFL, *Relazione del Consiglio d'amministrazione, 1906/7*, p. 4. All AFL reports are available in the Falck archive, Milan.
8. Ibid., *1907/8*, p. 3.
9. Ibid., *1908/9*, p. 3.
10. Frumento, *Imprese lombarde*, pp. 216–217.
11. Antonio Confalonieri, *Banca e industria in Italia dalla crisi del 1907 all'agosto 1914*, vol. 2 (Milan: BCI, 1982), p. 433.
12. Ibid., p. 86.
13. Ibid., pp. 433–434.
14. AFL, *Relazione, 1908/9*, p. 3.
15. Confalionieri, *Banca e industria*, p. 237.
16. See ibid., p. 437.
17. Ibid., p. 440.
18. Letter of BCI, 12 October 1909, in ibid., p. 442.

19. Confalonieri, *Banca e industria*, pp. 444–445.
20. Archivio Storico Banca Intesa, BCI, Sofindit, cartella 31, fasc. 5, fol. 100, note of 11 June 1908.
21. Confalionieri, *Banca e industria*, p. 447.
22. Ibid., p. 448.
23. Ibid.
24. AFL, *Relazioni del Consiglio d'amministrazione, 1911/12*, p. 3.
25. Confalionieri, *Banca e industria*, pp. 449–450.
26. Archivio Storico Banca Intesa, BCI, Sofindit, cartella 31, fasc. 4, fol. 39–41, contract of 22 December 1910.
27. Confalionieri, *Banca e industria*, p. 456.
28. Ibid., pp. 454–455.
29. Peter Hertner, "Deutsches Kapital in Italien: Die Società Tubi Mannesmann' in Dalmine bei Bergamo, 1906–1916," *Zeitschrift für Unternehmensgeschichte* 22 (1977), 183–204, and 23 (1978), 54–76.
30. Confalonieri, *Banca e industria*, table 16, p. 81.
31. Ibid., pp. 452–453.
32. This view is shared by most modern writers on the topic. See Franco Bonelli, *La crisi del 1907: Una tappa dello sviluppo industriale in Italia* (Turin: Fondazione Luigi Einaudi, 1971).
33. Figures from B. R. Mitchell, *European Historical Statistics, 1750–1970* (London: Macmillan, 1975).
34. Antonio Confalonieri, *Banche miste e grande industria in Italia, 1914–1933*, 2 vols. (Milan: BCI, 1994, 1997), 2: 458.
35. Ibid., p. 29.
36. L. De Rosa, "L'economia italiana fra Guerra e dopoguerra," in De Rosa, ed., *Storia dell'industria eletrica in Italia*, vol. 2: *Il potenziamento tecnico e finanziario 1914–1925* (Rome: Laterza, 1993), p. 65.
37. AFL, *Relazioni del Consiglio d'amministrazione, 1916–17*.
38. Confalonieri, *Banche miste*, 1: 23.
39. AFL, *Relazioni del Consiglio d'amministrazione, 1918/19*.

III. The Age of Organizationalism

1. See Alfred D. Chandler Jr., *Scale and Scope: The Dynamics of Industrial Capitalism* (Cambridge, Mass.: Belknap Press of Harvard University Press, 1990); also Louis Galambos, "The Emerging Organizational Synthesis in Modern American History," *Business History Review* 44 (1970), 279–290.
2. Andrea Colli, *The History of Family Business, 1850–2000* (Cambridge: Cambridge University Press, 2003), p. 38.

7. The Politician as Businessman

1. Two major biographies concentrate on François de Wendel's politics: Jean-Noël Jeanneney, *François de Wendel en République: L'argent et le pouvoir, 1914–1940* (Paris: Seuil, 1976); and Denis Woronoff, *François de Wendel* (Paris: Presses de Sciences Po, 2001).

2. "Arms and the Man," *Fortune*, March 1934, p. 118.
3. Roger Biard, *La sidérurgie française: Contribution à l'étude d'une grande industrie française* (Paris: Editions Sociales, 1958), p. 98.
4. Maurice Druon, *Les grandes familles* (Paris: René Juillard, 1948), p. 188.
5. Ministère du Commerce, *Rapport général sur l'industrie française, sa situation, son avenir* (Paris, 1919).
6. Chambre des Députés, *Procès-verbaux de la Commission d'enquête sur le rôle et le situation de la métallurgie en France: 1919* (Paris).
7. On 4, 5, and 10 February, 23 March, 5 April, 16 June, 12 and 22 July, 5, 9 and 23 September, and 29 October 1917; and 28 January, 21 and 30 May, 6 and 27 June, 15, 21, and 26 August, 16 September, and 28 October 1918: see René Sédillot, *Deux cents cinquante ans d'industrie en Lorraine: La Maison de Wendel de mil sept cent quatre à nos jours* (Paris: François de Wendel, 1958), pp. 293–294.
8. Ibid., p. 299.
9. Ibid., p. 310.
10. *"L'abominable vénalité de la presse . . ." d'aprés les documents des archives russes (1897–1917)* (Paris: Librairie du Travail, 1931).
11. There is a full discussion of the "querelle de Briey" in Jeanneney, *François de Wendel*, pp. 67–107.
12. *Le journal officiel, Chambre des Députés*, 31 January 1919, p. 351.
13. Ibid., p. 355.
14. Jeanneney, *François de Wendel*, p. 100.
15. See ibid. The letter was first published on 11 January 1928 in *Le nouvel âge*.
16. Jeanneney, *François de Wendel*, pp. 585–586.
17. Woronoff, *François de Wendel*, p. 229. On the overall politics, see Stephen A. Schuker, *The End of French Predominance in Europe* (Chapel Hill: University of North Carolina Press, 1976).
18. Jeanneney, *François de Wendel*, p. 591.
19. Ibid., pp. 569, 603.
20. William D. Irvine, *French Conservatism in Crisis: The Republican Federation of France in the 1930s* (Baton Rouge: Louisiana State University Press, 1979), p. 73.
21. See Jeanneney, *François de Wendel*, pp. 480–483 and 574.
22. Quoted in ibid., p. 175.
23. Ibid., p. 479.
24. Ibid., p. 613.
25. Ibid., p. 614.
26. Ibid., pp. 342–343.
27. See Kenneth Mouré, *Managing the Franc Poincaré: Economic Understanding and Political Constraint in French Monetary Policy, 1928–1936* (Cambridge: Cambridge University Press, 2002); also Emile Moreau, *The Golden Franc: Memoirs of a Governor of the Bank of France: The Stabilization of the Franc (1926–1928)*, trans. Stephen D. Stoller and Trevor C. Roberts (Boulder: Westview, 1991).
28. Julian Jackson, *The Politics of Depression in France, 1932–1936* (Cambridge: Cambridge University Press, 1985), p. 101.

29. The classic exposition of the view is Alfred Sauvy, *Histoire économique de la France entre les deux guerres*, 4 vols. (Paris: Fayard, 1965–1975).
30. See Crédit Lyonnais archive, Paris, DEFF 50724/1, Note, 6 January 1925.
31. The German owners were compensated by the German government.
32. See Claude Prêcheur, *La Lorraine sidérurgique* (Paris: SABRI, 1959), pp. 208–212.
33. Sédillot, *Deux cents cinquante ans*, p. 324.
34. AN, 189 AQ 186, Note de Daussy, directeur en chef de Fenderie, July 1930.
35. AN, 189 AQ 193, Lettre de Fr. de Wendel à A. Delage, April 1921.
36. AN, 189 AQ 201, Visite de François de Wendel à Joeuf, 5 April 1927.
37. Ibid., Visite de François de Wendel à Joeuf, 30 December 1927.
38. Jean-Marie Moine, "Histoire technique d'une innovation: La sidérurgie lorraine et le procédé Thomas 1880–1960," in Paul Wynants, ed., *Mutations de la sidérurgie du XVIe siècle à 1960* (Namur: Facultés Universitaires Notre-Dame de la Paix, 1997), p. 240.
39. Sédillot, *Deux centes cinquante ans*, p. 334.
40. Crédit Lyonnais archive, DEFF, 50724, Memorandum, 20 August 1929.
41. AN, 189 AQ 108, letter to Hochstrate, director of Zeche Wendel at Hamm, 15 June 1929.
42. AN, 190 AQ 43, Note by Maurice de Wendel, August 1936.
43. Maurice Lévy-Leboyer, "The Large Family Firm in French Manufacturing," in Akio Okochi and Shigeaki Yasuoka, eds., *Family Business in the Era of Industrial Growth: Its Ownership and Management* (Tokyo: University of Tokyo Press, 1984), pp. 228–229.
44. AN, 189 AQ 201, Lettre de François de Wendel à la Direction Générale de Joeuf, 26 March 1938.
45. AN, 189 AQ 115, Note sur la méthode Bedaux: Comité des forges et des Mines de Fer de l'Est de la France. Mémoire et note: dossier daté du 15 janvier 1935, 37 pp., document rédigé et réalisé par les ingénieurs des services techniques dont l'ingénieur en chef L. Boileau.
46. See Jean-Marie Moine, *Les barons de fer: Les maîtres de forges en Lorraine du milieu du XIXe siècle aux années trente: Histoire sociale d'un patronat sidérurgique* (Metz: Editions Serpenoise; Nancy: Presses Universitaires, 1989), p. 235; also Woronoff, *François de Wendel*, p. 205.
47. Moine, "Histoire technique," p. 245.
48. Crédit Lyonnais archive, DEFF 50724/1, Annexe la note 6343, n.d.
49. AN, 189 AQ 141, Note sur le régime des Mines de Joeuf novembre 1940, adressée à François, Maurice de Wendel, et de Mitry.
50. Historical archive of Deutsche Bank, Frankfurt, F167/0111, Notes of Deutsche Bank, Rheydt branch, 9 September 1941 and 15 June 1942.
51. Ibid., Reich Economics Ministry note, 5 April 1941.
52. AN, 189 AQ 139, Réponse française aux critiques allemandes, 18 March 1942.
53. Jean Chardonnet, *La sidérurgie française* (Paris: Armand Colin, 1954), pp. 204–205.
54. Crédit Lyonnais archive, DEFF 50724/1, Visite de M. de Mitry, 2 March 1944.
55. AN, 189 AQ 139, Voyage en Allemagne de Messieurs Gatelet et Martin du 2 au 17 janvier 1943.

56. AN, 189 AQ 141, Visite de l'usine de Joeuf, 7 March 1944.
57. Ibid., Visite aux forges de Joeuf et inventaire, May 1944.

8. A Family Concern

1. See Friedrich Zunkel, *Der rheinisch-westfälische Unternehmer, 1834–1879: Ein Beitrag zur Geschichte des deutschen Bürgertums im 19. Jahrhundert* (Cologne: Westdeutscher Verlag, 1962), p. 112; also Dolores L. Augustine, *Patricians and Parvenus: Wealthy Businessmen in Wilhelmine Germany* (Providence: Berg, 1994).
2. Alfred D. Chandler Jr., *Scale and Scope: The Dynamics of Industrial Capitalism* (Cambridge, Mass.: Belknap Press of Harvard University, 1990), p. 591.
3. Haniel archive, Duisburg, HB 444, Theobald Liebrecht, "Notizen zur Geschichte der Familie Haniel," manuscript, 1966.
4. Paul Reusch was born in 1868 in Königsbronn, Württemberg, the son of the director of the state foundry.
5. For instance, the influential list of the 100 largest companies in Germany compiled by Kocka and Siegrist omits the Wendels, presumably because their company was incorporated under French law; Jürgen Kocka and Hannes Siegrist, "Die hundert grössten deutschen Industrieunternehmen im späten 19. und frühen 20. Jahrhundert: Expansion, Diversifikation und Integration im internationalen Vergleich," in Norbert Horn and Jürgen Kocka, eds., *Recht und Entwicklung der Grossunternehmen im 19. und frühen 20. Jahrhundert: Wirtschafts-, sozial- und rechtshistorische Untersuchung zur Industrialisierung in Deutschland, Frankreich, England und den USA / Law and the Formation of the Big Enterprises in the Nineteenth and Early Twentieth Centuries* (Göttingen: Vandenhoeck & Ruprecht, 1979). The neglect is shared even in the study of Lorraine by Markus Nievenstein, *Der Zug nach der Minette: Deutsche Unternehmen in Lothringen 1871–1918* (Bochum: Brockmeyer, 1993).
6. Gerald D. Feldman, *Iron and Steel in the German Inflation, 1916–1923* (Princeton: Princeton University Press, 1977), pp. 34–35.
7. See idem, *Hugo Stinnes: Biographie eines Industriellen, 1870–1924*, trans. Karl Heinz Siber (Munich: C. H. Beck, 1998).
8. Fritz Büchner, *125 Jahre Geschichte der Gutehoffnungshütte* (Oberhausen: GHH, 1935), pp. 62–63.
9. Erich Maschke, *Es ensteht ein Konzern: Paul Reusch und die GHH* (Tübingen: Rainer Wunderlich, 1969), p. 93.
10. RWWA, GHH 300193000/5, Reusch (?) to August Haniel, 5 September 1923.
11. RWWA, GHH, 30001930025, GHH to Reich Justice Ministry, 15 December 1923.
12. Maschke, *Es ensteht ein Konzern*, p. 139.
13. Stinnes was the subject of endless commentary in the 1920s, and his life has been surveyed authoritatively in the fine biography by Gerald Feldman. Feldman also provides a detailed narrative of the MAN struggle in *Iron and Steel*, pp. 225–241.
14. Quoted in Feldman, *Stinnes*, p. 658.
15. Feldman, *Iron and Steel*, p. 232; Harald Wixforth, *Banken und Schwerindustrie*

in der Weimarer Republik (Cologne: Böhlau, 1995), pp. 151–157; Feldman, *Stinnes*, pp. 656–662.

16. Maschke, *Es entsteht ein Konzern*, p. 149, citing RWWA, GHH 300193017/2, Reusch to Cramer-Klett, 21 October 1920.
17. Maschke, *Es entsteht ein Konzern*, p. 154.
18. Ibid., p. 156.
19. Ibid., pp. 158–159.
20. RWWA, GHH 40810/0, Vereinheitlichung der Fabrikationsgebiete im Konzern der Gutehoffnungshütte: Verhandlungen in Nürnberg am 14. und 15. März 1921.
21. RWWA, GHH 40810/0, subfile 1, Konzernsitzung, Oberhausen, 24 October 1921.
22. Ibid., subfile 6, Konzernsitzung in Oberhausen, 28 November 1922.
23. From RWWA, GHH 40810/0.
24. RWWA, GHH 40810/2a, subfile 11, Konzernsitzung zu Oberhausen, 18 February 1929.
25. RWWA, GHH 40810/0, subfile 8, Konzernsitzung, 9 March 1925.
26. RWWA, GHH 300193000/5, Reusch (?) to August Haniel, 5 September 1923.
27. See Chandler, *Scale and Scope*, pp. 536–537.
28. See RWWA, GHH 3001900/4, for the credits.
29. Order books from RWWA, GHH 4080/1.
30. Büchner, *125 Jahre Geschichte der Gutehoffnungshütte*, p. 132.
31. Wixforth, *Banken*, p. 131.
32. Ibid., pp. 101–110; Alfred Reckendrees, *Das "Stahltrust"-Projekt: Die Gründung der Vereinigte Stahlwerke A. G. und ihre Unternehmensentwicklung 1926–1933/34*, Schriftenreihe zur Zeitschrift für Unternehmensgeschichte, No. 5 (Munich: C. H. Beck, 2000).
33. See Bernd Weisbrod, *Schwerindustrie in der Weimarer Republik: Interessenpolitik zwischen Stabilisierung und Krise* (Wuppertal: Peter Hammer, 1978), p. 395, and pp. 415–456 for the Ruhr iron lockout.
34. RWWA, GHH 40810/0, Konzernsitzung, 24 October 1921.
35. RWWA, GHH 300193000/5, August Haniel to Reusch, 13 March 1921.
36. Ibid., Reusch to August Haniel, 15 March 1921.
37. RWWA GHH 300193000/6, Karl Haniel to Reusch, 29 November 1922.
38. RWWA, GHH 4001012000/1b, Karl Haniel to Paul Reusch, 12 June 1926.
39. RWWA, GHH 40010145/3, Hermann Reusch to Karl Haniel, 7 June 1938.
40. The meeting and its significance are discussed extensively in Henry Ashby Turner Jr., *German Big Business and the Rise of Hitler* (New York: Oxford University Press, 1985), pp. 204–219. See also *60 Jahre Industrie-Club e.v. Düsseldorf* (Düsseldorf: Privately printed, 1972).
41. RWWA, GHH 3001900/1, Verhandelt im Werksgasthaus Oberhausen, 22 October 1931.
42. RWWA, GHH 40010110/1, Carp to Theodor Böninger, 9 October 1924.
43. Haniel archive, ZABW 50, fol. 263 ff., Pferdmenges to Carp, 15 December 1930.
44. See on this, and on the creation of Vereinigte Stahlwerke, Reckendrees, *Das "Stahltrust"-Projekt*, especially pp. 287–295.

45. E.g., RWWA, GHH 300193001/1, Reusch to Richard Jacobi, 8 January 1919.
46. RWWA, GHH 400100/95, Verkehr in Gutehoffnungshütte-Aktien, 15 June 1935.
47. Haniel archive, ZABW 50, fol. 276, Niederschrift über Telefongespräch mit Herrn Werner Carp am 3.12.30 abends (Welker).
48. Ibid., fol. 280, Aktennotiz (Welker), 1 December 1930.
49. Reusch to Welker, 29 November 1930, reproduced in Haniel archive, Walter Schäfer, "Die Entwicklung der Franz Haniel & Cie. GmbH im Spiegel der Bilanzen von 1917 bis 1976," manuscript, vol. 2, app. 10/1.
50. Haniel archive, ZABW 50, fol. 241, Welker to Carp, 19 January 1931 (also GHH 4001012026/7).
51. Haniel archive, ZABW 50, Reusch to Welker, 22 December 1930.
52. Ibid., Welker to Carp, 19 January 1931.
53. RWWA, GHH 4001012026/7, Welker to GHH (Reusch), 29 January 1931.
54. Ibid., Reusch to Edgar Haniel von Haimhausen, 8 March 1932.
55. Urkunde 205/1932 Duisburg-Ruhrort, reproduced in Schäfer, "Entwicklung der Franz Haniel & Cie.," 2: 345–346.
56. Karl Haniel to Reusch, 2 April 1932, quoted in ibid., p. 345.
57. Haniel archive, ZABW 49(2), fol. 240, Welker to Reusch, 7 April 1932.
58. Ibid., ZABW 49(1), Niederschrift (Welker), 19 October 1933.
59. RWWA, GHH 440010131/17, G. Lübsen to Kellermann (GHH), 10 February 1939.
60. Haniel archive, ZABW Di 314, Niederschrift über die Besprechung bei der Gutehoffnngshütte in Oberhausen am Freutag, 10 February 1939.
61. E.g., RWWA, GHH 40010124/14, Karl Haniel to Reusch, 12 January 1932 (on meeting of 11 January).
62. RWWA, GHH 40101220/11c, Reusch to Kastl, 6 September 1931.
63. RWWA, GHH 40810/2a, Bericht über die 11. Konzernsitzung in Oberhausen, 18 February 1929.
64. RWWA, GHH 400101293/10b, Reusch telephone conversation with Blank, 10 June 1930.
65. RWWA, GHH 400101290/32, Reusch to Poensgen, 25 August 1931.
66. For instance, RWWA, GHH 400101290/27a, Krupp to Poensgen, 28 July 1931; and Reusch to Krupp, 29 July, expressing agreement with the sentiment.
67. See RWWA, GHH 4000123/9, Paul Reusch memorandum, "Gelsenkirchen," 1932.
68. E.g., RWWA, GHH 4001012025/5b, Reusch to Blank, 17 November 1932.
69. RWWA, GHH 400101290/30a, Reusch to Luther, 20 July 1932, attaching memorandum "Erfahrungen mit der Devalvation in England."
70. RWWA, GHH 400101290/33a, Reusch to Schacht, 20 March 1932.
71. Ibid., Reusch to Schacht, 21 September 1932.
72. RWWA, GHH 400101290/30b, Luther to Gessler, 31 May 1933.
73. Ibid., Reusch to Luther, 17 June 1933.
74. RWWA, GHH 4001012026/3b, Reusch to Welker, 20 October 1934.
75. See Alfred Kube, *Pour le mérite und Hakenkreuz: Hermann Göring im Dritten Reich* (Munich: Oldenbourg, 1986), pp. 187–194; and Richard Overy,

"Heavy Industry in the Third Reich: The Reichswerke Crisis" in *War and Economy in the Third Reich* (Oxford: Clarendon Press, 1994), pp. 93–118.

76. RWWA, GHH 4001012026/26, Reusch to Victor Freiherr von der Lippe, 20 September 1939.
77. See Louis P. Lochner, *Die Mächtigen und der Tyrann. Die deutsche Industrie von Hitler bis Adenauer* (Darmstadt: Franz Schneekuth, 1955), p. 81.
78. FHC, *Jahresbericht 1935/6*. All FHC annual reports are in the Haniel archive.
79. FHC, *Jahresbericht 1937/8*.
80. Haniel archive, ZABW 217, Krum to Ahlers, 12 June 1938.
81. Ibid., Sonderbericht über die Reise nach Berlin, 6–9 April 1936.
82. Facsimile reproduction in Hermann Hecht, *Die Entstehung des Rhenania-Konzerns: Die ersten dreissig Jahre* (Mannheim: Privately printed, 1983), p. 57.
83. Haniel archive, ZABW 125(1), fol. 201, memorandum, 21 September 1938.
84. Ibid., fol. 200, Hecht to FHC (Welker), 25 September 1938.
85. Ibid., ZABW 125(2), fol. 7, Rhenania Mannheim Gesellschafter im Oktober 1950.
86. RWWA, GHH 4001482/24, Niederschrift über die Besprechung bei der Stadtverwaltung, 23 May 1945.
87. RWWA, GHH 400101301/3, Gestapo Düsseldorf to GHH Bergwerksdirektion, 13 July 1940.
88. RWWA, GHH 400101330/7, Arbeitsamt Kattowitz to Bezirksgruppe Steinkohlenbergbau der Wirtschaftsgruppe Bergbau, 27 June 1941.
89. Ibid., GHH letter to Bezirksgruppe Steinkohlenbergbau, 10 June 1942.
90. RWWA, GHH 400101301/3, Note: Sowjetische Kriegsgefangene, 21 October 1942.
91. RWWA, GHH 4001481/34, Kriegsgefangenenlohnlisten und -abrechnungen, Anlage. 1b, 23 January 1947.
92. RWWA, GHH 4001482/7, GHH letter to Deutsche Arbeitsfront, 31 May 1943.
93. RWWA, GHH 40010330/17, Merkblatt über den Einsatz sowjetrussischer Kriegsgefangener, n.d.
94. RWWA, GHH 4001481/34, Kriegsgefangenenlohnlisten und -abrechnungen, 23 January 1947.
95. E.g., RWWA, GHH 4001482/14a, Bericht über Einsatz, Leistung, Entlohnung, Unterbringung und Betreuung der Fremdarbeiter während der Jahre 1943 und 1944 bei der Gutehoffnungshütte Oberhausen A. G. Werk Sterkrade, n.d.
96. RWWA, GHH 400101293/28, anonymous letter to Reusch, 25 March 1941.
97. RWWA, GHH 400101293/23, Reusch to Reich Economics Minister, 5 February 1942.
98. Eugen Grolman (1902–1945): the OMGUS (Office of the Military Government of the United States) documents mistakenly refer to him as Groman.
99. NA, RG 260 (390/42/3/3), Decartelization papers, box 105, OMGUS report presented to James S. Martin, Chief, Decartelization Branch.
100. Peter Hoffmann, *The History of the German Resistance*, trans. Richard Barry (Montreal: McGill-Queen's University Press, 1996), p. 526 (original:

Widerstand Staatsstreich Attentat: Der Kampf der Opposition gegen Hitler [Munich: Piper, 1985], p. 647).

101. OMGUS report presented to James S. Martin.

9. Models of Italian Industrial Development

1. Giorgio Enrico Falck and Arturo Bocciardo, "La produzione della ghisa da fusione e da affizione: Le materie prime e le energie italiane: Relazione presentata al Consiglio superiore dell'economia nazionale nel febbraio 1926," *La metallurgica italiana* 18 (April 1926). See also Franco Bonelli, *Acciaio per l'industrializzazione: Contributi allo studio del problema siderurgico italiano* (Turin: G. Einaudi, 1982), pp. 67–68.
2. Oscar Sinigaglia, *Alcune note sulla siderurgia italiana* (Rome: Tipografia del Senato, 1946).
3. Falck archive, Milan, Verbale del Consiglio d'Amministrazione (hereafter VCA), 6 June 1930.
4. See on this issue Renato Gianetti, "Dinamica della domanda e delle tariffe," in Giuseppe Galasso, ed., *Storia dell'industria eletrica in Italia*, vol. 3: *Espansione e ologopolio, 1926–1945* (Rome: Laterza, 1993), pp. 282–284.
5. AFL, *Relazioni del Consiglio d'amministrazione, 1939*, p. 11. All AFL reports are available in the Falck archive.
6. Falck archive, VCA, 30 March 1928.
7. Antonio Confalonieri, *Banche miste e grande industria in Italia, 1914–1933*, vol. 2 (Milan: BCI, 1997), p. 356.
8. Ibid., pp. 111–112.
9. AFL, *Relazioni del Consiglio d'amministrazione, 1928.*
10. Ibid., *1929.*
11. Confalonieri, *Banche miste*, pp. 116–117.
12. Falck archive, VCA, 29 November and 10 December 1930.
13. Bonelli, *Acciaio per l'industrializzazione*, p. 192.
14. Falck archive, VCA, 23 October 1929.
15. Bonelli, *Acciaio per l'industrializzazione*, pp. 85–87.
16. AFL, *Relazioni del Consiglio d'amministrazione, 1931;* Falck archive, VCA, 17 July 1931.
17. AFL, *Relazioni, 1931;* Bonelli, *Acciaio per l'industrializzazione*, pp. 85–87.
18. Falck archive, VCA, 27 February 1932. There was another 30-million-lira bond issue in 1933 (VCA, 5 June 1933).
19. Ibid., VCA, 8 May 1934 and 6 February 1935.
20. Ibid., VCA, 12 April 1934. See also Valerio Varini, "Sesto San Giovanni: Il primato industriale," in Luigi Trezzi, ed., *Sesto San Giovanni, 1923–1952: Economia e società: La crescita* (Sesto San Giovanni: Banco di Credito Cooperativo, 2002), p. 85.
21. Bonelli, *Acciaio per l'industrializzazione*, p. 234.
22. Falck archive, Relazione sulla situazione, 1946.
23. Archivio Storico Banca Intesa, Milan, BCI, Sofindit, box 405, fasc. 3, subfasc. 1, Promemoria sull'Ilva, 12–13 April 1932.
24. Confalonieri, *Banche miste*, p. 151.
25. Bonelli, *Acciaio per l'industrializzazione*, p. 194.

26. Archivio Storico Banca Intesa, BCI, Sofindit, box 405, fasc. 3, subfasc. 2, fol. 6, Sinigaglia to Di Veroli, 9 August 1932.
27. Bonelli, *Acciaio per l'industrializzazione*, p. 234.
28. Archivio Storico Banca Intesa, BCI, Sofindit, box 405, fasc. 4, subfasc. 1, Consortio Siderurgica, 1 January 1933.
29. Ibid.
30. Ibid., box 405, fasc. 6, subfasc. 1, Luzzatto (BCI) to Sinigaglia, 9 July 1933.
31. Falck archive, VCA, 15 May 1936.
32. AFL, *Relazioni del Consiglio d'amministrazione, 1938*, p. 9.
33. Bonelli, *Acciaio per l'industrializzazione*, p. 233.
34. Ibid., p. 231.
35. Falck archive, VCA, 20 July 1938.
36. See Maximiliane Rieder, *Deutsch-italienische Wirtschaftsbeziehungen: Kontinuitäten und Brüche 1936–1957* (Frankfurt am Main: Campus, 2003), pp. 298, 324–334.
37. Falck archive, Lettera alla moglie e ai figli, 30 June 1942.

IV. The Age of the Postwar Miracle

1. Charles S. Maier, "The Politics of Productivity: Foundations of American International Economic Policy after World War II," in *In Search of Stability: Explorations in Historical Political Economy* (Cambridge: Cambridge University Press, 1987), pp. 121–152.

10. A Costly Miracle in Italy

1. Ada Ferrari, "Enrico Falck: Un moderno 'padrone delle ferriere'?" *Rivista Milanese di economia* 2 (1982), 34.
2. Giancarlo Galli, *Il padrone dei padroni: Enrico Cuccia il potere di Mediobanca e il capitalismo italiano* (Milan: Garzanti, 1995), p. 117.
3. Galli's book is an example of this kind of interpretation.
4. Quoted in Antonio Savignano, "Il regime normativo," in Valerio Castronovo, ed., *Storia dell'industria eletrica in Italia*, vol. 4: *Dal dopoguerra alla nazionalizzazione, 1945–1962* (Rome: Laterza, 1994), p. 95.
5. Margherita Balconi, *La siderurgia italiana (1945–1990): Tra controllo publico e incentivo del mercato* (Bologna: Il Mulino, 1991), pp. 82–83.
6. Ibid., p. 80.
7. Oscar Sinigaglia, "The Future of the Italian Iron and Steel Industry," *Banca Nazionale del Lavoro Quarterly Review* 4 (January 1948), 240, 244.
8. Luigi De Paoli, "Programmi di investimento e novità tecniche," in Castronovo, *Storia dell'industria eletrica*, 4: 203.
9. AFL, *Relazioni del Consiglio d'amministrazione, 1967*, p. 11. All AFL reports are available in the Falck archive, Milan.
10. Ibid., *1962*, p. 18.
11. Archivio Storico Banca Intesa, Milan, BCI, Research department note, 15 April 1939.
12. Bruno Bottiglieri, "L'industria eletrica dalla guerra agli anni del 'miracolo economico,'" in Castronovo, *Storia dell'industria eletrica*, vol. 4, table 4, p. 71.

13. AFL, *Relazioni del Consiglio d'amministrazione, 1966*, p. 13, figures relating to the average between 1963 and 1965.
14. Ibid., *1957*, p. 7.
15. Ibid., *1959*, p. 13.
16. Ibid., *1948*, p. 2.
17. Ibid., *1961*, p. 11.

11. A New Kind of Family Togetherness

1. NA, RG 260 (390/42/3/3), Decartelization papers, box 105, OMGUS report presented to James S. Martin, Chief, Decartelization Branch; S. Jonathan Wiesen, *West German Industry and the Challenge of the Nazi Past, 1945–1955* (Chapel Hill: University of North Carolina Press, 2001), p. 53.
2. Haniel archive, Duisburg, Geschäftsbericht FHC 1951/52.
3. NA, RG 466, HICOG (446/250/84/29/4), Central Subject Files, box 33, Shearman and Sterling and Wright to Allied High Commission, 6 October 1951.
4. *Die Welt*, 4 October 1950.
5. Haniel archive, WC 55, Wolfgang Curtius to Walter Kaecke, 27 December 1951.
6. Ibid., Curtius to Hans Böninger, 6 November 1951.
7. Walter Schäfer, *Franz Haniel & Cie. GmbH: Ein Fundament aus Tradition und Leistung* (Duisburg: Franz Haniel & Cie. GmbH, 1987), p. 44.
8. Haniel archive, WC 53.
9. Ibid., ZABW 14(2), fol. 7, Sitzung des Beratenden Ausschusses, 16 January 1962.
10. Ibid., ZABW 61(1), fol. 179, Unterredung mit den Herren Dr. Franz Haniel und Kaecke, 27 March 1958.
11. See Gloria Müller, "Montanmitbestimmung bei Eisen und Stahl. Ein Momentaufahme in der Geschichte," in Ottfried Dascher and Christian Kleinschmidt, eds., *Die Eisen- und Stahlindustrie im Dortmunder Raum: Wirtschaftliche Entwicklung, soziale Strukturen und technologischer Wandel im 19. und 20. Jahrhundert* (Dortmund: Gesellschaft für Westfälische Wirtschaftsgeschichte, 1992), pp. 511–524.
12. Haniel archive, ZABW 12(2), Aufsichtsrat FHC, 24 January 1958.
13. Ibid., ZABW 14(2), fol. 51, Sitzung des Beratenden Ausschusses, 21 April 1960.
14. Ibid., fol. 10, Sitzung des Beratenden Ausschusses, 16 January 1962.
15. Ibid., WC 53, fol. 33 ff., Familien-Kreis Haniel, 30 October 1959.
16. Ibid., ZABW 14(2), fol. 77–78, Sitzung des Beratenden Ausschusses, 24 February 1959.
17. *Handelsblatt*, 23–24 April 1965.
18. Haniel archive, ZABW 61(1), Alfred Haniel re: Fall Stinnes, 21 October 1963.
19. Ibid., ZABW 14(3) , fol. 91, Beratender Ausschuss, 24 June 1965.
20. Dietmar Petzina, "Zwischen Neuordnung und Krise die Entwicklung der Eisen- und Stahlindustrie im Ruhrgebiet seit dem Zweiten Weltkrieg," in Dascher and Kleinschmidt, *Die Eisen- und Stahlindustrie*, pp. 525–544.
21. See Horst A. Wessel, *Kontinuität im Wandel: 100 Jahre Mannesmann, 1890–*

1990 (Düsseldorf: Mannesmann, 1990), p. 446; Louis Galambos and Eric John Abrahamson, *Anytime, Anywhere: Entrepreneurship and the Creation of a Wireless World* (Cambridge: Cambridge University Press, 2002), p. 114.

22. Haniel archive, WC 9, Verhandlungen HOAG-Mannesmann, 1 March 1962.
23. *Frankfurter Allgemeine Zeitung*, 11 September 1967.
24. Dietrich Wilhem von Menges, *Unternehmensentscheide: Ein Leben für die Wirtschaft* (Düsseldorf: Econ, 1976), p. 177.
25. Ibid., p. 327.
26. Haniel archive, ZABW 14(3), Sitzung des Beratenden Ausschuses, 6 September 1967.
27. Ibid., WC 56, fol. 65, Kapitalerhöhung der GHH 1967/68.
28. Ibid., HB 1458, Wolfgang Curtius, memorandum, Tätigkeit für Haniel'sche Interessen nach 1968: GHH.
29. Ibid., WC 25, Besprechung bei der ALLIANZ München, 2 October 1969. Also Klaus Haniel, "Wichtige Entscheidungen, die allein von der Familie Haniel in den letzten 50 Jahren getroffen wurden," manuscript, dictated 19–20 October 2000, with the assistance of Ulrich Kirchner and Bernhard Weber-Brosamer.
30. The Commerzbank later took a one-third participation as well.
31. Haniel archive, WC 45, GHH Regina Sitzung, 29 June 1977.
32. Ibid., letter from Lennings to Klaus Haniel, 7 September 1983.
33. Curtius memorandum, Tätigkeit für Haniel'sche Interessen nach 1968, fol. 22.
34. Haniel archive, WC 45, Wolfgang Curtius, "Familienpolitik '75," August 1975.
35. Curtius memorandum, Tätigkeit für Haniel'sche Interessen nach 1968, fol. 17.

12. Postwar Reconstruction in France

1. Roger Biard, *La sidérurgie française: Contribution à l'étude d'une grande industrie française* (Paris: Editions Sociales, 1958), p. 112.
2. Jack Hayward, "The Nemesis of Industrial Patriotism: The French Response to the Steel Crisis," in Yves Mény and Vincent Wright, eds., *The Politics of Steel: Western Europe and the Steel Industry in the Crisis Years (1974–1984)* (Berlin: de Gruyter, 1986), pp. 502–533; Jean G. Padioleau, *Quand la France s'enferre: La politique sidérurgique de la France depuis 1945* (Paris: Presses Universitaires Françaises, 1981), pp. 32, 34.
3. Anthony Daley, *Steel, State, and Labor: Mobilization and Adjustment in France* (Pittsburgh: University of Pittsburgh Press, 1996), p. 50.
4. Biard, *La sidérurgie française*, p. 117.
5. Padioleau, *Quand la France s'enferre*, p. 33.
6. AN, 189 AQ 142, Dossier: sur les Sociétés de la famille de Wendel; Juin 1945, Dossier émanant des cadres de la famille de Wendel et remis le 5 juin 1945 à M. Gagne juge d'instruction.
7. AN, 189 AQ 216, Note du bureau d'étude, 11 December 1946.
8. *La Lorraine industrielle et la Société Lorraine de Laminage Continu* (Paris, 1949).

9. *Rapport de la commission de modernisation de la sidérurgie, République française, Commissariat général du Plan de Modernisation et d'Equipement* (Paris, 1947).
10. AN, 189 AQ 216, Direction d'Hayange note, 12 March 1947.
11. Crédit Lyonnais archive, Paris, DEFF 59810, Memorandum: Les Petit-Fils de François de Wendel et Cie., 1948.
12. AN, 189 AQ 107, Note, May 1946. See also Denis Woronoff, *François de Wendel* (Paris: Presses de Sciences Po, 2001), p. 206.
13. Woronoff, *François de Wendel*, p. 209.
14. AN, 189 AQ 217, Humbert de Wendel, Note, March 1947.
15. Ibid., Plan de modernisation de la sidérurgie: Observation et proposition de la Maison de Wendel [1947].
16. Ibid.
17. See the judgment of Michel Margairaz, "Les plans et la sidérurgie: Le Plan, mal nécessaire pour financer les investissements?" in Henri Rousso, ed., *De Monnet à Massé: Enjeux politiques et objectifs économiques dans le cadre des quatre premiers Plans (1946–1965)* (Paris: Editions du Centre National de la Récherche Scientifique, 1986), pp. 139–150.
18. Ibid., p. 143.
19. Daum to Plan investment committee, 7 January 1949, in ibid., p. 144.
20. Ibid., p. 150.
21. See on this episode John Gillingham, *Coal, Steel, and the Rebirth of Europe, 1945–1955: The Germans and French from Ruhr Conflict to Economic Community* (Cambridge: Cambridge University Press, 1991), p. 166; Hans Peter Schwarz, *Adenauer: Der Aufstieg 1876–1952* (Stuttgart: DVA, 1986), pp. 680–682.
22. François Roth, "Les milieux sidérurgiques lorrains et l'annonce du Plan Schuman," in Klaus Schwabe, ed., *Die Anfänge des Schuman-Plans, 1950/51 / The Beginnings of the Schuman Plan* (Baden-Baden: Nomos, 1988), p. 373. See also in the same volume the contribution of Philippe Mioche, "Le patronat de la sidérurgie française et le Plan Schuman en 1950–1952: Les apparences d'un combat et la réalité d'une mutation," pp. 305–318, in which Mioche describes how Wendel came gradually to accept the Coal and Steel Plan.
23. Crédit Lyonnais archive, DEFF 59810, Etude, July 1953.
24. AN, 189 AQ 218, Lettre de Henri de Wendel à Humbert de Wendel, 15 May 1952.
25. Ibid., Note de Maurice de Wendel adressé à M. Pierrard (membre de la direction générale de Fenderie), 23 September 1952.
26. Kenneth Warren, *Big Steel: The First Century of the United States Steel Corporation, 1901–2001* (Pittsburgh: University of Pittsburgh Press, 2001), pp. 252, 281.
27. Padioleau, *Quand la France s'enferre*, p. 79.
28. Henri de Wendel, "Face à face," interview with Roger Priouret, *L'Expansion*, July–August 1971, pp. 131–145, esp. 139.
29. Biard, *La sidérurgie française*, p. 268.
30. For instance, Société Générale archive, Paris, Sogenale, box 34.
31. Crédit Lyonnais archive, DEFF 59810, 59810/1.
32. Société Générale archive, Sogenal, box 34, Allocution du Président, 24 June 1954.

33. Ibid., Allocution du Président, 25 June 1955.
34. "New French Steel Plant May Be Sited at Marseilles," *The Times*, 8 October 1963.
35. "Critical Time for the Fos Complex," ibid., 8 June 1973.
36. Philippe Mioche, *Jacques Ferry et la sidérurgie française depuis la seconde guerre mondiale* (Aix-en-Provence: Publications de l'Université de Provence, 1993), pp. 240–241.
37. Société Générale archive, Sogenale, box B1604, memorandum, 17 February 1966.
38. Anthony Cockerill, *The Steel Industry: International Comparisons of Industrial Structure and Performance* (Cambridge: Cambridge University Pres, 1974), p. 42.
39. Hayward, "The Nemesis of Industrial Patriotism," pp. 513–514; Padioleau, *Quand la France s'enferre*, p. 47.
40. "Steel Hopes Pinned on New Plants," *The Times*, 15 June 1972.
41. "La sidérurgie française au sixième rang mondial," *Le Monde*, 19 April 1977.
42. Warren, *Big Steel*, p. 298.
43. *Le Monde*, 16 November 1971, p. 35.
44. See on this Yves Guéna, *Les Wendel: Trois siècles d'histoire* (Paris: Editions Perrin, 2004), pp. 214–215.
45. "Les députés renvoient dos à dos," *Le Monde*, 21 April 1977.
46. Laetitia de Warren, *Les fils de Vulcain: La saga des maîtres de forges* (Paris: Seuil, 1999), p. 167.
47. Hayward, "The Nemesis of Industrial Patriotism," p. 522.
48. Quoted in "Steel May Be at Centre of Industrial Storm," *The Times*, 31 May 1977.
49. "French Steel Group to Slash 2,500 Jobs," *Wall Street Journal*, 3 August 1977.
50. "France's Sacilor Says It Will Take Control of Ailing Steel Group," ibid., 25 July 1979.
51. Ray Hudson and David Sadler, *The International Steel Industry: Restructuring: State Policies and Localities* (London: Routledge, 1989), p. 90.
52. Ibid., p. 84.
53. Woronoff, *François de Wendel*, pp. 134–135.
54. Quoted in "Renaissance of a Dynasty," *Financial Times*, 5 June 1987.

V. The Age of Globalization

1. R[ichard] Passow, "Aktiengesellschaften," in Ludwig Elster, Adolf Weber, and Friedrich Wieser, eds., *Handwörterbuch der Staatswissenschaften*, 4th ed., vol. 1 (Jena: G. Fischer, 1923), p. 138.

13. Wendel Becomes a Conglomerate, French Style

1. For instance, Vivien A. Schmidt, *The Futures of European Capitalism* (Oxford: Oxford University Press, 2002).
2. Philip Gordon and Sophie Meunier, *The French Challenge: Adapting to Globalization* (Washington D.C.: Brookings Institution, 2001).

3. Christine Blondel and Ludo Van der Heyden, "The Wendel Family 'Affectio societatis,'" INSEAD case study, 1999.
4. "L'empire Seillière à la loupe," *La vie financière*, 4 August 2001.
5. CGIP, *Rapport annuel*, 1991.
6. Pierre Bourdieu and Monique de Saint Martin, "Le patronat," *Actes de la Recherche en sciences sociales* 20–21 (1978), 16.
7. Jean Bothorel and Philippe Sassier, *Seillière: Le baron de la République* (Paris: Robert Laffont, 2002), p. 208.
8. "Les nouveaux habits de Wendel Investissement," *Le Monde*, 20 July 2002.
9. Bothorel and Sassier, *Seillière*, p. 148.
10. "Après avoir soldé ses déboires," *Les Echos*, 27 November 2001:
11. Bothorel and Sassier, *Seillière*, pp. 173, 193.
12. Ibid., p. 85.
13. "Ernest-Antoine Seillière: Est-il un bon patron?" *Le Figaro*, 18 March 2002.
14. "Les mauvaises affaires du patron des patrons," *Le Monde*, 15 March 2001. This article gave the family wealth as 9 billion francs in Marine-Wendel and CGIP.
15. See, for instance, *Libération*, 7 April 2000.
16. E.g., *Le Monde*, 15 March 2001.
17. "SAirGroup—Swissair réunit aujourd'hui," *Le Figaro*, 25 April 2001.
18. "L'empire Seillière à la loupe."
19. Quoted in "Après avoir soldé ses déboires."
20. "Les nouveaux habits de Wendel Investissement."

14. The Crisis of Italian Steel

1. John Eisenhammer and Martin Rhodes, "The Politics of Public Sector Steel in Italy: From the 'Economic Miracle' to the Crisis of the Eighties," in Yves Mény and Vincent Wright, eds., *The Politics of Steel: Western Europe and the Steel Industry in the Crisis Years (1974–1984)* (Berlin: W. de Gruyter, 1987), p. 424.
2. Ibid., p. 427.
3. R&S, *L'accaio* (Milan: Mediobanca, 1982), p. 56.
4. Ibid., p. 103.
5. AFL-Falck, *Relazione e bilancio*, 1980, 1982. All AFL reports are available in the Falck archive, Milan.
6. Eisenhammer and Rhodes, "Politics of Public Sector Steel," p. 450.
7. Giorgio Pedrocco, *Bresciani: Dal rottame al tondino: Mezzo secolo di siderurgia, 1945–2000* (Milan: Jaca Book, 2000), pp. 313–314.
8. See Fabrizio Barca, ed., *Storia del capitalismo italiano dal dopoguerra a oggi* (Rome: Donzelli, 1997), pp. 155–183.
9. R&S, *L'annuario* (Milan: Mediobanca, 1999).
10. Quoted in *Il Sole–24 Ore*, 4 November 2003, p. 9.
11. See OECD, *Industrial Restructuring and Local Development: The Case of Sesto San Giovanni* (Paris, 1997), pp. 24, 36–37.
12. Mario Botta et al., *Linee guida per la trasformazione delle aree ex Falck di Sesto San Giovanni* (Milan, 2002).
13. *Bresciaoggi*, 19 August 2003; "Romain Zaleski: The Frenchman Who Is Shaking Up Italy Inc.," *BusinessWeek*, 18 June 2001.

14. "No a Montedison-Falck: Schiaffo a Mediobanca," *La Repubblica*, 27 February 2001; also "Some Light Shines at Last on Italian Investor Interests," *Financial Times*, 1 March 2001, p. 26.
15. AFL-Falck, *Relazione e bilancio*, 2002.
16. "An Emerging Generation of Business Leaders," *Financial Times*, 7 April 2003.
17. See Margherita Balconi, *La siderurgia italiana (1945–1990): Tra controllo publico e incentivo del mercato* (Bologna: Il Mulino, 1991).

15. German Diversification and Internationalization

1. Volker R. Berghahn, *The Americanisation of West German Industry, 1945–1973* (Leamington Spa: Berg, 1986).
2. See Lothar Gall, *Der Bankier Hermann Josef Abs: Eine Biographie* (Munich: Beck, 2004).
3. Cited in Hervé Joly, "Ende des Familienkapitalismus? Das Überleben der Unternehmerfamilien in den deutschen Wirtschaftseliten des 20. Jahrhunderts," in Volker R. Berghahn, Stefan Unger, and Dieter Ziegler, eds., *Die deutsche Wirtschaftseliten im 20. Jahrhundert: Kontinuität und Mentalität* (Essen: Klartext, 2003), p. 87.
4. "Auch die Wettbewerbeszentrale gibt klein bei," *Süddeutsche Zeitung*, 11 August 1993.
5. "Sollen die C&C-Betriebe mit Service und Beratung wieder mehr Anreize bieten?" *Handelsblatt*, 15 September 1986.
6. Haniel archive, Duisburg, ZABW 15(2), fol. 29, Wolfgang Curtius, Note on Metro, 1971.
7. "Mit Macht an die Spitze," *Die Zeit*, 8 May 1987.
8. "Metro Delivers the Message of the Moment," *Financial Times*, 26 February 2003.
9. Quoted in "Metro Delivers the Message of the Moment," *Financial Times*, 26 February 2003.
10. Haniel archive, ZABW 13(3), Supervisory board meeting, 5 December 1974.
11. Haniel, *Geschäftsbericht* (annual report), 1988, p. 3: "We supply stainless-steel producers with rust-free materials from scrap." All Haniel reports are available in the Haniel archive.
12. Hans G. Willers, "Haniel heute: Organisation, Strategie und Unternehmenskultur: Vortrag zum Jugendtreffen 22 Oktober 1988," manuscript (Willers papers).
13. John Roberts, *The Modern Firm: Organizational Design for Performance and Growth* (Oxford: Oxford University Press, 2004), pp. 215–216.
14. FHC, Kleiner Kreis, 9 October 1990 (Willers papers).
15. A term used by Jan von Haeften since 2001.
16. "Interview mit Prof. Willers: Entscheidungswege von Firma und Familie müssen klar sein," *Die Welt am Sonntag*, 8 September 1991.
17. See Theo Siegert, "Wertorientierte Unternehmensführung: Die Folge-Generation bei Haniel," in Klaus Macharzina and Heinz-Joachim Neubürger, eds., *Wertorientierte Unternehmensführung: Strategien—Strukturen—Controlling* (Stuttgart: Schäffer-Poeschel, 2002), pp. 35–44.

16. Family Capitalism and the Exit from Steel

1. Horst Albach and Werner Freund, *Generationswechsel und Unternehmenskontinuität: Chancen, Risiken, Massnahmen* (Gütersloh: Bertelsmann Stiftung, 1989), p. 266.
2. Kenneth Warren, *Big Steel: The First Century of the United States Steel Corporation 1901–2001* (Pittsburgh: University of Pittsburgh Press, 2001), pp. 311–312.

Conclusion

1. Jeff S. Wyles, Joseph G. Kibel, and Allan C. Wilson, "Birds, Behavior and Anatomical Evolution," *Proceedings of the National Academy of Sciences*, July 1993. This evolutionary parable was popularized in Arie de Geus, *The Living Company: Habits for Survival in a Turbulent Business Environment* (Boston: Harvard Business School Press, 1997).

Acknowledgments

I originally evolved the idea for this book in conversations with Jan von Haeften (as well as with my friend David Marsh); and the research for this project was in part supported by the Haniel Stiftung. I should like to thank Dr. Edith Hagenguth-Werner, and especially Dr. Rupert Antes of that foundation, for their constant encouragement. I also wish to thank the Haniel, Wendel, and Falck families for making available the archives of their companies and some family papers that elucidated further the interconnections of families with markets and states in shaping the character of entrepreneurial activity in three major European countries.

Dr. Bernhard Weber-Brosamer and Dr. Ulrich Kirchner helped me greatly in the Haniel archive in Duisburg-Ruhrort. The Haniel Stiftung provided a beautiful base for my research in the Rhineland, with a room in the house next door to the merchant Packhaus in which Franz Haniel was born in 1779. I also wish to thank Dr. Jürgen Weise, of the Rheinisch-Westfälisches Wirtschaftsarchiv in Cologne. In Paris, Vincent Dray helped me to use the Wendel family papers in the Archives Nationales, dealt brilliantly with bureaucratic hurdles, and worked on the rich papers of the Crédit Lyonnais and Société Générale. In Milan, Dr. Francesca Pini guided me through the papers of the former Banca Commerciale (now part of Banca Intesa). The Commerciale played a crucial role in creating the joint-stock company Società Anonima Acciaierie e Ferriere Lombarde, which became the modern Falck company, and its documentation constitutes the greatest archive of the modern industrial history of Italy. The archive of Banca Intesa is a model of organization and access. Dr. Maximiliane Rieder spent some time at the archives of Falck and helped me greatly in identifying issues and problems. My visits to Milan were made notable not only by the hospitality of Signor Federico Falck but also by the help of Signora Severina Erba. Signora Erba began to work for Falck in the 1940s, and in 2004 she drove me around the workers' settlement of Villagio Falck in her small Fiat, providing a powerful reminder of how family ownership can inspire exceptional loyalty.

I also benefited from interviews with some of the recent actors in these dynastic histories: Dr. Ernst Alers, Klaus Haniel, Günther Hülse (now deceased), Dr. Dieter Schadt, Professor Theo Siegert, and Professor Hans Willers in Germany; Pierre Celier, Comtesse Priscilla de Moustier, Madame Véronique Goupy, and Baron Ernest Seillière in France; and Alberto Falck (now deceased) and Federico Falck in Italy. I also received valuable suggestions from Carlo de Benedetti; Dr. Fulvio Coltorti, the head of research at Mediobanca; and Professor Marco Vitale in Milan. Jeffrey Fear helped me with an organizational chart for the Gutehoffnungshütte.

I presented some early conclusions of this study at a seminar conducted at the Wharton School by Dan Raff, where Caroline Fohlin and Jonathan Steinberg supplied very helpful comments; and in a joint paper with Chris Kobrak at a conference at Johns Hopkins University, organized by Louis Galambos and Caroline Fohlin. Douglas Forsyth shared some of his insights into Italian industrial development. But most of all the manuscript benefited from the close attention of a group of experts who included Christine Blondel and Professors Knut Borchardt, Gerald Feldman, and Peter Hertner. We met in the delightful setting of Schloss Elmau, largely constructed during the First World War with the financing of a member of the Haniel family, Gräfin Waldersee; Dietmar Müller-Elmau has made his family holding into a vital cultural and social institution in modern Germany. The discussion during this meeting helped me greatly to clarify for myself what the book was really about. Another meeting of this group in early 2006, with representatives of the three families, has been organized by the Haniel Foundation.

I also want to acknowledge the contributions of Michael Aronson and Christine Thorsteinsson of Harvard University Press, Dr. Claudia Althaus of C. H. Beck Verlag, the referees for Harvard University Press, and Ann Hawthorne for wonderful copy editing. Tsering Wangyal Shawa of the Princeton University Map Room helped greatly with cartography.

Marzenna James has raised a family that taught me about love as well as economics, and I wish also to thank Maximilian, Marie-Louise, and Montagu.

Index

Abs, Hermann Josef, 353
Adamoli, Ferdinando, 163–164
Adenauer, Konrad, 306
Afflelou, Alain, 331
AFL (Acciaierie e Ferriere Lombarde; later AFL-Falck), 13, 162–171, 245–258, 263–272, 341–352, 379, 383; and banks, 165–169, 248, 270–271; and change of name, 250; contraction of steel interests, 346–347; and family values, 250–252; and hydro-electric production, 169–170, 246–247, 270, 341–342; labor relations in, 164, 166, 266, 272, 342–343; steel technology in, 168, 246–247, 249, 269–270
Agnelli, Giovanni "Gianni," 13, 32
Agnelli family, 11, 13
Ahlers, Werner, 237–238, 288
Alexandre, François, 68
Ardissone, Vincenzo, 250, 254
Armaments manufacture, 43–45, 49, 85, 181–182, 200
ATH (August-Thyssen-Hütte), 291, 296, 312, 343
Aubertin, 54
Augusta, Queen of Prussia, 76
Aymaville, Gervasone di, 102

Badoni, Giuseppe, 103
Balconi, Margherita, 352
Balthasar, Alexandre-Georges, 54, 58–59
Balthasar, Louis-Ignace de, 49–50, 54
Balzac, Honoré de, 53
Banfield, T. C., 73
Bankruptcy law, 19–20
Banks: borrowing from, 61, 124, 128–129, 162–169, 198–199, 216, 221, 248–250, 270–271, 309–310, 367, 374–375; corporate governance and, 215, 290–291; technical reports on companies, 302–303
Barre, Raymond, 316–317, 319
Barthe, Édouard, 186–187
Bastogi Company, 165
BCI (Banca Commerciale Italiana), 30, 161–166, 248–249, 254
Bedaux method, 199–200
Beisheim, Otto, 355–358
Benedetti, Carlo de, 328–329
Berghahn, Volker, 353
Berle, Adolf, 116
Bernadotte, Jean Baptiste, 80
Berry, Charles Ferdinand Duc de, 61–62
Bertarelli, Irene, 108
Beukenberg, Wilhelm, 227
Beuth, Peter Christian, 89
BioMerieux, 328
Bismarck, Otto von, 130, 132, 140, 154, 156, 226
Bloch-Lainé, François, 305
Blondel, Christine, 329
Bocciardo, Arturo, 249, 256
Boecker, Hermann, 211
Bolis, Carlo, 105
Bolis, Giovanni, 105
Bolis, Giuseppe, 105
Bon, Michel, 340
Böninger, Adeline (née Haniel), 89–90, 97
Böninger, Hans, 280
Böninger, Theodor, 226
Bosch, Robert, Jr., 353
Botta, Mario, 348
Boulton, Matthew, 74
Bourdieu, Pierre, 14, 72, 329–330
Bourg de Bozas, Madame du, 16
Brantes, Anne-Aymone, 317
Bresciani mini-mills, 341, 344–345, 348
Briand, Aristide, 160, 185, 191
Brock, Günter, 360
Brooks, John, 381
Bruns, 281
Bülow, Bernhard von, 118, 176
Bureau Veritas, 328
Buz, Heinrich, 214

Cahen, Jacob, 55
Caillaux, Joseph, 192
Cap Gemini, 335, 339
Cargill, 5
Carli, Guido, 31

Carp, Carl Eduard, 242–243, 282
Carp, Eduard, 226
Carp, Elsa (née Windthorst), 226
Carp, Werner, 226–232, 243–244, 261, 275, 278–280, 282, 378
Carrefour, 358
Cartels: in France, 156–157; in Germany, 131–132, 136, 146, 207–208, 221
Cassin, René, 190
Catholicism: and entrepreneuship, 18; and paternalism, 145, 154, 252; and politics, 144, 159, 190, 264–267
Cattaneo, Carlo, 28
Cavalier, Camille, 160
Celesio, 11, 364
Celier, Pierre, 326–327, 330
CGIP (Compagnie Générale d'Industrie et des Participations), 319–320, 327–329, 335–337, 371, 383
Chaban-Delmas, Jacques, 333
Chandler, Alfred, 6–9, 175, 205, 340, 379, 381
Charles IV of Lorraine, 42
Chévènement, Jean-Pierre, 333
Chirac, Jacques, 335
Choiseul, Étienne-François Duc de, 45
CLIF (Compagnie Lorraine Industrielle et Financière), 316
Clos, Amidieu de, 197
Coal: and coking, 46, 60, 88–89; mining, 69, 78–79, 90, 151, 194; trade in, 78–79, 283–284
Coase, Ronald, 14
Cockerill, Friederike, 89
Cockerill, Heinrich, 89, *122*
Cockerill, John, 18, 89
Cockerill, Thusnelde (née Haniel), 89, 98, 121, *122*
Cockerill, William, 89
Colbert, Jean Baptiste, 23, 300
Colli, Andrea, 5
Conradi, Erwin, 355, 359–360
Corinth, Lovis von, 205
Cramer-Klett, Theodor von, 213–216
Cuccia, Enrico, 31–32, 352
Curel, Albert de, 150
Curel, François de, 150, 184
Curtius, Julius, 243
Curtius, Wolfgang, 273, 280, 286–287, 290, 294, 296–297, 357
CWS, 362, 364

d'Amico, Alfredo, 162, 166–167
Danton, Georges, 50
Davignon, Étienne, 317, 344
Debré, Michel, 313
Delbrück, Rudolf von, 94, 141
Delors, Jacques, 333
Demachy bank, 149
Devoto, Giovanni, 252
d'Hausen, Marguerite (Madame de Hayange), 44, 47–51, 55, 82
Dherse, Louis, 311, 314, 383
Dietrich, Jean-Albert Frédéric, 16
Dobson, 60
Dongo, 101–102, 105, 167–168, 246, 270, 344, 346
Doriot, Jacques, 190
Druon, Maurice, 25, 180, 199

ECSC (European Coal and Steel Community), 261, 281–282, 309–310, 315
Eiffel Tower, 24, 152
Engels, Friedrich, 2, 14, 74
Engels, Friedrich Sr., 73–74
Engerand, Fernand, 186–187
European Community steel restructuring plan, 344–345
Everard, Paul, 155

Falck, Alberto, 32, 266, 347, 349, 352
Falck, Bolis and Redaelli, 105–106
Falck, Bruno, 252, 266
Falck, Camilla, 106
Falck, Camille Ciceri, 266
Falck, Enrico (I.), 100, 103–106, 378
Falck, Enrico (II.), 252, 261, 263–266, *265*, 271–272, 347, 352
Falck, Federico, 347, 352
Falck, Giorgio Enrico (I.), 99–104, *100*, 377–378, 384
Falck, Giorgio Enrico (II.), 13, 106–109, 161–170, 245–252, *251*, 254–258, 261, 263, 266, 341, 347, 352, 379–380, 384
Falck, Giovanni, 252, 266, 268–271
Falck, Giulia Devoto, 266
Falck, Irene (née Rubini), 104, 106, *107*, 169
Falck, Jean Didier, 100
Falck, Luigia, 106, 108
Falck, Maly Da Zara, 266, 272
Fanfani, Amintore, 264
Fear, Jeffrey, 7
Feldman, Gerald, 214
Feltrinelli, Antonio, 252, 346
Feltrinelli, Carlo, 248
Ferry, Jacques, 312–313, 315

FHC (Franz Haniel & Cie. GmbH), 223, 230–239, 281–289, 354, 359–368, 370; Advisory Committee, 282, 288–289; internationalization, 354, 361–362; risk distribution, 364–365; role after World War II, 281–289; statutes of, 230; tensions with GHH, 229–231; youth meetings, 287
Fiat, 250, 268–269, 344, 349. *See also* Agnelli, Giovanni; Agnelli family
Fischer de Dicourt, Joséphine de (Madame Joséphine), 60, 63–66, *67*, 72, 137–138
Flacon, 151
Flick, Friedrich, 227
Foch, Ferdinand, 191
Ford Motor company, 5
Franco Tosi company, 170, 257, 269
Frederick the Great, 39, 77, 282
Frederick William III, 75–76
Frederick William IV, 22, 76, 94
Freisler, Roland, 243
Friederike, Princess of Mecklenburg-Strelitz, 76
Funk, Walther, 242

Galsworthy, John, 15, 17–18
Gandois, Jean, 333
Gargan, Théodore de, 62–66, 68–69, 141–142, 148–149
Gargan, Théodore de, Jr., 66, 150
Garibaldi, Giuseppe, 103
Garnier, 51
Gaulle, Charles de, 299
Gayssot, Jean-Claude, 336
Germany, as a model for technology, 102, 106–107, 142–143, 149, 384
Gerschenkron, Alexander, 26, 163
GHH (Gutehoffungshütte), 22, 120–135, 203–255, 382–383; and coking coal, 90; decartelization after World War II, 275–281; development of iron-working, 90–92, 95–98; establishment of joint stock company, 98, 120–123; and financial problems, 124–126, 128–129; as a *Konzern*, 123, 207, 210–218, 220; and MAN, 213–218, 295; and management, 132, 206–207, 218, 279–281; modernization in 1960s and 1970s, 290–295; pre-Haniel history, 81–83; purchase by Haniels, 84–85; and steel technology, 124–135
Gilchrist-Thomas process, 127, 144, 147–148, 152–153, 195, 290
Gille, Bertrand, 24
Giscard d'Estaing, Valéry, 24, 317, 330
Gnocchi, Carlo, 266
Goethe, Johann Wolfgang von, 52–53, 378
Goisis, Ludovico, 167, 249–250, 252, 346
Goody, Jack, 8
Göring, Hermann, 189–190, 201–202, 235, 237, 243
Grandet, Henri, 136–137, 142
Granthil, Louis, 51, 54, 56, 82
Great Britain, as a model for technology, 46, 60, 88, 101, 384
Grolman, Eugen, 243
Giulini, Graf, 101
Gutleben, Fritz, 238

Haase, Alfred, 292
Haeften, Barbara von (née Curtius), 243
Haeften, Hans-Bernd von, 243
Haeften, Jan von, 297, 359
Haniel, Aletta (née Noot), 51, 76–78
Haniel, Alfred, 223, 226, 261, 282, 284–289, *285*
Haniel, Alma, 225
Haniel, Alphons, 121, 128, 212
Haniel, August, 90, 212, 220, 223–224
Haniel, Bertha, 89, *122*
Haniel, Carl, 92, 96, 121, 128
Haniel, Clara, 90
Haniel, Curt, 280
Haniel, Eduard, 128
Haniel, Eduard James, 128–133
Haniel, Elsa, 205
Haniel, Erich, 90
Haniel, Franz (I.), 22, 73–80, 82–98, *86*, *97*, 101, 119, 121–124, 126, 128, 134–135, 223, 226, 243, 278, 283, 286, 377–378, 381–382, 384
Haniel, Franz (II.), *97*, 121–124, *122*, 204, 223
Haniel, Friedrich Wilhelm, 75, 121, 226, 283
Haniel, Friedrich Wilhelm Theobald, 76, 98
Haniel, Gerda, 90
Haniel, Gerhard, 77, 80, 82–85, 87–89, 91–92, 96, 121–122, 126, 128, 212, 243, 278, 382
Haniel, Henriette, 128
Haniel, Hugo, 89, 92, 96, 98, 119, 121–124, *122*, 127–131, 223, 283
Haniel, Hugo, Jr., 90
Haniel, Jacob Wilhelm, 76–77
Haniel, Joachim, 76
Haniel, Johanna (née Jacobi), *122*

Haniel, John, 89, 205
Haniel, Julius, 98, 121, 205
Haniel, Karl, 214–216, 218–219, 223–225, 230–232, 242–243, 275
Haniel, Klaus, 224–225, 279, 281, 286–287, 289–293
Haniel, Louis, 98, 121, 123
Haniel, Max (son of Franz), 89, 98, 121, 124, 128
Haniel, Max Berthold (son of Max), 90, 97, 123–124
Haniel, Nancy, 123
Haniel, Richard, 90, 205
Haniel, Sophia, 77, 80, 83–84, 87
Haniel, Wilhelm, 72, 79–80, 84, 87, 122
Haniel & Lueg, 123
Haniel-Niethammer, Gerhard, 205
Haniel von Haimhausen, Edgar, 124, 230
Hardy, Widow, 51
Harvey, Nicholas, 96
Hautecloque, Philippe. *See* Leclerc, Philippe
Hayange, 42–44, 47–51, 54–58, 62–63, 141–144, 147, 155, 182, 186–188, 195, 305–306
Hayward, Jack, 299
Hecht, Hermann, 238–239
Hecht, Jakob, 238–239
Henry, Emile, 156
Hereth, Hansjörg, 358
Herriot, Edouard, 185, 188, 190
Heyden, Ludo van der, 329
Hitler, Adolf, 188–189, 225, 234–235, 243, 355
HOAG (Hüttenwerke Oberhausen AG), 275–277, 282, 291
Hoppit, Julian, 19
Hoschiller, Max, 187
Hottenger, Georges, 155
Hülse, Günther, 359, 363
Hunolstein, Felix de, 63
Huyssen, Arnold, 82
Huyssen, Friederike, 82
Huyssen, Heinrich, 83–84, 92, 96
Hydro-electric power, 170, 245–248, 252–253, 270–271, 342

Ilva, 165, 248–250, 253–255, 345–347
IRI (Istituto per la ricostruzione industriale), 30–31, 343, 383
Iron-making technology, 45–46, 52, 58, 60, 101–102

Jackson, Julian, 194
Jacobi, Clementine, 96
Jacobi, Friedrich, 121–122
Jacobi, Gottlob, 80–81, 83–84, 96
Jacobi, Haniel & Huyssen, 84–85, 88, 91–92, 123
Jacobi, Hugo, 206
Japan, analogies with development in, 2, 13
Jars, Gabriel-Jean, 45–46
Jasson, Albert, 155
Jeanneney, Jean-Noël, 186, 188, 191–192
Jessen, Lambert, 213, 215–216
Joel, Otto, 162
Joeuf, 148–156, 160, 182, 195–197, 203, 302–303, 306
Joint stock companies, legislation establishing, 72, 96–98, 113–118, 161
Jospin, Lionel, 22, 333

Kampf, Serge, 328
Karl August of Saxony-Weimar-Eisenach, 52
Kellermann, Hermann, 237
Kerillis, Henri de, 187
Kindleberger, Charles, 7
Klett, Johann Friedrich, 213
Körber, Hans Joachim, 359
Kreuger, Ivar, 199
Krivine, Alain, 333
Krum (Vienna), 237
Krupp, Alfried, 274
Krupp, Helene Amalie, 51, 82–83
Krupp family, 11, 129, 136, 149, 205, 244, 274
Krupp von Bohlen und Halbach, Gustav, 274

Labor conflicts, 154–155, 164, 170, 308, 319–320, 342–344
Lafayette, Marquis de, 78
Lafonta, Jean-Bernard, 339
Lagardère, Jean-Luc, 6
Lagardère family, 6
Landes, David, 7, 379
Law, John, 44
Lazonick, William, 7
Lebrun, Albert, 159–160, 180, 190
Lecco, 103, 105
Leclerc, Philippe, 299
Leclerc de Hautecloque, Hubert, 332
Le Cresot, 46–47, 68–70, 148
Lejeune, Lt., 188

Lennings, Manfred, 294
Lennings, Wilhelm, 294
Le Play, Frédéric, 5, 72, 155
Liebrecht, Caroline (née Haniel), 97
Liebrecht, Franz, 90
List, Friedrich, 25
Longlaville, Jean-François, 46
Longwy-Briey, 34, 147, 159, 187–188
Lorraine, 34, 41–44, 50, 63, 70, 140–148, 158–159, 182–183, 197–198, 299, 301–306, 308, 310, 316, 319
Louis XIV of France, 23, 44
Louis XVI of France, 46–47, 49
Louise, Queen of Prussia, 22, 76
Lueg, Carl, 122–123, 126–127, 130–132, 206
Lueg, Heinrich, 123
Lueg, Wilhelm, 84, 88, 93, 96, 122–123, 132
Luther, Hans, 234
Luxembourg, 34, 50, 60, 70
Luyken, Georg, 88
Luzzato, Arturo, 255

Maier, Charles, 261
Malcor, Henri, 200
Malthusianism, 23, 137, 194, 298
Malzy, Benoît de, 43
Managerial capitalism, 20–21, 96, 127, 175–176, 205–207, 210, 323–324
Mannesmann, 135, 168, 290
Mannesmann, Max, 135
Maranghi, Vincenzo, 352
Marchi, Gioa, 347
Marie Antoinette, Queen of France, 39
Marin, Jean François, 55
Marin, Louis, 190
Marine-Wendel, 315–319, 327, 335–337, 370
Maroni, 185
Marriage strategies, 14–16, 59–60, 82–83, 89–90, 104, 108, 128, 149–150, 204–205
Marseille, Jacques, 63
Martignoni, Abramo, 266
Marx, Karl, 2, 14
Maupassant, Guy de, 185
Mazzanti, Manfredo, 343
Means, Gardner, 116
Medef, 25, 333–334
Mediobanca, 31–32, 347, 349–350, 352
Menges, Dietrich Wilhelm von, 291–294
Menichella, Donato, 31
Mérieux, Alain, 328
Mesnil, 58
Messier, Jean-Marie, 6, 340
Metro, 11, 34, 289, 354–359, 371
Metzsch, Thuisko von, 282, 286–289, 358
Meyer, Anne-Marguerite, 42
Michael, Fritz von, 205
Michelin, André, 16
Michelis, Gianni de, 344
Middelhoff, Thomas, 6
Migliavacca, Angelo, 162
Millerand, Alexandre, 160
Mitry, Emmanuel de, 184, 309–310, 326
Mitterand, François, 325
Moltke, Helmuth Graf, 141
Monnet, Jean, 299–301, 304
Monnet plan, 300–306
Montedison, 349–351, 371
Montini, Giovanni Battista, 267
Moody, John, 117
Moreau, Émile, 58, 192–193
Moselle, navigation of, 144
Moustier, Louis-Amédée, 332
Moyeuvre, 55, 63, 142, 150–151, 153, 182, 186–187
Müller, Johannes, 205
Mussolini, Benito, 175, 177, 188, 250, 252, 255, 257, 275

Nalèche, Étienne, 185
Napoleon I, 23, 40, 54, 59, 76, 80–81
Napoleon III, 23, 69–71
Narbonne-Lara, Louis de, 48–49
Necker, Jacques, 47
Nelson, Horatio, 88
Nitti, Francesco, 30
Nivelle, Robert, 186
Noblat, Barbara, 100
Noot, Diederike, 79
Noot, Jan Willem, 76–77

Ohnet, Georges, 149
OPDR (Oldenburg-Portugiesische Dampfschiffs-Rheederei), 283, 361
Orange Nassau (Oranje Nassau), 11, 145–146, 198, 329

Palavicini, Giacomo Durazzo, 109
Palteau de Veymerange, Gabriel, 46–47, 49
Papen, Franz von, 225

Parliamentary activities of industrial dynasties, 24–25, 61–62, 71–72, 93, 156–160, 180–181, 184–193, 263–264
Partible inheritance, 19, 64–66, 71–72, 155
Paschal, François, 303
Pastor, Robert, 182–183
Paternalism, 68–69, 95, 132, 153–154, 170–171, 208–209, 252, 272, 308
Peel, Sir Robert, 93
Pétain, Henri Philippe, 25, 186, 189–190
Pfandhöfer, Eberhard, 81, 90
Pferdmenges, Robert, 227, 306
PFFW (Société Les Petits Fils de François de Wendel et Cie.), 142–147, 150, 157–158, 184, 193–201, 208, 301–306; and banks, 143, 199, 305, 309; capitalization, 184; creation of, 142; labor force, 145, 184, 308; quotation of shares, 307; restructuring in 1970s, 314–319; share price, 310–311; technical retardation of, 157–158, 194–201, 303–304
Piérard, Paul, 200
Pietism, 73–74
Pinösch, 242
Pinot, Robert, 180
Pirelli family, 347
Poincaré, Raymond, 185, 188, 191, 193
Poupillier, Louis, 55
Protective tariffs, 61–62, 72, 93–95, 151, 168

Queirazza, Francesco Rodolfo, 165

Raffalovich, Arthur, 184
Rebua, Francesco Dandolo, 254
Redaelli, Costante, 106, 167
Redaelli, Giuseppe, 105
Redaelli, Pietro, 105
Reusch, Hermann, 116, 224, 242, 261, 279–280, 282–285, 288, 291, 353
Reusch, Paul, 20, 116, 133, 204, 206–208, *207*, 210–216, 218–235, 241–243, 261, 274–275, 278, 291
Rheinpreussen mine, 92–93, 191, 275–278, 287–289
Ridouet-Sancé, Louis de, 42
Rieppel, Anton, 213–216
Riva, Emilio, 345
Riva family, 345, 373
Robespierre, Maximilien de, 50
Rocca, Agostino, 255
Rochau, August, 26
Roche, Rodolphe de la, 42–43
Röchling, Hermann, 201
Rockefeller, David, 332
Roe, Mark, 21
Rossi, Ernesto, 29
Rostow, W. W., 26
Rothschild, Baron, 192–193
Rothschild family, 16, 65, 298
Roussely, François, 340
Rubini, Gaetano, 101
Rubini, Giuseppe, 101–105, *104*
Rubini, Pietro, 101
Rubini and Falck, 101–102
Ruhrort, 76–78, 87–88, 93

Sacilor, 314–315, 317–319, 345
Saintignon, Comte de, 197
Saint Martin, Monique, 329
Sarrail, Maurice Paul, 187
Sartine, Antoine Raymond Jean Gualbert Gabriel de, 46
Scalini, Enrico, 252, 263
Schacht, Hjalmar, 234
Schadow, Johann Gottlieb, 76
Schadt, Dieter, 360
Schäfer, Walter, 355
Schama, Simon, 47
Schiaffino, Rosanna, 347
Schlenker, Max, 143
Schlitter, Oscar, 215
Schmidt, Helmut, 278
Schmitz, Hugo, 211
Schneider, Achille, 68, 71
Schneider, Eugène, 72
Schneider, Henri, 147–149, 180
Schneider family, 11, 24, 64, 68–69, 71, 150, 299, 317
Schumpeter, Joseph, 74
Secchia, Pietro, 266
Seillière, Ernest-Antoine, 22, 320, 325, 327, 329–337, 339–340, 378
Seillière, Florentin, 55, 58
Seillière, Jean, 150, 201
Seillière family, 55, 149–150, 330
Sérilly, Megret de, 46–47, 54
Serre, Philippe, 59, 190
Sesto San Giovanni, 161–167, 250, 252–253, 269–270, 272, 341, 346, 348
Sidélor, 312–314
Sidona, Michele, 267
Siemens-Martin steel, 124–125

Sinigaglia, Oscar, 245–246, 254–255, 268
Skal, 182
Smith, Adam, 65
Sohl, Hans Günther, 312
Sollac, 205, 311
Solmer, 311–312, 315, 319
Solmssen, Georg, 227
Sombart, Werner, 74
Speer, Albert, 202, 257
Speer, Edgar, 314
Spielhagen, Friedrich, 121
Stalin, Joseph, 189
Starace, Achille, 257
Stinnes, Fanny, 89
Stinnes, Gustav, 89
Stinnes, Hugo, 18, 208, 213–216, 220, 222, 225, 233
Stinnes, Mathias, 93
Stiring-Wendel, 69, 142, 145
Stock market: comparative performance, 32–33, 117–118; suspicions of speculation, 126, 143
Stresemann, Gustav, 212
Stringher, Bonaldo, 164, 248
Strousberg, Bethel, 121
Stumm, Karl Ferdinand, 156
Stumm family, 129–130
Sturzo, Luigi, 264
Suermondt, Barthold, 123

Tange, Kenzo, 348
Tansini, Emilio, 162, 165
Taxation, 176–177, 205, 379
Templeton, Jack, 332
Téry, Gustave, 179
Thiers, Adolphe, 141
Thomas, Sidney Gilchrist, 147–148
Thyssen, August, 7
Thyssen, Fritz, 225, 274
Toeplitz, Giuseppe, 248–249
Togliatti, Palmiro, 266
Tolstoy, Leo, 16
Tourneur, Jacques, 49
Tronville, Françoise-Cécile, 45
Trudaine, Daniel-Charles, 45
Tuttmann, 83

Ulrich, Franz, 290
United States, as a technological and business model, 158, 196–197, 224–225, 269, 301, 307, 327, 337, 384
Urbig, Franz, 215
Usinor, 301, 310–313, 315, 319, 383
U.S. Steel corporation, 8, 307–308, 314, 372

Valeo, 328–329, 339
Vereinigte Stahlwerke, 201, 227–232, 378
Veroli, Giorgio di, 254
Villèle, Joseph de, 62
Vincke, Ludwig von, 76, 87
Visconti, Luchino, 27
Vito, Francesco, 264
Vlissingen, Fentener van, 242
Voltaire, 160

Waldersee, Alfred Graf, 288
Waldersee, Franz von, 205
Walrand, Charles, 149
Wars: Franco-Prussian, 136–137, 141; French Revolution and Napoleonic wars, 49–51, 54, 78–80; Seven Years' War, 45; World War I, 169–170, 181–183, 185–188, 208–209, 211; World War II, 189, 201–203, 239–244, 257–258
Watt, James, 74, 88, 384
Weber, Max, 74, 116–117
Weil, Federico, 162
Welker, Johann, 116, 206, 229, 231, 234, 238
Wendel, (Alexie-)Charles de (son of François I), 19, 63, *64*, 66, 68–72, 137–140, 145, 150, 377
Wendel, Benoît, 49
Wendel, Caroline de, 66
Wendel, Charles de (brother of François I), 54–57
Wendel, Charles de (grandfather of François I), 16, 44–45
Wendel, Charles de (son of Robert), 145, 157–159, 194, 307
Wendel, Christian, 42
Wendel, François de (I.), 18, 53–63, 65–66, 71, 75, 88, 101, 137, 157, 377–378, 384
Wendel, François de (II.), 22, 25, *154*, 156–157, 159–160, 179–201, *181*, 232, 261, 298, 300, 303, 306–307, 309, 320, 330, 332–333, 339, 382
Wendel, Guy de, 155, 159, 180, 182, 189, 194

Wendel, Henri de (son of Alexie-Charles), 137, 142, 148–149, 151–152, 154–157, 189, 261, 378
Wendel, Henri de (son of François), 306–308, 314, 326
Wendel, Humbert de, *154*, 156–159, 182, 184, 201, 303–304
Wendel, Ignace de, 45–55, 68, 378, 384
Wendel, Jean-Georges, 41
Wendel, (Jean-)Martin, 42–44, 46, 60
Wendel, Louis de, 54, 56–58
Wendel, Marguérite-Joséphine, 63, 65
Wendel, Maurice de, *154*, 155–156, 158, 182, 184, 198, 307, 330
Wendel, Pauline de, 149
Wendel, Renée de, 150
Wendel, Robert, 137, 142, 151–152, 156–157, 378
Wendel, Ségolène de, 201
Wendel, Victor-François, 63, 65, 149
Wendel et Cie. SA, 150–156, 184, 198, 306; labor force, 153; technical change in steel-making, 147–149, 152
Wendel Investissement, 338–339, 370
Wenge zu Dieck, Franz Ferdinand Freiherr von, 81
Wiesner, Eugenie, 90
Wiesner, Gustav, 219
Wilhelm I, German Emperor, 76
Wilhelm II, German Emperor, 205
Wilkinson, John, 46
Wilkinson, William, 46
Willers, Hans, 353, 362–363, 366
Windthorst, Ludwig, 226
Winkhaus, Hermann, 290–291
Winkler, Carl, 216
Wolff, Otto, 227
Women and management, 16, 50–51, 65–66, 77–78, 106, 137

Zaleski, Romain, 349–351
Zeppelin-Aschhausen, Friedrich von, 159
Ziegler, Gottfried, 206
Zimmermann, Paul, 257